HOW TO USE THE INTERNET FOR LEGAL RESEARCH

HOW TO USE THE INTERNET FOR LEGAL RESEARCH

BY JOSH BLACKMAN

Find®/SVP

For information, contact:
Find/SVP
625 Avenue of the Americas
New York, NY 10011

Library of Congress Catalog Card Number: 96-86120
ISBN 1-56241-398-2
Printed in the United States of America

COVER AND TEXT DESIGN BY BERNARD SCHLEIFER

3rd Printing

To the women in my life
who have made it possible and worthwhile
Sandy and Liz

In my opinion, the great thing in this world
is not so much where we stand
as in what direction we are moving.

—TANH QUYEN, *South Vietnamese Colonel
who survived the Khmer Rouge and moved
to the U.S. as quoted in Forbes FYI, 9/25/95*

Preface

I REALIZED A WHILE BACK THAT IT WAS IMPOSSIBLE TO WRITE THE DEFINITIVE encyclopedia for lawyers who want to use the Internet for research, communication and marketing. This is bad and good. It's bad that we can't fully get a handle on the resource, but it's good that the Internet continues to grow and change. I like to think that growth connotes improvement.

When I wrote my first book on this subject in the fall of 1993 (*The Legal Researcher's Internet Directory*), I thought of the Internet as an additional resource in the lawyers' arsenal. Since then, the idea that the public ought to have greater access to public information, including the law, has grown along with the Internet. Today many nonlawyers are using online services and other self-help media to find what they need to know about the law.

This book is designed to serve legal professionals (practicing lawyers, law librarians, paralegals, law professors and students) and the lay public. This is not to say that the Internet simplifies the dense legal language one often finds in statutes, judicial opinions and contracts. It does suggest that the Net provides greater access to these documents, and that there is a great market of people who are interested in achieving better understanding of their rights and responsibilities. If this book can help you find the information you need, it will have achieved its purpose.

—JOSH BLACKMAN
May 1996

Acknowledgments

TAKING A BOOK FROM CONCEPT TO REALITY IS HARD WORK. IF I GAINED nothing else from the experience of transporting these words from my mind to yours, that lesson has been worth the effort. Along the way, many people have helped in the creative process.

A number of people with the foresight and energy to get involved early in using the Internet in legal practice provided the benefit of their experience in the form of interviews. The following people lent their considerable insight to this book's development: Dan Appelman, Ken Bass, III, Neal Friedman, Robin Diane Goldstein, Lyonette Louis-Jacques, Tim Muth, and Lewis Rose.

The people I work with daily at FIND/SVP have provided the inspiration and a testbed for many of the ideas you'll find in the following pages. Dana Rachlin shared her significant online research expertise and has been an ally when no one seemed to understand what we were talking about. Sean Jenkins has worked on the book throughout its long development, and continues to teach me things about using the Internet for legal research. Sean is largely responsible for the Mailing List section. Brian Wilcove did whatever it took to help get this book done. Barbara Kessler, Kim Collins and Tara Barker have helped build the Legal Research Group into a business we can be proud of.

On the publishing side, Andy Garvin, David Weiss and Michael Shor have ensured that these words make it into print. Ellen Greenberg has not only helped with copyediting and design, but also made cogent suggestions that have made the book better. Finally, thanks to Tim O'Reilly who encouraged me to expand my original concept to include specific portions of the narrative.

Contents

PART I. INTRODUCING THE INTERNET

PART II. PRACTICAL USES OF THE NET

PART III: INTERNET LEGAL RESEARCH DIRECTORY

PART I

INTRODUCING THE INTERNET

WHAT THE INTERNET IS

The Internet is an international interconnection of millions of computers over ordinary telephone lines. Since the net is a new phenomenon and generally requires some time to truly understand, it may be helpful to compare the Net to similar networks that you're familiar with.

For example, the familiar communication device known as the fax machineis part of an international network that enables people to share documents. Using the fax machine, you and I can transmit anything on paper from one machine to another via the telephone lines. The technical details of electronic fax communication have been worked out so that the document I send is virtually identical to the document you receive. No single entity "owns" the fax network, although telephone companies facilitate it through their telephone lines. The endpoints, or "nodes" of the fax network are the fax machines themselves that you and I control.

Like the fax network, the local area networks (LANs) that exist in many companies interconnect computers using copper wire. Some of those computers are used by people to do work, run software and exchange messages. Some of the computers connected to the LAN are not on an employee's desk, but rather sit alone in the company computer room. These computers are simply processing and storage devices designed to serve everyone on the network. Such computers are known as servers. Servers are used to distribute email, to store copies of software that everyone on the LAN uses, and to maintain the network overall.

The Internet is a sort of gigantic local area network, and can be described as a wide area network. It connects many smaller networks, including many LANs, and many other wide area networks. CompuServe is an example of a wide area network that connects some three million international subscribers. CompuServe in turn is connected to the Internet. Therefore, all three million Compuserve members can send email to people who are connected to the Internet, but who do not have Compuserve accounts. In this way, the Internet has become the network of networks, connecting many millions of people.

Estimates vary regarding the number of people who use the Internet. The research and consulting firm FIND/SVP issued a survey in January 1996, indicating some 10 million people access the Net for email and at least one other reason (to use the World Wide Web, for example). It is difficult to be precise about such estimates, because there are varying definitions of what being "on" the Internet means. Generally, being on the Net means you can not only send email to anyone who's Net-connected, but also that you can access Internet server computers to read and download documents, and explore databases. Some people who have a mere email connection to the Net claim to be "on the Net," which in a way they are. Email can be used to access Internet server computers, though email is not as simple an access method as the menu and graphically-driven software available to those with full Internet access.

Chapter 1

How the Net Fits with Legal Practice

A SILENT REVOLUTION IS TRANSFORMING THE LEGAL PROFESSION INTO A business. Along with the rise of alternative dispute resolution, fixed-fee billing, and outsourced legal research, computer networking is the most noticeable sign of change in the way lawyers work. The most prominent instrument of this change is the Internet, which offers lawyers dramatic cost savings in legal research and entirely new ways to market services and communicate with colleagues, government agencies, and clients.

Practitioners who are not online are out of touch and may soon be out of business. The client who gets charged high fees for Lexis research and hours spent in the county records hall, may soon take his or her business elsewhere. This is especially likely when the clients find they can pay a lower rate to another lawyer who uses one Internet government site to retrieve statutes, an online database to check real estate records, and email rather than courier services to send documents.

The Internet is not a threat to lawyers, but rather a watershed opportunity. Rather than limiting your personal network to work colleagues and others you know through direct contact, the Net provides for contact with a universe of people.

For example, the Legal Research Group in New York's FIND/SVP has a manufacturing client who required counsel in an antidumping matter. Within an hour or two of posting the referral request on an online discussion forum (an Internet newsgroup), a number of qualified private firm resumes were on their way to the manufacturing firm's corporate counsel. The dollar and time costs involved for all parties, including the corporate counsel, the Legal Research Group personnel, and the private firm attorneys who responded to the request, were minimal. In addition, all activity relevant to the referral was conducted by the parties without leaving their desks.

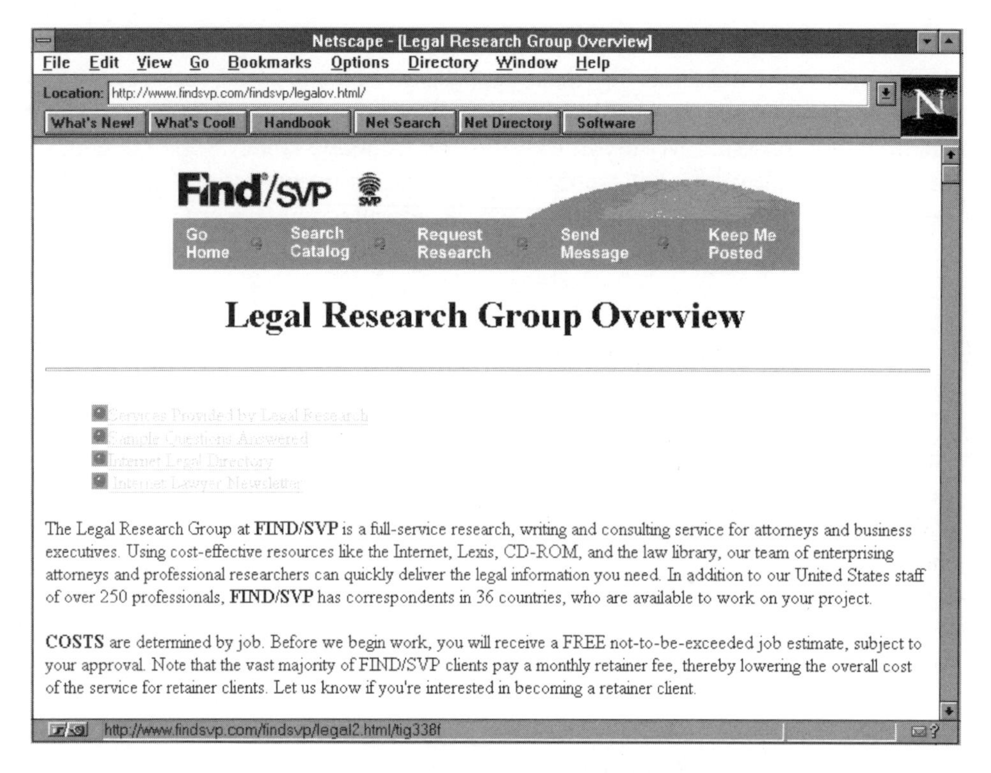

Figure 1-1: http://www.findsvp.com/findsvp/legalov.html/

The Legal Research Group at FIND/SVP has its own Web site on the Internet. The site enables anyone with Internet access, from anywhere on the planet to find out what the group offers, and to even submit research requests online.

The same sort of referral activities, whether for legal representation, or the computer address for free access to the entire text of NAFTA, or Supreme Court opinions, or SEC filings (to name but a few examples) take place every moment on the Internet. By means of newsgroups and Internet mailing lists, the Net exponentially increases the number of personal contacts one person can have.

The Internet is also a boon to lawyers'clients and those who seek access to the law on their own. Clients gain from lawyers' ability to reduce costs, and electronically reach out to a network of colleagues. Clients also benefit from the very efficient means of communication that the Internet provides. Clients with their own Internet connection can receive and transmit messages to counsel whenever convenient, versus merely during business hours.

For the nonlawyer seeking to find the law independently, the Net offers easy access to some of the same court, legislative and regulatory materials lawyers use in practice. Anyone with the basic hardware,[1] software, and ability to learn where to go online, can retrieve the statutes, government documents and other legal materials that comprise the law. The way laws and court opinions are written has not changed merely because such documents are available on the Internet.

Knowing how to work within the legal system, however, still requires know-how. Access to legal materials is no substitute for an understanding of the legal system, and the ability to use that system effectively to protect rights and interests. The Internet easily increases the individual's ability to communicate with a

1. To get on the Internet, three pieces of hardware are required: (1) a computer (any type will do); (2) a modem (again, any will do, but the faster the better; the standard fast-speed modem runs at 14.4 bits per second (bps); and (3) a telephone line that plugs into the modem.

wide audience, to share ideas and information. The Internet can also enable anyone to review the materials that make up the law. In some cases, such review can provide valuable insight into legal issues. It is important to keep in mind that interpretation is an art. My favorite expression from law school was "it depends." The law is not always what it appears to be, and its interpretation "depends" on the particular facts of each situation. So take advantage of the virtual law library known as the Internet, but handle your own legal affairs with caution.

WHY SHOULD LAWYERS CARE?

It is ironic that the legal community, which arguably can make better use of automation than any other profession, is traditionally very resistant to using computers in the practice of law. Large law firms that support large clients with large staffs generally have large computer budgets. The big firms have therefore been the early adopters of technology. But such firms make up only about 17% of U.S. lawyers. Of the 900,000 lawyers in the country, over 54% are in small firms (one- to twenty lawyer firms). Small firm practitioners that lack the big firm benefits of on-site computer staffers, on-site law libraries, and access to large computer budgets, actually have the most to gain from automation. Computers can, in many ways level the playing field, giving the small firm many big-firm advantages at very reasonable prices. The personal computer (PC) was the first evidence of this advantage.

Before the PC, having a computer meant paying megabucks for a mainframe or minicomputer and a staff to maintain it, an expensive maintenance contract, and no real access to computing power for the practicing lawyer. When the PC debuted in 1981, however, suddenly anyone could use a computer for word processing or accounting. Although the machines were not simple to use (even today, some don't find computers simple, though we've certainly come a long way since 1981), they put computing power on the lawyers' desk at a reasonable price.

The Internet is revolutionizing digital communication and online research in the same way that the PC revolutionized access to computers. The Internet provides access to global email and electronic legal research materials to everyone at a very reasonable price. The value of email and cheap online research may not yet be obvious to everyone, but that will change soon, for many reasons.

First, many of your current and prospective clients are either already online or will be soon. The convenience of email communication, and the fact that it is rapidly becoming a standard way to communicate (much like the fax machine became standard in the 1980s) is making it a requirement for all law firms. Those firms that fail to use email are already missing out on the opportunity to bid for work that requires email connectivity between lawyers and clients.

Second, your competitors are already online or will be there very soon. Such competitors will be more attractive to clients who expect their lawyers to use the most efficient tools to save the client's money. Not being at the leading edge of the wave sends a message to clients and competitors alike that you either don't care or don't know how to practice in the most cost-efficient way.

Third, many courts and government agencies are online, using the Internet to distribute agency notices, court opinions, legislative history materials, you name it. You can continue to pay Lexis and Westlaw five dollars a minute for materials available on the Net for free or you can stop wasting money. An easy example of the distinction between Lexis and Internet agency documents are those available from the Securities and Exchange Commission. Every year, every public corporation in the United States files numerous documents with the SEC, including 10-Ks, 10-Qs, etc. These documents provide important insight into U.S. companies. For example, section C of every 10-K reports the litigation that each company is involved with. If your firm is considering representing a new corporate client, or if you're considering targeting a company as a prospective client, or if you're litigating against a company, and you want to know quickly, easily and cheaply about a firm's court matters, section C is a great start.

Pulling a 10-K from Disclosure costs $36 plus $8 to $12 for delivery, and takes four hours. Pulling the same document from Lexis costs about $6 plus $1.50 per printed page, and is available anytime. Pulling the document from the Internet takes seconds, and costs nothing. This is one of endless examples of how the Net can save you and your clients money.

The Internet is a practice efficiency tool. If your law firm does not get online, you will not be practicing as efficiently as possible. You could choose to be reactive and scramble to get online when one of your important clients asks why you don't have email to exchange documents, or why you're sending a lawyer to the courthouse to go through records that are available online. It is clearly a better idea to be proactive in this regard. It is quite simply a business imperative to get online.

COST SAVINGS USING THE NET FOR DOCUMENT RETRIEVAL

The Internet is commonly discussed in terms of how complex it is to use. For those who have never accessed the Net, it is complex. There is a lot to know if you want to use it effectively. Of course, the same thing can be said of researching legal precedent, or negotiating a contract. The lawyer who wants to survive in today's market will learn how to use the best tools.

A recent experience bears this out. I needed to locate a recent report printed in the Federal Register.[2] The report was well over 400 pages. Retrieving the report via Lexis would have cost a total of $626.50 ($20 to search the FEDREG library, plus online charges of 65 cents per minute, plus about $600 for the print charges). I found the report on the Internet, for a total cost, of about $10 (phone call cost of two cents per minute (the download took about 10 minutes), plus prorated Internet access cost of $19 per month, plus three minutes of my time). The value of the Internet in this case is plain. [Note that Lexis pricing has since been changed.]

Such cost-savings was possible because I knew where on the Internet to find the Federal Register document. I have this knowledge because I subscribe to several Internet mailing lists. Everyday, the mailing lists send messages to my email box reporting what's new and interesting on the Net. As with conventional mail, there's also lots of junk in my daily messages, but I've learned to quickly scan email, discarding the junk and keeping the gems.

Although there are several thousand Internet mailing lists, for the most part, I only subscribe to those that discuss new Internet legal documents and databases. One of those lists is LAW-LIB, also known as the Law Libraries list. Not long ago, I received the following message from the LAW-LIB list:

2. The Federal Register is a daily listing of federal agency documents, including Notices, Rules, Proposed Rules, Presidential Documents, Code of Federal Regulations Parts Affected and other releases.

GPO GIVES THE PUBLIC FREE, 24-HOUR ACCESS
TO ONLINE FEDERAL INFORMATION

The U.S. Government Printing Office (GPO) announced today the first site giving the public free access to many of the Nation's most important Federal documents with a phone call.

The Congressional Record, Federal Register and Congressional Bills databases are now available to off-site callers through the Columbia Online Information Network (COIN) located at the Daniel Boone Regional Library in Columbia, MO.

In cooperation with the Federal depository library at the University of Missouri at Columbia, COIN is offering free public access to the GPO databases as part of an expanding gateway program which will extend nationwide. Users may reach COIN by dialing 314-884-7000, or by telnet to 128.206.1.3.

. . .

Inquiries about GPO Access - subscription services should be directed to the Access User Support Team at (202) 512-1530, or Internet e-mail <help@eidsO5.eids.gpo.gov>.

Free access to essential data like the Federal Register, the Code of Federal Regulations, the United States Code and the Congressional Bills database makes it clear that the Internet is worth lawyers' time, and is similarly valuable to anyone who needs access to the law. The amount of free legal data available on the net is increasing at a substantial pace.

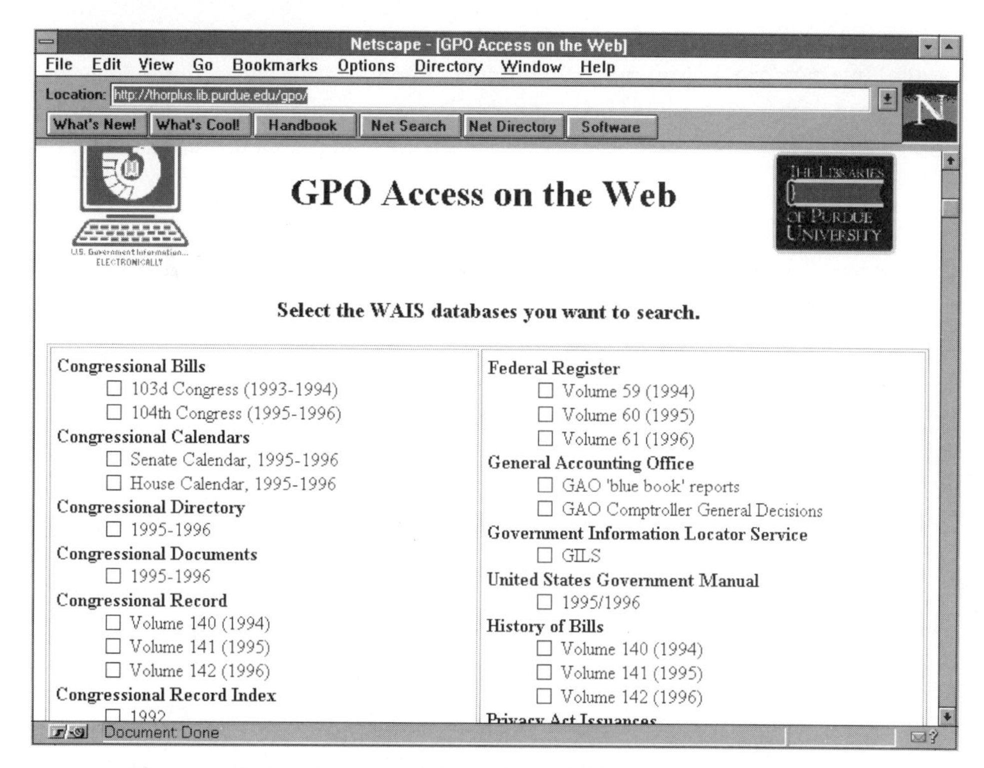

Figure 1-2: http://thorplus.lib.purdue.edu/gpo/

One of the best Internet sources for federal data, providing free access to the Federal Register, United States Code and Congressional Record is known as GPO Access on the Web, and is maintained by Purdue University.

HOW THE NET DIFFERS FROM LEXIS

When most lawyers think of electronic legal research sources, they invariably think of Lexis and Westlaw. New low-cost technologies such as CD-ROM and online bulletin board systems have enabled other legal publishers to offer electronic legal research products. However, Lexis' and Westlaw's mainframe computer-based databases remain the most used and most recognized electronic sources. So it is common to expect the Internet to fit the model of the virtual law library advanced by these two established and costly services. But the Net does not fit that model. The Net is not a centrally-owned and coordinated service maintained by multimillion dollar development and customer support budgets. The Net is a public network. Anyone who wishes to make information available via the Net can do so. Therefore, there are some great, accurate sources, and some that are questionable.

As a research resource, the Internet complements Lexis and Westlaw. The Net provides some information at vastly reduced costs (the Americans with Disabilities Act and NAFTA can be downloaded for free), doesn't provide other information at all (most state and trial-level (versus appellate-level) federal court opinions are not available yet) and provides other information not available anywhere else (for example, access to the House of Representatives Internet Law Library, mailing lists and newsgroups).

Several other factors distinguish Lexis from the Net. Most significant is the Internet's provision for interactive communication, which Lexis lacks. Users of the Internet can communicate amongst themselves, exchanging ideas and documents. On Lexis, individuals can retrieve documents, but can not then use Lexis to modify those documents and then electronically send those documents to others.

HOW LAWYERS ARE USING THE INTERNET

I personally got involved with the Internet in 1991, while I was working on an article that was ultimately published in the *Santa Clara Computer and High Technology Law Journal*.[3] In the course of writing that article, I attended a fascinating conference titled "Computers, Freedom and Privacy." In attendance were an unusual mix of people, including FBI agents, computer hackers, attorneys, journalists and others interested in the nexus of technology and civil liberties. Of the many things I learned at that conference, the most important was that virtually everyone there was already communicating via this thing called the Internet. I resolved that when I returned home, I would have to get online. Since that time, I've left legal practice to start a company that supports lawyers and business people with legal research services. The Internet has continued to play a vital role in that work, from the communication, research and marketing standpoints.

Now the Internet is a popular phenomenon, no longer the obscure medium it was a few short years ago. Many lawyers are online, using the Net in daily practice. Tim Muth is an attorney with Reinhart, Boerner and others in Milwaukee, Wisconsin, who has been online a short time, but is already proficient at using the range of Internet services. When I caught up with Tim he was surfing[4] around the

3. The article is titled "A Proposal for Federal Legislation Protecting Informational Privacy Across the Private Sector," November 1993, page 431, and can be found on the net at: gopher://gopher.panix.com:70/00/SEA/Privacy/Federal%20Information%20Privacy%20Proposal%20%28J.%20Blackman%29.

4. "Surfing" in the Internet context (versus the beachboy context) means visiting various Internet computers from the comfort of your computer (bikinis and beer optional).

net, and that seemed like a good place to start our conversation. I wondered whether partners at his firm worry that lawyers might waste time online. Tim responded:

> "At this point we don't have lots of people with full access to the Net, although the plan is to have everybody with Netscape[5] and access to the Net directly. And so people do raise that as a concern. I have mixed emotions about it. I can relate to having situations when I'm spending time surfing the Net when there's probably other things I should attend to. On the other hand, I think that it just makes my day longer, it doesn't mean that the work doesn't get done; it just means that there are these intermissions.
>
> "I haven't had any situations where I have had to defend the value of [the time involved in establishing] the home page.[6] I mean generally the reaction whenever anyone sees it—at least for the younger ones—is 'that's cool.' The firm is very supportive of the home page and generally supportive of giving people access to the Internet as a whole, although you have to affirmatively ask for it. We're not going to suddenly have it appear as an icon on everybody's screen. But I don't know that we have any plans to make people justify that they have a real need for it.
>
> "I first started using the Internet last summer. I had my own account through a local Internet provider. One thing that provider offered was that anybody who had

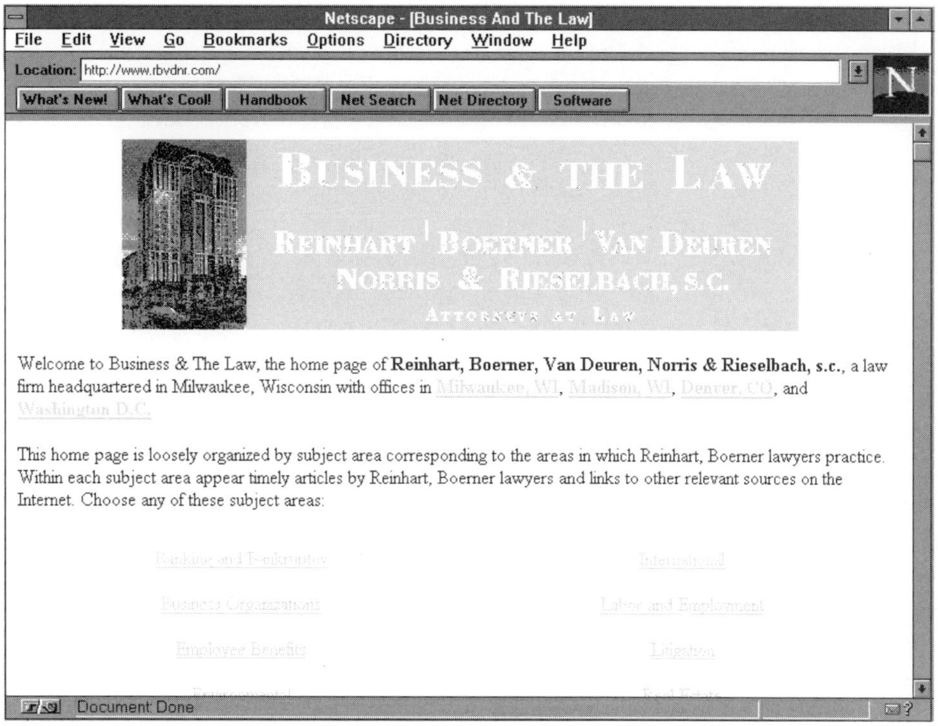

Netscape - [Business And The Law]
File Edit View Go Bookmarks Options Directory Window Help
Location: http://www.rbvdnr.com/
What's New! What's Cool! Handbook Net Search Net Directory Software

BUSINESS & THE LAW
REINHART | BOERNER | VAN DEUREN
NORRIS & RIESELBACH, S.C.
ATTORNEYS AT LAW

Welcome to Business & The Law, the home page of **Reinhart, Boerner, Van Deuren, Norris & Rieselbach, s.c.**, a law firm headquartered in Milwaukee, Wisconsin with offices in Milwaukee, WI, Madison, WI, Denver, CO, and Washington D.C.

This home page is loosely organized by subject area corresponding to the areas in which Reinhart, Boerner lawyers practice. Within each subject area appear timely articles by Reinhart, Boerner lawyers and links to other relevant sources on the Internet. Choose any of these subject areas:

Document: Done

Figure 1-3. http://www.rbvdnr.com/

This is the home page of the law firm Reinhart, Boerner, Van Deuren, Norris & Rieselbach S.C. Attorney Tim Muth maintains the page.

5. Netscape is a web browser. That means that it is software that can be used to go to various computers (or Browse) that are interconnected via software that comprises the World Wide Web. The Web provides graphically oriented hypertext documents. By using browsers such as Netscape, one can hypertextually "jump" from documents on various computers in various geographic locations, by using your mouse and cursor to click on documents that appear on the browser screen

6. A home page is a screen of information that is accessible on the Internet using software known as a web browser. Common browsers are Netscape, Mosaic and Lynx. Tim Muth created a home page for his firm that displays information about the firm and that enables anyone on the net to access memos written by firm attorneys and other materials. To view the memos, you can simply click your mouse on particular parts of the home page.

a subscription, could set up a home page. I initially started just playing around with creating my own links. But then, gradually, as I saw other legal sites, I thought that it was something that might be useful for the firm as a whole. I took what I had been playing around with and I developed it into something that people could take a look at. The reactions were, Wow, this is great. Go ahead and take it the rest of the way.

"I don't think that we have real expectations of getting a large number of clients through the fact that we have a presence on the Net. I think if that were our expectation we'd be sadly disappointed. We have long viewed ourselves as being a technological leader in the legal community in terms of the level of automation of the firm. We had terminals on everybody's desktops nine, 10 years ago, which was well before anybody else. I guess we viewed the home page as giving us both sort of a presence and adding to our image as sort of at the cutting edge, forward looking. It was as much image enhancement as anything.

"We also view it as a communication tool with clients to a certain extent. In the next mailing of our firm newsletter that generally goes to our entire client base, there's going to be an article letting people know about the site. If they want to get information about the attorneys or see what we're doing on the Internet, or see latest updates and articles on particular areas within the firm, [the home page enables that]. Just the fact that we announce it to our client base, even if some of them have no connection to the Internet, it has a certain advantage in the image department.

"[In setting up the home page] one thing that we spent time thinking through were the disclaimers that are at the bottom of that first page. We thought those were important to include. I don't see them on many other law firm pages. [We thought they were important because first,] you have to think through the issues of legal advertising. We looked at the Wisconsin ethics rules and we think that we are complying with them. The other thing is, we don't want to have a situation where someone sends us email, particularly for me since I'm a litigator. If an opposing party, or someone who was thinking that I might represent their opponent, sent me email with some kind of confidential information saying we want to hire you, [that] could conflict me out. We thought it was important to try and eliminate that possibility. We also wanted to let our clients know about the lack of security of communications on the Net and [that] if you do send us an email, be careful about what you do.

"I'm real pleased with the results and the reaction I'm getting from people online. I think that the payback is right for the amount of time I put into it. I really did do it at night and on weekends. It helped that there was someone like me that enjoys doing it. I've always done a little bit of computer programming on the side as a hobby. And while this is nowhere nearly as complicated as programming, it has sort of the same attraction to me. A lot of this stuff is taking materials that already exist in word processing documents someplace within the firm and simply taking the steps to convert them into HTML[7] format, which can really be done fairly simply. The part that is my favorite is the page called "Legal Sites."[8] It is a collection of excerpts from the NET-LAWYERS mailing list of every URL[9] that has been listed on the mailing list since January 1995."

7. HTML stands for HyperText Markup Language, the programming language used to compose home pages. Writing HTML largely consists of inserting codes like <bold> into documents so that they can be properly displayed by Web browsers.

8. Sites on the Internet are virtual places, that exist on some computer hard disk somewhere (could be in the next room, or in the next country; the Internet cares little for borders). If you have an "address" for a site, you can get there and take advantage of the material at that site, which may be a database, or a document, or a picture, or a combination of these things.

9. URL stands for Uniform Resource Locator. This has evolved into the standard citation method for the Net. The URL for the firm Reinhart, Boerner, Van Deuren, Norris & Rieselbach home page created by Tim Muth is: http://www.rbvdnr.com/.

Chapter 2

Internet BASICS

HOW TO GET CONNECTED

IT MAY BE THAT THE INTERNET OFFERS THE BEST OPPORTUNITY YET TO DRAG THE legal profession into the information age. The Net offers free access to government documents, statutes and case opinions, as well as the opportunity to directly communicate with global and neighborhood colleagues. In order to take advantage of the Internet's offerings, the first step is to get online. Access requires a computer, a modem, communication software and an account with an Internet access provider.

Hardware and Software

You can use any computer to access the Internet. The age, speed and memory of the machine are of little consequence for basic Internet access purposes. If you don't already have a computer and plan to buy one, it's generally a good idea to purchase the machine that has the most advanced central processing chip (the Pentium chip is the current top-end chip for IBM-compatible machines), the most random access memory (RAM) and the largest hard disk you can afford. The speed of the machine is important if you run sophisticated graphics-intensive software like Windows and Netscape. Computer speed is also known as clock speed, and is measured in megahertz (Mhz). Today's high-end machines run at higher than 150 Mhz. You'll get by okay with a machine running at half that speed. The Windows operating system, for example, will run faster as your clock speed increases. Windows will also run faster as you increase RAM (a minimum of 16 megabytes (MB) is recommended). Windows is necessary (for IBM-compatible machines) if you plan to use graphical Web browsers such as Netscape, Netcruiser or Internet Explorer.

The vast majority of Internet uses that apply to the law office are text-based, so it matters little whether you have a color or monochrome monitor. Most people, however, use their computer for more than accessing the Internet, and color generally makes using computers a bit more stimulating. Furthermore, high resolution color monitors are generally standard issue with new computers, so for many readers, this discussion of color is moot. However, if you're using an older machine with a black and white monitor, the Internet will appear the same as in color, except for the graphical images found on the World Wide Web.

In addition to a computer, most people need a modem and telephone line to reach the Net. There are those who don't need a modem because they have access to a "direct Internet connection," a perpetually open line to the Net. For example, if your firm provides Net access through the company LAN, or if you're at a university that provides a Net connection through a mainframe computer to which your personal computer is linked, you won't need a modem (unless you want to access the Net when away from the office). But most people access the Internet by dialing an Internet access provider. The modem is the device that does the dialing. It is either internal or external to the computer, and is plugged into a telephone line. By using communication software, your computer directs the modem to dial the phone number of your Internet access provider, and connect to the Internet.

The modem is one of the key elements that will determine how fast your Internet connection runs. Modem speed is measured in bits per second (bps). The average fast speed modem is 14,400 (14.4 bps), although there are 28.8 bps modems available now. If you're shopping for a modem, get the fastest one you can afford.

The communication software you will use to access your Internet provider will depend on that provider. Some providers give you access software, and some do not. If your provider does not, you will need to use off-the-shelf software such as ProComm or Xtalk (note that most modems are packaged with communication software). These programs enable you to dial into electronic bulletin board systems as well as your Internet provider. Communications software is similar to other software types, such as word processing programs, in that each type of software does the same basic thing (communicate or write). The differences are in how well the software is designed, how it "looks and feels," and what sort of features are built in.

Types of Internet Connections

Deciding which provider to use is critical. Although you may switch around among providers before you settle on one (or more) you're happy with, you do want to settle on one you'll use for email. In order to avoid confusing your colleagues and yourself, you'll want to have only one email address, so that all your email goes to one place where you can retrieve it. Just like postal mail, if you have multiple addresses, it's likely you won't get some of your mail in a timely fashion. Therefore, you need to choose a primary online provider.

For someone who is new to online services, the best idea is to choose a provider who makes access to and use of the service as easy as possible. Such ease of use includes software that is fairly intuitive, and stable, and telephone support to help out when you run into problems. Understanding what each provider offers will help you make that decision. The various providers offer five ways for individuals to connect to the Internet.

1. Commercial online services. All of the commercial services (America Online, CompuServe, Prodigy, Counsel Connect, etc.) offer Internet access. It is often limited access, and more expensive and slower than other types of connections. On the plus side, the access software is pretty easy to use, and the commercial services have telephone support people (if you can get through). This is often the best option for people who are new to online services.
2. Shell account. Before the world realized the Internet existed, the only sort of connection available to most people was a shell account. This sort of connection is text only (there's no graphical interface). It's usually necessary for you to know some minimal UNIX commands (similar to understanding DOS). Shell accounts are cheap (under $20 per month), but require a willingness to figure things out, as there is little provided in the way of technical support.
3. SLIP (Serial Line Internet Protocol) or PPP (Point-to-Point Protocol) accounts are the next generation in Internet access after shell accounts. Usually, the same providers who offer shell accounts also offer SLIP/PPP. The most noticeable difference is that SLIP and PPP allow the use of the graphical Web browsers (Netscape and Mosaic) that are so popular. You can't use a graphical browser with a mere shell account. SLIP/PPP software is usually tricky to set up, however. Don't bother with a SLIP or PPP connection unless you're willing to tinker with it.
4. Hybrid (aka integrated) dial-up account. Netcom is one of the most popular providers who offer this sort of account. Essentially, Netcom access consists of proprietary graphical software (provided by Netcom) that includes everything you need to access the Internet, including a Web browser, email, and telnet/gopher/ftp/newsgroup access. When you start up the Netcom software, it establishes a hassle-free PPP connection for you. Cost is reasonable ($20 for 30 hours). If you're not interested in the additional services available on a commercial service such as America Online, or the particular legal services available on Counsel Connect, then a Netcom account might be for you.
5. LAN connection. If your firm or institution connects its local area Network (LAN) to the Internet, you will have the fastest sort of access available. Unlike dial-up connections, a LAN connection (also known as a dedicated connection) is available 24 hours a day. It costs several thousands dollars per month, and requires expensive dedicated computer hardware and a technical staff to maintain it.

If you're shopping around for a provider, you can usually try them out on a monthly basis for little cost. Many services even offer a free introductory period. You might want to give several providers a try to find the one that works best for you.

Finding an Access Provider

There are plenty of Internet providers, with ever-changing prices and features. The better-known providers include CompuServe, Prodigy, America Online, the Microsoft Network, Netcom, and PSI, with additional players entering the market every day. There is a legal-specific provider (Counsel Connect) that offers email, access to the Internet, and access to legal resources.

You may find that access is already available if you're affiliated with a university or a technically-oriented firm. If not, you can contact a provider and arrange access for yourself. For a list of Internet access providers (in the U.S. and abroad), call the Internet Network Information Center (InterNIC) at (800) 444-4345.

Figure 2-1. http://www.thelist.com

The List Web site enables you to search for Internet providers by name, country, state or country.

One of the most comprehensive lists of providers is known simply as The List. A problem with The List is that it is only accessible from the Net, so if you're not already online, it will be hard to get, and if you are online, you probably already have a provider. In any case, The List is a searchable collection of thousands of Internet providers, and can be found at http://www.thelist.com .

Another list of providers is the Public Access Dial-up Provider List or PDIAL. Like The List, PDIAL is only available online, although unlike The List, PDIAL can be retrieved using email. I can imagine a situation where you're using a system that provides email-only access to the Internet, and you want to find a provider that offers a more robust Internet connection. In such a situation, PDIAL can be a useful document. You can retrieve it by sending an email message to info-deli-server@Netcom.com. In the body of the message, type: Send PDIAL

The PDIAL list is also available from the Web at the following address:

http://www.cis.ohio-state.edu/hypertext/faq/useNet/pdial/faq.html

ACCESSING INFORMATION ON THE Internet

URLs

Throughout this directory, you will find the address of an Internet-connected computer, or Internet-accessible document displayed in a format known as URL, or Uniform Resource Locator. For example, the URL for Cornell Law School is: http://www.law.cornell.edu The URL is a standard way to display an Internet address, and can be used in a Web browser (such as Netscape or Mosaic) to take you directly to the site designated by the address.

Note the "http" designation at the beginning of the Cornell URL. This stands for hypertext transfer protocol and tells you that this URL will take you to a Web site. By definition, Web sites are hypertextual, meaning Web sites generally include on-screen links, or highlighted words that you can select to jump to related documents that may be on another portion of the hard disk at Cornell, or could be on a computer in another country. This hypertextual feature is one of the hallmarks of the World Wide Web.

In addition to identifying Internet sites that are accessible using a Web browser, URLs can identify the location of documents and databases that are accessible using other Internet tools, including gopher, ftp and telnet. For example, here's a gopher address in URL format for the Murdoch University Law Library in Australia:

gopher://infolib.murdoch.edu.au/11/.ftp/pub/subj/law

Notice that rather than starting with "http," this URL starts with "gopher." This indicates that once you get to this site (for example, by inserting the URL into the Location option in your Netscape Web browser) you will be presented with a menu of options from which you can choose. This menu format is produced by the gopher software running at the Murdoch University site.

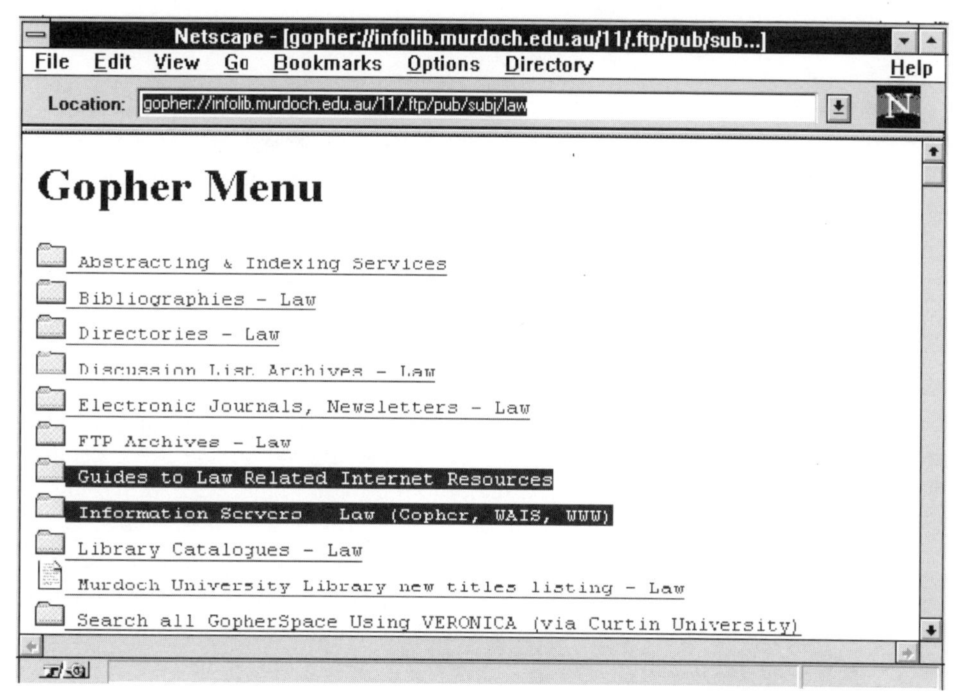

Figure 2-2.
gopher://infolib.murdoch.edu.au/11/.ftp/pub/subj/law

A gopher site from the Murdoch University Law Library in Australia, displayed in the Netscape Web browser.

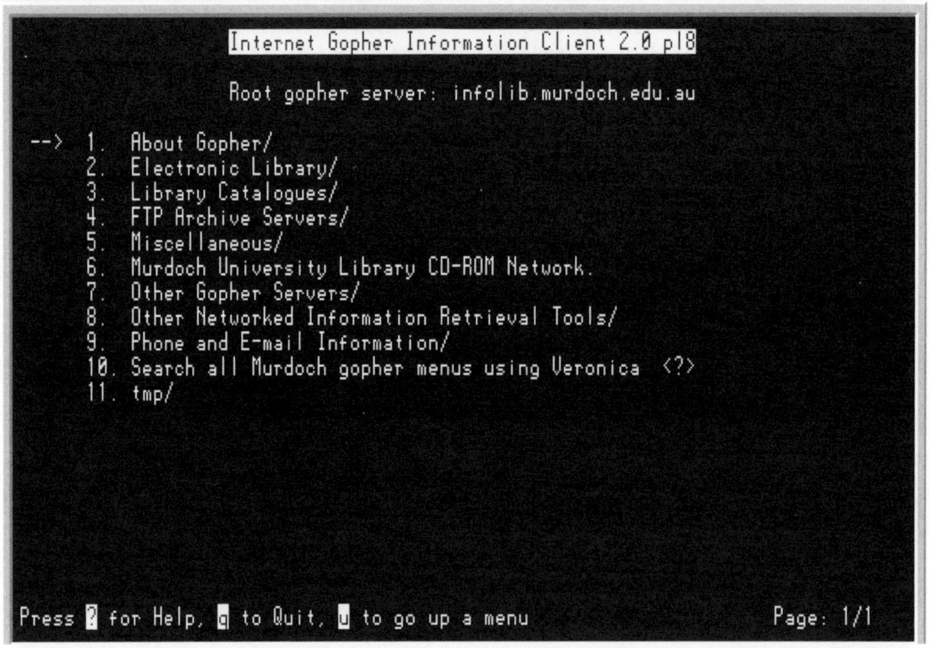

```
                    Internet Gopher Information Client 2.0 pl8

                    Root gopher server: infolib.murdoch.edu.au

 -->  1.  About Gopher/
      2.  Electronic Library/
      3.  Library Catalogues/
      4.  FTP Archive Servers/
      5.  Miscellaneous/
      6.  Murdoch University Library CD-ROM Network.
      7.  Other Gopher Servers/
      8.  Other Networked Information Retrieval Tools/
      9.  Phone and E-mail Information/
      10. Search all Murdoch gopher menus using Veronica  <?>
      11. tmp/

Press ? for Help, q to Quit, u to go up a menu                    Page: 1/1
```

Figure 2-3.

The Murdoch Law Library gopher site displayed using the Lynx non-graphical Web browser.

Before graphical Web browsers became common, the Internet was usually accessed through a strictly-text Web browser, such as Lynx. In order to get to Internet addresses using a shell account, you have to enter commands, rather than use your mouse to click on graphical icons. For example, to get to the Murdoch Law Library using Lynx, you would type: "G" to bring up the "go to" prompt in Lynx, and then type: gopher infolib.murdoch.edu.au . The resulting gopher menu looks like the screen in figure 2-3.

Notice that the list of gopher menu options on this root gopher screen are not identical to the menu options retrieved using Netscape. This is because when using Lynx to go to a gopher menu, you must navigate your way through the menu options to get to the precise page of options you desire. When using a URL in a Web browser, however, you can get directly to the menu page, without having to burrow down through the gopher menu options.

Through trial and error, I found the identical menu page displayed in figure 2-2 by choosing the following options. From the root menu, I chose Electronic Library. This brought up another screen, from which I chose Subject Information, and then Subject Information from Murdoch University and then Law. The end result is the screen in figure 2-4.

The benefits of using a URL are pretty plain, if you are using a Web browser. You can simply plug the URL string into your browser and go directly to the page you want. If you are not using a browser, however, it can be difficult to use a URL to figure out how to get to a Web address.

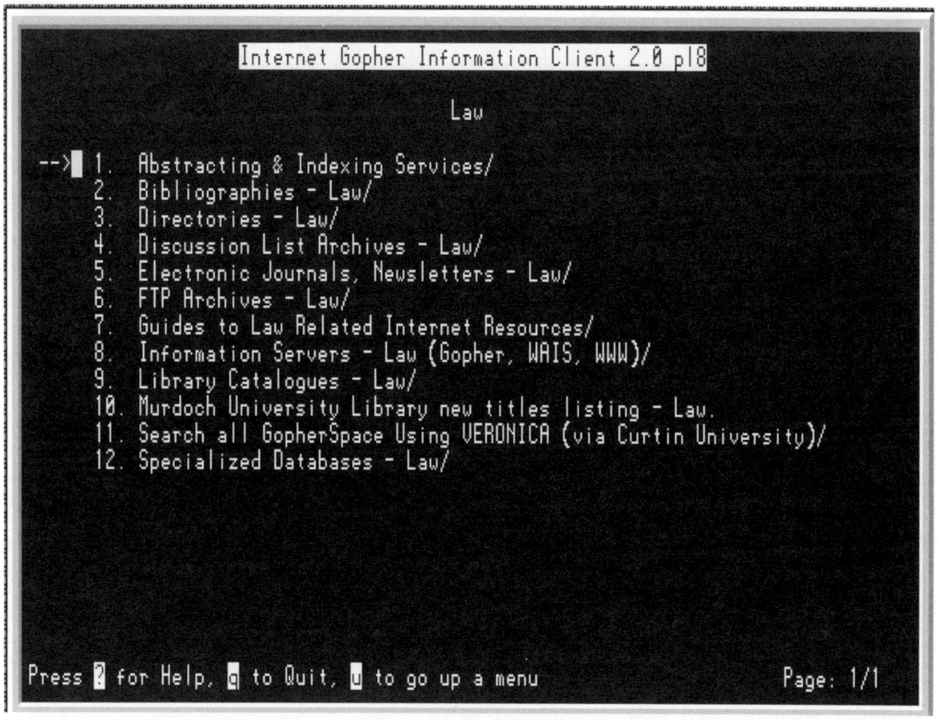

```
Internet Gopher Information Client 2.0 pl8

                         Law

-->  1.  Abstracting & Indexing Services/
     2.  Bibliographies - Law/
     3.  Directories - Law/
     4.  Discussion List Archives - Law/
     5.  Electronic Journals, Newsletters - Law/
     6.  FTP Archives - Law/
     7.  Guides to Law Related Internet Resources/
     8.  Information Servers - Law (Gopher, WAIS, WWW)/
     9.  Library Catalogues - Law/
     10. Murdoch University Library new titles listing - Law.
     11. Search all GopherSpace Using VERONICA (via Curtin University)/
     12. Specialized Databases - Law/

Press ? for Help, q to Quit, u to go up a menu                Page: 1/1
```

Figure 2-4.

Here's the Murdoch Law Library site again, showing the same gopher menu options as displayed in the Netscape image in figure 2-2.

Searching for Information Online

There is no point to getting online if you don't know what to do once you get there. For example, if you wish to "go to" the Library of Congress, you need to know the Library's Internet address (gopher://marvel.loc.gov). There are several ways to get this information. You could ask for it on one of the legal mailing lists or newsgroups. You could acquire one of the directories of legal resources (such as this book) available either on the Internet, or on bookstore shelves. You could also search for it online using an Internet search engine.

Accessing a search engine is a way to use the Internet's powerful computers to filter through large amounts of data to find what you need. Search engines (also known as indexes, crawlers, spiders, worms and robots) are attached to large databases of Internet addresses that are searchable by key word. These tools allow you to look for particular documents or to search for materials that address a particular subject.

Using a search engine is pretty simple. You just fill in a box with a word or words and hit the return key. Results are usually returned to your screen in seconds. Whether you're looking for a section of the Americans with Disabilities Act, or trying to find a railroad expert based in London, search engines will often help you find what you need.

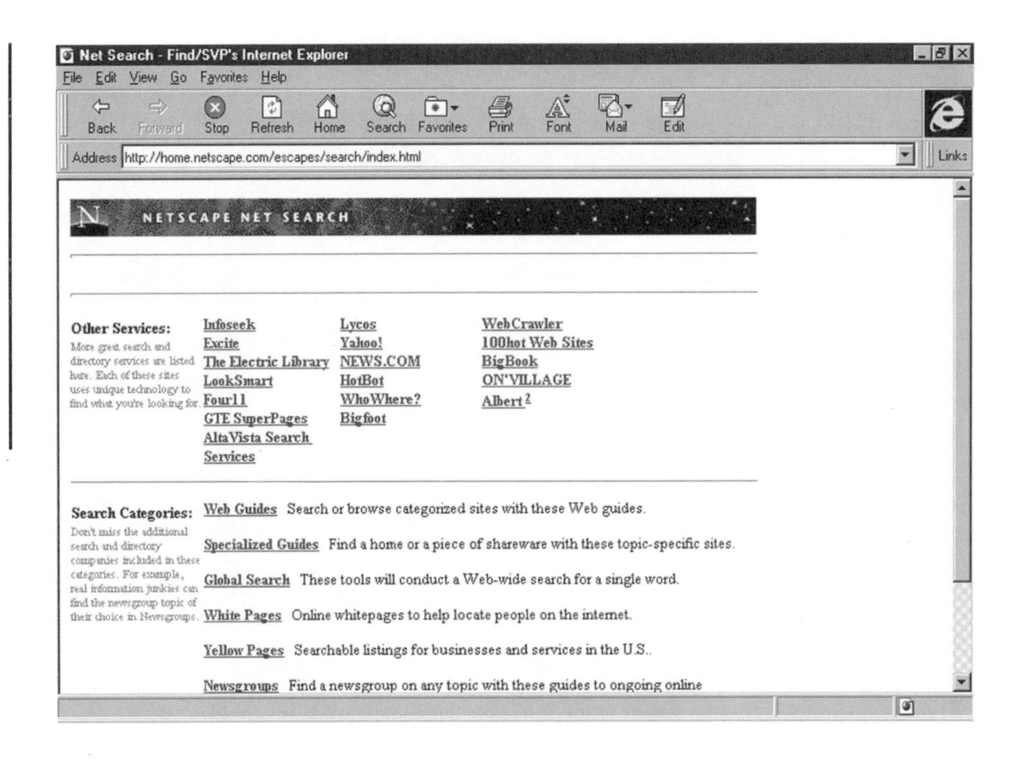

Figure 2-5.
http://home.netscape.com/escapes/search/index.html

A collection of Internet search engines.

There are several search engines, and they all work slightly differently. Some have more complete databases than others. The most popular search engines can run slower than those that are used less frequently. Following are a few of the best search engines. Remember that different engines produce different results, so if one doesn't return what you need, try another.

- Internet Search Engine Page is a collection of various search engines.

  URL: http://home.Netscape.com/home/interNet-search.html

- Yahoo is one of the most popular Web search engines. As a result of its popularity, you may experience delays in receiving results. The Yahoo database is very large, and therefore provides excellent coverage of Internet resources. It also provides subject-specific indexes, including one for law.

  URL: http://www.yahoo.com/Government/Law/

- Lycos is similar to Yahoo in terms of its breadth. It includes some four million Web addresses, and is very popular.

  URL: http://lycos.cs.cmu.edu

- Veronica is an engine that will search through gopher sites only. That means it will not search Web sites. It allows for both general and specific searches.

  URL: gopher://info3.scs.unr.edu:8117/7

  URL: gopher://gopher.tamu.edu

Centralized Legal Connections

In addition to Internet search engines, a number of centralized services have been set up to make it easier to find legal information on the Internet. See the Publications section of the directory for a list of such services. For example, Cornell Law School's Legal Information Institute, operates a gopher server rich with legal resources. The URL is: gopher://fatty.law.cornell.edu . Below is the opening menu from the Cornell site. Choosing any one of these menu options will reveal several layers of additional legal resources.

- Cornell Law School Information
- Directory Of Legal Academia
- Discussions And Listserv Archives
- U.S. Law: Primary Documents and Commentary
- Foreign And International Law: Primary Documents And Commentary
- Government (US) And Agency Information
- Information Services: Academic Institutions
- Library Resources (Online Catalogs)
- Periodicals, News, And Journals
- Other Gophers And Information Services
- Internet (Ftp Sources, Archie, etc)
- Locators (Where To Find People And Things)
- Miscellaneous
- Other Internet Law Sites

ACCESSING Internet INFORMATION USING THIS DIRECTORY

In Part III, the directory portion of this book, a unique format has been used to present information about legal resources available on the Internet. Following is an example of one of those resources.

COMMUNICATIONS LAW MEMOS

DESCRIPTION: This site is provided by the law firm Pepper & Corazzini. It includes attorney-written memos on a variety of current issues related to broadcasting, cable, equal employment opportunity (EEO), common carriers, PCS and information law. The WWW server has a direct link to the FCC gopher.

PROVIDER: Pepper & Corazzini, L.L.P.

ADDRESS:	1776 K St., N.W., Washington, DC 20006
PHONE:	(202) 296-0600
FAX:	(202) 296-5572
CONTACT:	Neal J. Friedman
EMAIL:	nfriedma@clark.Net
URL:	http://www.commlaw.com
URL:	ftp://ftp.iis.com/pub/pepper/memos/

Note that the entry for Communications Law Memos includes an identification of the provider of the information, as well as the providers' address and other contact information. This is included to help you determine whether this data is credible and accurate. In chapter 5 of this book, you will find a discussion of the accuracy of Internet information, as well as opinions on this subject from several experts.

Note also that this entry includes two access methods. These are provided because there are two ways to retrieve the Pepper & Corazzini memos from the Internet. Some Internet resources are accessible only by one method, and some via multiple methods. In this case, the memos are first accessible by using a Web browser to reach the http[10] site. Second, one can use ftp[11] to retrieve the file. Both methods will provide you with the same document.

FAQS

Since there is so much to know about the Net, and so many people ask the same questions, files of frequently asked questions or FAQs, have been compiled and are commonly available for free on the Net. Whether you want to know what particular newsgroups are concerned with, or how to set up a firewall in your firm, there's probably a FAQ that will give you the basic information you want to know. There is a central repository for FAQs available at the following URL: http://www.cis.ohio-state.edu/hypertext/faq/useNet/FAQ-List.html

DOWNLOADING

If you access the Internet by dialing into a public access provider, your desktop computer will generally not actually be on the Internet as a node such that other people on the Net could visit your computer. Rather, you will be accessing your provider's computer (which is an Internet node) through which you will access the wider Net. In such a case, if you retrieve a file from a remote site, for example, if you retrieve a Supreme Court opinion from Cornell Law School's site, you will be retrieving the opinion (which is in the form of a text file) to your provider's computer. If you want to get that file onto your desktop machine, you will need to download the file.

Downloading is a process whereby you direct software to move a file from your provider's computer memory to your desktop machine's hard disk (or floppy disk). The download software is imbedded within your communication software.[12] There are various standard names for the imbedded software, including XMODEM, ZMODEM and Kermit. These are also known as download proto-

10. "http" stands for hypertext transfer protocol, which is the program that enables you to retrieve information on the World Wide Web.

11. "ftp" stands for file transfer protocol, which is a program that one can use to retrieve files located on remote computers. If you know the computer address, directory, and file name where a particular file is located, you can ftp to that site and copy the file to your provider's computer. If you wish, you can then download it to your desktop machine.

12. Downloading to a floppy disk is a little-known security method. Although Internet access providers routinely scan their machines to check for computer viruses (as should you), it is possible that such potentially damaging programs could get through to you. As an added security step, rather than downloading to your hard disk, and potentially infecting it, you can download to a floppy disk, which has no data that could be potentially harmed. Then you can virus scan the floppy prior to moving the downloaded file to your hard disk.

cols. In some communications software, for example, the software provided by Counsel Connect, or CompuServe, the name and technical aspects of the download portion of the software are hidden from the user. All you have to know when using these interfaces is that you want to download a file. You'll find a download option in one of the menus. You'll choose the option; the software will tell you that the download will take a few minutes or seconds, and the download will begin. The size of the file, the speed of your modem and the efficiency of the download protocol will determine how long each download takes.

UPLOADING

Uploading is the opposite of downloading, but works in essentially the same way. Uploading denotes moving a file from your desktop computer to your provider's computer. Once you get the file to your provider's machine, you can then email it to a colleague, or store it on the provider's hard disk for later retrieval. Again, some providers' software makes the upload process more or less invisible. If you choose to email a file to a friend, and you're using Counsel Connect's interface, you can simply direct the email software to "attach" a file that may reside on your hard disk, and send it to your friend. In such a case, the file is dynamically copied from your hard disk and sent directly to your friend's email box, without requiring an intermediary upload process.

COMPRESSED FILES

In order to save hard disk space, and transmission (upload/download) time, sometimes files are compressed. Compression software is used to compress and decompress files. Common compression software includes Winzip and pkzip. This software is available free on the Internet, and can also be purchased. There are many other compression programs as well. You can generally identify a compressed file by its extension, or the characters that appear after the dot in the file name. For example, a file compressed using pkzip or Winzip has a zip extension as follows: bigfile.zip . A compressed file is not usable in its compressed form. It must be decompressed in order to be usable or readable. If you want to know more about compressed files, read the Compressed files FAQ, which you can find at: http://www.cis.ohio-state.edu/hypertext/faq/useNet/compression-faq/top.html

UNIX

If you do not choose a provider who offers easy-to-use graphically-driven Internet access software, such as Counsel Connect, or Netcom, you may choose a provider who offers a simple text-only interface. Effective use of such an interface may require a basic understanding of the Net's common operating system - UNIX. For DOS users, this is not all that complex. There are UNIX commands that are functionally equivalent to the DOS commands for directory creation and deletion, copying of files, etc.

The Internet is, of course, a network of computers. As in any foreign land, it helps to know the native tongue. So, here are a few useful UNIX commands and their functions. In order to enter the following commands, you must enter them at a UNIX prompt, which may be: $ or %

pwd	print working directory (displays current directory)
ls	lists files in current directory
rm FILENAME	removes file
mkdir DIRECTORY	creates (makes) a directory
cd DIRECTORY	change to a new directory
<ctrl> c	Break character; stops an operation; in some cases, must be used twice

Chapter 3

Introduction to Internet Information Access Tools

ESPECIALLY FOR THE UNINITIATED, THE INTERNET CAN BE INTIMIDATING. MERELY understanding what it is and how it practically applies to your life can be most difficult of all. From a functional perspective, the Net is a communication tool, just as the telephone and fax machines are devices that let you speak to other people. Some fax machines resemble Internet-connected computers by behaving interactively. For example, it is common to use fax machines to distribute product literature. Using the buttons on your touch-tone telephone, you can direct a properly configured manufacturer's fax machine to send literature to your fax machine. On the Internet as well, there are computers that you can contact to request information.

Sometimes that information is stored on a government computer. Sometimes that information comes directly from another person responding to your request. Therefore, the Internet enables both communication, and information retrieval. Information can be a document or a person's opinion. For the many knowledge workers in our society (including lawyers), who work intensively with bits of such information, the Net is a very cost-effective way to get through the days chores.

There are essentially six mechanisms or software tools in use on the Internet that let you get the information you want:

1. email,
2. discussion forums (including mailing lists and newsgroups),
3. World-Wide-Web (also known as WWW and the Web),
4. gopher,
5. telnet, and
6. ftp.

This chapter will briefly discuss the most important things you need to know to use each of these tools effectively.

USING INTERNET EMAIL

In order to use email on the Internet, you need access to email software (sometimes referred to as a mailreader). There are many mailreaders available. Which one you use will depend on which provider you choose for Internet access. Providers with unique interfaces, like Counsel Connect or America Online, provide their own mailreaders, with custom-designed features. Most public Internet providers, such as Panix, for example, do not provide proprietary software interfaces. On Panix, you can choose from one of the several common Internet mailreaders that are freely available. These software packages reside on the hard disk of the provider. When you log on to the Panix computer, for example, you can then invoke your mailreader. Mailreaders on Panix have names like PINE and ELM.

All mailreaders do essentially the same thing. They let you read, create, send, reply and forward mail. Most mailreaders enable you to "attach" a file to your mail message. For example, you might want to attach a word processed document to your message. Alternatively, you can include documents within the body of mail messages. Some mailreaders have address books that you can customize so you don't have to remember your colleagues' addresses. Some of them have better (more intuitive) word processing capabilities for composing mail messages. The slicker packages have spell checking and other fancy features.

Another sort of mailreader that can be useful, is the offline mailreader. While most mailreaders enable you to receive and send mail while you are logged on, an offline mailreader will capture all your mail and download it to your hard disk. The idea is that you then log off, and respond to your mail offline, without incurring any online charges. For some providers, such as Panix, this serves little purpose, because Panix doesn't charge an online (or per-minute) fee. However, if you're using a business telephone line, you are incurring local phone charges while online.

INTERNET ADDRESSES

As the Internet transitions toward broad public use, many of its characteristics are being streamlined. The way the Net appears on your screen, for example, is changing from a text-based interface into a friendlier, graphical screen. One of the lingering, and perhaps unavoidable aspects of Internet use is addressing. Since the Net consists of interlinked computers, in order for each computer (and each document stored on each computer) to be identifiable, each requires a unique address.

Internet addresses have certain characteristics that are important for you to be aware of in order to get things done online. First, addresses are case sensitive. An upper case "B" and a lower case "b" are not the same character. In the digital world, precision is essential. So whenever you type an Internet address, whether you are using it for email, gopher, or Web access, be sure to reproduce the address exactly as you see it.

The format of addresses is also very important. Internet addresses are divided by periods "." into domains. Originally, there were six so-called high-level domains that appeared at the far right of email addresses. There are now many more high-level domains. For example, there are domains for each Internet-connected country in the world. The original six domains, which represent the different entities that own computers connected to the Internet, are:

- com = commercial organization
- edu = educational organization
- gov = governmental organization
- mil = military organization
- org = other organizations
- net = network resources

To the left of the high-level domain are unique domain names, which identify each Internet-connected computer, or node. These unique names are registered with the Internet Network Information Center (InterNIC) to ensure uniqueness. Examples include the "mcdonalds" portion of mcdonalds.com and the "internetlawyer" portion of internetlawyer.com.

To the left of the unique domain name are domains created by the administrator of each Internet node. For example, in the address: sunsite.unc.edu, the high-level domain is edu, so we know that the computer is based at an educational institution. To the left of edu, unc is the unique designator for the University of North Carolina. The administrator of that site created a subdomain, named "sunsite," where certain menus and documents exist.

In email addresses, domains are to the right of the @ symbol. In other addresses, for example, those used for gopher, telnet, ftp and web addresses, you will see domains simply strung together by periods (for example: fatty.law.cornell.edu). Here are some examples of Internet addresses:

Email addresses:	joshb@panix.com president@whitehouse.gov
Gopher addresses:	fatty.law.cornell.edu ecix.doc.gov
Uniform Resource Locator (URL) for a gopher site:	gopher://gopher.ora.com:70/11/features
Uniform Resource Locator (URL) for a Web site:	http://www.law.cornell.edu/

The latest innovation in Internet addressing is the URL, or Uniform Resource Locator, described in chapter 2. The nice thing about the URL is its uniformity. If you type the URL (or paste it using a graphical operating system like Windows) into your Web browser you will get directly to the place you want to go. The URL will be clearly interpreted by your browser every time (unless, the computer you're trying to access is disconnected from the Net, or the document is removed or moved to another location on the computer, all of which can happen). On the other hand, a human being may have difficulty deciphering the URL. Although browser software can understand what a URL represents, it's not as clear to a human.

MAILING LISTS

The primary function of email is communication between people. Whether sending a quick note to say hi or transmitting large documents, email is a simple, fast and cheap way to get your message across. The Internet offers a powerful feature known as mailing lists (also known as listserves) that enables communication with many people at the same time. Overall, there are thousands of mailing lists available online that discuss every imaginable topic. There are several hundred that focus on legal issues (see the Mailing Lists section of the Directory).

Email can be used to subscribe to any and all of the mailing lists described in the directory. As a subscriber, you (and everyone else subscribed to the list) will receive (and can participate in) the on-going discussions that occur on that list. For example, to participate in discussions concerning government documents, you can subscribe to the Government Documents mailing list by using email to send the message:

subscribe govdoc-l <Your Name>
(at <Your Name>put your first and last names), to the email address:
listserv@psuvm.bitnet

NEWSGROUPS

Like mailing lists, newsgroups provide Internet access to discussions concerning thousands of specific subject areas. Also like mailing lists, newsgroup discussions generally stay focused on the subject area designated for each group. Groups that no longer generate interest disappear, while new ones appear regularly. Some groups are moderated by an individual who screens the messages released into the group, and some groups are not moderated, thus allowing every and any posting to appear online. Some commercial providers provide for-pay access to some newsgroups. The vast majority, however, are free.

While mailing lists conveniently send messages directly to your email box, newsgroups require that you have access (through your Internet access provider) to software known as a newsreader. This software will display any and all of the 9000 or so newsgroups available on the net. There are several different newsreaders, each of which have their individual characteristics and features. Consult with your access provider to find out which newsreaders are available to you.

Newsgroup messages are displayed in a bulletin board format, which enables you to see the name of the person who authored the message, the subject of the message, and whether anyone has appended comments to the original message. Figure 3-1 is an example of a newsgroup screen.

The newsgroup displayed in figure 3-1 is known as misc.legal. It is one of the many legally-related newsgroups. You can see the newsgroup title in the upper

```
Newsgroup: misc.legal                         Articles: 528 of 2982819/4538 *NO*UPDATE*

a Michael Stone       33  >personal injury
b Conway Chu          20  Need Advice on State Sales Tax Liability
c Jonah Seiger        50  >Attention: New Bill "Title IV of S-652"
d Howard Kass         32  >Can someone with a prior felony conviction become a CPA?
e A Technology        38  Science Law Journal Paper Call
f Daniel Goldberg      1  Mexico
g Daniel Goldberg    120  Mexican Incorporation
h Aileen Kawabe       10  Privatization
i Async User          29  Lawyer Advertising
j Ken Rudd            55  >
k Steve Brinich       10  >>>>Attention: New Bill
l Seth Finkelstein    17  >>>
m Name request       453  SCIENTOLOGY'S WAR AGAINST JUDGES <<< Must read!
n Mike Zorn           14  >>>>>earthlink.com = Scientolo<> Re: Scientology harasses
o J.D. Falk           12  >
p Mark G.             21  >>>>>>
q JESSE M FALK        17  >>
r Alex Shapiro        16  Any expert in Israel Criminal law?
s Mike Zorn           18  >>>>Rogue Site Consideration?<>ink.com = Scientology?...)

-- 08:11 -- SELECT -- help:? -----50%-----<level 2>--
```

Figure 3-1

This screen displays 19 of the hundreds of messages in the misc.legal newsgroup. Each of these 19 messages can also be viewed in full text.

left portion of the screen. Notice the message authors listed along the left side of the screen, identified by the characters a - s. To the right of each name are numbers that identify the number of lines in each message. To the right of that number is the subject of each message. Where you see a subject consisting of one or more "greater than" symbols: ">>," that means that the message is in response to the prior message in the list. For example under the message "Lawyer Advertising," Ken Rudd has appended a comment, identified as ">."

This screen displays only a list of messages. Messages can also be displayed in full text. In this particular newsreader, known as nn, full text can be displayed by typing the character associated with the message you want to see (a - s). If you wanted to read the message whose subject is "Lawyer Advertising," you would hit "i" on your keyboard to highlight the message, and then, holding down the Shift key, hit "z" to display the message. Note that this is a technique particular to nn.

Creation of new newsgroups is not as easy as creation of mailing lists. There is a protocol that must be followed to set up a newsgroup, which often takes time. As a result, newsgroups are not created as dynamically, nor as quickly as mailing lists. Newsgroups have the benefit of organizing conversations in a fairly easy to read format, and are ideal as research resources. For example, many FAQs are regularly posted to newsgroups. Eric Heel's Legal List (a collection of online legal resources), is regularly posted on misc.legal. Should you need to access the Legal List, you can always find a recent version on the newsgroup. Documents found on newsgroups, whether they are messages from individuals or documents like the Legal List can easily be emailed (using newsreader software) to your email box.

WORLD WIDE WEB

The World Wide Web (also known as WWW and the Web) is the primary force driving the Internet into popular consciousness and usage. Its ability to display graphics and provide easy, point-and-click-your-mouse access to information is enabling the majority of people, who won't take the time to figure out how to use the cruder text-only Internet interfaces, to access and use the Internet.

Just as special software is required to read email (a mailreader) and newsgroups (a newsreader), so a Web browser is required to access documents on the Web. There are essentially two sorts of browsers: those that can display graphics (Netscape, Mosaic, Netcruiser) and those that cannot display graphics (Lynx and Cello). The graphical browsers are more fun, because they display color and pictures, and enable you to use your mouse to move from document to document and from computer to computer on the Web. The graphical browsers also have more features, since they are very popular, are competing for attention, and are produced by for-profit companies (versus the text-only browsers that have historically been produced by universities). However, graphical browsers generally require a more sophisticated and more expensive connection to the Internet, and require a computer that has the capability to run a graphical operating system like Windows.

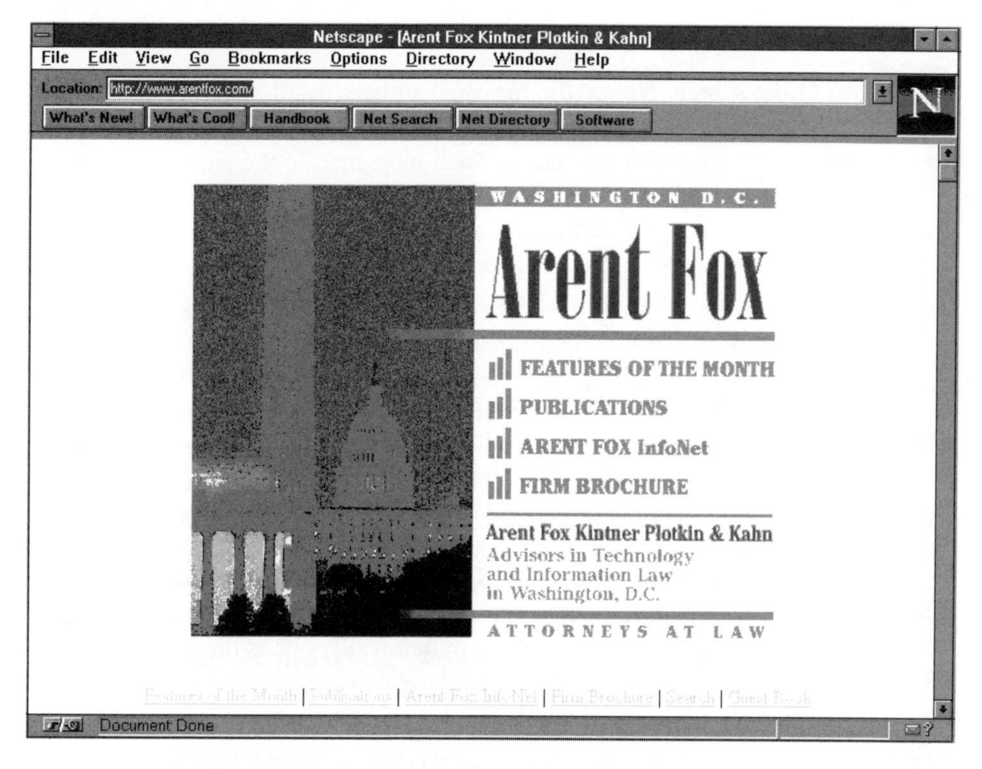

Figure 3-2. http://www.arentfox.com/

Arent Fox Kintner Plotkin & Kahn were one of the earliest firms with an Internet Web site. Their excellent site demonstrates the firm's experience in using the Net for promotion.

Due to the size of files that contain graphics (size refers to the number of bytes that such files take up), graphical browsers generally run slower than non-graphical (text-only) browsers. Text-only browsers generally do not allow you to use your mouse. Rather, you navigate in such browsers using the cursor keys on your keyboard.

Both graphical and text-only Web browsers can display the content of documents on the Web. For the legal professional, the graphical browsers are not as effective as the text-only. Graphical browsers run slower, are generally more expensive, and will not necessarily help you get your work done any more efficiently. The text-only browsers display the documents you need just as well as those that include graphics. One law-firm situation where graphical browsers are the better choice is in the marketing realm. Many law firms are setting up home pages on the web for promotional purposes, and pictures make such pages more interesting (see figure 3-2).

One of the nice things about Web browsers is they can be configured to access gopher, telnet and ftp sites. So, rather than using text-only interfaces to run each of these data access programs on the Net (see descriptions of each on the pages that follow), you can run them from within your browser. If you're using a browser that enables use of your mouse, running gopher, telnet and ftp through the browser will be that much easier.

For those who don't have access to a Web browser, but do have access to telnet, you can use telnet to get to a public Web browser (these public sites offer text-only Lynx browsers). Here are the instructions for accessing these public Web sites:

ACCESS: telnet www.law.cornell.edu
LOGIN: www
ACCESS: telnet www.law.indiana.edu
LOGIN: www

GOPHER

Gopher is software that displays menus of documents and databases. Figure 3-3 is an example of a gopher menu retrieved using an Internet access provider (Panix) that offers a text-only interface. The screen is the first menu offered by the Library of Congress. The menu was retrieved by executing the command: gopher marvel.loc.gov (where marvel.loc.gov is the address for the Library of Congress). Each of the options in the menu represents several layers of menus. You can tell that a menu option has options "behind" it because the option ends with the symbol "/". When a menu option ends in a period "." you can tell that this option is the end of the line, and there are no further options behind it.

You can also use a Web browser to access gopher sites. Figure 3-4 is an image of the same Library of Congress menu retrieved in the Web browser Netscape. In order to get to this gopher site, the URL: gopher://marvel.loc.gov was entered into the Web browser, which effectively tells the Web browser to retrieve the gopher menu that resides at that URL address, and represent it as in the figure.

The two menus represent the same data. What distinguishes them is their look and feel. The Web browser screen enables you to use your mouse to choose menu

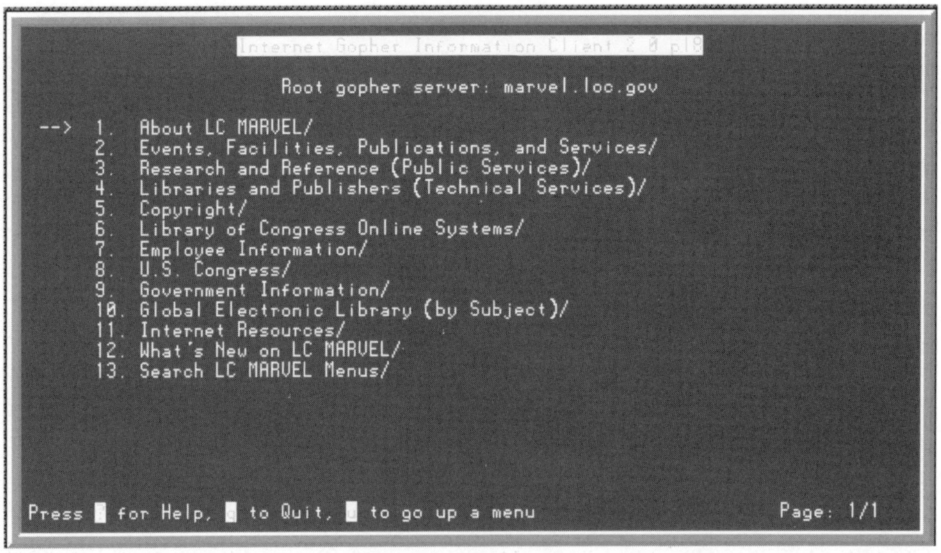

Internet Gopher Information Client 2.0 pl8
Root gopher server: marvel.loc.gov
--> 1. About LC MARVEL/
2. Events, Facilities, Publications, and Services/
3. Research and Reference (Public Services)/
4. Libraries and Publishers (Technical Services)/
5. Copyright/
6. Library of Congress Online Systems/
7. Employee Information/
8. U.S. Congress/
9. Government Information/
10. Global Electronic Library (by Subject)/
11. Internet Resources/
12. What's New on LC MARVEL/
13. Search LC MARVEL Menus/
Press for Help, to Quit, to go up a menu
Page: 1/1

Figure 3-3.

This is the initial gopher menu at the Library of Congress. Using the cursor keys on your keyboard, you can move the arrow (on the left side of the screen) to the option of your choice, and hit the Enter key to go to that option.

gopher://marvel.loc.gov/
Directory
Gopher Menu
About LC MARVEL
Events, Facilities, Publications, and Services
Research and Reference (Public Services)
Libraries and Publishers (Technical Services)
Copyright
Library of Congress Online Systems
Employee Information
U.S. Congress
Government Information
Global Electronic Library (by Subject)
Internet Resources
What's New on LC MARVEL
Search LC MARVEL Menus

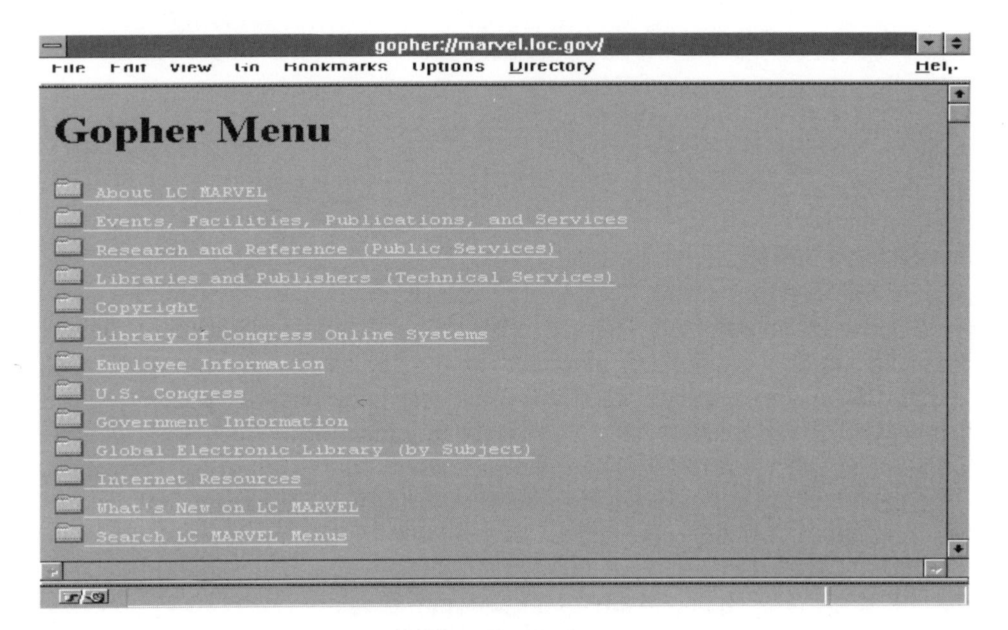

Figure 3-4.

This screen displays the Library of Congress gopher in the Netscape Web browser. Using Netscape to access gopher sites enables you to click on gopher options with your mouse.

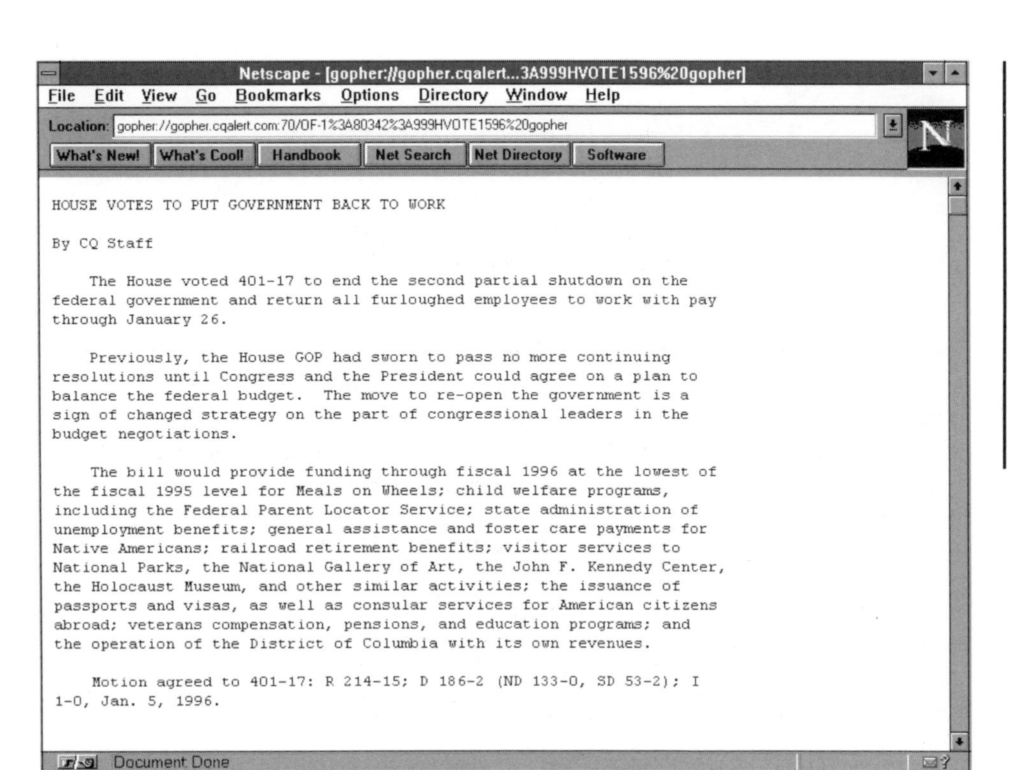
Netscape - [gopher://gopher.cqalert...3A999HVOTE1596%20gopher]
File Edit View Go Bookmarks Options Directory Window Help
Location: gopher://gopher.cqalert.com:70/0F-1%3A80342%3A999HVOTE1596%20gopher
What's New! What's Cool! Handbook Net Search Net Directory Software

HOUSE VOTES TO PUT GOVERNMENT BACK TO WORK

By CQ Staff

The House voted 401-17 to end the second partial shutdown on the federal government and return all furloughed employees to work with pay through January 26.

Previously, the House GOP had sworn to pass no more continuing resolutions until Congress and the President could agree on a plan to balance the federal budget. The move to re-open the government is a sign of changed strategy on the part of congressional leaders in the budget negotiations.

The bill would provide funding through fiscal 1996 at the lowest of the fiscal 1995 level for Meals on Wheels; child welfare programs, including the Federal Parent Locator Service; state administration of unemployment benefits; general assistance and foster care payments for Native Americans; railroad retirement benefits; visitor services to National Parks, the National Gallery of Art, the John F. Kennedy Center, the Holocaust Museum, and other similar activities; the issuance of passports and visas, as well as consular services for American citizens abroad; veterans compensation, pensions, and education programs; and the operation of the District of Columbia with its own revenues.

Motion agreed to 401-17: R 214-15; D 186-2 (ND 133-0, SD 53-2); I 1-0, Jan. 5, 1996.

Document Done

Figure 3-5. gopher://gopher.cqalert.com:70/0F-1%3A80342%3A999HVOTE1596%20gopher

House of Representatives Voting Records from the Library of Congress gopher.

options, whereas the text-only screen requires you to use your keyboard to move the cursor to the menu option you want, and hit Enter to choose the option. The Web browser screen offers larger typefaces, and small graphical representations of folders, which some may find easier to understand and use than the text-only screen. The documents you will find behind each menu option, however, are exactly the same.

The range of available data on this one site is extremely broad. When you consider that there are thousands of individual gopher sites on the Internet, and that each one offers access to many other gopher sites, you may begin to understand the enormity of resources the Net has to offer. From the researcher's perspective, gopher is an easy way to find information. Gopher software enables rapid access to a remote computer, where available resources are listed in tidy menus. Gopher menus can be several layers deep however, so to find a particular document within a gopher, directions can be invaluable. Since the Web browser has become the ubiquitous way to access Internet information, wherever possible, this directory provides a URL, or uniform resource locator, to guide you directly to the document you require. As an example, House Voting Records are seven layers deep into the Library of Congress gopher. Here are the directions for stepping down through the Library of Congress menu to get to the Voting Records:

ACCESS: gopher marvel.loc.gov
==> Government Information/
==> Federal Information Resources/
==> Information By Branch of Government/
==> Legislative Branch/
==> Congressional Voting Records/
==> Major Congressional Votes/
==> House Votes.

To get the Voting Records, you could log on to your access provider's computer, enter the command gopher marvel.loc.gov, and then choose the menu options listed above in succession, until you reach the GAO Transition Reports. Alternatively, and as presented in this directory, you could simply enter the following URL into your web browser to retrieve the same document:

gopher://gopher.cqalert.com:70/0F-1%3A80342%3A999HVOTE1596%20gopher

It is very easy to navigate within gopher. If you use a Web browser to access gopher, simply use your mouse to point at and click on menu options. If you use a text-only interface, use the up and down arrows on your keyboard to browse the items on a menu. Press the right arrow to choose a menu item, and use the left arrow to back out again.

TELNET

Telnet is software that allows you to gain access to a remote computer. Both gopher and Web software also enable you to "go to" a remote computer connected to the Internet and access information that resides on that computer. Gopher and Web software, however are very particular software applications. They arrange the data in a particular, organized fashion on the screen. Some data, however, exists in databases that are not easily represented via gopher or the Web. In such cases, you need to log on (via telnet) to the computers where these databases exist, and view the data through the database software that exists on those computers.

After executing the telnet command, and perhaps entering a login or password, you may enter the remote computer's directory structure or a database, depending on what's available. This is where a rudimentary knowledge of UNIX may be necessary. As an example, the State of Hawaii provides access to a wonderful system that provides all sorts of state legislative information for free. The telnet command for access is: telnet fyi.uhcc.hawaii.edu . (If you're accessing telnet via a Web browser, enter the following URL: telnet://fyi.uhcc.hawaii.edu) After the Hawaiian computer responds, hit the Return key twice and the computer will take you into its access menu.

Telnet itself is very easy to use. Simply type "telnet" (or telnet:// if you're using a Web browser) followed by the Internet address of the computer system you wish to access. For example, here's how to access the gopher at Washington & Lee University via telnet: Simply type: telnet liberty.uc.wlu.edu

or, if using a Web browser:

telnet://liberty.uc.wlu.edu

The Washington & Lee machine will prompt you for a LOGIN. In response, type: lawlib . Then the machine will prompt you for a password. In response, type: lawlib .

That's all there is to it. Should you wish to escape from telnet, back to your local machine, you can exit the remote machine gracefully by following the on-screen instructions for "quitting," or you can use the telnet escape sequence. To escape from telnet, hold down the CTRL key and press:"]". The computer will respond with the telnet prompt: telnet> Type: quit and you will be returned to your local machine.

FTP

The file transfer protocol (ftp) is software that enables you to transfer a file from a remote (distant) computer to your local (Internet access node) machine. In most cases, ftp access involves logging on to the remote computer as an anonymous user. Note the following example:

URL: ftp://ftp.cwru.edu/hermes

Using the above example, after entering the ftp URL (ftp://ftp.cwru.edu/hermes) to access the remote machine at Case Western Reserve University (ftp.cwru.edu), you will be presented with the screen in figure 3-6.

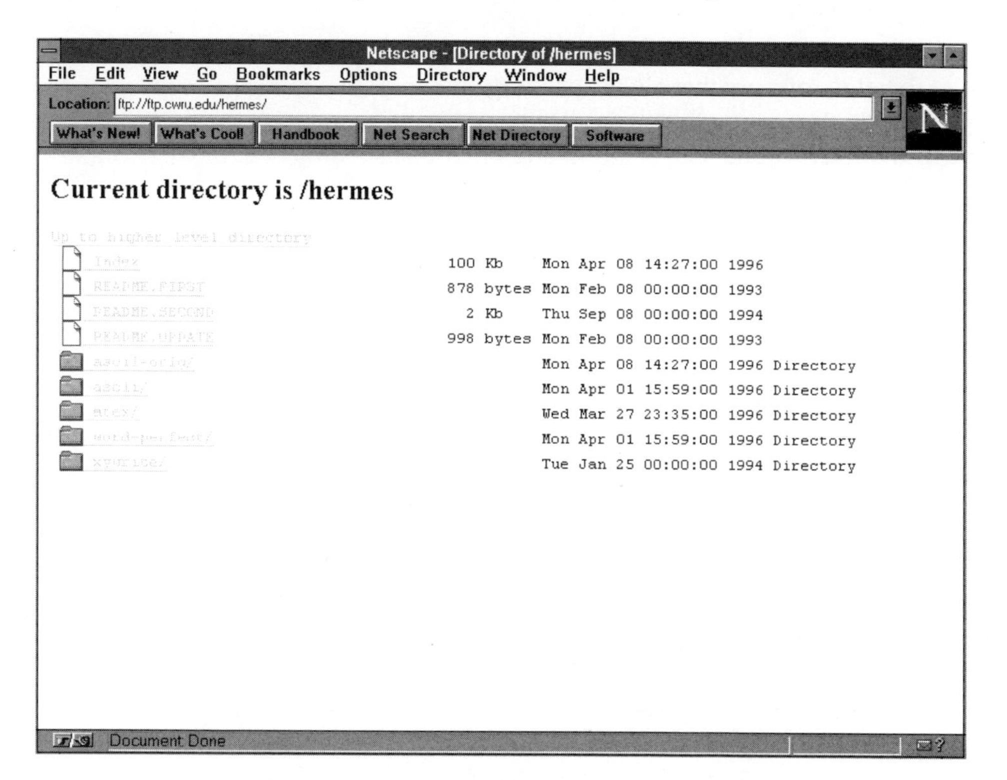

Figure 3-6. ftp://ftp.cwru.edu/hermes

This is the ftp site at Case Western Reserve University. It provides the primary archive of U.S. Supreme Court opinions on the Internet.

From the screen represented in figure 3-6, you can easily access the documents at the Case Western site. Before Web browsers, if you wanted to use file transfer protocol software to retrieve files, you had to step through a series of complex steps. Web browsers simplify the process of retrieving files stored in ftp directories. However, using Web browsers, instead of the more complex method (which requires a basic understanding of UNIX commands), prohibits you from retrieving files in binary format. This means that, for example, you can use your Web browser to go to the Case Western site to retrieve nonformatted versions of U.S. Supreme Court opinions. These ASCII versions of the opinions lack any word-processing formatting (such as bold, varying fonts, and footnotes integrated into the text). You cannot use your Web browser to retrieve the WordPerfect versions of the opinions, which retain the formatting in the original opinions.

In order to retrieve opinions from Case Western using your Web browser, the procedure is as follows. You must first know the docket number. Armed with that information, the next step is to open the Index file. This file contains a list of all opinions on the site. The file is the first option on the above screen. Simply click on the word "Index," and the file will open. The Index file will tell you the file number of the opinion you need. Then, you'll close the Index file, and retrieve the opinion from the ASCII directory. You can then cut and paste the opinion from your screen into a file on your desktop computer's hard disk. This file can, in turn, be read using your word processor.

PART II

PRACTICAL USES OF THE NET

Chapter 4

Communication on the Internet

Communication is the fundamental Internet feature. Indeed, the network was created as a way for people using computers to communicate with each other over great distances. From the human standpoint, the Net presents a new communication paradigm. Other mass media that connect millions of people (newspapers, television and radio) are essentially unidirectional. They enable one communicator (often an institution like the New York Times, NBC or the federal government) to communicate to many people. The Internet, in contrast, is interactive. It enables many people to communicate to many other people, who can answer back.

Communication on the Internet occurs via four tools that will be discussed in this book. First there's the most essential: email. Each of the following communication tools build on email. Second, there are mailing lists that enable a single email message to be sent to everyone who subscribes to an email list. Some lists have thousands of subscribers. In turn, there are several thousand lists in existence, serving every special interest group you can imagine.

Newsgroups are the third communications mechanism on the Internet. These are similar to mailing lists, in that they serve every conceivable special interest group. What distinguishes them from mailing lists is that newsgroup messages are not sent directly to your email box. Rather, you must go to the newsgroup to read and post messages. In addition, newsgroup messages are generally not as personal as email, since newsgroups can be read by anyone. Email list messages, by contrast, reach only those who subscribe to the list.

The fourth way to communicate on the net is via the World Wide Web. While many are aware that millions of colorful Web sites (also known as home pages) exist, and are continually being created for marketing and informational purposes by companies, law firms, organizations and individuals, it's easy to miss the unique communication components of the Web. The average home page starts where a magazine ad leaves off. Hopefully it's eye-catching and provocative, and makes the viewer want to see more and remember the source. But more than that, Web sites communicate a message about the source. Web sites say the source is computer savvy and aware of current technology. Many Web sites also allow for more direct communication by providing a button that reveals an email page. If you hit this button you will be able to send email directly to the owner of the Web page. In this way, web site purveyors open a direct communication link with potential customers that magazines cannot provide.

There's a fifth Internet communication tool that won't be discussed at length in this book. Internet Relay Chat or IRC is a chat system that allows people to correspond with each other onscreen in real time. As comments are typed in at the keyboard, they appear onscreen, and can be read by all participants wherever they are in the world.

Just like newsgroups and mailings lists, IRC allows participants to divide up into interest groups and chat away. Although this is a fun technology, it is not a business tool that lawyers would tend to use. If lawyers need to have a live, real-time conversation, conference-call technology is far more appropriate for several reasons. For example, conference call-technology does not anchor participants to a keyboard, but allows a group to sit around a table and converse with another group via telephone. IRC is rather clunky to use and limits communication to the speed each party can type. Finally, telephones are everywhere, whereas computers are not. Yet.

ESSENTIAL EMAIL

If you've never used email, it may seem like an unnecessary and confusing burden. There are details to understand and procedures to learn. However, the advantages to using email are so dramatic that its use is simply essential. Not adopting email means being left out of the stream of business conversations. Not adopting means giving business away to your competitors, and not fully serving your clients. Not adopting means going out of business. This is strong language for a technology that under 10% of American consumers have begun using, but the fact remains that lawyers are getting clients because they're online, while other lawyers are losing work because they have not had the foresight to embrace the technology.

To better understand what email is all about, let's take a look at fax technology, another communication innovation that was not universally embraced when it debuted. The fax machine burst upon the business scene in the 1980s to supplement the existing document delivery mechanisms, which included postal mail, overnight delivery and same-day messenger. Each of the existing mechanisms involved at least one human courier who hand-carried documents from sender to recipient. The fax machine eliminated the courier, placing the sender and recipient in more direct communication.

The earliest fax machines required hand-feeding of individual pages, which took time and required human involvement. Still, once the pages had been fed in, they were immediately available at the recipient's machine, whether across the street or around the planet. The fax machine thereby eliminated not only the courier, but the delay inherent in human locomotion. No human can compete with the speed of electrons moving along a telephone wire.

There are other benefits in addition to speed. Faxed documents are very convenient. They can be read when the recipient has time. As opposed to verbal phone messages that can be misunderstood, written fax messages may more clearly articulate the sender's intent, and have the added advantage of relative permanence. Faxes can be reviewed and easily sent on to others, whereas voice messages are not usually so flexible. Faxed pages are also much cheaper to send than human-delivered pages. Although the initial investment in a fax machine is greater than any one packet sent via courier, the incremental cost of each faxed document is far cheaper than the cost of hand-carrying the same document.

There are also negative aspects to faxing. Fax machines break, and require maintenance. They encounter busy signals. They often require a human monitor (although the newer direct-to-computer fax devices don't require much human attention). Faxed pages are not identical to original pages. The former are usually less sharp, and are not in color. Faxed documents are not easy to edit. They must be retyped or copied if they are to be modified by the recipient. Faxed messages do not have the vocal inflections that a phone message conveys. What is sarcastic to one person is insulting to another. Therefore, faxed (written) messages need to be composed with this consideration in mind. However, not everyone has the writing ability, nor the time to avoid such problems.

Email picks up where the fax machine leaves off. It retains some of the great fax benefits, like speed and cheapness; eliminates some problems, like busy signals and the inability to edit documents; and adds additional benefits, like easy routing to multiple parties. But email is much more than a mere advance over the fax machine. Email is a quantum leap akin to the telephone in terms of the new ways it enables humans to communicate. Such an expansion in functionality is hard to understand until you actually spend time using email. For example, one might not bother using the fax machine or telephone, and certainly not a letter to simply say hi to a colleague. Email makes this easy and fun. Informal communications are simple via email, and enable building and maintaining relationships with people you may never meet in person.

For those who are comfortable in front of a computer, and have learned to smoothly transmit their thoughts into the keyboard, email is the keystroke that further transmits those thoughts to other people (thousands of people at a time if you send your thoughts to a list of email addresses). You can similarly immediately respond to the thoughts of others by replying to email that you receive. Once you become comfortable with email, the number of ideas and documents you can receive and transmit are increased many times. Thus your mind becomes connected to a network of people through the computer network. Poised at the keyboard and monitor, you become visually and tactilely connected to the thoughts of other people who share your interests, no matter where on earth they are located. This is not quite the same thing as receiving your club newsletter from the postman, or getting a letter via fax.

Not only is email fast in terms of its transmission rate, it is also immediate in the way that speech is immediate. Once uttered, an idea is unalterably released. You can utter follow-up statements to modify your original idea, but the first utterance remains intact. Similarly, once the email Send button has been hit, the message scurries away irretrievably. Your message immediately (this is a relative term; immediacy depends on your email provider) appears in your recipients' email box. This can have dangerous side-effects, of course. Judicious use of email requires that care be taken before hitting the Send key. You want to be sure you mean what you say, that your words are not prone to misinterpretation, and that you are not releasing information that may find its way to inappropriate parties.

Email as a Legal Practice Tool

Email is the most easily understood Internet tool. It is already in place in most U.S. companies. It's a small leap to understand that if you can email the person in the next building, you can email the person on the next continent. For the legal researcher, email can make daily chores much more efficient. Email can be used to reach out and brainstorm with colleagues, and to communicate with courts, bar associations and government agencies. In addition, it is increasingly a way to communicate with clients.

For example, partner Ken Bass explains that his firm, the 260-lawyer general business firm Venable, Baetjer, Howard & Civiletti in Washington, DC. uses the Internet

> "primarily as a means of electronic communication with clients and colleagues. Hopefully someday, we'll use the Net to facilitate the transaction of our practice, exchanging drafts, instead of playing telephone tag. Using email, which is on the desk of many, but not all, of our lawyers, is the bulk of our use of the Internet. Secondly, it is being used as a research tool, largely by the library, as a means of finding some things that are not otherwise accessible; or accessible not nearly as cheaply as they are over the Net.
>
> "The third element that we are using the Net for is our World Wide Web server, which is an expansion of what we've done for years in terms of newsletters and periodicals; fairly common marketing activities by law firms for a long period of time. We are now doing it electronically as well as in print. The reasons for going to electronic communication are the same as the other reasons in terms of using more efficient means of communication.
>
> "There's no question that email is a far more efficient means of communication in many ways than the telephone, particularly with busy individuals who have trouble sometimes even answering the phone. Email is a lot easier when you're doing multiple addressing as we do repeatedly. It's a lot easier to transmit documents when you have compatible email systems and you can send binary attachments too [i.e., computer files that contain formatting and information more than simply text; for example, a WordPerfect document, which contains special WordPerfect information, would be a binary file or attachment]. It is international and it's cheap. We have no additional marginal cost for sending messages anywhere in the world, which you can't duplicate with fax or any other system.
>
> "We don't track email time, if you will. I do have some sense of how much time I personally spend maintaining the Web, because I track that time. In the first year of creating it, which was 1994, the Web was my biggest client. Its rate of return, in terms of immediacy was not very high. This past year the time has dropped off to maybe 15 minutes a day. [I've never had to defend the value of putting that time in] to people here. There have been a lot of discussions outside for doing it. But when you show people 2000 contacts a week with the firm that did not exist before, almost all of which are new contacts, you have people convinced that the exposure in and of itself is of utility. You take that and you lay that out, plus the fact that we have a couple of substantially productive clients who have come in as a result of our being out on the Net in a variety of forms. I don't think there's much difficulty justifying what was done when it was largely my soft time, if you will, last year.

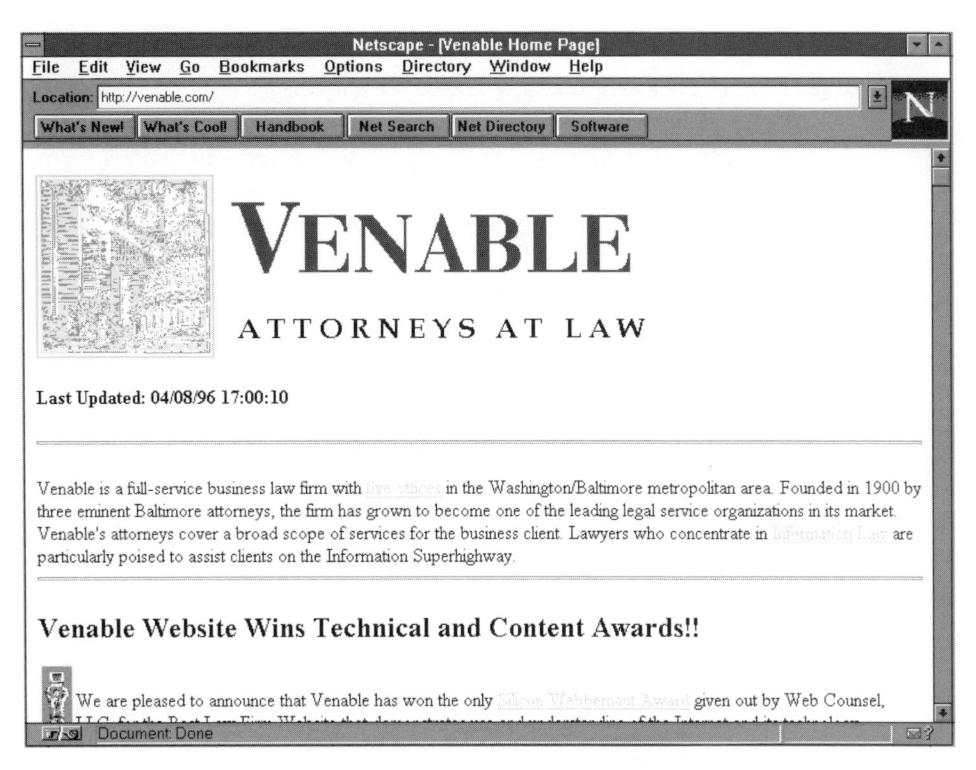

Figure 4-1. http://venable.com/

Home page of Venable, Baetjer, Howard & Civiletti.

"[The Net's reach is just beginning] to penetrate beyond the Net techies into the type of clients that we do normally reach. That said, we do have a strong intellectual property practice, particularly in intellectual property litigation. We are aware that a lot of the people that you really want to reach, in terms of that practice, are the technicians in the companies, rather than necessarily the general counsels in companies. I think that particular method of publication does reach those people and does communicate that we practice what we litigate, if you will. That we understand the technology and can use it. But certainly as the Web rolls out through the online services (Prodigy, AOL, CompuServe, Counsel Connect, and what have you) and as everybody jumps on the Web as the hottest thing on the net and begins offering it, then our message will reach a much broader audience.

"Technicians are people who, in the long run, matter more in terms of winning technical cases. The communications between the technicians and the lawyers are critical to winning a technical case. We believe, when it comes to picking lawyers in what has become a commodity market, that a law firm's ability to convince the client that it understands their business, that it understands their modes of thinking, that lives where they live, if you will, is an important marketing factor.

"In terms of today, I don't think [Internet use in law firms] is a high priority item. But in terms of firms who have their eye on the future, it is an essential item. You are going to be playing catch-up five years from now. Law firms will not use fax in the year 2000. Email will have replaced fax; it will be a totally dead technology. I think we are going to wind up increasingly using email and encryption as techniques for recording and exchanging all kinds of things. I think that the Web will never replace traditional media, but will certainly supplement it. When we started in March of 1994, there were two law firms who had services on the Net, us and Heller Ehrman. Last count I had a day or two ago, it was in excess of 30 now, that are out on the Web with some provider. I think all but two of them are through third-party providers. I think that will increase.

"[By the year 2000, a firm that is not email-connected is going to be in trouble.] We've already had competitive solicitation responses in which the terms of bidding are compatible email. There is no sense of putting in a bid [if the firm doesn't have email]. You can tell them how much more efficient and how much everything else you are and they'll say, 'Have you got email that we can communicate to your desk?' And if the answer is no, they say, 'Thank you very much. Good-bye.'"

Getting Started with Email

Getting started with email is much easier than it was just a few years ago, but it's still not quite as push-button-simple as faxing. To fax a document, one needs merely to buy a fax machine, plug it into a phone line, and begin faxing immediately. To use email, one needs more. In addition to the hardware (a computer, a modem, and a telephone line), email requires an account with an online service provider and software to access that provider. Depending on the provider you choose, access software may be the generic, off-the-shelf sort, or it may be proprietary and supplied by the provider.

Once you have chosen your provider, and logged on, you will have access to email. If your Internet connection is through your firm's local area network (LAN) then you'll use the firm's email software to send Internet email. Either way, the point is to get your hands on the email software. The basic features of all email software include the ability to:

- send messages,
- attach documents to the messages you send,
- read the messages you receive,
- save, print or delete the messages you send and receive,
- reply to messages that have been sent to you,
- forward messages you receive to third parties, and
- maintain an address book of frequently used email addresses.

Attachments

The ability to attach documents to the messages you send is very useful. If you're drafting a document with a colleague who's out of the office, sending the document via email will provide both drafters with the exact same document, not merely a faxed paper copy. When both drafters have the identical electronic version, editing is much easier.

There are two ways to send a document via email. First, you could send the document within the body of the message. This method usually requires that you save the document (from within your word processor) as a text document. Most word processors offer this option. Then, when you are creating your email message, you will insert the text document into the email message. The problem with this method is that you will not be able to send the formatting and various fonts (including bold, underline and italics) that you may have created in your word-processed document. All of that formatting will be stripped away when you save the document as mere text. Such simple text is also known as ASCII text (American Standard Code for Information Interchange). In many cases, however, this option will be quite appropriate.

If, however, you want to send the document in all its word-processed glory, you have another option. You can send the document as an attachment. Most email software offers this option. Assuming that your correspondent has email software that is compatible with your email software, meaning that the attachment arrives intact and readable, you're all set. It's a good idea to confirm this compatibility before you find yourself in a "must get it done now" situation.

An alternative to attaching a file is to simply transfer a file. Again, access to such a transfer feature depends on the provider you use. CompuServe, for example, has an excellent, dependable transfer feature that allows you to send files right to other CompuServe subscribers. You won't likely have a compatibility problem, because your correspondent will be using the same provider (CompuServe) that you are.

Netiquette

Much has been written of the idea that the human interaction that happens online forms a sort of "community," with established customs and acceptable behavior. When new people visit this community (for example, by sending a message to a mailing list) they may upset the status quo if they behave contrary to the established norms. Therefore, to maintain relative peace online, a code of recommended behavior has evolved, known as netiquette. As with all rules, there are exceptions to these, but it is a good idea to pay heed until you learn the parameters. Failure to observe these guidelines may result in hostile responses being directed at you (also known as being flamed). Note that many of these guidelines apply particularly when using mailing lists.

- Be aware that once you hit the Send button, you are giving away control of your message. Email is easily forwarded, and your message can end up anywhere, and may be saved perpetually in various archives. Before you hit Send be sure that you haven't written something you'll be sorry about later.
- Include information about yourself at the end of your messages. Failure to include such signature information will cause your messages to lack credibility, and will make it difficult for others to contact you, especially if your message asks for feedback. The common practice is to include your name, email address, and perhaps phone and postal address. Most email software allows you to create a standard signature file that will appear at the end of every message you send, so you won't have to create the signature from-scratch each time you send email.

- Use CAPITAL letters sparingly. Using ALL CAPS is akin to shouting. Don't do it unless you mean it. There are many other techniques to express emphasis, including surrounding a word with *asterisks.*
- Sarcasm and humor are easily misinterpreted online. One person's joke is another's insult. There are various techniques to indicate humor online (ha ha). Emoticons or smileys are commonly used to express humor and other emotions. Emoticons are images created from punctuation. For example, if you turn this page (or your head) 90 degrees, you can view this smiley face: :-) There are endless variations on this theme. My personal favorite is smiley with glasses: B-).
- If you quote an earlier message in your message, edit out irrelevant material. Nothing's more annoying than receiving an enormous message full of irrelevant junk.
- You'll find after a while that email tends to proliferate in your email box. The shorter messages are, the better. Therefore, abbreviations are favored. Here are a few abbreviations that are in common use online:

IMHO	=	in my humble/honest opinion
FYI	=	for your information
BTW	=	by the way
Flame	=	antagonistic criticism

- Know the difference between Reply and Forward. When you reply to a message sent from a mailing list by using the Reply function in your mailer, your message will be sent back to the mailing list, not only to the individual who wrote the message to which you are replying. In order to reach the individual only, use the Forward function, or simply email (without using the Reply or Forward functions) a message to the individual. The correlative to using reply and forward properly is: don't send personal mail, intended for one person, to a mailing list.
- Don't type articles from the newspaper into your email, especially not when sending email to a list. Such widespread, nonpermissioned distribution of published material is usually a copyright infringement.
- Be aware that certain mailing lists do not allow commercial messages. If you're seeking to promote your firm, and you want to send a press release, for example, be sure that the lists you send allow the sort of message you're sending. Otherwise, your message may do more damage than good. In order to determine what lists allow, read the Frequently Asked Question file (FAQ) if one exists for the list (the FAQ may be forwarded to you when you subscribe), and subscribe to the list for a while to see what sort of traffic is typical on the list.
- Personal messages do not belong on legal email lists. The lists are for public discussion of issues relating to each list's purpose. Personal messages should be sent directly to the relevant party.

Using Email to Retrieve Documents

Across the Internet, computers (often referred to as servers) have been programmed to respond to particular email messages. These automated response systems can deliver promotional or other material to anyone who requests it using email. For example, if you are interested in retrieving information describing the procedure for accessing White House publications and documents, send email to:

publications@whitehouse.gov

In the body of the message, include the following text: send info

Here's another example. Vice President Al Gore's report on reinventing government, titled "From Red Tape to Results: Creating a Government that Works Better and Costs Less," can be retrieved by sending a message to:

almanac@ace.esusda.gov

In the body of the message, include the following text:

send npr nprintro
send npr npr01
send npr npr02
send npr npr03
send npr npr04
send npr nprconc
send npr end
send nappena
send nappenbc

For those who do not have access to a full or direct Internet connection which provides access to such functions as gopher, telnet, ftp and the Web, email can provide an alternate method to retrieve some of the Internet's legal resources. The Send command, as indicated in the examples above, can be used to retrieve files from servers when you know the names of the files you want. If you don't know what files may be available from a particular server, you can use the Index command to get a list of available files.

Email Addresses for Lawyers

An email address is similar to a street address. Both identify where your mail goes. Therefore, if you're interested in receiving mail, it's best to have one address that you don't change frequently, if at all. Anyone who has moved their residence or office knows how annoying it can be when important mail is delayed because of an address change. It's best to minimize such moving around, especially online, where there is no U.S. Postal Service attaching yellow change of address labels to your mail. If you change your online address, it's likely that lots of people will never find you again.

This is especially important for lawyers and other business people. Businesses depend on a certain amount of new business that walks in the door, so to speak. Clients need first to find your door. If you make it difficult, clients may go elsewhere.

There are essentially two ways to acquire an email address. First, you can acquire an account on a commercial online access provider such as CompuServe or Counsel Connect, and an address will be assigned to you. Second, you can create your own domain name such that you or your firm has a unique address in cyberspace which identifies you, like janelawyer@lawfirm.com There are things to consider with each option.

Commercial providers each have their own conventions for creating online addresses. CompuServe, for example, has historically used a numeric system. My CompuServe address, looks like this:

71357.525@compuserve.com

Counsel Connect's (CC) scheme is a bit less arcane. My address on CC looks like this:

jblack00@counsel.com

These addresses are very easy to acquire. All I had to do was pay the subscription fee, and an address was created for me, enabling email to immediately flow to my email box. However, neither of these addresses is particularly easy to remember. If someone wants to find my email address, they would either have to ask me, or use the directory that each of these private services (CompuServe and CC) offer privately online. That means unless you have an account on CC or CompuServe, you can't find my email address by using the relevant directory. Even though both CC and CompuServe are Internet-connected, such that email sent from any Internet connection can get through to CC or CompuServe, unless you know the specific email address of the person you want to reach, your email will not get through.

If I were to distribute both of these addresses to people I meet, I would need to stay on these services forever, or risk losing touch with people. No matter how much rates may rise, I would be stuck. Similarly, if any of those online services go out of business, I would lose touch with anyone who had my defunct address.

It is theoretically possible that I could send change-of-address notices to those who need to know my new email address, although that would cost money and time. And there's little chance that I could reach everyone who has stored my email address. Some of those are people I don't know. Finally, there's no assurance that those notified of my new address will record the change.

A common question regarding email addresses, is whether there exists a centralized directory of email addresses. Attempts will continue to be made to compile such a directory, but as yet there really is no authoritative email directory. The best way to find an individual's email address is simply to ask them for it.

Your Own Domain

Although it is very common and easy to establish an email address through a third-party provider (such as CompuServe or Counsel Connect), for the reasons noted above, such a choice is not always the best idea for businesses. An alternative is to set up your own Internet domain, or address. Rather than your mail going to 12345@compuserve.com, your mail can go to yourname@yourfirm.com . Establishing your own domain will provide you with a customized address, and your placement in an Internet-wide look-up directory known as Whois. Private domains can provide a level of visibility and convenience not attainable from large-scale commercial providers.

You don't need to have your own Internet-connected computer to set up a domain. Rather, you can set it up through your Internet access provider. Registration of domains is $100 for the first two years, and $50 per year thereafter. However, you've got to know where that domain will "reside." That is, if you register the domain name lawfirm.com where will mail sent to that address end up? Will it be sent directly to your firm's local area network? Will it be sent to your Internet service provider? It's essential that you resolve this issue before you register the domain. If you don't have a computer professional within your firm, discuss this question with your provider. If you'd like to explore this issue on your own, you can access the information provided by the Internet Network Information Center (InterNic) at http://www.internic.net/ Maintaining a domain through an Internet service provider commonly requires payment of a monthly fee starting at about $50.

EMAIL LISTS

Law-Related Mailing Lists

Email really gets interesting when it provides access to regional and international mailing lists (also known as listservs). The Net supports thousands of such lists for special interest groups, such as tax attorneys, international law librarians and people interested in copyright issues. The Legal Mailing List section of the directory describes some 250 listservs of particular interest to legal researchers, and that number is growing. Don't confuse Internet mailing lists with the sort of postal mailing lists that direct marketers use. Internet mailing lists are usually not commercially-oriented at all. Rather, email lists are used for the email distribution of discussions, announcements and electronic newsletters.

The content of messages sent to listservs vary widely. For example, on the Government Documents list (GOVDOC-L), as well as the Law Librarian's list (LAWLIB-L), there are frequent queries and discussions about free Internet access to government documents. When Vice President Gore's National Performance Review task force released its report on reinventing government, GOVDOC-L participants posted the Internet address for the report. With this information, anyone with access to the appropriate net tools (ftp, telnet, gopher or WWW could immediately retrieve the entire document for free.

Subscribing to Mailing Lists

To subscribe to a list, send the following message in the body of an email message:

subscribe <listname> <Your Name>

Replace "listname" with the name of the list, and replace "Your Name" with your first and last names. Note that this command will work with nearly all listservs. However, there are several varieties of listserv software running on the Internet, and you will occasionally need to vary the subscription request. When a variation from this standard command is required the Mailing List section of the directory entry will explain the appropriate subscription procedure. You don't need to put anything in the subject field of your message when you send a message, such as a subscription request to a listserver. If you do put text in the subject field, it will be disregarded.

Here's an example from the directory:

BANKRLAW

DESCRIPTION: Internet discussion group that focuses on all aspects of bankruptcy. This includes business and financial aspects, legal aspects, teaching aspects as well as practical aspects.

SUBSCRIPTION ADDRESS: listserv@polecat.law.indiana.edu
subscribe bankrlaw <Your Name>
MAIL ADDRESS: bankrlaw@polecat.law.indiana.edu

If you want to subscribe to the BANKRLAW list, send email to the subscription address above. Note that each listing in the Mailing List section of the directory also includes a mail address. It is very important to note the difference between the subscription and mail addresses. The former is used strictly to subscribe and unsubscribe, and to send various other commands to the listserv computer. Messages sent to the subscription address will not be read by people on the list. If you wish to send a message that will be distributed to everyone who has subscribed to the listserv, send it to the mail address. Confusing these two addresses is very common. You will frequently see people erroneously sending messages to the list (rather than to the listserver) requesting they be unsubscribed.

If your subscription request is made properly, the computer serving the list (the listserver) will respond to the subscriber acknowledging the subscription. Thereafter, all messages sent to the mailing list (the listserv) will be sent (via email) to you as a list subscriber. It is a good idea to retain the confirmation message sent to you by the listserver when you subscribe. That message will include instructions for unsubscribing, and other useful information about the list.

To signoff from a list (also known as unsubscribe), send a message to the subscription address as follows: signoff <listname>

Note that you need to replace "listname" with the name of the list (for example BANKRLAW). Note also that you don't need to include your name in the signoff command.

Mailing List Archives

Archives provide access to past discussions on mailing lists. Where possible, the location of mailing list archives have been identified in the directory. There are a few central sites for mailing list archives. For example, Cornell Law School provides access to the archives of several legal listervs. For a variety of reasons (reader convenience, disk space, disk space and disk space) Cornell doesn't keep the postings forever. Some of the lists archived include:

TEKNOIDS	List for legal techie wonks
INT-LAW	List for foreign and international law librarians
LAW-LIB	Law librarian list
AI-LAW	Artificial Intelligence and the law list
HISTLAW	History of the law list

Here are the access instructions for various listserv archives:

URL:	gopher://gopher.law.cornell.edu:70/11/listservs
URL:	http://www.kentlaw.edu/lawnet/lawnet.html
URL:	http://barratry.law.cornell.edu:5123/notify/buzz.html

Listservs as Research Tools

The opportunity to share information about products and business practices, and seek referrals for both is another valuable use of listservs. The Legal Research Group (LRG) (which the author founded and directs) in New York's FIND/SVP, frequently uses listservs and online discussion forums on Internet-connected services (such as Counsel Connect) to find appropriate attorneys to whom work may be referred.

The procedure for making such referrals starts with determining where to post the work opportunity. By reviewing the list of legal listservs and newsgroups, an LRG attorney identifies several appropriate forums. The message describing the client's need is composed and sent via email to each lists' mail address. Similarly, the message is posted in each relevant newsgroup. Within a couple of hours of sending the messages, a number of qualified private attorneys generally have responded, contacting the LRG by telephone and email. Soon thereafter, qualified firm resumes are on their way to the party who requested the referral. Rather than limiting our personal network to work colleagues and others we know through direct contact, the Net provides for contact with a universe of people. One can keep aware of pertinent issues and opportunities in a way never before possible by subscribing (at no fee) to subject-specific mailing lists.

The directory portion of this book makes an effort to catalog the entire range of legal resources available on the Internet. The very nature of the Net makes this task impossible, however. Therefore, it is useful to know about other resources that collect legal resources, and that can be used in addition to this book. One which catalogs legal listservs is known as the Law Lists. It is maintained by Lyonette Louis-Jacques, Foreign and International Law Librarian & Lecturer in Law at the University of Chicago Law School. Ms. Louis-Jacques is also responsible for the valuable, and well-trafficked listserv INT-LAW, which focuses on international legal resources. She has a number of thoughts on using listservs for research purposes.

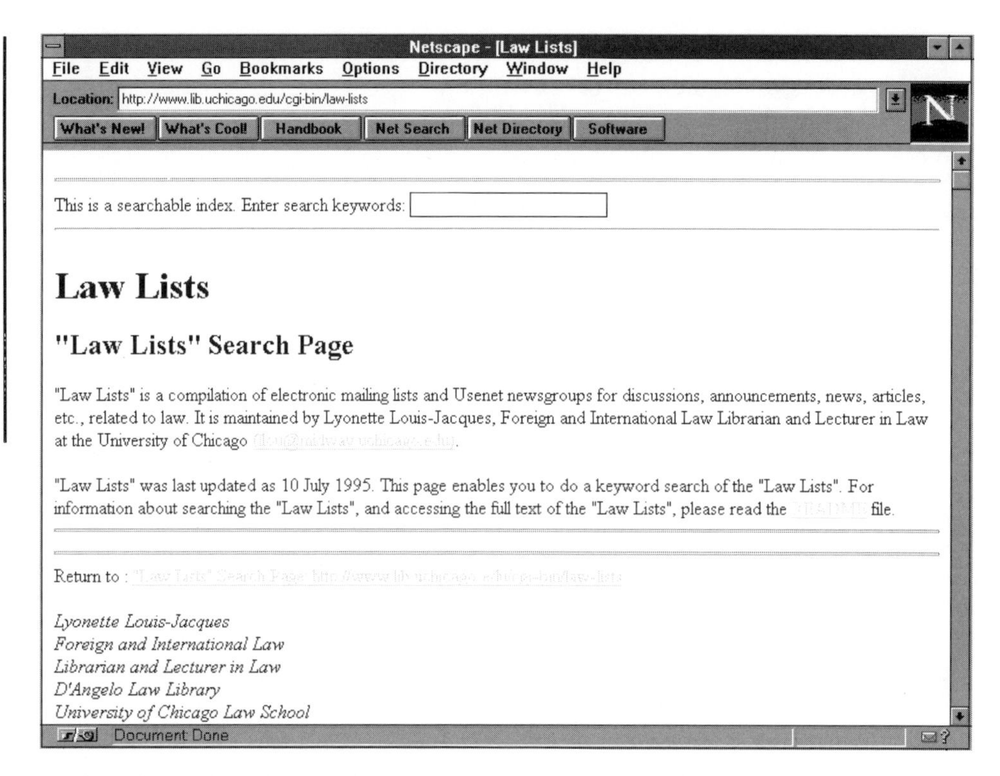

Figure 4-2. http://www.lib.uchicago.edu/cgi-bin/law-lists

The Law Lists is the foremost catalog of legal mailing lists. It is available at this URL: http://www.lib.uchicago.edu/cgi-bin/law-lists

"I'm a reference librarian. In the past, to help a patron, if I knew something off the top of my head, I would tell them that this statute or case is in this resource and I would tell them the title of the resource. When it was something I didn't know for sure, I would tell them to check our online catalog or something like that. But now, if I don't know (or don't have a good guess) where something is, I can send an email message to a mailing list to see who else might know. It is sort of like I am drawing on resources that didn't exist before. It is something new because it is a group of people who have a reasonable likelihood of being interested in the subject that I'm interested in finding information about.

"Before the Internet existed, you would [start legal research with] Lexis or Westlaw, an online repository that actually has the stuff full text. Or you could go to paper. Then you would find yourself calling people. In international law that happens a lot. If you can't find a recent treaty in *International Legal Materials*, or a standard treaty series set, then you find yourself calling all over the place to see who has it. The Internet is part of that level of research. The first person you call might not work. They may refer you someplace else. Except that when you send your message to an email list on the Internet, someone in that group of people, depending on which groups you choose, might actually have the document in hand.

"I use email lists to get an idea of where I should go next. You know, like, I checked this and that and that, is there anything else I can check? What happens is that sometimes you will have someone who is keen on that particular topic. Even if they don't have it on their desk, they are intrigued by the question and then they are willing to put out the effort to go find the information and give it to you. I do use the Internet to get other ideas. I consider myself to be someone who still has a lot to learn. I probably will consider that 20 years from now if I'm still in this position.

"I'm always trying to develop a standard way of approaching things, so that next time I get the question, which doesn't happen that often, if I get a particular question again that gave me a hard time, I will have a pattern of approaching it. I've already done a lot of initial searching on my own, and then I will post a question on INT-LAW [the Foreign and International Law Librarian's list] asking what else can I search. How else can I approach this question. Sometimes I get an answer, sometimes I don't, and sometimes if it is a document I'm looking for, I get the document. Most of the time I get people asking me that whatever I hear, to let them know. Then I've created another burden on myself, because now I have to remember to tell this other person what I found. Sometimes the Internet creates more work. It is not like you go in there and people will help you. People ask you for help because you are asking the same question they would have asked if they had thought about it.

"A lot of people are overwhelmed by what is available [on the Net]. I think it is because they don't realize, just like with any other research tool, you have to have an approach. When you go into a library, yeah they have tons of books, but you make some determination how to approach it. Sometimes you just decide to go to Cornell or something. You have to have an approach to it.

"I think that listservs are the most important thing on the Internet. Because you can't rely on people to put up stuff on gopher and the Web that will answer your questions all the time. It is mostly the basic stuff, like the U.S. Code and Supreme Court. So a lot of your questions may not be answered [by those sources]. It is good to be kind of familiar with listservs; at least how to find them. If you could get to a listserv on a topic that you are researching, then you know there is a group of people on that list that would be able to be interested in that question and might be able to answer it.

"You have to keep in mind that people get email at different times of the day, sometimes their feed is slow. For me, I get INT-LAW the next day. People don't always check their mailboxes. The people who know might not always check their mailboxes; they might be on vacation. A list, if you've not been on it before, might not be a very active one. So it is always good to send email to a list you are familiar with or a list that has a reputation for being a really good list.

"Some people post on listservs that they have never been on before. So someone [may] post on CYBERWONKS or something like that [without] realizing that maybe that list has had one message in a year. Because they don't have familiarity with the list, they don't realize they probably are not going to get an answer. One message in a year means there aren't that many people actively using it. If I had more time in a day and I could clone myself, I could annotate my Law Lists and say what the traffic is like. That would be useful. Then you could look at some guide and know that people on a certain list are very responsive and really wonderful and that for most questions you get a response. Even some of the more odd, esoteric ones."

Setting Up Your Own Listserv

There are currently some 250 legal listservs and more being created all the time. But law is a very broad discipline. There are far more than 250 areas of discussion concerning the law. If you are interested in setting up your own mailing list, there's a Frequently Asked Question (FAQ) document that will get you on your way at the following

URL: http://www.cis.ohio-state.edu/hypertext/faq/usenet/mail/list-admin/software-faq/faq.html

NEWSGROUPS

Newsgroups are similar to listservs in that both provide interest groups of every persuasion with a place to electronically gather and share ideas. Just as email software is required to send and receive listserv messages, newsgroup software is required to view and post messages to newsgroups. In addition, newsgroups (like listservs, and maybe even more so) are populated by people who can be extremely zealous in maintaining each group's posting rules. If a group is non-commercial, and you post an advertisement (or something construed as an ad) it is likely that you will be bombarded by hate email and your posting will be removed forthwith by the newsgroup moderator (if there is one). This is one of the paradoxes of the Internet from a marketer's standpoint. Although people online divide themselves (via listservs and newsgroups) into perfect target groups (the lawyers, the boating enthusiasts, etc) these same groups are often vehemently against finding commercial messages within their forums.

Newsgroups and listservs are also very different. In order to read listserv messages, you need to subscribe. Thereafter, all new list messages will be sent to your email box. If you want to read listserv messages sent prior to your subscription, you'll need to find the listserv archive, if one exists for the particular list you're interested in.[1] As a result of this subscription requirement, the average Internet browser (who is not subscribed to the thousands of existing listservs) does not have access to listserv messages.

Newsgroup messages on the other hand, are not delivered to your mailbox, and you don't need to subscribe to read, respond to and create (post) newsgroup messages. Newsgroup messages are available to anyone with newsgroup software. Newsgroup messages are listed in a bulletin board format (see screen at figure 4-3 below), and historical messages are kept for varying lengths of time (depending on the newsgroup). Therefore, if you're interested in seeing what's been discussed on a legal newsgroup like misc.legal, for the last several months, all you've got to do is start up your newsgroup software, and browse misc.legal.

Networking with potential clients does occur in newsgroups, but even more significantly, the forums serve as meeting places for like-minded people. Taking another look at misc.legal, since it is one of the busiest legal newsgroups, one can find regular postings of Erik Heel's Legal List, (a compilation of law-related resources on the Internet and elsewhere) endless discussions of civil liberties issues, requests for referrals to lawyers in particular states and practice areas, comments on legal software, and on and on.

1. Listserv archives are available for some lists, and not for others. A number of legal lists are archived at:http://www.kentlaw.edu/lawnet/lawnet.html and gopher://gopher.law. cornell.edu:70/ 11/listservs .

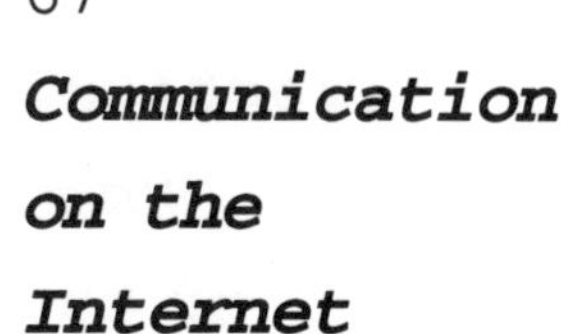

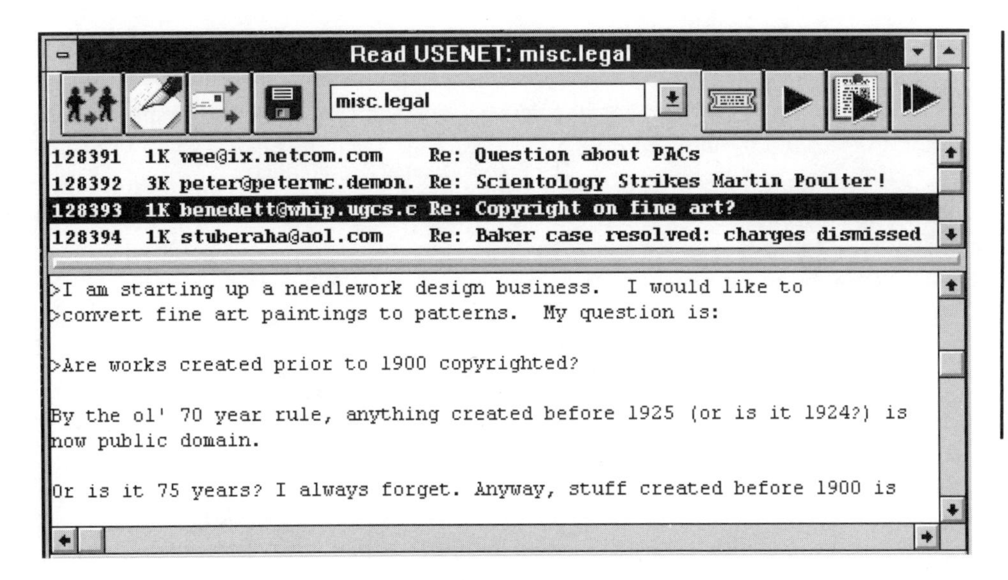

Figure 4-3.

An example of a message in the misc.legal newsgroup. This particular newsgroup view is through the Netcruiser newsreader software.

Searching through Newsgroups

There are hundreds of thousands of newsgroup messages available for you to read and respond to. Combined, these messages offer a wealth of information. Somewhere in that morass of messages may be the answer you're looking for. Finding it, however, can be a time-wasting chore. You may recall reading something in a newsgroup last week that is right on point for a project you're working on today, but have no clue where the message is now.

A solution has been created in the form of a newsgroup search service known as Dejanews. The service (http://www.dejanews.com) lets you leverage the millions of pages of information in newsgroups by quickly searching based on your criteria. Dejanews gives you access to most of the usenet postings from the past month (articles posted to groups that match alt.*, soc.*, talk.* or *.binaries are excluded). In addition, the service provides a profile of anyone who has posted in a newsgroup. If you click on the author's name, you get a list of all the posts he has in the Dejanews database. (See figure 4-4 on the following page.)

PRIVACY AND SECURITY ONLINE

Security and privacy are critical issues for lawyers using online networks for communication. Email that flows through the Internet (versus email that stays within your firm's in-house network) passes through several channels from the time it leaves your fingers to the time it reaches your correspondent. Unless you encrypt your messages, assume that no email you send or keep in an accessible place (for example on network storage) is completely private or secure. It is con-

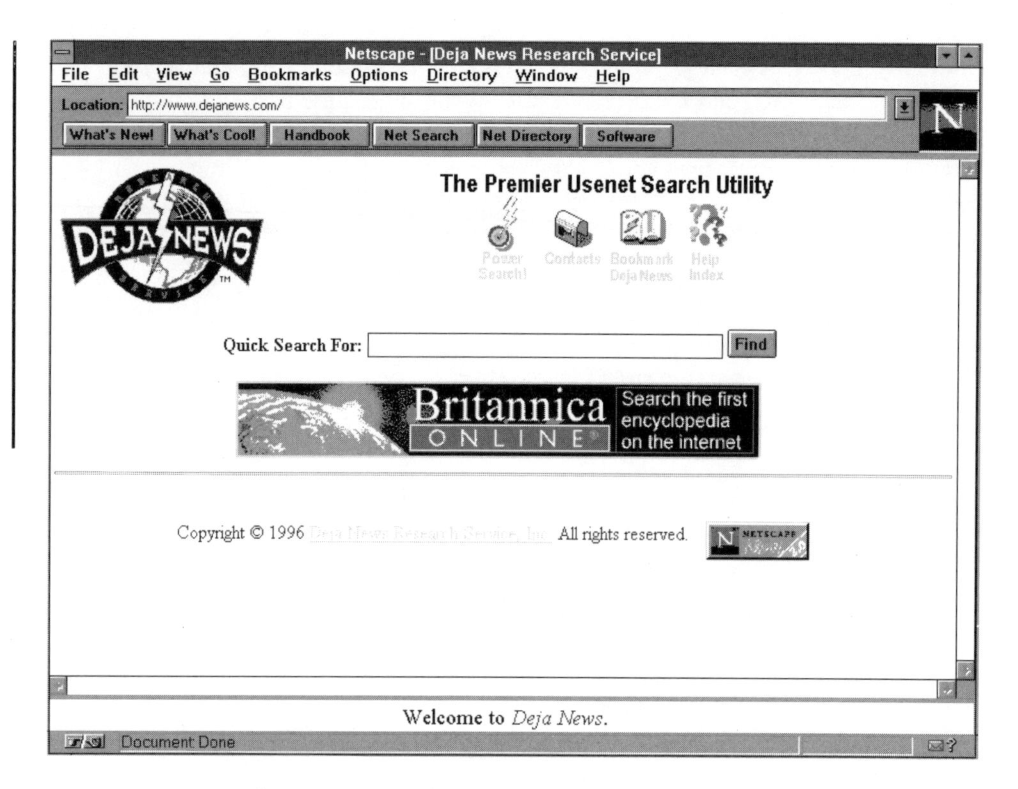

Figure 4-4. http://www.dejanews.com

Dejanews is a quick and easy way to search through newsgroups.

ceivable that someone may gain unauthorized access to your email box, or that someone who has authorized access somewhere along that chain (for example, in your firm's systems department, at your online service provider, or at your correspondent's firm) may peer into, alter or even forge your messages. As trustees of privileged information, lawyers have a special obligation to ensure that trust is not breached.

The only sure way to prevent such privacy infringement is to encrypt your mail when you send it, and for the email recipient to decrypt it when he or she receives it. Encryption is a technique for scrambling messages such that they are unreadable by anyone who does not have the private software key.

The issue of whether public encryption systems (versus systems authorized and controlled by the federal government, such as the Clipper Chip) should exist continues to be contentious, although such public systems have been available for some time, and some say the cat is out of the bag, and it would appear too late to stuff it back in. The government argues that such public systems prevent effective law-enforcement. The government believes that criminals will be able to hide their activities through the use of impenetrable encryption software. However that issue is resolved, so-called public-key encryption systems are available now.

Public-key encryption works as follows. I acquire a copy of public-key encryption software such as PGP (see below for more information). I use the software to create a program known as my personal public key. This is a software program that anyone can use to encrypt a private message they wish to send me. I place my public key on a public-key server on the Internet, so that anyone can grab it and use it to send me private mail. At the same time that I create that public key, I also create a private key that is a second software program. This private key decrypts any messages scrambled using my public key. If I'm smart, I keep only one copy of this private key, and I don't tell anyone about it. I keep it in a secret place, not on a network anywhere, so no one can get to it, except me. When someone sends me a message encrypted using my public key, I take out my private-key software, and decrypt and read the message. If I want to send you a private message, I need your public key.

It is likely that encryption technology will become an integrated option in online services in the future, such that you could simply choose the Encrypt option when composing email, thereby making the message unreadable until decrypted. So far, however, encryption has not been commonly integrated into email software. There are many encryption methodologies on the market, however, that are being used to protect the privacy of email correspondents.

The most well-known publicly available software (as opposed to those technologies kept under lock and key by the National Security Agency) is known as PGP, or Pretty Good Privacy. You can find books on how to use PGP at your local bookstore. There are both commercial and free versions of the software. Free versions can be found on the Internet. Since encryption technology is perceived as a volatile tool that could threaten the security of the United States, the product is protected by law, such that it may not be exported out of the country. To prevent such distribution via the Internet, prospective users of the product must agree with certain license agreements. If you are interested in pursuing this, the PGP Distribution Authorization Form is at: http://web.mit.edu/network/pgp-form.html

RSA Data Security, Inc. is a leading producer of software encryption and authentication software. PGP contains some proprietary technology owned by RSA (encryption algorithms). If you're interested in reading RSA's Frequently Asked Question file about cryptography, it is available at: http://www.rsa.com/faq/faq_toc.html

Digital Signatures

A separate, though very related issue to protecting the privacy of digital communication, is protecting the integrity of digital documents. As email becomes a common way to communicate, so will sending important documents, such as contracts online. There is concern in the online community that digital documents are too insecure, too easy to copy and modify to be used in commerce. There are those who disagree with this idea,[14] who say that agreements struck via email have the same essential properties of verification and alterability as those committed to paper. Whether or not this is what courts will decide, there are technological ways to ensure that email correspondence is authored by a particular individual.

Public-key encryption is one way to ensure that a particular document was signed by a particular person. Sometimes it is also important to verify when a particular document was written. A particular software product capable of this sort of verification is the Digital Notary System (DNS) available from Surety Technologies. DNS can establish the time when a digital document was sealed

2. See The Verdict on Plaintext Signatures: They're Legal by attorney Ben Wright, available at: http://infohaus.com/access/by-seller/Benjamin_Wright

with a specific set of contents. For more information on DNS, send email to info@surety.com

Protecting Internet-Connected Computers

In addition to securing the documents and email transmissions that are sent to and from lawyers, another key security issue is how to protect computers that are set up as servers on the Internet. Certainly, the average firm is not setting up its own domain, although many firms have done so. Some of these domain addresses may lead to computers maintained by third-party providers. There are also law firms that are setting up computers on the Internet that may physically exist at the firm's location.

A computer that is Internet-connected, and that enables access from the Internet, into a Web or gopher site for example, is vulnerable to those who may try to gain unauthorized access to the machine through the Internet. One of the dangers of such unauthorized access is that intruders may alter or destroy information on the machine, or may otherwise use the machine for purposes not in the firm's interest. However, a far greater danger may arise if the Net-connected machine also contains sensitive client or firm data, or is connected to other firm computers that contain such data.

To avoid such problems, the common technical solution is to construct what are known as firewalls between the Internet-accessible portion of the computer, and any other portion of the firm's computers. Although this book will not explore the technical details involved in setting up a firewall, it is useful to simply know what firewalls are, and what problem they can help avoid. If you're interested in knowing more about firewalls, you can find the Internet Firewalls Frequently Asked Questions file at: ftp://ftp.tis.com/pub/firewalls/faq.current

Chapter 5

Legal Research on the Internet

TRADITIONALLY, LEGAL RESEARCH INVOLVES FINDING THE MATERIALS A LAWYER needs to support an argument, and to ensure he or she acts in accord with current law. Those materials include primary legal sources (court opinions, statutes and regulations), and secondary sources that analyze and point to the primary materials. Secondary sources include treatises, digests, journal articles, etc. Understanding the organization of this information, how to locate it, navigate through it, and cite it is the basis of traditional legal research.

In practice, however, legal research extends way beyond traditional boundaries. As the practice of law is transformed from a profession into a business, and as wider access to information (through online services) enables people to answer their own basic legal questions, the definition of legal research is expanding.

A product liability suit, for example, might require an investigation into non-legal research sources, such as consumer newspapers, trade periodicals, scientific journals, and even biographical sources. Proving that someone owned a piece of property at a given time can involve research through public record data that can be found at the County Records Hall, and increasingly, online. Medical malpractice cases frequently require research using medical texts and journals. Essentially, every sort of resource has a role in resolving legal issues.

In order to be an effective legal researcher, one must understand the structure of the legal system. In the U.S., for example, one must understand the nature of federalism, which divides authority between the federal and state governments. This means that some areas of law, such as family law (which includes divorce and estate law), are governed by the states, while others, as directed by the U.S. Constitution, are the responsibility of the federal government. The Constitution states, for example, that "Congress shall have Power ... To promote the Progress of Science and useful Arts...." This phrase is the basis for Congress' authority over intellectual property protections (copyright, patent and trademark).

Recognition of the three areas of government (executive, legislative and judicial), and how they work together to make law is also vital. For law is not simply found in statutes passed by Congress and signed by the President. Law is also found in judges' interpretations of those statutes. Law is found in state and federal agency regulations. Law is found in zoning ordinances passed by town councils. Legal research involves determining which level of government, and which branch of government is relevant for deciding each legal issue.

To sort through the complexity of law, one must also understand the structure of the U.S. Court system, and the relationship between legislation and regulations (law created by legislatures and government agencies, respectively) and the law made by judges' opinions, also known as common law or case law. Law school teaches that law is rarely black and white, but most often gray. The answer to most every legal question is "it depends." It depends on the facts of a given situation. It depends on the interpretation of a statute or a judge's opinion. It depends on the social forces of the day. Although there may be a statute or court opinion that appears to decide a legal issue, the lawyer's task is to argue that the present fact situation is alike or distinguishable from the facts described by the statute or opinion. Which side will the lawyer argue? It depends whom the lawyer represents.

Legal research is concerned with criminal matters, which involve violation of criminal statutes, and civil matters, which involve disputes between businesses and people. Legal research may take place in the judge's chambers, in the lawyer's office, in the legislator's office, in the jail cell or at the kitchen table. The easy access to legal materials that the Internet and other online services provide make it relatively easy for anyone to access the body of law.

Just reading the law, however, can lead one to the wrong conclusions. It is critical to be aware that courts interpret laws. Often the literal meaning of a statute is quite different from the legal meaning. One of the benefits of a legal education is awareness of the interlocking complexity of statutes, regulations and court decisions. Although one needn't be a lawyer to read the law, truly understanding it and working through the legal system often does require a trained attorney. However, whether legally trained or not, any person can use the Internet to access the law, and use it as a basis for proceeding to engage an attorney. Such self-education can often save time and money, and help the researcher determine if he or she needs to consult a lawyer.

For those interested in further understanding of legal research, the Internet offers a Frequently Asked Questions file on the subject. A current version of the Legal Research FAQ may be obtained at URL: ftp://rtfm.mit.edu/pub/usenet/news.answers/law/research/

In addition, you can retrieve the FAQ via email. Send email to: mail-server@rtfm.mit.edu In the body of the message, type the following:

send usenet/news.answers/law/research/part1
send usenet/news.answers/law/research/part2

MANUAL VERSUS ONLINE LEGAL RESEARCH

In the online age, it is often easy to forget that there are other ways to get information than sitting in front of a computer. Books are a good example. Books were around before computers, and will likely be around for some time to come.

Books are accessible to anyone who can walk into a library. Books contain information that requires no access skills beyond the ability to read. No further skills, nor hardware are required. Similarly, the telephone is an essential low-tech research resource. Calling up a government agency is often the fastest, easiest and cheapest way to get information.

The benefits of online research, however, are also great. Sometimes online is the only source available. For example, libraries are not open 24 hours a day. Books get lost, misplaced, and damaged. Government employees are sometimes unavailable. Online services, by contrast, never sleep. Internet resources based on computers in Washington, DC, for example, are accessible anytime from anywhere. Whether the researcher is in China or Chicago, Internet resources such as the U.S. Congress' THOMAS legislative database are available day or night for free.

In law school, generally after manual research techniques are taught, students are introduced to Computer-Assisted Legal Research (CALR). Although CD-ROM and the Internet have widened the electronic research options, CALR is still predominantly thought of in terms of the major online services: Lexis and Westlaw. These vast "virtual law libraries" are available free to law students. By giving their services away to students, Lexis and Westlaw encourage a dependence that can obscure other effective research sources.

Traditional manual research is often less appealing to the researcher who can sit at a computer, type in a phrase, and within seconds, retrieve precise, full-text material to the screen. However, not all questions are best answered using CALR services. In general, such services are best when used to answer questions that can be stated in clear, specific terms. That is to say, CALR is an excellent way to quickly retrieve a specific case, statute, regulation or article, to check citations, and to research well-defined issues. Books are preferable over traditional computer research in situations where the researcher has not clearly defined the issue. In such a case, using Lexis would be most inefficient in terms of time and money. Printed indexes and digests are usually the best way to focus an issue. Over the history of legal study, scholars have created vast outlines of every conceivable legal topic and issue for every jurisdiction. The outlines are perpetually updated and published in the form of digests and treatises.

In order to determine how a particular issue has been dealt with and categorized by the law, a treatise can guide the researcher to a summary of the issue and leads to relevant cases and statutes. The very process of browsing a treatise often provides the researcher with relevant research directions to follow. Using Lexis is not an analogous process. Although the major CALR services have invested millions of dollars to develop powerful search software, using such software to search for relevant case law, for example, effectively hides the search process from the researcher. Search software commonly uses proximity-based techniques to find documents wherein particular words (selected by the researcher) exist near each other. This is not the optimal way to determine the relevancy of particular documents to a legal issue, because language is difficult to categorize absolutely. There are any number of ways to express a given idea, and searching for that idea using particular words, may or may not find it.

Recently, both Lexis and Westlaw have developed so-called natural language search software that employs complex algorithms to find documents that match a researcher's English-language query (versus a cryptic boolean query that uses logical connectors: "and," "or," etc.). Such software searches on a relevancy versus a proximity basis. That is, it looks for documents that are relevant to the researcher's question, rather than merely containing particular words. But no matter how sophisticated the software, it is no match for the mind of a trained researcher who can perceive the nuance in a judge's opinion. In most cases, CALR will pull up the most relevant material. But in the law, many issues turn on fine points that can not be identified by an algorithm that weights the importance of documents based on some programmer's criteria. Research on legal issues is too important to delegate to software.

The power of digital technology is clear. There is no doubt that computers have a prominent role to play in the law office. But there is a danger when personal discretion, particularly in weighing the importance of relative legal arguments, is sacrificed. Although the virtual law libraries have a secure place in the legal researcher's arsenal, they are but one of many valuable tools. The Internet is another.

HOW THE NET DIFFERS FROM LEXIS

The Lexis and Westlaw databases are the gold standards for computer-assisted legal research. These online services are the most comprehensive virtual law libraries available to the legal researcher. Their collective computer memories include nearly every U.S. court opinion of import, every statute and bill, many government agency documents, public records, law journal articles, legal directories, some foreign law, and enormous periodical and newspaper databases. In addition, both services have developed sophisticated computer search mechanisms and 24-hour support staffs to enable anyone to find whatever research materials they need whenever they need it.

There are, however, a few problems with Lexis and Westlaw. First, they are very expensive, averaging five dollars per minute. Second, they charge this hefty sum for access to materials that we, as taxpayers, have already paid for. Third, neither service provides the ability to communicate via email with other legal researchers. Finally, there are regional and other niche databases that are not of interest to the major online services' global clientele, and therefore are not offered by Lexis or Westlaw.

The materials that issue from our courts and legislatures are the property of the citizens of the country. The law, and the materials that comprise that law can therefore not be owned by anyone. What Lexis and Westlaw are really charging for, of course, is not the law itself. They are charging for access to the law. They are charging for convenience.

There are libraries throughout this country that anyone can use to peruse the miles of documents that comprise the law. Unfortunately, however, libraries are not open 24 hours every day. Even when the library is open, sometimes the book you want is not on the shelf. Or perhaps you live far from the nearest library. Online services, therefore, serve a very useful purpose. They make the law easy to get to whenever you want it. Computer searching is far faster, and more cost-effective than manual methods. To be sure, there are times when manual research is preferable. Very often, however, it is simply too slow. While research via Lexis and Westlaw is relatively fast, there is a high cost to pay for that speed.

The Internet eliminates this cost problem. Access to the Internet, depending on the access provider you choose, can be as little as $15 per month. Once you gain access, the vast majority of data available via the Net is completely free.

On Lexis, if you need to know where to find a particular document, you can simply call Lexis' phone support. That sort of convenience is why Lexis costs five dollars per minute. There is no analogous Internet phone support. Some Internet service providers offer phone support to help out with the technical details of accessing the Net, but they do not help you find documents on the Net. The interactive nature of the Net and the existing online "community" ensures that you can always find plenty of help to be had online. There are, for example, many opportunities to ask for help by using email or reading newsgroup postings. But for those having trouble accessing the newsgroups, a friendly voice on the other end of the telephone can be invaluable.

The cost distinction is also evident in the "look and feel" of Lexis versus the Net. Lexis' corporate owners have invested a lot of time and money to make the database serve the needs of its users. Its screens are strictly-text (that is, Lexis screens do not use graphical icons). However, the organization of its database, and its standardized search commands, epitomize a centralized, planned service. The Internet, in contrast, has no owner. Its evolution as a global source of information has not been centrally planned. Rather, the Internet is being shaped by those who use it.

Since access to the Internet is available from many different providers, the on-screen "look" or interface of the Internet varies considerably. The most common interface is a strictly-text screen. Frequently, an elementary knowledge of the UNIX operating system is required to use such interfaces effectively. On the other hand, the growing popularity of the Internet has resulted in the development of graphical interfaces. Particularly, World Wide Web-based legal servers that enable hypertextual access to documents (jumping from one document to another by choosing a highlighted word) are becoming common. While Lexis also offers the ability to jump from one document to another, the fact that Lexis users accrue costs at the average rate of five dollars per minute inhibits the sort of free-wheeling exploration one can do on the Internet. This is especially important for the neophyte legal researcher, who's poking around and trying to learn about the law and how to conduct research. Lexis is great for the professional who knows exactly what he or she's looking for. The cost-benefit of being able to immediately pull the digital version of a decision is clear. But for the researcher who can't charge the cost of research back to a client, or who wishes to research at a more leisurely pace, the Internet is a natural alternative.

Beyond cost and interface considerations, the primary difference between the Internet and Lexis is the sort of materials available on each. Lexis is a virtual law library in the sense that it makes available online most of the primary and many secondary materials found in a traditional law library. Lexis includes most federal and state appellate court opinions. (Court opinions rendered at the trial level, that is the pre-appellate level, are rarely available from law libraries or Lexis. Such opinions are generally available only from the courts themselves.) Lexis also includes all federal and state statutes, and all federal regulations.

The Net's resources are nowhere near as comprehensive. Still, there is a great deal of valuable legal data available on the Net. All branches of government are Internet-connected and offering free access to the law. State and federal legislatures provide Internet access to statutes and pending bills. The U.S. Congress provides Internet access to the entire body of codified U.S. law in the U.S. Code, as well as access to the Code of Federal Regulations and Federal Register. Courts provide Internet access to opinions. Government agencies provide access to rules, information releases, advisory opinions, and other important documents.

In short, while the Internet is not yet a substitute for Lexis/Westlaw, it is a supplemental source. For some researchers the Net provides everything required; for others it is not yet comprehensive. Clearly, the Internet has some catching up to do to match the holdings of Lexis/Westlaw. While Lexis has been a legal resource since 1975, the Internet only became a recognized source for legal documents in 1993.

For some limited purposes (for example, tracking new legislative bills, or accessing the Library of Congress' copyright database), the Internet is a cheap alternative to Lexis. For direct access to particular government agency documents, current Supreme Court or federal Courts of Appeals' rulings, the Internet can't be beat. For access to proprietary materials, like legal memoranda and unpublished articles, the Internet offers access to previously unavailable material. For direct online contact with colleagues, for communicating via email with clients, the Internet is the only choice. Neither Lexis nor Westlaw provide email, nor group discussions. But for comprehensive access to traditional research materials, especially historical data (prior to a couple years), Lexis and Westlaw are still ahead of the Net.

Lexis and Westlaw also have more sophisticated search engines than the Internet. Both services have recently begun offering natural language search software that enables you to search vast databases using English-language queries, rather than the more obscure boolean search expressions (these are essentially logical connections of words, e.g., "copyright" and "cyberspace" or "Internet").

There are many different search mechanisms on the Internet. Some enable you to search through a broad range of material on many different computers, others enable searching through databases located on individual machines. A rapid evolution of this search software is occurring. Due to the decentralized nature of the Net, the fact that virtually anyone can provide data, and the fact that no central organization is responsible for the "look and feel" of that data, using the Net for research is not the consistent experience one has using Lexis or Westlaw. Data on the Net occasionally gets moved to a new location. Internet computers can become hard to access due to heavy user traffic or technical problems. Since the computers offering data on the Net are not owned by a central organization, there is essentially no one to call for help when these problems occur. The Net researcher is essentially on his own.

Such independence is the flip-side of free access. You pay dearly for 24-hour support on Lexis/Westlaw. It might seem that paying a high price for access to computer-based information would guarantee dependability and absolutely comprehensive access. One would hope that for five dollars a minute, Lexis/Westlaw could do everything. But of course, this is not the case. There is simply too much information in the world for all of it to be included in one place. The Internet has enabled anyone to publish legal data online. While the government, for example, once found it not to be cost-effective to publish court opinions itself, and therefore legal publishers established a foothold, now the government is publishing court and legislative material on the Internet. Similarly, law firms, which churn out reams of legal materials that can benefit the researcher, have begun publishing their materials on the Net.

Simply put, the Net is an efficient publishing mechanism. Electronic distribution is cheaper than shipping books. Electronic publishing enables rapid updating of material, and quick access by anyone at anytime. The fact that the Net is not centralized, and therefore not an overhead-burdened commercial creation is a great strength. It is different from Lexis/Westlaw. There are both positive and negative aspects to that difference. Lower cost is balanced against less convenience. As the Net evolves, its efficiencies will continue to establish it as an important tool for the legal researcher.

USING THE NET FOR LEGAL RESEARCH

The communication and marketing advantages of the Internet are clearly unique and unavailable from Lexis or Westlaw. In addition, the Internet is a valuable research tool. However, effective research use of the Net requires an understanding of its unique properties. When most lawyers think of electronic legal research, they think of Lexis and Westlaw. Due to their longterm domination of the field, these two services have, by default, determined the nature of online research. The emergence of alternative electronic resources (including CD-ROM, electronic bulletin boards (BBSs) and the Internet) has demonstrated that Lexis and Westlaw have not exploited all the features of electronic research media.

The Internet in particular, offers many new and valuable ways to conduct research. For example, one can access Internet documents from central "collections" created by lawyers and law librarians, one can access databases provided for free by public and private organizations, and one can use the Net to find experts for consultative purposes. One of the most unique research uses of the Net is the ability to ask the legal community for help in locating a source that may not be available from traditional media. Only three years ago, there was no way to access a well-trafficked mailing list to ask the international community of law librarians for example, where to find the new Commercial Code from the United Arab Emirates (UAE). When this question was posed recently to the FIND/SVP Legal Research Group, and no traditional source had the code (including Lexis, Westlaw, the Library of Congress, the U.S. Commerce Department, and the many excellent international law collections in North America), the INT-LAW list provided the answer. Within hours of posting the request to the list, several responses were received that identified an Abu Dabai source for the Code, as well as a recommended translator.

Mailing list archives are also valuable sources of information. Rather than reinvent the wheel every time a question comes up, it may save you time and your client money if you check to see if your peers have already resolved the issue. Mailing list archives contain the history of discussions that have occurred on the list. For example, to review the archive for the INT-LAW list, try this URL: gopher://gopher.law.cornell.edu:70/11/listservs

The idea that researchers can benefit from the past work of others is not new to lawyers. It is very common for brief writers to plagiarize language right out of judicial opinions. Court decisions are not copyrighted, therefore, it is not a copyright violation to copy language into new court documents. In addition, it can be persuasive when trying a case before Judge Smith to use Judge Smith's own opinion to argue a point in a subsequent trial.

Similarly, a recent research innovation are CD-ROMs that contain exemplary legal briefs in particular practice areas. For example, there are disks that contain the best, and most notable briefs concerned with intellectual property. The idea is, why not learn from the best? Why not benefit from the best legal minds and writers? Following this logic, use of mailing list archives to resolve research questions is natural and in fact, essential. A series of forces is transforming the legal industry into a more cost-effective mechanism. Retooling research methods is another way to achieve this transformation.

In addition to offering communication as a revolutionary way to answer legal questions, the Net provides very cost-effective access to print sources. In many cases, individual lawyers and law librarians (rather than corporate entities), are driving the effort to identify and centralize Internet resources relevant to particular practice areas. In some cases, these people are not only creating centralized Internet legal sites, but are adding materials supplied by their academic, government and/or private law firm employers. Such material is generally unavailable elsewhere. Before Web sites became the preferred method to offer and access such collections, gopher sites and ftp archives were common, and still abundantly exist.

For example, at the Advertising Law site provided by law firm Arent Fox Kintner Plotkin & Kahn, there are memos and articles authored by Arent Fox lawyers. These materials are ostensibly provided to market the firm. The idea is that a researcher, in the course of considering the firm's materials, may choose to employ Arent Fox. The materials are also very valuable in their own right, as sources of professionally prepared information about focused topics. Here is a listing of some of the materials available at the Arent Fox site.

- Fundamental Advertising Principles
- Articles About Advertising Law
- FTC Advertising Guidelines And Enforcement Policy
- Statements
- FTC Trade Regulation Rules
- FTC Consumer Brochures
- FTC Business Compliance Manuals
- Testimony And Speeches
- European Commission Advertising/Consumer Law

Similarly, solo patent lawyer Robin Diane Goldstein has set up a home page (http://www.zoom.com/robins_sandbox/robinlaw.html) that collects intellectual property resources that are available in various places on the Internet. Here's an example of the resources collected by Ms. Goldstein:

- US Patent And Trademark Office
- US Copyright Office Gopher
- Smart Patents
- Patent Faq
- Sunnyvale Patent Library
- League for Programming Freedom
- Search PTO Archives

- Sto's Internet Patent Search Service
- Shadow Patent Office
- International Trademark Classifications
- Patent Law Documents
- Cornell Law School—Information Institute
- Trademark Law Documents
- Villanova Center for Information Law
- Indiana Law School Virtual Law Library

The Internet is an excellent way to find expert witnesses. Lawyers need experts to testify at trial, to evaluate materials and situations, and for advisory purposes. The PSYCH-LAW mailing list is a well-trafficked and excellent place to post a request for psychological experts. Access to computer and other technical people are available in profusion online. If you need a computer security expert, or someone familiar with setting up a local area network within a law firm, or someone to rebuild a corrupted hard disk, you'll find plenty of offers of help if you post a request in one of the relevant newsgroups or mailing lists.

The experienced researcher picks and chooses from available resources, to establish a personal library, shaped to the individual's needs. The Internet itself can be used in this way by the researcher. In order to take advantage of the Net as a research tool, one must seek out resources, by reviewing directories (like this book), and by communicating with others who are using this evolving resource, via mailing lists and newsgroups. In this way, the researcher will compile a personal virtual library of numerous resources, none of which need to take up shelf space, but all of which are always available virtually for free.

The directory portion of this book seeks to catalog all of the legal research resources identifiable at the time of its publication. By its very nature, however, the Internet is not able to be completely captured. All we can hope to do is provide a photograph of the Net's offerings at a given moment in time. Despite their imperfection, there is value in such photographs. Just as the central patent site put together by Robin Goldstein can make it easier to find particular materials, this directory is a ready source that puts together in one concise volume, a substantial amount of the Internet's legal offerings, so you don't have to go find them yourself. The Net is an evolving resource that changes daily. Therefore it is incumbent on the researcher to be informed of new relevant resources as they become available. The best way I've found to do this is to subscribe to relevant mailing lists, such as LAW-LIB, and GOV-DOC. For those researchers who focus on specialized legal areas, there are even more relevant lists to subscribe to, such as TAX-L for tax and INT-LAW for international law. In the following sections are identified resources one can turn to for particular legal practice areas.

GENERAL PRACTICE

General legal practitioners are involved with areas of law that affect small business people and average citizens. Such people do exchange real estate, get injured, need wills, and enter into contracts. Each of these activities can require the services of an attorney. The Internet can help both individuals and lawyers who find themselves in general practice situations.

Each of these areas of law depends on access to legislation and court-case decisions. The Internet case law collection is focused on federal law. Very little state case law is on the Net so far. On the federal side, the U.S. Supreme Court provides Internet-access to opinions dating to 1990, and Courts of Appeals' opinions dating back a few years are also on the Net. However, due to the current lack of a vendor-neutral page numbering scheme for court opinions, Internet-accessible decisions are not citable in legal documents. This doesn't mean you can't use the Internet versions for reading or informational purposes, however, and the cost can't be beat.

There's a good deal of state and federal legislation available on the Net. The Net provides easy access to state bill tracking databases (collections of pending laws) and state codes (collections of existing laws). The U.S. Congress, through the Library of Congress, has provided access to a federal bill tracking database as well as the texts of new federal laws. The Government Printing Office (GPO: http://thorplus.lib.purdue.edu/gpo/) provides free access to the body of U.S. laws (the U.S. Code) as well as federal agency issuances (in the Federal Register). In addition, the House of Representatives Internet Law Library (HILL: http://law.house.gov) provides a fine collection of legislative material. Here's the top-level menu from HILL:

- Federal Laws (Arranged By Original Published Source)
- Federal Laws (Arranged By Agency)
- State And Territorial Laws
- Laws Of Other Nations
- Treaties And International Law
- Laws Of All Jurisdictions (Arranged By Subject)
- Law School Law Library Catalogues And Services
- Attorney And Legal Profession Directories

For Personal Injury (PI) practitioners, the Net can provide a way to locate expert witnesses. If, for example, you need someone familiar with ski-boot construction, you might try posting to one of the skiing mailing lists or newsgroups, or perhaps find out whether competitors of the boot manufacturer in question have online sites. (For example, try a Web or gopher search.) Another source for expert witnesses via the Net is LERN, the Legal Research Network designed to help lawyers network with expert witnesses. At LERN's home page (http://www.witness.net/) you'll find a listing of all the curriculum vitaes (CVs) maintained on the LERN service. The listing includes expert name, and a very brief description of the areas of expertise. All the CVs are in a database with full-text search capability. This list is updated roughly once per month and contains over 400 experts.

An additional Internet source of use to PI lawyers are motor vehicle records. For example, if you have a client who has been injured in a traffic accident, you can use one of the databases accessible online to get the vehicle registration and driver's license history of the pertinent parties. Only a few states currently make this information available on the Net. It is not free (though it's only a few dollars per record) and you'll need an account with the relevant provider. But access to this data from the comfort and convenience of your desktop computer is hard to beat. Since you'll be accessing the data on the Internet, you'll also be saving the long-distance charges you'd have to pay if you dialed into a remote BBS.

General practitioners can also benefit from the information made available by the many federal agencies that have set up shop on the Internet. For example, PI lawyers may be interested in consulting the Consumer Products Safety Commission's (CPSC) gopher site (gopher://cpsc.gov/) to keep aware of press releases or Federal Register notices relevant to current litigation. Here are some of the entries in the CPSC menu:

- Reporting Product Related Hazards To CPSC
- CPSC Public Calendar
- CPSC Press Releases
- Federal Register Notices
- CPSC Hotline Information
- CPSC Information For Manufacturers, Retailers And Distributors
- How To Receive Information From CPSC

INTERNATIONAL PRACTICE

For firms that do significant international work, the Internet is particularly useful. The INT-LAW mailing list is a primary way to stay aware of international legal materials available on the Internet. One of the more outstanding sites, at the Fletcher School of Law and Diplomacy in Medford, Massachusetts, offers free access to a large catalog of international treaties.

As part of its Multilaterals Project, the Fletcher School provides the text of a wide variety of multilateral conventions. Although the primary focus of the project has been on international environmental instruments, conventions dealing with human rights, the laws of war, and other fields are also included. Following is a partial list of available documents.

- Action Plan for the Human Environment (Stockholm, 1972).
- Agreement Governing the Activities of States on the Moon.
- Charter of the United Nations (1945).
- Conv. on Fishing & Conserv. of Living Res. of the High Seas.
- Conv. on the Territorial Sea & the Contiguous Zone (1958).
- Convention on the Continental Shelf (1958).
- Convention on the Elimination of All Forms of Discrimination.
- Convention on the Rights of the Child (1989).
- International Covenant on Civil and Political Rights (1966).
- International Covenant on Economic, Social, & Cultural Rights.
- International Tropical Timber Agreement (1983).
- Paris Conv. for the Protection of Indus. Property (rev.1967).
- Patent Cooperation Treaty; with Regulations (1970).
- Protocol relating to the Status of Refugees (1967).
- Statute of the International Court of Justice (1945).
- The General Agreement on Tariffs and Trade (1947).
- United Nations Convention on the Law of the Sea (1982).

To access the Multilaterals Project, you can use gopher or ftp as follows:

URL: ftp://ftp.fletcher.tufts.edu/pub/diplomacy
URL: gopher://gopher.law.cornell.edu:70/11/foreign/fletcher

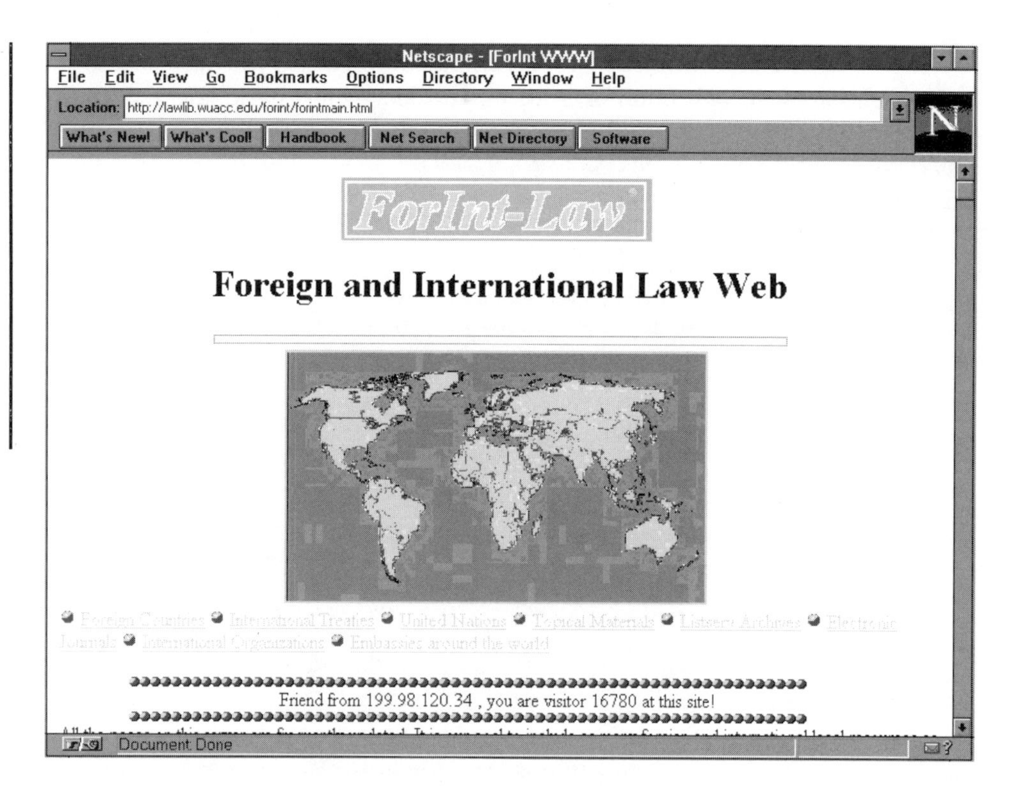

Figure 5-1. http://lawlib.wuacc.edu/forint/forintmain.html

Washburn University's international law collection can help you find the foreign law you need.

Many foreign countries are beginning to provide direct access (in English) to laws and other-country information. Many enterprising librarians and system operators are taking the initiative to provide one-stop Internet sites that access large collections of foreign materials. These one-stop sites make it much easier for internauts to find information, especially if you find it burdensome to collect and retrieve hundreds of disparate email messages that describe interesting sites.

One of these one-stop sites is provided by the Law Library at Washburn University in Topeka, Kansas (http://lawlib.wuacc.edu/forint/forintmain.html). System administrator Mark Folmsbee provides access to a wide-ranging, and easy to use international law server. The site provides links to primary and secondary legal sources in many countries. All files are arranged by geographic region and subject.

At this point in the Internet's development, there is a lot of information about some sources, and none about others. On the domestic side, for example, California has made an enormous amount of legislative and political information freely available, while Connecticut provides very little. The same is true internationally. Some countries have provided little or no access to statutory or other legal data, while others, like Israel, for example, provide a lot. It would seem the provision of such materials via the Internet could offer countries a cost savings from the standpoint of answering telephone requests for information, a superb public relations tool, and a boon to legal researchers all over the world.

The Israeli Foreign Ministry (gopher://israel-info.gov.il/) provides access to an English-language collection of government documents, basic law and court decisions on notable issues (such as the Demjanjuk appeal). Following are examples of the available documents:

- Justice Ministry on Supreme Court HAMAS Ruling.
- Israel's Policy on Selective Conscientious Objection.
- Israel's Interrogation Policies and Practices.
- Justice Minister Liba'i on Demjanjuk Appeal Decision.
- Decision Israel Supreme Court on Demjanjuk Petition.
- Attorney General's Opinion on Kach and Kahane Chai.
- Basic Law: The Government (new law).
- Basic Law: Judicature.
- Basic Law: Israel Lands.
- Basic Law: The State Economy.
- Law of Return, 57101950.
- Nazi and Nazi Collaborators (Punishment) Law, 57101950.

SECURITIES AND TAX RESEARCH

Just a short time ago, there was very little tax, security-related and financial data available on the Internet. Today, there is a wealth of great material online that has significant practical value for lawyers, accountants, investment analysts and plain folks who need financial-related information, forms, and other resources.

Federal agencies provide some of the most impressive materials available online. The Securities and Exchange Commission provides the Electronic Data Gathering and Retrieval (EDGAR) database of corporate information (http://www.sec.gov/edgarhp.htm). Through a very friendly Web interface, EDGAR provides direct, full-text access to all electronic corporate filings made to the SEC dating back to 1994. All publicly traded domestic companies are subject to electronic filing requirements as of May 1996, and most documents filed with the Commission will be available on EDGAR.

These filings provide a wealth of insight into American corporations. For example, section C of the annual 10-K filing made for every U.S. corporation details the legal matters that each company is involved with. If you're trying to determine whether a firm is a good investment, or whether it is involved in litigation, section C is a good place to look.

The SEC also provides information on Fedworld, which is an Internet site that brings together some 75 federal bulletin board systems. To reach the SEC site on Fedworld, telnet to fedworld.gov, choose: Regulatory Information Mall, and then choose option: B. The docket library contains the full text of final rules, proposed rules, and a variety of information releases. The docket library also offers various legislation, including:

- Securities Exchange Act Of 1934
- Public Utility Holding Company Act
- Investment Advisers Act Of 1940
- Investment Company Act Of 1940

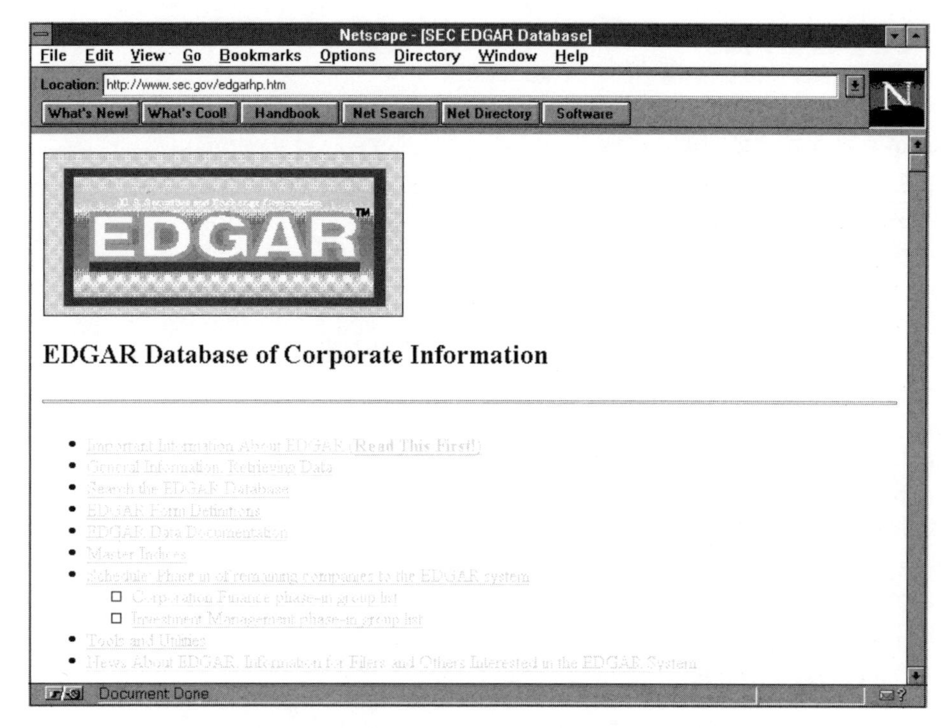

Figure 5-2. http://www.sec.gov/edgarhp.htm

As of May 1996, all domestic public corporations are required to make their SEC filings electronically. These documents will be available on the EDGAR database on the Net.

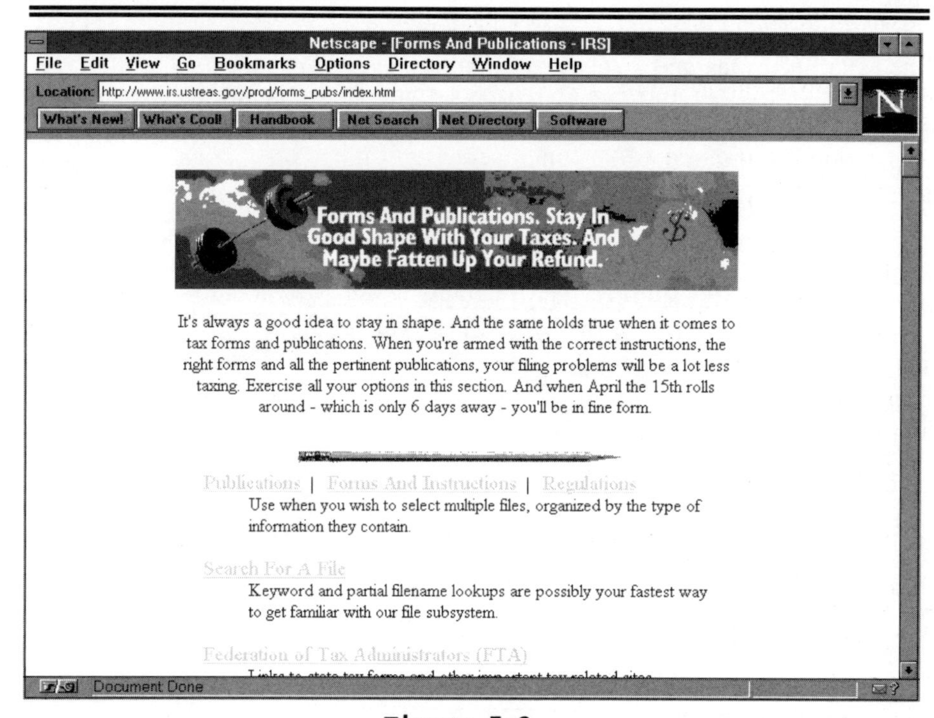

Figure 5-3. http://www.irs.ustreas.gov/prod/forms_pubs/index.html

The IRS provides 24-hour free access to tax forms, publications and regulations at this Web site.

Tax Forms

There are at least two sources for tax forms on the Internet. One is the IRS. (See figure 5.3.) The other is the Web site provided by Maxwell Labs, and known as Taxing Times. The Maxwell site (http://www.scubed.com/tax/index.html) has current-year federal, state and Canadian tax information and forms, and public domain tax software. The forms are available for you to download and print using your local printer. They are available in three different formats: TIFF image format, printer-downloadable Adobe PostScript(TM), and Adobe Portable Document Format (PDF). Not all of the 750 + forms are available in every format. It depends on the form Maxwell Labs received them in. State forms are only available in TIFF and PostScript (converted from the TIFF images) formats. If you're interested in downloading a free copy of the Adobe Acrobat Reader (this is the forms reader of choice for many government agencies), go to Adobe's site: http://www.adobe.com

The IRS provides all tax forms and instructions along with Taxpayer Information Publications (TIPS). IRS files are available in pcl, pdf, ps and sgml formats at this site: http://www.irs.ustreas.gov/prod/forms_pubs/index.html

Tax Discussion Archive

The Federal Taxation mailing list (FedTax-L) provides a generally unmoderated environment for the discussion of federal taxation issues from both a practical and academic viewpoint. The discussions are intended to include latest trends, regulatory actions, and, of course, a lively exchange of ideas and concerns.

The archive for the Federal Tax List is searchable back to 1991. There is a wealth of information here, including many points of view on many tax-related issues, and identification of many individuals with viewpoints and expertise on these subjects. If you're looking for an expert, or a quick lesson on a tax subject, the archive is a quick, cheap way to gather varied input.

URL: gopher://Niord.shsu.edu:70/11gopher_root%3A%5B_DATA.FILESERV.FEDTAX-L%5D

URL: gopher://gopher.shsu.edu

Then choose:

- Economics (SHSU Network Access Initiative Project)/
- Archives of Pol-Econ, FedTax-L and sci.econ.research/
- List Archives for FedTax-L@SHSU.edu/

Tax Journal

A compilation of student and faculty tax papers, known collectively as the Villanova Tax Law Compendium, is online, courtesy of Villanova Law School's Tax Law Society and the Villanova Center for Information Law and Policy. Here's a sampling of some of the faculty articles:

- New LIFO Recapture Tax and Its Effect On State Income Taxation
- Treatment of Multistate Income Taxes
- Adjusted Basis for State Income Tax Purposes: Modification Problems
- Adjusted Basis for State Income Tax Purposes: Nonresident Shareholders
- Adjusted Basis When S Election Not in Effect for State Income Tax Purposes
- Adjusted Basis for State Income Tax Purposes: Newly Enacted State Income Taxes and State Audit Adjustments
- The Model Act: Overview
- The Model Act: Taxation of the S Corporation; Corporate Filing and Tax Remission Obligations
- The Model Act: Taxation Of S Corporation Shareholders

The Tax Law Compendium also welcomes submissions. If you are a tax attorney or tax accountant and are interested in making your material available on the World Wide Web and Villanova's gopher server, you can contact amajor@mail.law.vill.edu . To reach the Compendium:

gopher://ming.law.vill.edu/11/.taxlaw/
http://www.law.vill.edu/vill.tax.l.compen/index.html

Other Valuable Financial Sites

INTERNET BANKRUPTCY LIBRARY

URL: http://bankrupt.com

FINANCENET

URL: http://www.financenet.gov
URL: gopher://gopher.financenet.gov
URL: ftp://ftp.financenet.gov
Newsgroup: news.financenet.gov

FREE STOCK QUOTES

URL: telnet://telnet.quote.com
URL: http://www.quote.com
URL: ftp://ftp.quote.com

FIDELITY INVESTMENTS

URL: http://www.fid-inv.com

PARKVIEW FINANCIAL INC.

URL: http://www.usit.net/pfi.html

ACCURACY OF INTERNET RESOURCES

Accuracy of materials used for research is an essential issue to legal researchers. There's really no point in using material that will be cited in a legal memo if there is a question that the material is up-to-date and letter-perfect. Therefore, in the past, many Internet materials, were not suitable for this purpose. Even U.S. Supreme Court opinions issued by the Court itself may have posed a problem for research purposes because the citations in those opinions did not match the page numbers in official reporters (see the section below, Citing Internet Information, for more on this subject).

There have traditionally been many sources for access to legislation on the Internet, often provided by special interest providers, such as Computer Professionals for Social Responsibility (CPSR), an organization concerned with cyberspacial civil rights. Therefore, CPSR has long provided access to such documents as the Privacy Act of 1974. However, CPSR wasn't the original provider on the Internet of this document. CPSR's computer actually pointed to a server in California known as the Internet Wiretap (wiretap.spies.com). I have never been able to figure out who actually maintains the wiretap machine, or who is responsible for the online version of the Privacy Act.

In any case, without actually comparing the Wiretap/CPSR version of the document with the official United States Code (U.S.C.) version of the document, it's impossible to know whether the Internet version is completely accurate. Therefore, citing to such a document in a brief is a bit risky. However, using the Internet document for informational purposes, or when you don't have the U.S.C. handy, or when you don't need to be letter-perfect, and you don't want to pay an expensive commercial database for access, is completely appropriate.

More recently, however, government entities such as the U.S. House of Representatives have been getting into the practice of making data (current bills and legislation for example) available via the Internet. Although this practice only began in January 1995 for the U.S. Congress, it would seem that one can depend on the accuracy of the materials made available by this legislative body. As this practice becomes more common, it would seem likely that use of Internet-retrievable materials will become accepted, and even expected by clients that want to see costs kept to a minimum.

In order to determine the accuracy of an Internet resource, attorney and international law librarian Lyonette Louis-Jacques says she looks "to see who is putting it up. If it is a government agency, I would tend to be more willing to accept its accuracy, just like with regular sources. But I look to see where it is coming from. Even if the source is at a government site, it might be a link to some nongovernmental site. Is it actually at that site or is it from someplace else? Then you look for things within the document, like date of publication, who put it up. So you sort of scrutinize the resource for indication of date, any indication of how often it is updated.

> "If you go there frequently enough you will get an idea of how often it is updated. If you are actually following that area of law, you get an idea. Since I'm on a lot of [email] lists, I tend to know the names of the people who are actually putting up and sometimes the process in which they get a document. Who they got the document from is important. So it is not only the site, but the origin of that document, and then the dates on the document.

"For instance, there was this PLO agreement with Israel that everyone was looking for. It showed up on the Israel Information Service. I know, from having visited their gopher site and their Web site, that from the way they set up their site and the way they have done everything, I have utter faith. And because it is from the Ministry itself, you are getting the true text.

"But, for things that are coming from [some other sites], I [may] know who is putting it up, but I don't know how he is putting it up. I don't know if he's typing or scanning the information in. Who is he getting it from? Does it vary with each text of the treaty? See, I don't know that. So, you can get hold of the [Internet] text to start with, and you could work with it, but when it comes to citing, I would want to know more about it. Especially if I'm going to quote a particular section, I would want to verify its accuracy from an official source.

"Lexis and Westlaw are going through a similar process that the people who are putting stuff on the Internet are. Except [the individuals posting data on the net] don't have the budget I don't think, to establish a reputation for accuracy. I think you just have to take each source on its own and evaluate it on its own, [depending] on who puts out the source, where is it located, and any indication on the document of how up-to-date it is and how often it is updated."

Another Viewpoint on Internet Accuracy

Attorney Elliot Chabot heads up the automated legal support team for the U.S. House of Representatives. Chabot explains that when House staffers became aware of the resources available on the Internet, they said:

"'We've seen publicity about the Internet, but the publicity says it is a big mish mash of information. We still have access to the more traditional ways of doing legal research; does this offer an advancement? Does this offer us easier access to the materials? If we've got to spend more time hunting for something on the Internet than it would take to phone the Library of Congress Law Library or the Congressional Research Service, then we really haven't gained anything.

"My response was to build the House Internet Law Library [http://law.house.gov], which we released on January 3rd of 1995. That is a library mostly of pointers to specific law resource items on the Internet. It is arranged by jurisdiction and arranged by subject. What we've tried to do is to go deeply into the resources, so that we won't simply point to, for instance, the Cornell University gopher. We will go down and point to their collection of treaties and have that on our list of treaties and international law. Also, on behalf of the Office of the Law Revision Counsel we set up a searchable copy of the U.S. Code at that address. We've also thrown in the whole CFR [Code of Federal Regulations] from title one to title fifty since that is so closely associated with the U.S. Code.

"Because almost none of the material actually originates on servers under the control of the House, and because accuracy depends on whoever is maintaining each particular database, we made a point to put in a disclaimer. What we've put on the disclaimer is a message that says, '...We make no guarantees or warranties as to the accuracy or the timeliness of the data. On the other hand, we have not deliberately included any inaccurate data in our directories. If you believe any material referenced by these directories is inaccurate, please contact us....'

"Someone with legal training is likely to understand the need right off to verify the accuracy of the information and to be wary of the timeliness of the information. When you get to the public doing [legal research], you run into the same situation as law libraries that are open to the public. They are there, open to the public, the public is welcome. Federal depository libraries are set up that way. But the lay user of legal resources needs to be wary.

"Of course, none of these pitfalls justify closing it off. We will have a rehash of the problems that exist currently when laymen attempt to use legal resources. You will have some successes and you will have some enormous failures. People will publish treatises and people are now starting to publish, on the Net, material aimed at the lay audience. Fairly early on, there were groups that were putting material on the Net about how to use the Freedom of Information Act. Over time I think you will see more and more of that. I think in fact Nolo Press has a server out and they specialize in how to use the law for laymen. I think you will see an expansion of that.

"[The choice whether to use Internet versus conventional sources] becomes a function of how important is it to have the most accurate and the most up-to-date version of the material. My general approach to Internet legal research now, because it's in such a state of infancy, is to suggest that people use it as a starting point. But if it is important to verify that you are completely accurate, once you've got your citations, once you believe you have found what you need, check it against the official version. Go to the books. People start off with the best intentions when they put law and other material on the Internet. But people also discover, I think, what a drudgery it is to maintain databases and some folks carry on, and others don't. There is a lot of material that was timely when it was placed on the Internet, but is no longer particularly timely.

"Because of my position supporting House offices with legal research, I wind up covering a wide variety of legal areas. Some of the material that is available now through the House Internet Law Library was the result of offices wanting to know 'Where can I find such and such information? I want to find a copy of the Japanese Instruments of Surrender at the end of W.W.II.' My task was to find it. In this particular case they wanted it on a floppy disk. So that if I could find it on the Net, that was the simplest thing in the world to download. Fortunately, it was available. I did a Veronica search and got it through Gopher.

"I monitor a fair number of listservs in search of folks announcing the availability of law resources. I think that is one of the great things about the Internet; it really encourages sharing. Perhaps this will change the image of the profession. There is somewhat of a leveling effect here. It is not just lawyers that are participating , it is other legal professionals as well. It's law librarians and it is other researchers that are involved with legal questions or government document questions, and those people are participating as equals in this whole sharing of information."

CITING INTERNET INFORMATION

The ability to accurately cite to court opinions is critical to their usefulness. Generally, court opinions are used to support or oppose legal arguments made in court-filed documents. Such documents must specify the source of referenced opinions, so that the judge (and the opposition) reading the document can easily retrieve the referenced case.

Whenever a court opinion or statute is referenced in a legal memo, the opinion is identified, or cited, using a standard format. For example, the standard citation* to the landmark Supreme Court decision in Roe v. Wade, is: 410 U.S. 113. This means Roe is in volume 410 of the U.S. Reporter, page 113. Such standard citations enable anyone reading the memo to precisely retrieve the referenced document. Citations to statutes are determined by legislatures, and therefore are standard and nonproprietary. Court opinion citations, however, are created by the companies that publish opinions in book form (known as official court reporters, such as the U.S. Reporter).

The commonly followed reference source for accurate citing to opinions, known as The Blue Book, requires that citations first be made to the jurisdiction's "official reporter." Often, a second or parallel cite must be made to the "unofficial reporter" (usually a West publication). Since such official and unofficial reporters were designated long before CD-ROM or the Internet existed, such newer sources of opinions cannot be cited to in court documents.

Compounding this problem for publishers seeking to enter the case law market, and for lawyers who want to use the new and often more efficient media, is the fact that West Publishing asserts a copyright over its page numbering scheme. Any publisher without a license from West (Lexis seems to be the only licensee) is thereby prevented from inserting West's page numbers into opinions as they are issued by courts. In the case of federal district and appellate courts, The Blue Book provides that citations should be made to the relevant West reporters. Since Internet opinions cannot include the West page numbers, Internet opinions cannot be cited to in federal court pleadings.

The citation issue is contentious. CD-ROM publishers have challenged West's copyright assertion in court. Various organizations are expressing support for a "vendor-neutral" citation system. Two court systems in the nation have thus far established noncommercial citation systems. Louisiana uses a public domain citation that includes the case name, court docket number and court name. South Dakota adopted its "universal" citation system in January 1996 citing cases with the year and opinion number. Otherwise, however, no standard public domain citation system exists to identify opinions published anywhere other than in the official reporters or in other media owned by the publishers of the reporters.

The Internet poses an additional problem for those who need to identify the source of documents found on the Net. As the Net's role as a publishing medium continues to expand, more and more documents will be retrieved from the Net, as opposed to other sources. The sheer convenience of the Net, which provides for retrieval at any time from anywhere, in combination with its very low cost of distribution, ensures that it will be increasingly important as a source for documents. In fact, it seems likely that the Net may develop into the primary source of distribution for government documents, including court opinions, legislative material and administrative agency documents. Therefore, it is essential that a standard public domain citation system be developed for materials found on the Internet.

Generally, if you are citing to material that is available somewhere other than the Internet, it is unnecessary to indicate the Internet as a source. For example, a journal article that happens to be available on the Internet, but is also available from a hard-copy journal, can be cited to the journal using standard bibliographic or legal citation form.

*For a primer on standard legal citation, go to: http://www.law.cornell.edu/citation/citation.table.html .

If there is no alternative citable source, however, or if such alternative source is very obscure, it is appropriate to use a citation to the Internet. Keep in mind that the primary purpose of citations is to enable the reader to retrieve the original material to which you cite. Citations should therefore provide sufficient information for the reader to identify the material. In the realm of nonelectronic sources, citations often include such information as: author, title, date, page(s), and source. Internet citations similarly ought to include the traditional document identification (author, title, etc.), and an Internet location. Where a document exists in more than one place on the Net, cite to the original Internet source, where the document still resides. You may also wish to provide a secondary, or parallel Internet source, in order to provide your reader with a "backup" location for the document.

Uniform Resource Locater

The predominant Internet citation form is the URL, or Uniform Resource Locator. This format can be used to cite to Web, ftp, telnet and gopher sites. The syntax for a URL reveals its representation of a computer address. It includes the method of access (ftp, gopher, etc.), the computer or server name on which the document resides, the specific port if it is not a standard or default port, and finally, the directory and file name. The full syntax for a URL is:

access-method://server-name[:port]/directory/file

Alternatively, the book *Electronic Style, A Guide to Citing Electronic Information* by Xia Li and Nancy B. Crane offers a citation format that has the following basic form:

> Author, (date). Title (edition), [Type of medium]. Available [insert Internet retrieval method: ftp, email, telnet, www, gopher, newsgroup]: [insert relevant data; eg for ftp, insert "Directory: File:"; for email, insert: "Message:"; for telnet, insert: "Directory: File:"; for www, insert "URL:"; for gopher, insert "URL:"; and for newsgoup, insert "USENET Newsgroup:"]

Here are examples of suggested formats when citing to the Internet:

Newsgroups Message
Frank, G. (1994, January 7). Looking for environmental counsel [Discussion], [Online]. Available email: USENET NEWSGROUP: misc.legal

Mailing List Message
Milligan, Stuart (1991, March 19) Database of scanned reserve readings [Online] Available email: LISTSERV@UHUPVM1.BITNET

Gopher Site: State Law
Computer Crime Act, Alabama, Ala. Code § 13A-8-10 (1975) [Online]. Available GOPHER: gopher://sulaw.law.su.OZ.AU:70/00/Law Documents/Collection of various Laws (mainly from U.S.)/alabama.law

Telnet Site: Court Decision

Independence Party of NY v. Board of Elections, NY Court of Appeals, (March 13, 1995) [Online]. Available TELNET: freenet.buffalo.edu LOGIN: freeport Directory: Legal Center, NY Court of Appeals. File: March 1995

FTP Site: Article

Reichertz, Peter S. and Micheli, Alison J., "Choosing a Corporate Name: Tips On What Should Be Done to Avoid Legal Problems" [Online]. Available FTP: ftp.wecom.com Directory: pub/lewrose/www File: ChoosingABusinessName

PART III

INTERNET LEGAL RESEARCH DIRECTORY

Substantive Resources

FEDERAL

Executive Branch

GENERAL RESOURCES

EXECUTIVE BRANCH DIRECTORY

DESCRIPTION: Contains addresses, phone numbers, fax numbers, and email addresses for executive branch personnel, including President, and cabinet.

PROVIDER: University of California, Santa Cruz Science Library
PHONE: (408) 459-2886 or (408) 459-2711
CONTACT: Steve Watkins
EMAIL: watkins@scilibx.ucsc.edu
URL: gopher://gopher.ucsc.edu:70/00/The%20Community/Guide%20to%20Government--U.S.%2C%20State%20and%20Local/Executive%20Branch%20Addresses

EXECUTIVE OFFICE OF THE PRESIDENT

WHITE HOUSE INFORMATION SERVICE

DESCRIPTION: Texas A&M University maintains an outstanding collection of White House information from 1992 through the present. Menu options include:

- Domestic Affairs/
- International Affairs/
- Business and the Economy/
- Press Briefings and Conferences/
- Memoranda, Executive Orders, & Proclamations/
- Remarks during Photo-Ops/
- Speeches and Town Halls/
- Appointments, Nominations, and Awards/
- President's Daily Schedule/

PROVIDER: This server is run by the Computing & information Services at Texas A&M University. The data are obtained from the clinton@marist.bitnet listserv or the alt.politics.clinton Usenet newsgroup, both of which receive the information from MIT White House information server.
EMAIL: whadmin@tamu.edu
URL: gopher://gopher.tamu.edu:70/11/.dir/president.dir

WHITE HOUSE WEB SERVER

DESCRIPTION: Also known as The White House an Interactive Citizen's Handbook, this site appears designed for the consumer market, with many images and other nonresearcher-oriented material. However, the Publications option provides links to many White House Documents (press briefings, etc., current as well as in archive form). In addition, the Executive Branch option enables access to documents from Executive Branch agencies.

URL: http:www.whitehouse.gov

DEPARTMENT OF COMMERCE

COMMERCE BUSINESS DAILY

DESCRIPTION: The Commerce Business Daily (CBD) is a daily list of U.S. government procurement invitations, contract awards, subcontracting leads, sales of surplus property and foreign business opportunities.

PROVIDER: Counterpoint Publishing, Inc.
ADDRESS: PO Box 928, 84 Sherman Street, Cambridge, MA 02140
EMAIL: info@counterpoint.com
PHONE:: (800) 998-4515 or (617) 547-4515
FAX: (617) 547-9064
URL: gopher://cfr.counterpoint.com:2003/11/
PROVIDER: Internet Express
PHONE:: (719) 592-1240 or (800) 592-1240
EMAIL: service@usa.net

URL: gopher://earth.usa.net:71/11/cbd
PROVIDER: USIC
ADDRESS: 48 Harbor Park Drive, Port Washington, NY 11050
PHONE: (800) 275-7455 or (516) 626-2090
FAX: (516) 626-2099
EMAIL: cbd@savvy.com
URL: gopher://usic.savvy.com/

INFORMATION INFRASTRUCTURE TASK FORCE

DESCRIPTION: Many different agencies make policies that affect different components of the National Information Infrastructure (NII). In addition, federal agencies will use and contribute to the NIIe. The task force will ensure that the entire administration is acting in concert to accelerate the development and use of the NII.

The task force consists of high-level representatives of the key federal agencies involved in telecommunications and information policy. Participating agencies include the Department of Commerce, the Department of Defense, the Department of Justice, the Department of State, and the General ServicesAdministration. Menu options at this site include:

- List of Committees & Working Groups/
- Press Releases/
- Speeches, Testimony, and Documents/
- Selected Legislation/
- NII Advisory Council/

PROVIDER: Department of Commerce, National Telecommunications and Information Administration
CONTACT: Charles Franz
EMAIL: cfanz@ntia.doc.gov
PHONE: (202) 482-1835
URL: gopher://iitf.doc.gov/

NATIONAL TELECOMMUNICATIONS AND INFORMATION ADMINISTRATION (NTIA) BBS

DESCRIPTION: The NTIA serves as the principal executive branch adviser to the President on telecommunications and information policy, and develops and presents these policies before Congress, the FCC, and other federal and international agencies. Menu options include:

- National Information Infrastructure Initiatives
- Teleview – Testimony/Notices/Comments
- Press Releases and Public Notices
- Legislation – Existing/Pending/Initiatives
- NTIA Organization Act of 1992
- Title VI – Omnibus Budget Reconciliation Act of 1993
- Section 706 of the Communications Act of 1934

PROVIDER: Department of Commerce, NTIA
CONTACT: Norbert Schroeder
PHONE: (202) 482-6207
URL: telnet://ntiabbs.ntia.doc.gov

NATIONAL TRADE DATA BANK

DESCRIPTION: The Commerce Department's trade database provides a wealth of export-related information, including legislative, regulatory, licensing and tax documents. Following are just a few of the 117 menu options:

- A Basic Guide to Exporting/ (provides overview of relevant regulations, licenses, customs and tax issues)
- Copyright Protection for Computer Software
- Country Reports on Economic Policy and Trade Practices/
- Country Reports on Human Rights Practices/
- Directory for Trading and Investment/
- Export Administration Regulations/
- Export Assistance Contact List/
- Export Licensing Information/Δ
- GATT - Final Act..../
- GATT Standards Code Activities of NIST/
- Impact of the Caribbean Basin Economic Recovery Act/
- International Social Security Agreements/
- Legal Aspects of International Trade and Investment/
- NAFTA Implementation Resources Guide/
- North American Free Trade Agreement/
- North American Free Trade Agreement Information/
- North American Free Trade Agreement Treaty/
- Tariffs & Other Taxes on Computer Hardware and software/

PROVIDER: U.S. Department of Commerce
PHONE: (202) 482-1986 or (800) USA-TRADE
URL: gopher://gopher.stat-usa.gov/
URL: http://www.stat-usa.gov/BEN/Services/ntdb home.html

ECONOMIC CONVERSION INFORMATION EXCHANGE GOPHER

DESCRIPTION: This site provides many materials pertinent to military base closures/conversions. There is a rich collection of relevant federal laws and regulations, information concerning federal, state and other programs, contact information, and economic and environmental data.

PROVIDER: U.S. Department of Commerce
CONTACT: Amy Williams
EMAIL: amy@sunny.stat-usa.gov,awilliams @esa.doc.gov
URL: gopher://ecix.doc.gov:70/11/ecix

PATENT AND TRADEMARK OFFICE (PTO) BBS

DESCRIPTION: PTO BBS provides access to the weekly issue file of patent data, including Official Gazette notices for patents and trademarks, PTO news bulletins, press releases, directory information and product and services information. The BBS allows for searching and downloading of weekly issue files for patent titles, abstracts and classes. Directories of PTO personnel are also available. All access is free. Users are given 60 minutes of logon time for each call. Total access per day is 240 minutes. Registration is required.

PROVIDER: U.S. Patent and Trademark Office
URL: telnet://fedworld.gov

then choose:
- -[F] Regulatory, Government Administration and State Systems
- -[B] Government Administration Mall
- -[1] GOVADMIN GateWay Systems (Connect to Gov't systems/databases)
- -116 (PTO-BBS)

PATENT SEARCH

DESCRIPTION: Greg Aharonian, who runs the patent search and technology analysis firm Source Translation & Optimization, has created a web site with, according to Mr.Aharonian, 500 MB of PTO & patenting information, including the beginning of an Internet site that provides full searching capabilities of the PTO's patent text databases for free. The site allows for retrieval of patent titles in any class/subclass by clicking through a few screens. The patent title data goes from 1970 to Dec. 1993." This is indeed an impressive collection. Note the Internet Patent News Service option below, which provides for weekly email of all patents issued by the PTO during the last week (or more specifically, all of the patents listed in the most recent issue of the USPTO Patent Gazette). Other options are:
- Determine patent class/subclass using Manual of Classification
  - Master list of all 400+ patent classes
  - Design patent groups
  - ELECTRONIC patent groups
  - MECHANICAL patent groups
  - ENGINEERING patent groups
  - CHEMICAL patent groups
- Determine patent class/subclass using Index to Classification
- RETRIEVE patent titles using class/subclass code
- Patent documents from the PTO, PCT, EPO, etc.
  - PHONE numbers for various PTO offices
  - PTO Examining Groups - key personnel and contact points
  - Special PTO P.O. boxes for sending materials to the PTO
  - PTO depository libraries across the country
  - US Patent filing fees
  - Massachusetts roster of attorneys
  - Preparation of Patent Drawings - PTO guide
  - 37 CFR 1.84 appendices to Patent Drawings guide
  - Current PCT countries and future expansion
  - Paris Convention for int. property protection
- US Code Section 35 - federal patent laws
- IPNS - Internet Patent News Service

PROVIDER: Source Translation & Optimization, in cooperation with theUniversity of North Carolina
ADDRESS: PO Box 404, Belmont, MA 02178
PHONE: (617) 489-3727
EMAIL: patents@world.std.com
CONTACT: Greg Aharonian
URL: http://sunsite.unc.edu/patents/intropat.html

WEEKLY PATENT SERVICE

DESCRIPTION: This free service offers a weekly emailing of all patents issued by the Patent Office during the last week (or more specifically, all of the patents listed in the most recent issue of the USPTO Patent Gazette). For each patent, the patent title and number is listed. The mailing consists of three files, each on the average totalling 50K of ASCII text - one file with the mechanical patents, one file with the chemical patents and one file with the electronic patents. With each file there is information on how to order paper and electronic versions of patents. The files are not copyrighted, so you are free to do whatever you want with the information.

PROVIDER: Source Translation & Optimization, in cooperation with the University of North Carolina
ADDRESS: PO Box 404, Belmont, MA 02178
PHONE: (617) 489-3727
EMAIL: patents@world.std.com
CONTACT: Greg Aharonian
URL: Send your name and postal and email addresses, the words MECHANICAL, CHEMICAL and/or ELECTRONIC (depending which groups you care to receive), and the words ASCII or UUZIP (depending on which format you want - UUZIP means you can receive and UNZIP a UUDECODED file, which are about half the size of the ASCII files). If you want to receive patent news information (PTO announcements, lawsuit outcomes), send the word NEWS. If you want to receive all of the files, send the word ALL. Also, the provider requests, that you include some information on what you do and how you might use this patent information. Forward your requests to: http://sunsite.unc.edu/patents/intropat.html
URL: http://sunsite.unc.edu/patents/intropat.html

PATENT OFFICE REFORM PANEL FINAL REPORT

DESCRIPTION: This 1992 report issued by the Patent Office reviews current patent practices in the United States. It makes suggestions regarding such issues as first to file, software patents, excessive secrecy orders, international harmonization, challenging patents, reexamination, excessive legal costs and other issues. This gopher includes the entire report in full text, split into five files.

PROVIDER: The Internet Wiretap, Cupertino, CA
EMAIL: gopher@wiretap.spies.com
URL: http://wiretap.spies.com/Gopher/Gov/Patent/
URL: gopher://wiretap.spies.com:70/11/Gov/Patent

PATENT LICENSING SYSTEM

DESCRIPTION: Provides the earliest possible information (new postings approximately every two weeks) concerning hundreds of new government R&D inventions available each year for licensing—often exclusively. Full text of the patent applications are available from the National Technical Information Service (NTIS). The inventions can be licensed through NTIS' Center for the Utilization of Federal Technology (CUFT). The inventions represent new technologies from federal laboratories of the following agencies:

- Agriculture
- Commerce
- Transportation
- Environmental Protection Agency
- Health and Human Services
- Interior
- Veteran Affairs

PROVIDER: National Technical Information Service
PHONE: (703) 487-4650
URL: telnet://fedworld.gov

then choose:

-[F] Regulatory, Government Administration and State Systems
-[B] Government Administration Mall
-[1] GOVADMIN GateWay Systems (Connect to Gov't systems/databases)
-14 ELISA System (DOD)

DEPARTMENT OF ENERGY

FEDERAL ENERGY REGULATORY COMMISSION ISSUANCE POSTING SYSTEM (FERC-CIPS)

DESCRIPTION: The Commission Issuance Posting System is rich with information and documents. It provides search and download access to the daily list of all filings made at the Commission, rulemaking notices and orders, regulatory proceedings, including formal documents filed with the Commission or issued by it, identified by docket numbers. Files are listed by the broad topics of Electric, Gas, Hydro, Miscellaneous, Oil, and Rulemaking. Registration is required, but no fees are involved.

FILES AVAILABLE (partial list):
EL - Formal proceedings related to electric power
ES - Issuance of securities, assumption of liabilities and merger of facilities by electric utilities
GP - General docket category for matters under the NGPA where the assignment of a docket number would be useful for purposes of noticing and tracking the proceeding
AI - Interpretations of the Chief Accountant on accounting, reporting, and record retention matters.
CA - FERC Commission Agenda
DC - Daily calendar of Commission events
DF - Daily list of filings made at the Commission
FD - A list of all documents issued on a particular day, consisting of the docket number, the applicant name, the date issued, and the title of the document
IS - Suspension and Investigations into rates, fares, charges and practices of oil pipelines under section 15(7) of the Interstate Commerce Commission Act, 49 U.S.C. § 15(7)
OR - Oil pipeline rate cases
RA - Appeals from denials of requests for adjustments issued by the Economic Regulatory Administration of DOE
RO - Appeals from Remedial Orders issued by the Economic Regulatory Administration of DOE
RM - Rulemaking notices and orders (including any former Interstate Commerce Commission reference)

PROVIDER: The Federal Energy Regulatory Commission, U.S. Department of Energy
URL: telnet://fedworld.gov

then choose

-[F] Regulatory, Government Administration and State Systems
-[B] Government Administration Mall
-[1] GOVADMIN GateWay Systems (Connect to Gov't systems/databases)
-19 (Federal Energy Regulator Commission)

DEPARTMENT OF HEALTH AND HUMAN SERVICES

FOOD AND DRUG ADMINISTRATION (FDA) BBS

DESCRIPTION: The FDA's online information service includes the following information options:

- News releases

- Enforcement Report
- Drug and Device Product Approvals list
- Center for Devices and Radiological Health
- Text from Drug Bulletin
- Current Information on AIDS
- FDA Consumer magazine index and selected articles
- FDA Federal Register Summaries by Subject
- Summaries of FDA information
- Index of News Releases and Answers
- FDA Federal Register Summaries by Publication Date
- Text of Testimony at FDA Congressional Hearings
- Speeches Given by FDA Commissioner and Deputy
- Veterinary Medicine News
- Upcoming FDA Meetings
- Import Alerts
- On-Line User's Manual

Technical Support: Parklawn Computer Center
PHONE: (301) 443-7318
CONTACT: For help finding a specific report or article, contact Karen Malone in the FDA Press Office (301) 443-3285
URL: telnet://fdabbs.fda.gov
LOGIN: bbs
PASSWORD: bbs
URL: telnet://fedworld.gov

then choose:
-[F] Regulatory, Government Administration and State Systems
-[B] Government Administration Mall
-[1] GOVADMIN GateWay Systems (Connect to Gov't systems/databases)
-17 FDA-BBS

SOCIAL SECURITY NUMBER (SSN) FAQ

DESCRIPTION: This document answers the question: What to do when they ask for your Social Security Number? It examines use of the SSN in the context of health insurance, and credit issuance, and relevant privacy issues.

PROVIDER: Computer Professionals for Social Responsibility
CONTACT: Chris Hibbert
ADDRESS: 1195 Andre Avenue, Mountain View, CA 94040
EMAIL: hibbert@netcom.com
URL: http://www.cpsr.org/cpsr/privacy/ssn/ssn.faq.html
URL: ftp://ftp.cpsr.org/cpsr/privacy/ssn/Social_Security_ Number_FAQ
URL: EMAIL: send mail to listserv@cpsr.org
Body of message:
GET/cpsr/privacy/ssn/Social_Security_Number_FAQ

DEPARTMENT OF THE INTERIOR

NATIVE AMERICAN INFORMATION

DESCRIPTION: Cornell University provides an Internet site for the purpose of distributing information having to do with Native Americans and Native American issues. See also: Listserv:
NATIVE-L@TAMVM1.BITNET, Newsgroup: soc.culture.native
URL: ftp://ftp.cit.cornell.edu/pub/special/NativeProfs
DIRECTORY: /general
FILES: List of Federally Recognized Tribes (/fed_rec_tribes.txt)
Letter to Congress from Tribal Leaders (/igra-ltr.txt)
343 Tribal Address & Phones (tribelist.txt)
URL: ftp://ftp.cit.cornell.edu/pub/special/NativeProfs
DIRECTORY: /law
FILES: Court decision re: religious use of peyote (boyll.txt)
DIRECTORY: /newsletters
FILE: Native American Newsletter Volume 13 (native_ american_news.13)

DEPARTMENT OF JUSTICE

DEPARTMENT OF JUSTICE GOPHER

DESCRIPTION: This site was established in July 1994. It provides many interesting documents concerning recent litigation matters, including court documents, consent decrees, reports, Attorney General office speeches and press releases. Examples of documents available include selected Microsoft antitrust case documents (the Complaint, Final Judgment and Stipulation), and the Reginald Denny Case settlement. Other options include DOJ orders, statistics and lots more. Some of the menu options are:

- Agency Procurement Requests/
- Antitrust Division/
- Civil Rights Division/
- DOJ Attorney Job listings/
- Department of Justice Orders/
- National Institute of Justice/
- Office of Public Affairs/

PROVIDER: U.S. Department of Justice, Systems Technology Staff
PHONE: (202) 514-0733
EMAIL: gopher@usdoj.gov
URL: gopher://gopher.usdoj.gov/

AMERICANS WITH DISABILITIES ACT (ADA) BULLETIN BOARD

DESCRIPTION: The ADA authorizes the DOJ to provide technical assistance to individuals and entities that have rights or responsibilities under the Act. This BBS has been established to assist the public in obtaining access to information for understanding and complying with the ADA. Registration is required. Provides access to files in the following categories:

- Regulatory: contains the ADA statute, and the regulations promulgated by the federal agencies with statutory responsibilities for implementing specific titles of the ADA.
- Overview: contains documents developed to assist in understanding the ADA, such as Q&A booklets, fact sheets. This library also contains info on miscellaneous provisions such as available tax credits, and definitions.
- Enforce: contains details of ADA-related Department of Justice activities, and lawsuits filed under ADA (and related laws such as section 504 of the Rehabilitation Act).
- Government: contains files of public service provisions by state and local governments under title II of the ADA.

PROVIDER: U.S. Department of Justice, Public Access Section, Civil Rights Division
PHONE: (202) 514-0301. Operators are available to answer questions about titles II and III of the Act, 1-5 p.m. Eastern time, Monday through Friday.
URL: telnet://fedworld.gov

then choose:
-[F] Regulatory, Government Administration and State Systems
-[B] Government Administration Mall
-[1] GOVADMIN GateWay Systems (Connect to Gov't systems/databases)
-9 ADA-BBS

NATIONAL CRIMINAL JUSTICE REFERENCE SERVICE (NCJRS)

DESCRIPTION: The NCJRS was established in 1972 by the National Institute of Justice of the DOJ, to serve as an international criminal justice information network for policymakers and criminal justice professionals. NCJRS provides users with comprehensive and current information about the latest criminal justice studies and projects from around the world. The NCJRS gopher and the NCJRS bulleting board (which is accessible thru the gopher and independently), serve as central information sources for the following DOJ offices:

- National Institute of Justice
- Office of Juvenile Justice and Delinquency Prevention
- Office of Victims of Crime
- Bureau of Justice Statistics Clearinghouse
- Bureau of Justice Assistance Clearinghouse
- Drugs and Crime Data Center Clearinghouse

Available files include:

- Directory of Criminal Justice Info. Sources
- Bureau of Justice Statistics Press Releases

PROVIDER: Aspen Systems Corporation
ADDRESS: 1600 Research Boulevard, Rockville, MD 20850
PROVIDER: National Criminal Justice Reference Service
ADDRESS: 600 Research Boulevard, Rockville, MD 20850
CONTACT: William Browning
EMAIL: wbrownin@aspensys.com
PHONE: (301) 251-5507
FAX: (301) 251-5212
URL: http://www.aspensys.com
URL: gopher://ncjrs.aspensys.com
PROVIDER: National Institute of Justice
CONTACT: G. Martin Lively, NIJ Program Manager
EMAIL: lively@usdoj.gov
PHONE: (800) 851-3420 or (202) 514-6211
FAX: 202) 307-639
URL: telnet://fedworld.gov

then choose:
-[F] Regulatory, Government Administration and State Systems
-[B] Government Administration Mall¡
-[1] GOVADMIN GateWay Systems (Connect to Gov't systems/databases)
-75 (NCJRS-BBS)

BUREAU OF JUSTICE STATISTICS (BJS)

DESCRIPTION: BJS is an agency of the U.S. Department of Justice, and is part of the Office of Justice Programs, which also includes the National Institute of Justice, the Bureau of Justice Assistance, the Office of Juvenile Justice and Delinquency Prevention, and the Office for Victims of Crime. The BJS issues reports on a range of criminal justice issues including capital punishment, law enforcement, sentencing and prison. This database provides access to the full text of the reports, as well as a directory of Bureau of Justice Statistics personnel. Available options include:

- U.S. Bureau of Justice Statistics Telephone contacts
- Drug Enforcement and Treatment in Prisons, 1990
- Jail Inmates, 1991
- Justice Expenditures and Employment, 1990
- Drunk Driving
- Capital Punishment, 1989

- Drug Enforcement by Police, 1990
- Police Departments
- Drugs and Jail Inmates, 1989
- Felony Sentences in State Courts, 1989
- Prisoners in 1990
- Prisoners in 1991.
- Probation and Parole, 1990
- Recidivism of Felons on Probation, 1986-1989
- Tracking Offenders, 1988
- Women in Prison
- Capital Punishment, 1989
- State and Local Police Departments, 1990

URL: gopher://justice2.usdoj.gov:70/1/ojp/bjs
URL: gopher://UMSLVMA.UMSL.EDU:70/11/LIBRARY/SUBJECTS/CRIMINAL

DEPARTMENT OF LABOR

OSHA DATABASE

DESCRIPTION: This site is known as the Labor News BBS. It provides access to the OSHA Computer Information System (OCIS), which includes full text of regulations, compliance directives and memoranda, the OSHA Field Operations Manual and OSHA Federal Register entries from 1971 to date. Registration is required; no fees are involved.

PROVIDER: U.S. Department of Labor, Secretary of Labor's Office of PublicAffairs
CONTACT: Labor News Sysop is David Dickerson
PHONE: (202) 219-8831
CONTACT: OCIS Help Desk
PHONE: (801) 487-0680 x234
URL: telnet://fedworld.gov

then choose:
-[F] Regulatory, Government Administration and State Systems
-[B] Government Administration Mall
-[1] GOVADMIN GateWay Systems (Connect to Gov't systems/databases)
-26 Labor News (DOL)
O ... OSHA (OCIS) Database

OSHA REGULATIONS

DESCRIPTION: Full text of OSHA Standards (29 CFR - Parts 1900-1999, Occupational Safety and Health Act of 1970, and Federal Register sections, by month (1971 to date).

PROVIDER: Department of Energy's Office of Environment, Safety and Health
EMAIL: support@tis.inel.gov
PHONE: (208) 526-8955
URL: gopher://gabby.osha-slc.gov/

DEPARTMENT OF THE TREASURY

INTERNAL REVENUE SERVICE (IRS)

DESCRIPTION: The IRS offers this bulletin board for the exchange of information about electronic filing and other IRS/tax information. Registration is required, but no fees. Access is limited to 10 minutes per call, up to 60 total minutes per day.

Files available:
- Electronic filing Conferences and Exhibitions
- Federal/State Electronic Filing State Roster
- 1040PC - Accepted Software List for 1994
- Federal/State Electronic Filing Bulletin Software
- Developer Specifications
- Advance Copy of Publication 1346
- 1040PC Record Layouts/File Specifications - 1995

URL: telnet://fedworld.gov

then choose:
-[F] Regulatory, Government Administration and State Systems
-[B] Government Administration Mall
-[1] GOVADMIN GateWay Systems (Connect to Gov't systems/databases)
- 33 (1040 BBS)

ADMINISTRATIVE AGENCIES

CONSUMER PRODUCT SAFETY COMMISSION (CPSC)

DESCRIPTION: CPSC's mission is to protect the public from unreasonable risks ofinjury and death associated with consumer products. This server currently provides access to all press releases from 1991 to the present and the agency's public calendar. Other information, such as the Commission's Annual Report and executive summaries of briefing packages submitted to the Commission may soon be made available.

PROVIDER: U.S. Consumer Product Safety Commission
EMAIL: info@cpsc.gov
URL: gopher://cpsc.gov/

ENVIRONMENTAL PROTECTION AGENCY (EPA)

ONLINE LIBRARY SYSTEM

DESCRIPTION: The EPA's Online Library system (OLS) is an electronic card catalogof environmental materials compiled by the EPA library network. The system includesthe following databases:

- The National Catalog Database contains EPA report bibliographic data and abstracts.
- The Hazardous Waste Database is a copy of the Hazardous waste collection that is administered by EPA headquarters. It contains references to key materials on hazardous waste in the EPA library network. Bibliographic descriptions, keywords, abstracts, locations and other information are listed for books, EPA reports, Office of Solid Waste and Emergency Response policy and guidance directives, periodicals and commercial databases containing information on hazardous waste.
- The National Center for Environmental Publications and Information is a listing of EPA publications. It is updated biweekly.

CONTACT: ELFIN hotline at (202) 260-0420
URL: telnet://epaibm.rtpnc.epa.gov

then choose: public

ACCESS EPA DIRECTORY

DESCRIPTION: Access EPA is an annually-updated document that compiles every identifiable information resource within the Environmental Protection Agency. It includes publications, databases, libraries, dockets, hotlines, bulletin boards, records contacts, and clearinghouses. The hardcopy version of Access EPA is document number: EPA/220-B-93-008.

PROVIDER: EPA Office of Administration and Resources Management, Office of Information Resources Management, Information Management and Services Division, Information Access Branch
ADDRESS: U.S. Environmental Protection Agency, Public Information Center, PM™211B, 401 M Street, S.W., Washington, DC 20460
CONTACT: Michael Lingenfelter
EMAIL: lingenfelter.michael@epamail.epa.gov
PHONE: (202) 260-2049
FAX: (202) 260-6257
URL: telnet://epaibm.rtpnc.epa.gov

then choose:
- Public
- OLS
- A

ENVIRONMENTAL LEGISLATION

DESCRIPTION: This site provides full text access to many critical U.S. environmental laws, regulations and policies.

PROVIDER: U.S. Department of Commerce
CONTACT: Amy Williams
EMAIL: amy@sunny.stat-usa.gov, awilliams@esa.doc.gov
URL: gopher://ecix.doc.gov:70/11/ecix/adprog/lawpol

EPA GOPHER

DESCRIPTION: This is a very rich gopher server, offering EPA-generated or related rules, regulations and legislation, EPA directories, standards, full-text access to the EPA Journal, press releases, announcements, free software, etc. It also gateways to over a dozen other environmental (non-EPA) gophers, and provides a menu keyword searchfunction.

PROVIDER: U.S. Environmental Protection Agency, Washington, DC 20460
CONTACT: John Shirey, National Data Processing Division, U.S. EPA
EMAIL: internet_support@unixmail.rtpnc.epa.gov
URL: gopher://gopher.epa.gov
URL: ftp://ftp.epa.gov
URL: http://www.epa.gov

CLEANUP INFORMATION BULLETIN BOARD (CLU-IN)

DESCRIPTION: Provides access to regulatory, legislative information, and CommerceBusiness Daily announcements relevant to various environmental acts (including Superfund, RCRA, EPCRA, etc.). No fees, requires registration.

PHONE: (301) 589-8368
URL: telnet://fedworld.gov
then choose:
-[F] Regulatory, Government Administration and State Systems
-[B] Government Administration Mall
-[1] GOVADMIN GateWay Systems (Connect to Gov't systems/databases)
- 7 (CLU-IN)

TECHNOLOGY TRANSFER NETWORK (TTN)

DESCRIPTION: The TTN is a network of electronic bulletin boards that provide information related to the control of air pollution. Registration is required. Availability is 24 hours except: Mondays from 8:00 a.m. to 12:00 noon EST. The bulletin boards accessible through TTN include:

- CAAA (Clean Air Act Amendments) - provides information on the Clean Air Act amendments of

1990, regulatory requirements, implementation programs, criteria pollutants, and technical analyses.
- AMTIC (Ambient Monitoring Technology Information Center) - provides all Federal Regulations pertaining to ambient monitoring.
- COMPLI includes two databases:
  1. NARS National Asbestos Registry System -contains a listing of all asbestos contractors, their inspections and the results of them. This database is used to target contractors for inspection.
  2. Determinations Index. This is a compilation of clarifications and determinations used by EPA concerning selected subparts of the Federal Register.

PROVIDER: EPA Office of Air Quality Planning and Standards
PHONE: (919) 541-5384
CONTACT: Walter White
PHONE: (703) 308-8704
URL: telnet://ttnbbs.rtpnc.epa.gov
hit return to begin

EPA FEDERAL REGISTER MAILING LISTS

DESCRIPTION: EPA distributes, via listserv, selected Federal Register documents automatically on the day of publication. Documents are extracted directly from the Government Printing Office (GPO) database to establish an electronic federal government-wide Environmental Sub-Set of the daily issue accessible via the Internet. This effort is part of the Agency's paperless information initiative. The listserves provide ASCII files with graphic notes. Both ASCII files and the corresponding TIFF graphics are also be accessible via the EPA public access gopher (gopher.epa.gov). The listserves are described as follows:

LISTSERVE NAME	DESCRIPTION
EPAFR-CONTENTS	This will contain the full-text table of contents with page number cittions.
EPA-MEETINGS	This will contain all meeting notices.
EPA-SAB	Material relating to the Science Advisory Board.
EPA-IMPACT	All environmental impact statements published in the Federal Register.
EPA-SPECIES	All endangered species documents published in the Federal Register.
EPA-GENERAL	All general EPA nonprogram specific documents, Presidential documents related to environmental issues, and other Agency documents other than environmental impact and endangered species actions.
EPA-AIR	All Office of Air and Radiation documents.
EPA-PEST	All Office of Pesticide Programs documents.
EPA-TOX	Office of Pollution Prevention and Toxic Substances documents excluding Community-Right-To-Know (Toxic Release Inventory) documents.
EPA-TRI	Community-Right-To-Know Toxic Release Inventory documents.
EPA-WASTE	All Hazardous and Solid Waste documents.
EPA-WATER	All Office of Water documents.

CONTACT: John A. Richards
PHONE: (202) 260-2253
FAX: (202) 260-3884
EMAIL: richards.john@epamail.epa.gov
URL: To subscribe to any of the above Listserves address your messages to: Listserver@unix mail.rtpnc.epa. gov. In the body of the message, type: Subscribe <Listserve name> <your first name> <your last name>

FEDERAL COMMUNICATIONS COMMISSION (FCC)

FCC GOPHER

DESCRIPTION: This site provides current common carrier regulatory information, including the FCC Daily Digest, news releases, orders, public notices, and speeches by Commission officials. Availability is between 9:30 a.m. - 10:30 a.m. and 1:00 p.m. - 1:30 p.m. EST. The BBS is restricted to FCC use.

PROVIDER: Federal Communications Commission, Office of Public Affairs
CONTACT: Rosa Prescott
PHONE: (202) 418-0500
CONTACT: Industry Analysis Common Carrier
PHONE: (202) 418-0940)
URL: gopher://gopher.fcc.gov
URL: http://www.fcc.gov

NATIONAL ARCHIVES

NATIONAL ARCHIVES GOPHER

DESCRIPTION: This gopher provides descriptions of National Archives nationwide. Also included at this site are data from the Office of the Federal Register, including:
- Daily Table of Contents to the Federal Register: Each table of contents (toc) file includes a descriptive entry and page number for every document published in a single day's Federal Register.
- Public Laws Index: These lists (not full text) of Public Laws from the current Congress provide: bill number, public law number, name of act, approval

date, U.S. statutes at-large page citation, number of pages in the published law.

PROVIDER: The National Archives
CONTACT: Jon Radel, Synetics Inc.
EMAIL: Technical Help: postmaster@ nara.gov; Research questions: inquire@nara.gov
URL: gopher gopher.nara.gov
URL: http://www.nara.gov.

then choose:

-[F] Regulatory, Government Administration and State Systems
-[B] Government Administration Mall
-[1] GOVADMIN GateWay Systems (Connect to Gov't systems/databases)
-87 FREND #1 (NARA)

SECURITIES AND EXCHANGE COMMISSION (SEC)

EDGAR

DESCRIPTION: EDGAR is the Electronic Data Gathering, Analysis and Retrieval System established by the SEC. EDGAR allows companies to make required filings to the SEC via direct transmission, diskette, or magnetic tape. All publicly traded domestic corporations are required to electronically file as of May 1996. EDGAR on the Internet provides access to any filings to the SEC that are available to the public starting in 1994. Nonelectronic filings, filings that are not available to the public, and any data prior to 1994 are not available here.

URL: http://www.sec.gov/edgarhp.htm

SMALL BUSINESS ADMINISTRATION (SBA)

SMALL BUSINESS ADMINISTRATION

DESCRIPTION: This gopher provides access to:

- address/phone lists for all SBA offices'
- training aids such as how to create a business plan
- instructions on how to obtain all of SBA's publications (many available on the gopher)
- calendars of classes and events held by local SBA offices
- summaries of federal acts and regulations pertinent to small businesses, including the following:
  - Consumer Credit Protection Act (15 U.S.C. 1601 et seq.)
  - Debt Coll. Act of 1982 Deficit Reduction Act of 1984 (31 U.S.C. et seq.)
  - Equal Credit Opportunity Act (15 US.C. 1691)
  - Executive Order 11738 – Environmental Protection (38 F.R.)
  - Flood Disaster Protection Act (42 U.S.C. 4011)
  - Freedom of Information Act (5 U.S.C. 552)
  - Lead-based Paint Poisoning Prevention Act (42 U.S.C. 4821 et seq.)
  - Privacy Act (5 U.S.C. 552a)
  - Right to Financial Privacy Act of 1978 (12 US.C. 3401)

URL: gopher://www.sbaonline.sba.gov/
URL: http://www.sbaonline.sba.gov
URL: ftp://www.sbaonline.sba.gov

U.S. INFORMATION AGENCY

VOICE OF AMERICA GOPHER

DESCRIPTION: Full text of Voice of America news reports, program schedules, shortwave radio frequency and satellite downlink information. Full text of federal legislation concerning broadcasting to Cuba can be found under the "Radio and TV Marti (Broadcasting to Cuba)" menu option.

PROVIDER: U.S. Information Agency, Voice of America, Computer Services Division
PHONE: (202) 619-2020
EMAIL: postmaster@voa.gov
URL: gopher://gopher.voa.gov

LEGISLATIVE BRANCH

CONGRESSIONAL DIRECTORIES

STATE-BY-STATE LISTING OF CONGRESSIONAL DIRECTORY

DESCRIPTION: Lists Representatives and Senators of the 104th Congress by postal code abbreviations of the states they represent. Provides political party, state, telephone numbers, fax numbers and office addresses.

PROVIDER: Compiled from the *Congressional Yellow Book* and amplified with addresses using the Commerce Clearing House Congressional Index
CONTACT: Grace York
PHONE: (313) 764-0410
EMAIL: grace.york@um.cc.umich.edu

URL: gopher://una.hh.lib.umich.edu:70/11/socsci/poliscilaw/uslegi/congdir/state

SEARCHABLE CONGRESSIONAL DIRECTORY

PROVIDER: University of California, Santa Cruz Science Library
CONTACT: Steve Watkins
EMAIL: atkins@scilibx.ucsc.edu
URL: gopher://gopher.ucsc.edu:70/7waissrc%3A/.WAIS/Congress-104.src

U.S. SENATE

SENATE GOPHER

DESCRIPTION: This gopher provides general information about members and committees of the Senate. It is remarkably barren, especially compared to the House of Representatives gopher. Perhaps this balance will shift over time. Note that Senate policy restricts a Senator's use of the Senate Internet servers during the 60 days before an election. As a result, during election times, the "Available Documents Distributed by Member" options are empty.

PROVIDER: Office of the U.S. Senate Sergeant at Arms and the Senate Committee on Rules and Administration
EMAIL: ftpadmin@scc.senate.gov
URL: gopher://gopher.senate.gov/
URL: http://www.senate.gov/

SENATE COMMITTEE ASSIGNMENTS FOR 103RD CONGRESS

PROVIDER: The Internet Wiretap (Archives)
URL: http://wiretap.spies.com/Gopher/Gov/US-Gov/

SENATE COMMITTEE INFORMATION

DESCRIPTION: The U.S. Senate has 16 standing committees. Senate committees providing information on this gopher include:

- Agriculture, Nutrition and Forestry/
- Democratic Policy/
- Environment and Public Works/
- Indian Affairs/
- Republican Conference/
- Republican Policy/
- Rules and Administration/
- Small Business/

PROVIDER: The information provided here is maintained by the individual Senate committees, so the amount and type of information varies. Examples of the data provided by some com mittees: committee structure, general informa tion about the committee, press releases, standing rules of the Senate.
URL: gopher://ftp.senate.gov:70/11/committee

SENATE ACTIONS AND COMMITTEE ACTIONS

DESCRIPTION: Senate and committee actions for the last three legislative days.

URL: gopher://gopher.house.gov:70/0F1%3A947%3ASenate%20Committee%20Actions

U.S. HOUSE OF REPRESENTATIVES

HOUSE OF REPRESENTATIVES GOPHER

DESCRIPTION: This gopher provides access to information about members and committees of the House. The main menu options include:

- Congressional Information/
- House Schedules/
- Legislative Resources/
- House Committee Information/
- House Directories/
- House Email Addresses/
- House Member Information/

MAINTAINER: House Administration Committee Internet Working Group in cooperation with individual House committees
EMAIL: househlp@hr.house.gov
URL: gopher://gopher.house.gov
URL: http://www.house.gov/Orgpubs.html

HOUSE COMMITTEE ASSIGNMENTS FOR 104th CONGRESS

MAINTAINER: House Administration Committee Internet Working Group in cooperation with individual House committees.

EMAIL: househlp@hr.house.gov
URL: http://www.house.gov/Orgpubs.html

HOUSE COMMITTEE INFORMATION

DESCRIPTION: The U.S. House of Representatives has 19 standing committees and one select committee. There are 86 subcommittees.

URL: http://www.house.gov/Orgpubs.html

HOUSE ACTIONS AND HOUSE COMMITTEE ACTIONS

DESCRIPTION: House actions and committee actions for the last three legislative days.

URL: http://www.house.gov/Legproc.html

CONGRESSIONAL BILLS

HOUSE BILLS

DESCRIPTION: The U.S. House of Representatives provides full text of the printed versions of House bills and resolutions. This database works best if you already have the bill number.

URL: http://www.house.gov/Legproc.html
URL: gopher://wgate.house.gov:70/7waissrc%3A/USHOUSE_house_bill_text_104th
URL: gopher://gopher.house.gov:70/1D1%3A3983%3ABills

LEGI-SLATE

DESCRIPTION: The following Legi-Slate services are available over the Internet on an annual subscription basis: Congressional Service, Federal Register Service, Transcripts Service, BNA Online News Services, Daily CFR Service and Current USC Service.

PROVIDER: Legi-Slate is owned by the Washington Post Company
EMAIL: legislate@mudhoney.micro.umn.edu.
ADDRESS: Legi-Slate, Inc., 777 North Capitol Street, Washington, DC 20002
PHONE: (202) 898-2300 or 1(800) 733-1131
FAX: (202) 898-3030
URL: gopher://gopher.legislate.com/
URL: http://www.legislate.com/

WATER QUALITY: FEDERAL LEGISLATIVE PROPOSALS

DESCRIPTION: Provides access to full text of Congressional bills concerning water quality.

PROVIDER: Purdue University Agricultural Communication Service Cooperative Extension Management System W. Lafayette, IN
EMAIL: cems@ecn.purdue.edu
MAINTAINER: Eldon Fredericks
PHONE: (317) 494-8679
EMAIL: freder@ecn.purdue.edu
URL: gopher://hermes.ecn.purdue.edu:70/11/Extension/Environment/Water%20Quality

JOINT COMMITTEES

JOINT COMMITTEE ACTIONS

DESCRIPTION: The Joint Committee Actions includes information for the last three legislative days on which Joint Committees met and acted.

URL: gopher://gopher.house.gov:70/0F1%3A947%3AJoint%20Committee%20Actions

JOINT COMMITTEE ASSIGNMENTS FOR 103RD CONGRESS (Archives)

PROVIDER: The Internet Wiretap
URL: http://wiretap.spies.com/Gopher/Gov/US-Gov/jt-com.103

GENERAL ACCOUNTING OFFICE (GAO)

GAO DAYBOOK

DESCRIPTION: The GAO DayBook is the daily listing of released GAO reports. It is prepared by GAO's Office of Public Affairs, primarily for distribution to the press and wire services. Each month, GAO publishes *Reports and Testimonies Issued in Month/Year*, which contains abstracts of the reports and testimony issued that month, arranged by subject.

PROVIDER: The General Accounting Office can be reached at (202) 512-6000. Online access to current DayBook listings and most recent month's "Monthly List" is provided by CapAccess, the National Capital Area Public Access Network. CapAccess is a community access network serving the Washington, D.C., metropolitan area.
PHONE: (202) 994-4245
EMAIL: info@cap.gwu.edu
PROVIDER: Information Services Center, Office of Information Management and Communications, U.S. General Accounting Office, Room 6430, Washington, DC 20548
EMAIL: kbonney@cap.gwu.edu

PHONE: (202) 512-4448
URL: telnet://cap.gwu.edu
Login: guest
Password: visitor
At main menu type: go gao

GOVERNMENT PRINTING OFFICE (GPO)

DEPOSITORY LIBRARIES LIST

DESCRIPTION: Legal research frequently requires retrieving federal government documents from a U.S. depository library. This current comprehensive list presents depository libraries by state (including Guam, Panama, Saipan, Samoa, Puerto Rico and the U.S. Virgin Islands). Information is arranged by individual files for each state. Within each state arrangement is alphabetical by institution.

PROVIDER: These files are extracted from ftp.fedworld.gov as a "zipped" DBase file dlprof.zip in the \misc subdirectory. The DBase files were then used to create these ASCII text files. University of Missouri-St. Louis Thomas Jefferson Library Reference Department, St. Louis, MO 63121
CONTACT: Raleigh Muns, Reference Librarian
PHONE: (314) 553-5059
EMAIL: srcmuns@umslvma.umsl.edu
URL: gopher://umslvma.umsl.edu/11/library/govdocs.gdep

FEDERAL BULLETIN BOARD

DESCRIPTION: The Federal Bulletin Board provides public access to GPO documents. Documents are available for free and for sale. Registration is required. Theboard also enables users to email comments and inquiries to GPO and other federal agencies that participate in the BBS.

EXAMPLES OF AVAILABLE FILES:

- BBSUSER.DOC - Introductory file, explains the Board, free.
- Biographies of each state's Congresspeople, $2 - $3 each.
- Overviews of public laws from current Congress, $2 each.
- House and Senate bills as introduced, $5 - $25 each.
- Title 40 CFR Parts 1 - 52A, $2 - $24 each.
- Merit System Protection Board (MSPB) Case Opinions and orders of the Board. All files in MSWord 5.5, $2 each. MSPB case summaries, free.

AVAILIBILITY: The Board is available 22 hours each day, seven days a week. It is unavailable from 3:00 a.m. to 5:00 a.m., Eastern time when maintenance is performed.

USER ASSISTANCE: Available from 8:00 a.m. until 5:00 p.m. Eastern time, Monday through Friday (except federal holidays) by calling the GPO Office of Electronic Information Dissemination Services.
PHONE: (202) 512-1003
PROVIDER: Superintendent of Documents, U.S. Government Printing Office, 700 4th St., N.W., Washington, DC. 20401
PHONE: (202) 512-1530
URL: telnet://federal.bbs.gpo.gov 3001
hit return to start
URL: telnet://fedworld.gov

then choose:
-[F] Regulatory, Government Administration and State Systems
-[B] Government Administration Mall
-[1] GOVADMIN GateWay Systems (Connect to Gov't systems/databases)
- 22 (Federal BBS)

GPO ACCESS

DESCRIPTION: This site provides free access to The Congressional Record, Federal Register, and Congressional Bills.

URL: http://thorplus.lib.purdue.edu/gpo/
URL: http://www.lib.utk.edu/gpo/GPOsearch.html
URL: http://ssdc.ucsd.edu/gpo/
URL: http://www.okstate.edu/cgi-bin/gpo-gateway

GPO PUBLICATIONS REFERENCE FILE (PRF)

DESCRIPTION: The GPO PRF, which is updated every two weeks, includes everything currently for sale by the Government Printing Office except titles available on subscription and titles sold through the Congressional Sales Office. Any government publications found in the PRF can be ordered from the provider of this file, private publisher Bernan. According to information supplied by Bernan, the GPO price and the Bernan price are always the same, except in those cases where a GPO price is under $5. In those cases, Bernan charges $5.

PROVIDER: Bernan/UNIPUB is a private company that distributes government-related publications.
ADDRESS: 4611-F Assembly Drive, Lanham, MD 20706
PHONE: (800) 274-4447
FAX: (301) 459-0056
URL: telnet://kraus.com
LOGIN: gpn

ORDERING PUBLICATIONS FROM THE GPO

DESCRIPTION: This document explains how to order publications for sale by the Government Printing Office.

URL: gopher://marvel.loc.gov:70/0/0/federal/fedinfo/byagency/general/gpo/gpopubs.txt

MONTHLY GPO CATALOG

DESCRIPTION: This database contains titles published by agencies of the U.S. government since 1976. You can search by document name or by word (title, subject, or date), and browse by title, call number or series. Each catalog entry includes author, title, shipping list number, call number and where document can be found (for example in depository libraries in microfiche, or available for sale by the GPO).

URL: telnet://pac.carl.org
then choose:
- PAC (Public Access Catalog)
2. Open Access Databases
42. U.S. Government Publications

FEDERAL REGISTER (FR)

DESCRIPTION: The full text of the U.S. Internet Federal Register (IFR) is available free from the Government Printing Office (and from Counterpoint Publishing for a fee) the same day that the GPO makes it available in electronic format. Access to IFR abstracts, searches for FR citations, and a demo version of the full text IFR is available on the Net for free. If you want to evaluate the IFR service, you can receive an evaluation account by sending a request, including the name, email address, and telephone number of a technical contact person in your organization to: fedreg@internet.com

ACCESS: Full-text access is available via telnet, gopher, and usenet. For telnet, and usenet access, or to set up an account, contact Counterpoint Publishing at 1(800) 998-4515, or send email to fedreg@internet.com with your name, affiliation, and telephone number.
URL: gopher://gopher.counterpoint.com:2002/11/
ALSO SEE GPO ACCESS for Federal Register access

LIBRARY OF CONGRESS

LEGISLATIVE DATABASE

DESCRIPTION: These files track and describe legislation (bills and resolutions) introduced in the U.S. Congress, from 1973 (93rd Congress) to the current Congress (at this writing the 104th). Each file covers a separate Congress.

AVAILIBILITY: Note that this database is subject to limited hours of availability (Mon.-Fri.: 6:30 a.m. 9:30 p.m., Sat: 8:00 a.m.-5:00 p.m., Sun: 1:00 p.m. 5:00 p.m.).
URL: telnet://locis.loc.gov

then choose:
2. Federal Legislation

COPYRIGHT OFFICE

DESCRIPTION: The U.S. Copyright Office provides forms and publications free on the Net, including:
- Copyright Basics
- Copyright Registration
- Copyright Application Forms
- Copyright Information Circulars
- Form Letters -- In Answer to Your Query
- Copyright Office Records -- How to conduct a search
- Copyright Office Announcements, including Federal Regulations
- International Copyright, Fair Use, Publication and More
- Internet Resources Related to Copyright

PROVIDER: U.S. Copyright Office, Library of Congress
EMAIL: copyifno@loc.gov
URL: http://lcweb.locgov/copyright/

OFFICE OF TECHNOLOGY ASSESSMENT (OTA)

DESCRIPTION: Selected OTA publications.

PROVIDER: OTA Congressional and Public Affairs, Washington, DC 20510
PHONE: (202) 224-9241
EMAIL: cpa@ota.gov
URL: ftp://otabbs.ota.gov/pub/

SAMPLE FILES:
- OTA Catalog of Publications, March 1994,updated regularly
  FILE: catalog
- Making Government Work: Electronic Delivery of Federal Services
  FILE: making.government.work
- Protecting Privacy in Computerized Medical Information
  FILE: protecting.privacy.medical.info
- Psychiatric Disabilities, Employment and the Americans with Disabilities Act
  FILE: psych.disability

• Defensive Medicine and Medical Malpractice
  FILE: defensive.medicine.medical.malpractice

JUDICIAL BRANCH

U.S. SUPREME COURT

SUPREME COURT DECISIONS

DESCRIPTION: The U.S. Supreme Court has distributed its opinions via the Internet since 1990. There are several ways to access the documents, although there is one primary Internet source: a set of files at Case Western Reserve University (CWRU) that are received directly from the Court. This collection provides the opinions in ASCII and in WordPerfect format. The ASCII versions omit the Court's original formatting (including bold, underline and italics) and include footnotes at the end, rather than throughout the opinions. The WordPerfect versions retain the court's original formatting.

Although Case Western provides the most current Internet access to Supreme Court opinions, this site is not easy enough for most people to use. First of all, the access procedure is time consuming. Secondly, Web browsers are not designed to allow for retrieval of (binary) WordPerfect files. Therefore, unless you're accessing Case Western using software other than a Web browser (for example, native ftp software), you won't be able to retrieve the WordPerfect versions.

You could use your Web browser to get the ASCII opinions from CWRU, however. The procedure is as follows. In order to retrieve opinions from Case Western, you must first know the docket number. Armed with that information, the next step is to open the Index file. The Index file will tell you the file number of the opinion you need. Then, close the Index file, and retrieve the opinion from the directory of your choice (ASCII or WordPerfect). The whole process takes time, and is more than most people will tolerate.

It's easier to use the Cornell site. Cornell provides keyword-searchable access to the ASCII files stored at Case Western. You don't need to know the docket number at Cornell. Rather, you can search by topic, date, party name or keyword. One thing to be aware of regarding the Supreme Court decisions at Cornell is that it can take up to a week for cases to be keyword indexed and available there. If you require Internet access to opinions as soon as they are issued, you'll need to get them directly from Case Western.

PROVIDER: Case Western Reserve University
URL: ftp://ftp.cwru.edu/hermes/
PROVIDER: Cornell Law School Legal Information Institute
URL: http://www.law.cornell.edu/supct/supct.table.html

SUPREME COURT DECISION SUMMARIES

DESCRIPTION: Summaries (syllabi) of all Supreme Court decisions issued are prepared by the Court's Reporter of Decisions. To have the full text of a decision emailed to you, send email to: liideliver@fatty.law.cornell.edu. In the body of the message, type: request docket _number [where docket_number is the docket number of the case you want sent (e.g. "request 91-611" is the proper format for a request). Docket numbers are specified in the syllabi. You can request several decisions at once by putting the docket numbers on separate lines.

PROVIDER: Case Western Reserve University
URL: ftp://ftp.cwru.edu/hermes/atex/
PROVIDER: Legal Information Institute at Cornell Law School
URL: send the following message (all on one line) to listserv@fatty.law.cornell.edu:
subscribe liibulletin Name, Address, Telephone Number
URL: gopher://marvel.loc.gov:70/11/federal/fedinfo/byagency/judiciary
URL: http://www.law.cornell.edu/supct/supct.table.html
URL: telnet://www.law.cornell.edu
LOGIN: www

SUPREME COURT ORDERS (LIST)

DESCRIPTION: The Order Lists of the Supreme Court serves many functions. In many instances the Orders List serves as the formal way the Supreme Court makes known its decision on whether to hear a case or not. Included in the Orders List are the following:

• Orders in Pending Cases
• Certiorari Granted
• Certiorari Denied
• Habeas Corpus Denied
• Mandamus Denied
• Prohibition Denied
• Rehearing Denied
• Recess Order

Look for the current Orders List by most recent date in the directory of the most recent term, i.e., 1992term/01-13-order-list to current 1993term/06-01-order-list

URL: gopher://gopher.inform.umd.edu:70/11/EdRes/Topic/UnitedStatesAndWorld/United_States/National_Agencies/Judicial/SupremeCt

DRAFT SUPREME COURT RULES

DESCRIPTION: The Supreme Court released and invited comment on a set of revised rules governing proceedings before the Court. The LII has now mounted them on its WWW site with links connecting all cross references within the rules and associated comments, and all references to the U.S. Code as well.

PROVIDER: Cornell Law School Legal Information Institute
URL: http://www.law.cornell.edu/rules/supct/overview.html

SUPREME COURT JUSTICES

DESCRIPTION: Biographies of the sitting Justices, and a few former Justices.

URL: gopher://gopher.inform.umd.edu:70/11/EdRes/Topic/US+W/US/Agencies/Judicial/SupremeCt/Justices

FEDERAL CASE LAW

As case law and seemingly everything else is added to the Internet "collection" the most difficult thing remains knowing where to find the information you need. Search engines and indexes like Yahoo and InfoSeek are helpful, but legal professionals benefit even more from legal-specific resource locators. There are several Internet collections of federal case law. The most colorful is the Federal Courts Finder at Emory University Law School.

- **THE COURTS FINDER** provides a map of the U.S. which you can click on with your mouse to go directly to federal opinions relevant to the jurisdiction. For example, if you click on New York State on the map, you'll be taken to the Second Circuit Court of Appeals opinions at Touro Law Center. *(See figure D-1.)*

URL: http://www.law.emory.edu/FEDCTS/

- **THE CORNELL UNIVERSITY LEGAL INFO INSTITUTE** has built a search engine that permits comprehensive searching of most U.S. Circuit Courts of Appeals' decisions on the net (as of this writing, the Eighth Circuit had not been added to the Cornell search, nor does it cover the opinions pro

Figure D-1.
URL: http://www.law.emory.edu/FEDCTS/

Clicking on the numbered federal circuits will take you directly to that circuit's opinions.

vided by LawJournal Extra). You can search by keyword or phrase, party name and citation (this generally means docket number, since most, if not all Internet case law does not include a citation).

URL: http://www3.law.cornell.edu/Harvest/brokers/circuit-x/fancy.query.html

- **WASHBURN UNIVERSITY SCHOOL OF LAW** In Topeka, Kansas typifies the fine efforts made by many law schools and other entities to collect Internet legal resources on one easy-to-use menu. Washburn not only provides links to all the Courts of Appeals' opinions on the Net, but also other relevant federal practice materials, including Supreme Court opinions, court rules and administrative office information.

URL: http://lawlib.wuacc.edu/washlaw/doclaw/fedres5m.html

- **LAW JOURNAL EXTRA** (LJX) provides a very extensive collection of opinions for all federal circuits, including for the First Circuit which, as of this writing, has no other Internet presence. The opinions generally go back at least a year, and may have been downloaded from thefederal court bulletin boards (also known as the PACER system), but that's just a guess. LJX provides no information describing the opinions, thereby raising concern about the accuracy of the material. *(See figure D-2.)*

URL http://www.ljextra.com/courthouse/feddec.html

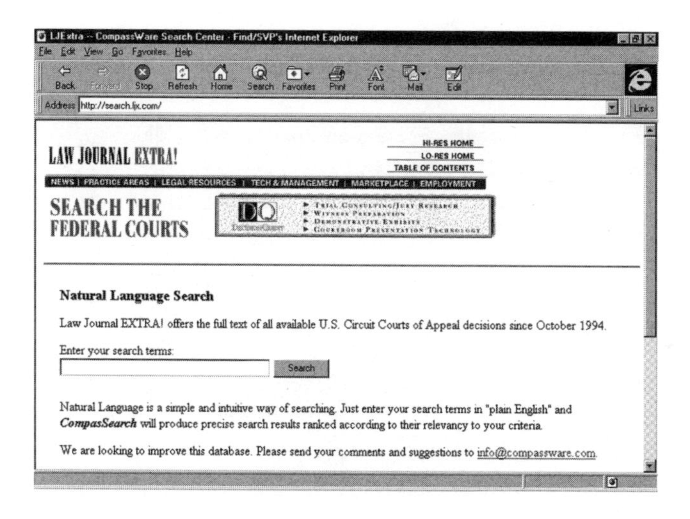

Figure D-2.
URL: http://search.ljx.com

Law Journal Extra provides a centralized collection of courts of appeals decisions.

FEDERAL COURTS OF APPEAL

COURT: First Circuit Court of Appeals
PROVIDER: Emory University School of Law
OPINIONS FROM: February 1995
URL: http://www.law.emory.edu/1circuit/

COURT: Second Circuit Court of Appeals
PROVIDER: Pace University School of Law and Touro Law Center

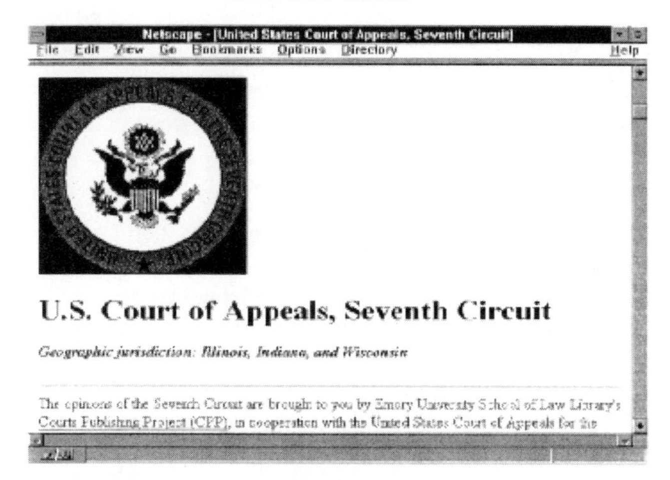

Figure D-3.
URL: http://www.law.emory.edu/7circuit/

The court's official seal symbolizes the Court's sanction of the Internet publication of its opinions.

OPINIONS FROM: August 1995
URL: http://www.law.pace.edu/legal/us-legal/judiciary/second-circuit.html
URL: http://WWW.TouroLaw.edu/AboutTLC/2nd Circuit/

COURT: Third Circuit Court of Appeals
PROVIDER: Villanova University Law School
OPINIONS FROM: May 1994
URL: http://www.law.vill.edu/Fed-Ct/ca03.html

COURT: Fourth Circuit Court of Appeals
PROVIDER: Emory University School of Law
OPINIONS FROM: January 1995
URL: http://www.law.emory.edu/4circuit/

COURT: Fifth Circuit Court of Appeals
PROVIDER: University of Texas at Austin Tarlton Law Library
OPINIONS FROM: 1992
URL: http://www.law.utexas.edu/us5th/us5th.html

COURT: Sixth Circuit Court of Appeals
PROVIDER: Emory University School of Law
OPINIONS FROM: January 1995
URL: http://www.law.emory.edu/6circuit/

COURT: Seventh Circuit Court of Appeals
PROVIDER: Chicago-Kent College of Law and Emory University School of Law
OPINIONS FROM: August 1995
URL: http://www.kentlaw.edu/7circuit/
URL: http://www.law.emory.edu/7circuit/

COURT: Eighth Circuit Court of Appeals
PROVIDER: Washington University School of Law
OPINIONS FROM: October 1995
URL: http://www.wulaw.wustl.edu/8th.cir/

COURT: Ninth Circuit Court of Appeals
PROVIDER: Villanova University Law School
OPINIONS FROM: July 1995
URL http://www.law.vill.edu/Fed-Ct/ca09.html

COURT: Tenth Circuit Court of Appeals
PROVIDER: Emory University School of Law(
OPINIONS FROM: August 1995
URL: http://www.law.emory.edu/10circuit/

COURT: Eleventh Circuit Court of Appeals
PROVIDER: Emory University School of Law
OPINIONS FROM: November 1994
URL: http://www.law.emory.edu/11circuit/

COURT: Federal Circuit Court of Appeals
PROVIDER: Emory University School of Law
OPINIONS FROM: March 1995
URL: http://www.law.emory.edu/fedcircuit

COURT: DC Circuit Court of Appeals
PROVIDER: Georgetown University Law Center Library
OPINIONS FROM: March 1995
URL: http://www.ll.georgetown.edu:80/Fed-Ct/

FEDERAL RULES OF EVIDENCE AND CIVIL PROCEDURE

PROVIDER: Cornell Law School Legal Information Institute
URL: http://www.law.cornell.edu/rules/fre/overview.html
URL: http://www.law.cornell.edu/rules/frcp/overview.htm

VERA INSTITUTE OF JUSTICE

DESCRIPTION: Vera has traditionally been involved in many different areas of the U.S. justice system. Information available at this Web site includes:

- Computer Technology at the New York City Midtown Community Court
- Federal Crime Control Bill
- Links of Other Criminal Justice Sites

ADDRESS: 377 Broadway, New York, NY 10013
CONTACT: Julie Eigler
EMAIL: elj@vera.org.
URL: http://broadway.vera.org/

FEDERAL LAWS

ADVERTISING LAW

DESCRIPTION: This site offers articles concerning the legal aspects of marketing and advertising products, with particular emphasis on advertising substantiation, intellectual property, product demonstrations, endorsements, and related issues. It also offers FTC policy statements, Trade Regulation Rules, and 1994 Amendments to the Federal Trade Commission Act.

PROVIDER: Arent Fox Kintner Plotkin and Kahn
CONTACT: Lewis Rose
ADDRESS: 1050 Connecticut Avenue, N.W., Washington, DC 20036
EMAIL: lewrose@netcom.com
PHONE: (202) 857-6012
URL: http://www.webcom.com/~lewrose/home.html
URL: ftp://ftp.webcom.com/pub/lewrose

AMERICANS WITH DISABILITIES ACT

DESCRIPTION: Several sites provide access to the full text of the Americans with Disabilities Act of 1990 in addition to related materials.

PROVIDER: State University of New York, Buffalo, NY
URL: gopher://val-dor.cc.buffalo.edu:70/11/.legislation/
PROVIDER: St. John's University, Queens, NY
CONTACT: Ms. Tzipporah BenAvraham
URL: gopher://SJUVM.stjohns.edu:70/11/disabled/easi/easilaw

BERNE CONVENTION IMPLEMENTATION ACT OF 1988

DESCRIPTION: The Act is codified at 17 U.S.C. 101.

PROVIDER: The Internet Wiretap, Cupertino, CA
EMAIL: gopher@wiretap.spies.com
URL: http://wiretap.spies.com/Gopher/Gov/Copyright/US.Berne.Convention.txt

BRADY HANDGUN VIOLENCE PREVENTION ACT

DESCRIPTION: Before passage in 1993, this Act was known as the Brady Bill and H.R. 1025. It provides for a waiting period before the purchase of a handgun, and for the establishment of a national instant criminal background check system to be contacted by firearms dealers before the transfer of any firearm.

PROVIDER: The Internet Wiretap, Cupertino, CA
EMAIL: gopher@wiretap.spies.com
URL: http://wiretap.spies.com/Gopher/Gov/brady.act

BROADCASTING ACTS

DESCRIPTION: Full text of Voice of America news reports, program schedules, shortwave radio frequency and satellite downlink information. Full text of federal legislation concerning broadcasting to Cuba can be found under the "Radio and TV Marti (Broadcasting to Cuba)" menu option.

PROVIDER: U.S. Information Agency, Voice of America Computer Services Division

PHONE: (202) 619-2020
EMAIL: postmaster@voa.gov
URL: gopher://gopher.voa.gov:70/11/marti/policy

CIVIL RIGHTS CODE

DESCRIPTION: This is the full text of the civil rights provisions of the U.S. Code (title 42, chapter 21). The ASCII source used was found on a CD-ROM prepared and published by the Office of the Law Revision Counsel of the House of Representatives. It contains the laws in force on January 2, 1992. This site also provides for boolean searching of the entire statute.

PROVIDER: Cornell Law School Legal Information Institute
CONTACT: Brian T. Shelden
EMAIL: bts1@cornell.edu
PHONE: (607) 255-9093
URL: http://www.law.cornell.edu/usc/42/21/overview.html

CLEAN AIR ACT

DESCRIPTION: Codified at 42 U.S.C. 7401.

PROVIDER: U.S. Department of Commerce
CONTACT: Amy Williams
EMAIL: amy@sunny.stat-usa.gov
URL: gopher://ecix.doc.gov:70/00/ecix/adprog/lawpol/cplpm529.txt

CLEAN WATER ACT

DESCRIPTION: Codified at 33 U.S.C. 1251.

PROVIDER: U.S. Department of Commerce
CONTACT: Amy Williams
EMAIL: amy@sunny.stat-usa.gov
URL: gopher://ecix.doc.gov:70/00/ecix/adprog/lawpol/pilwm513.txt

CLEAN WATER ACT REGULATIONS

DESCRIPTION: Codified at 40 C.F.R. 122, 125, 130, 131, 133, 135.

PROVIDER: U.S. Department of Commerce
CONTACT: Amy Williams
EMAIL: amy@sunny.stat-usa.gov, awilliams@esa.doc.gov
URL:
- gopher://ecix.doc.gov:70/00/ecix/adprog/lawpol/pgrwm521.txt (Water Quality Planning Mgt, Regs.)
- gopher://ecix.doc.gov:70/00/ecix/adprog/lawpol/pgrwm522.txt (Water Quality Standards Regs.)
- gopher://ecix.doc.gov:70/00/ecix/adprog/lawpol/pgrwm523.txt (Secondary Treatment Regulation.)
- gopher://ecix.doc.gov:70/00/ecix/adprog/lawpol/pgrpm524.txt (Clear Water Act Regs.)
- gopher://ecix.doc.gov:70/00/ecix/adprog/lawpol/pgrpm519.txt (National Pollution Discharge System, Regs.)
- gopher://ecix.doc.gov:70/00/ecix/adprog/lawpol/pgrwm517.txt (National Pollutant Discharge Elim. System.)

CODE OF FEDERAL REGULATIONS (C.F.R.)

DESCRIPTION: The U.S. Code of Federal Regulations contains all federal agency rules and regulations.

PROVIDER: Cornell Law School Legal Information Institute
CONTACT: Peter W. Martin
EMAIL: martin@law.mail.cornell.edu
URL: http://www.law.cornell.edu/copyright/regulations/regs.overview.html
URL: telnet://www.law.cornell.edu
LOGIN: www
PROVIDER: General Services Administration
URL: http://www.gsa.gov/far/
PROVIDER: U.S. House of Representatives
URL: http://www.pls.com:8001/his/cfr.html

COMMUNICATIONS LAW MEMOS

DESCRIPTION: This site is provided by the law firm Pepper & Corazzini. It includes attorney-written memos on a variety of current issues related to broadcasting, cable, equal employment opportunity (EEO), common carriers, PCS and information law. The WWW server has a direct link to the FCC gopher.

PROVIDER: Pepper & Corazzini, L.L.P.
ADDRESS: 1776 K St., N.W., Washington, DC 20006
PHONE: (202) 296-0600
FAX: (202) 296-5572
CONTACT: Neal J. Friedman
EMAIL: nfriedma@clark.net
URL: http://www.commlaw.com/
URL: ftp://ftp.iis.com/pub/pepper/memos/

COMMUNITY ENVIRONMENTAL RESPONSE COMPENSATION & LIABILITY ACT

DESCRIPTION: Codified at 42 U.S.C. 9601, this law is also known as the Superfund law, and as the Community

Environmental Response Facilitation Act. This is the version of the Act prior to its U.S. Code codification.

PROVIDER: U.S. Department of Commerce
CONTACT: Amy Williams
EMAIL: amy@sunny.stat-usa.gov, awilliams@esa.doc.gov
URL: gopher://ecix.doc.gov:70/00/ecix/adprog/lawpol/pgrpm509.txt

COMPUTER LAW CASES

DESCRIPTION: This site provides documents from many important computer litigation cases.

PROVIDER: Electronic Frontier Foundation
URL: ftp://ftp.eff.org/
Directory: /pub/EFF/Legal/Cases
URL: gopher://gopher.eff.org:70/11/Legal/Cases
URL: http://www.eff.org/pub/EFF/Legal/Cases

COPYRIGHT ACT

DESCRIPTION: Full text of the Copyright Act of 1976 (17 U.S.C. 101-810). The Cornell site (see below) provides the Act by chapter, rather than in one long file. Note: For more information oncopyright, see Copyright Office in Legislative Branch section.

PROVIDER: The Internet Wiretap, Cupertino, CA
EMAIL: gopher@wiretap.spies.com
URL: http://wiretap.spies.com/Gopher/Gov/Copyright/US.Copyright.1976.txt
PROVIDER: Cornell Law School Legal Information Institute
EMAIL: tom@law.mail.cornell.edu, bts1@cornell.edu
URL: telnet://fatty.law.cornell.edu 8210
LOGIN: www
URL: http://www.law.cornell.edu/usc/17/overview.html

COPYRIGHT REGULATIONS

DESCRIPTION: Cornell's Web server indicates the source for these regulations (37 C.F.R. 201-202, General Provisions, and Registration of Claims to Copyright) is the Government Printing Office tape for title 37 updated to February 12, 1994.

PROVIDER: Cornell Law School Legal Information Institute
CONTACT: Peter W. Martin
EMAIL: martin@law.mail.cornell.edu
URL: http://www.law.cornell.edu/copyright/regulations/regs.overview.html
URL: telnet://fatty.law.cornell.edu
LOGIN: www

COPYRIGHT FAQ

DESCRIPTION: The Copyright FAQ (Frequently Asked Questions file) is a series of six articles that contains frequently asked questions with answers relating to copyright law, particularly that of the United States. The contents of the six articles is as follows:

Part 1: Introduction
Part 2: Copyright Basics
Part 3: Common Miscellaneous Questions
Part 4: International Aspects
Part 5: Further Copyright Resources
Part 6: Appendix

PROVIDER: Massachusetts Institute of Technology
AUTHOR: Terry Carroll
EMAIL: tcarroll@scuacc.scu.edu.
URL: ftp://rtfm.mit.edu/pub/usenet/news.answers/law/copyright/faq/
Files: part1 through part6
URL: The FAQ files can be retrieved using email.

Send a
message to: mail-server@rtfm.mit.edu
with the following lines in it:
send usenet/news.answers/law/Copyright-FAQ/part1
send usenet/news.answers/law/Copyright-FAQ/part2
send usenet/news.answers/law/Copyright-FAQ/part3
send usenet/news.answers/law/Copyright-FAQ/part4
send usenet/news.answers/law/Copyright-FAQ/part5
send usenet/news.answers/law/Copyright-FAQ/part6
quit

URL: The FAQ is posted monthly to the following usenet newsgroups:

- misc.legal.computing
- misc.legal
- misc.int-property
- comp.patents
- misc.answers
- comp.answers
- news.answers newsgroups

PROVIDER: Coalition for Networked Information
ADDRESS: 21 Dupont Circle, N.W., Washington, DC 20036
CONTACT: Craig A. Summerhill
EMAIL: craig@cni.org
PHONE: (202) 296-5098
URL: gopher://gopher.cni.org:70/11/cniftp/forums/cni-copyright/other

CORPORATE LAW

DESCRIPTION: Basic information about corporations, including corporate types, reasons to incorporate in Delaware, and commonly asked questions. The provider offers incorporation services.

PROVIDER: The Company Corporation
PHONE: (800) 542-2677
URL: gopher://gopher.service.com:70/11/The%20Company%20Corporation

COUNCIL ON ENVIRONMENTAL QUALITY

DESCRIPTION: Codified at 42 C.F.R. 4321, the purposes of this law are to declare a national policy that will encourage productive and enjoyable harmony between man and his environment, and to establish a Council on Environmental Quality. The Indiana University site provides regulations codified at 40 C.F.R. 1500.

PROVIDER: U.S. Department of Commerce
CONTACT: Amy Williams
EMAIL: amy@sunny.stat-usa.gov, awilliams@esa.doc.gov
URL: gopher://ecix.doc.gov:70/00/ecix/adprog/lawpol/pilwm511.txt
PROVIDER: Indiana University School of Law, Bloomington, IN
CONTACT: Will Sadler
EMAIL: sadler@law.indiana.edu
URL: http://www.law.indiana.edu/envdec/envdec.html

CRIME CONTROL BILL

DESCRIPTION: This site contains the entire "Crime Bill," also known as the Public Safety Partnership and Community Policing Act of 1994. It also provides the legislative history of the Crime Bill, and Joint Explanatory Statements of the Committee of Conference. The conference committee report that contains the text of the final version of the Crime Bill is available at the C-SPAN site.

PROVIDER: Vera Institute of Justice
ADDRESS: 377 Broadway, New York, NY 10013
CONTACT: Richard Zorza
EMAIL: zorzar@vera.org
PHONE: (212) 334-1300
FAX: (212) 941-9407
URL: http://broadway.vera.org/pub/crimebill/cb.html
PROVIDER: Cable-Satellite Public Affairs Network (C-SPAN)
CONTACT: Paul Hanulya
EMAIL: ph@c-span.org
URL: gopher://c-span.org:70/11/Resource/Congress/bills/crime/crime.txt.

DECLARATION OF INDEPENDENCE

DESCRIPTION: This was the first electronic text released by Project Gutenberg, early in 1971.

PROVIDER: The Internet Wiretap, Cupertino, CA
EMAIL: gopher@wiretap.spies.com
URL: http://wiretap.spies.com/Gopher/Gov/US-History/decind.txt

DEFENSE BASE CLOSURE AND REALIGNMENT ACT OF 1990

DESCRIPTION: This is the precodification text of the Act.

PROVIDER: U.S. Department of Commerce
CONTACT: Amy Williams
EMAIL: amy@sunny.stat-usa.gov, awilliams@esa.doc.gov
URL: gopher://ecix.doc.gov:70/00/ecix/adprog/lawpol/xclwm512.txt

DISPOSAL OF SURPLUS PROPERTY

DESCRIPTION: Codified at 40 U.S.C. 484, this law provides for the disposal of federal property by the General Services Administration. See also 41 C.F.R. 101-47, regulations dealing with property disposal.

PROVIDER: U.S. Department of Commerce
CONTACT: Amy Williams
EMAIL: amy@sunny.stat-usa.gov, awilliams@esa.doc.gov
URL: gopher://ecix.doc.gov:70/00/ecix/adprog/lawpol/cxdwh920.txt
gopher://ecix.doc.gov:70/00/ecix/adprog/lawpol/cxrwm528.txt

EDUCATE AMERICA ACT

DESCRIPTION: The full text, as signed into law on March 31, 1994.

PROVIDER: U.S. Dept. of Education
EMAIL: gopheradm@inet.ed.gov
URL: gopher://gopher.ed.gov:10001/11/initiatives/goals/legislation
URL: http://www.ed.gov

ELECTRONIC COMMUNICATIONS PRIVACY ACT

DESCRIPTION: This is the preenactment bill text version of the 1986 Act.

PROVIDER: The Internet Wiretap, Cupertino, CA
EMAIL: gopher@wiretap.spies.com
URL: http://wiretap.spies.com/Gopher/Gov/ecpa.act

ENDANGERED SPECIES ACT

DESCRIPTION: The Act is codified at 16 U.S.C. 1531-1544. Indiana University provides the Act, plus selected Endan-gered Species Act Regulations, cited at 50 C.F.R. 402.

PROVIDER: U.S. Department of Commerce
CONTACT: Amy Williams
EMAIL: amy@sunny.stat-usa.gov, awilliams@esa.doc.gov
URL: gopher://ecix.doc.gov:70/00/ecix/adprog/lawpol/pilwm514.txt
PROVIDER: Indiana University School of Law, Bloomington IN
CONTACT: Will Sadler
EMAIL: sadler@law.indiana.edu
URL: http://www.law.indiana.edu/envdec/envdec.html

FAIR CREDIT REPORTING ACT

DESCRIPTION: The Act is codified at 15 U.S.C. 1681.

PROVIDER: Computer Professionals for Social Responsibility
EMAIL: cpsr@csli.stanford.edu
PHONE: (415) 322-3778
URL: ftp://ftp.cpsr.org/cpsr/privacy/law/fair_credit_reporting_act.txt
PROVIDER: The Internet Wiretap, Cupertino, CA
EMAIL: gopher@wiretap.spies.com
URL: http://wiretap.spies.com/Gopher/Gov/faircredit.act

FAMILY EDUCATIONAL RIGHT TO PRIVACY ACT

DESCRIPTION: This Act is also known as the Buckley Amendment, and is codified at 20 U.S.C. 1232.

PROVIDER: Computer Professionals for Social Responsibility
EMAIL: cpsr@csli.stanford.edu
PHONE: (415) 322-3778
URL: ftp://ftp.cpsr.org/cpsr/privacy/law/education_records_privacy.txt

FEDERAL ADMINISTRATIVE PROCEDURE ACT (APA)

DESCRIPTION: The APA was originally enacted in 1946. Later additions include the Freedom of Information Act (section 552) and the Privacy Act (section 552a). The APA is codified at 5 U.S.C. 551-59, 701-06, 1305, 3105, 3344, 5372, 7521.

PROVIDER: Cornell Law School Legal Information Institute
CONTACT: Peter W. Martin
EMAIL: martin@law.mail.cornell.edu
URL: http://www.law.cornell.edu/apa/apa.table.html

FEDERAL PROPERTY UTILIZATION LAW

DESCRIPTION: Codified at 42 U.S.C. 6921. This gopher entry is labeled "summary." However, the entry includes several U.S.C. sections, and is clearly full text, not a summary.

PROVIDER: U.S. Department of Commerce
CONTACT: Amy Williams
EMAIL: amy@sunny.stat-usa.gov, awilliams@esa.doc.gov
URL: gopher://ecix.doc.gov:70/00/ecix/adprog/lawpol/xclgy005.txt

FEDERAL SECURITIES ACT OF 1933

DESCRIPTION: This is the full text of the Act of May 27, 1933, codified at 15 U.S.C. 77a-77aaa, as amended.

PROVIDER: Cornell Law School Legal Information Institute
CONTACT: Peter W. Martin
EMAIL: martin@law.mail.cornell.edu
URL: http://www.law.cornell.edu/usc

FEDERAL SECURITIES EXCHANGE ACT OF 1934

DESCRIPTION: Full text of the Act.

PROVIDER: Cornell Law School Legal Information Institute
CONTACT: Peter W. Martin
EMAIL: martin@law.mail.cornell.edu
URL: http://www.law.uc.edu/CCL/34Act/index.html

FREEDOM OF INFORMATION ACT (FOIA)

DESCRIPTION: A variety of FOIA documents, including

the Act of 1966 and Amendments as of 1991 (5 U.S.C. 552), and the Congressional Report "A Citizen's Guide to Using the Freedom of Information Act and the Privacy Act of 1974". The Internet Wiretap also offers the Citizen's Guide.

PROVIDER: Electronic Frontier Foundation
URL: ftp://ftp.eff.org/pub/EFF/Legal/FOIA
URL: gopher://gopher.eff.org/
URL: http://www.eff.org/pub/EFF/Legal/FOIA
PROVIDER: The Internet Wiretap Cupertino, CA
EMAIL: gopher@wiretap.spies.com
URL: http://wiretap.spies.com/Gopher/Gov/foia.cit

FREEDOM OF INFORMATION ACT REGULATION

DESCRIPTION: Cornell's Web server indicates the source for these regulations (37 C.F.R. 203 Freedom of Information Act: Policies and Procedures) is the Government Printing Office tape for title 37 updated to February 12, 1994.

PROVIDER: Cornell Law School Legal Information Institute
CONTACT: Peter W. Martin
EMAIL: martin@law.mail.cornell.edu
URL: http://www.law.cornell.edu/copyright/regulations/regs.overview.html

FREEDOM OF INFORMATION ACT REQUEST PACKAGE

DESCRIPTION: These six files provide instructions for making a FOIA application to a federal agency.

PROVIDER: The Internet Wiretap, Cupertino, CA
EMAIL: gopher@wiretap.spies.com
URL: http://wiretap.spies.com/Gopher/Gov/US-History/foia.req

GENERAL AGREEMENT ON TARIFFS AND TRADE (GATT)

PROVIDER: U.S. Department of Agriculture
PHONE (202) 720-8155
EMAIL: gopher-admin@cyfer.esusda.gov
URL: gopher://cyfer.esusda.gov:70/11/ace/policy/gatt

HAZARDOUS WASTE ACT

DESCRIPTION: Codified at 42 U.S.C. 6921. This gopher entry is labeled "summary." However, the entry includes several U.S.C. sections, and is clearly full-text, not a summary.

PROVIDER: U.S. Department of Commerce
CONTACT: Amy Williams
EMAIL: amy@sunny.stat-usa.gov, awilliams@esa.doc.gov
URL: gopher://ecix.doc.gov:70/00/ecix/adprog/lawpol/pilwm515.txt

HIGH PERFORMANCE COMPUTING ACT

DESCRIPTION: The House-Senate compromise version of S. 272, the High Performance Computing Act, was signed into law on December 9, 1991. The Act provides for a coordinated federal program to ensure continued United States leadership in high-performance computing. This ftp directory also contains testimony from individuals and organizations who appeared before the Senate Subcommittee on Science, Technology and Space hearings on the Senate bill in March of 1991.

PROVIDER: Merit Network, Inc.
ADDRESS: Information Services, 2901 Hubbard, Pod G, Ann Arbor, MI 48105
URL: ftp://nis.nsf.net/internet/internet/nren/hpca.1991/nrenbill.txt
URL: gopher://nic.merit.edu:7043/11/internet/nren/hpca.1991nrenbill.txt

MCKINNEY ACT FEDERAL PROPERTY FOR HOMELESS

DESCRIPTION: Codified at 42 U.S.C. 11411, this law provides for the use of underutilized public buildings to assist the homeless.

PROVIDER: U.S. Department of Commerce
CONTACT: Amy Williams
EMAIL: amy@sunny.stat-usa.gov, awilliams@esa.doc.gov
URL: gopher://ecix.doc.gov:70/00/ecix/adprog/lawpol/pglhm503.txt

NATIONAL ENVIRONMENTAL POLICY ACT OF 1969

DESCRIPTION: Codified at 42 U.S.C. 4321-4345.

PROVIDER: U.S. Department of Commerce
CONTACT: Amy Williams
EMAIL: amy@sunny.stat-usa.gov, awilliams@esa.doc.gov
URL: gopher://ecix.doc.gov:70/00/ecix/adprog/lawpol/xglpm504.txt
PROVIDER: Indiana University School of Law, Bloomington IN
CONTACT: Will Sadler

EMAIL: sadler@law.indiana.edu
URL: http://www.law.indiana.edu/envdec/envdec.html

NATIONAL HISTORIC PRESERVATION ACT

DESCRIPTION: Codified at 16 U.S.C. 470. Also see Protection of Historic and Cultural Properties (36 C.F.R. 800), and National Register of Historic Places (36 C.F.R. 60).

PROVIDER: U.S. Department of Commerce
CONTACT: Amy Williams
EMAIL: amy@sunny.stat-usa.gov, awilliams@esa.doc.gov
URL: gopher://ecix.doc.gov:70/00/ecix/adprog/lawpol/ocrwm510.txt
gopher://ecix.doc.gov:70/00/ecix/adprog/lawpol/cirwm538.txt

NATIONAL PERFORMANCE REVIEW

DESCRIPTION: Vice President Al Gore's proposal on reinventing government, in full text, by section.

PROVIDER: Sun Microsystems and the University of North Carolina at Chapel Hill
MAINTAINER: The Office of Information Technology
CONTACT: Jonathan Magid or Chris Colomb
PHONE: (919) 962-6501
EMAIL: ftpkeeper@sunsite.unc.edu
URL: gopher://sunsite.unc.edu:70/11/../.pub/Politics/National_Performance_Review .../

NORTH AMERICAN FREE TRADE AGREEMENT

PROVIDER: The Internet Wiretap, Cupertino, CA
EMAIL: gopher@wiretap.spies.com
URL: http://wiretap.spies.com/Gopher/Gov/NAFTA/
PROVIDER: U.S. Department of Agriculture
PHONE: (202) 720-8155
EMAIL: gopher-admin@cyfer.esusda.gov
URL: gopher://cyfer.esusda.gov:70/11/ace/policy/nafta
PROVIDER: University of North Carolina
EMAIL: GopherMaster@SunSITE.unc.edu
URL: gopher://sunsite.unc.edu:70/11/sunsite.d/politics.d/international.d

OCCUPATIONAL SAFETY AND HEALTH ACT OF 1970 (OSHA)

DESCRIPTION: This site offers the full text of the Act, as well as OSHA Standards (29 C.F.R.—Parts 1900-1999) and relevant Federal Register sections, by month, (1971 to date).

PROVIDER: Department of Energy's Office of Environment, Safety and Health
EMAIL: support@tis.inel.gov
PHONE: (208) 526-8955
URL: gopher://gabby.osha-slc.gov/

PATENT ACT

DESCRIPTION: The U.S. Patent Act (35 U.S.C.1-376) by chapter.

PROVIDER: Cornell Law School
EMAIL: tom@law.mail.cornell.edu, bts1@cornell.edu
URL: telnet://www.law.cornell.edu 8220
LOGIN: www
URL: http://www.law.cornell.edu/patent/patent.table.html
URL: http://www.law.cornell.edu/usc/35/i_iv/overview.html

PRIVACY ACT OF 1974

DESCRIPTION: This version of the Act was retrieved from the Government Printing Office U.S. Code on CD-ROM. It provides the Privacy Act and Amendments as of January 2, 1991. The Act is codified at 5 U.S.C. 552a.

PROVIDER: Computer Professionals for Social Responsibility
EMAIL: cpsr@csli.stanford.edu
PHONE: (415) 322-3778
URL: ftp://ftp.cpsr.org/cpsr/privacy/law/privacy_act_1974.txt
PROVIDER: The Internet Wiretap, Cupertino, CA
EMAIL: gopher@wiretap.spies.com
URL: http://wiretap.spies.com/Gopher/Gov/privacy.act

PRIVACY ACT REGULATION

DESCRIPTION: Cornell's Web server indicates the source for this regulation (37 C.F.R. 204 Privacy Act: Policies and Procedures) is the Government Printing Office tape for title 37 updated to February 12, 1994.

PROVIDER: Cornell Law School Legal Information Institute
CONTACT: Peter W. Martin
EMAIL: martin@law.mail.cornell.edu
URL: http://www.law.cornell.edu/copyright/regulations/regs.overview.html
URL: telnet://www.law.cornell.edu
LOGIN: www

PRIVACY ARTICLE

DESCRIPTION: This article is titled "A Proposal for Federal Legislation Protecting Informational Privacy Across the Private Sector," was first published in the Santa Clara Computer and High Technology Law Journal in November 1993. The author is Josh Blackman.

PROVIDER: Society for Electronic Access
ADDRESS PO Box 7081, New York, NY 10116-7081
EMAIL: sea@sea.org
PHONE: (212) 592-3801
URL: gopher://gopher.panix.com:70/11/SEA/Privacy

RESOURCE CONSERVATION & RECOVERY ACT REGULATIONS

DESCRIPTION: This Code of Federal Regulations Section (40 C.F.R. 124) is pursant to the Resource Conservation and Recovery Act (42 U.S.C. 6901), the Safe Drinking Water Act (42 U.S.C. 300(f), the Clean Water Act (33 U.S.C. 1251) and the Clean Air Act (42 U.S.C. 1857).

PROVIDER: U.S. Department of Commerce
CONTACT: Amy Williams
EMAIL: amy@sunny.stat-usa.gov, awilliams@esa.doc.gov
URL: gopher://ecix.doc.gov:70/00/ecix/adprog/lawpol/cgrpm539.txt

RULES OF PROFESSIONAL CONDUCT

DESCRIPTION: The American Bar Association (ABA) promulgates Model Rules of Professional Conduct. All states have similar rules governing the conduct of lawyers. The Idaho Rules provided by Cornell's Legal Information Institute are based on the ABA Model Rules, and are therefore representative of most state's professional conduct rules. This document includes comments borrowed from the ABA Model Rules.

PROVIDER: Legal Information Institute Cornell Law School, and the Idaho State Bar
CONTACT: Peter W. Martin
EMAIL: martin@law.mail.cornell.edu
URL: http://www.law.cornell.edu/lawyers/ruletable.html

SUPERFUND LEGISLATION

DESCRIPTION: Codified at 42 U.S.C. 9601, this law is also known as the Comprehensive Environmental Response, Compensation and Liability Act of 1980 (CERCLA).

PROVIDER: U.S. Department of Commerce
CONTACT: Amy Williams
EMAIL: amy@sunny.stat-usa.gov, awilliams@esa.doc.gov
URL: gopher://ecix.doc.gov:70/00/ecix/adprog/lawpol/cplpm551.txt

TELECOMMUNICATION BILLS AND OTHER MATERIALS

DESCRIPTION: This site provides information on regulatory and policy issues associated with the ongoing telecommunications policy reform debate. Materials available include information on issues such as cable-TV competition, American universal service polices and practices, and the impact of regulations on consumers. Legal materials available include court decisions and many congressional bills related to telecommunications.

PROVIDER: MFJ Task Force - an ad hoc committee of the seven regional Bell Operating Companies, which is coordinating the legislative strategy for removing the restrictions on the Bell companies contained in the 1982 AT&T Consent Decree and the Cable Act of 1984
EMAIL: info@bell.com
CONTACT: Jeff Richards
EMAIL: mfjtf@bell.com
URL: ftp://bell.com/pub/
URL: http://bell.com
URL: gopher://bell.com/

TELECOMMUNICATIONS LAW

Provides links to U.S. state and international Internet sites dealing with telecom law and policy. Sites included are U.S. National Telecommunications Information Administration, FCC, Office of Telecom Policy Analysis, and International Telecommunications Union.

PROVIDER: St. Louis University
CONTACT: Jim Milles
EMAIL: millesjg@sluvca.slu.edu
URL: http://lawlib.slu.edu/misc/telecomm.htm

TOXIC POLLUTANT EFFLUENT STANDARDS

DESCRIPTION: Codified at 40 C.F.R. 129, these regulations were created pursuant to the authority of the Federal Water Pollution Control Act (33 U.S.C. 1251).

PROVIDER: U.S. Department of Commerce
CONTACT: Amy Williams
EMAIL: amy@sunny.stat-usa.gov, awilliams@esa.doc.gov

URL: gopher://ecix.doc.gov:70/00/ecix/adprog/lawpol/pgrpm520.txt

TRADEMARK ACT

DESCRIPTION: The Trademark Act of 1946 (the Lanham Act; 15 U.S.C. 1051-1127).

PROVIDER: Cornell Law School
EMAIL: tom@law.mail.cornell.edu, bts1@cornell.edu
URL: telnet://fatty.law.cornell.edu 8230 LOGIN: www
URL: http://www.law.cornell.edu/lanham/lanham.table.html
URL: http://www.law.cornell.edu/usc/15/22/overview.html

UNIFORM COMMERCIAL CODE

DESCRIPTION: Cornell Law School provides section-by-section access to the entire Uniform Commercial Code, articles 1 through 9 as follow:

- Article 1 General Provisions
- Article 2 Sales
- Article 2A Leases
- Article 3 Negotiable Instruments
- Article 4 Bank Deposits and Collections
- Article 4A Funds Transfers
- Article 5 Letters of Credit
- Article 6 Bulk Transfers and Bulk Sales
- Article 7 Warehouse Receipts, Bills of Lading and other Documents of Title
- Article 8 Investment Securities
- Article 9 Secured Transactions

PROVIDER: Cornell Law School Legal Information Institute
CONTACT: Peter W. Martin
EMAIL: martin@law.mail.cornell.edu
URL: telnet://fatty.law.cornell.edu 8260 LOGIN: www
URL: http://www.law.cornell.edu/ucc/ucc.table.html

UNIFORM CODE OF MILITARY JUSTICE

DESCRIPTION: The files in this directory contain, in ASCII format, subchapters 1 through 12 of the U.S. Uniform Code of Military Justice.

URL: http://wiretap.spies.com/Gopher/Gov/UCMJ/

UNIVERSAL COPYRIGHT CONVENTION

DESCRIPTION: The source for this version of the Convention is International Copyright Conventions, Circular 38c, Copyright Office, Washington, DC, pages 23-35. The Convention was revised in Paris in 1971 and ratified by the U.S. Senate in 1982.

PROVIDER: The Internet Wiretap, Cupertino, CA
EMAIL: gopher@wiretap.spies.com
URL: http://wiretap.spies.com/Gopher/Gov/Copyright/US.Universal.Copyright.Conv.txt

U.S. BUDGET

DESCRIPTION: The President's budget proposals dating from 1993 to date are available here. Available files include the President's Message, separate files for each Budget chapter, and additional detailed budget data.

PROVIDER: Sun Microsystems and the University of North Carolina at Chapel Hill
MAINTAINER: The Office of Information Technology
CONTACT: Jonathan Magid or Chris Colomb
PHONE: (919) 962-6501
EMAIL: ftpkeeper@sunsite.unc.edu
URL: gopher://sunsite.unc.edu:70/11/../.pub/Politics

U.S. CODE

DESCRIPTION: The United States Code contains all federal laws (the Code of Federal Regulations contains all federal regulations). The Government Printing Office offers the entire U.S. Code (many books worth) on a CD-ROM for under $40. The problem with the disk is currency. Congress continually passes new laws that find their way into the U.S. Code. The books are updated via "pocket parts," paper inserts that law libraries receive regularly. In any case, someone at the University of Michigan has apparently com- pressed the contents of the CD-ROM and made it available online. Note that the files are compressed. Title 28 of the U.S. Code, sections 1251-1259, which deal with the jurisdiction of the U.S. Supreme Court is also available at Cornell Law School.

PROVIDER: University of Michigan
URL: ftp://etext.archive.umich.edu/pub/Politics/Conspiracy/AJTeel/USC
PROVIDER: Cornell Law School Legal Information Institute
URL: http://www.law.cornell.edu/courts/28usc.table.html

U.S. CONSTITUTION

DESCRIPTION: This edition of the Constitution of the United States is based on many hours of study of a variety of editions. This edition does not include the amendments.

PROVIDER: The Internet Wiretap, Cupertino, CA
EMAIL: gopher@wiretap.spies.com
URL: http://wiretap.spies.com/Gopher/Gov/US-History/us-const.txt

U.S. OLYMPIC COMMITTEE LAW

DESCRIPTION: The Amateur Sports Act of 1978 amended the statute chartering the U.S. Olympic Committee. The act is codified at 36 U.S.C. 371-396.

PROVIDER: Cornell law School Legal Information Institute
CONTACT: Peter W. Martin
EMAIL: martin@law.mail.cornell.edu
URL: http://www.law.cornell.edu/sector/sports/36usc.overview.html

VIDEO PRIVACY PROTECTION ACT

DESCRIPTION: This Act is also known as the Bork Bill (after Judge Robert Bork) and is codified at 18 U.S.C. 2710.

PROVIDER: Computer Professionals for Social Responsibility
EMAIL: cpsr@csli.stanford.edu
PHONE: (415) 322-3778
URL: ftp://ftp.cpsr.org/cpsr/privacy/law/video_rental_privacy_act.txt

WAR POWERS RESOLUTION OF 1973

DESCRIPTION: This law concerns the war powers of Congress and the President. It's also known as Public Law 93-148, enacted November 7, 1973.

PROVIDER: The Internet Wiretap, Cupertino, CA
EMAIL: gopher@wiretap.spies.com
URL: http://wiretap.spies.com/Gopher/Gov/warpower.act

STATES

ALABAMA

STATE HOME PAGE

DESCRIPTION: The State of Alabama's Official home page includes topics such as Government, Tourism and Travel, Newspapers, State Education.

PROVIDER: State of Alabama
CONTACT: Carla J. Gilmore
ADDRESS: Governor's Correspondence Office 600 Dexter Ave. Montgomery, AL 36104
EMAIL: webmaster@asnmail.asc.edu
PHONE: (334) 242-4429
FAX: (334) 242-4541
URL: http://alaweb.asc.edu

LEGISLATIVE BRANCH

CONSTITUTION

DESCRIPTION: This site provides Article I of the 1901 Constitution of Alabama, as amended through 1966.

PROVIDER: HarborNet
CONTACT: Dan Rubin
ADDRESS: 4810 Pt Fosdick Dr. NW, Gig Harbor, WA 98335
PHONE: (206) 858-8839
EMAIL: support@harbornet.com
URL: http://www.harbornet.com/rights/alabama.txt

LEGISLATIVE DIRECTORY

DESCRIPTION: Unusual collection here, although not surprising given that the provider is an archive. Site includes a directory of all state representatives, committees, speakers and clerks, a log of all legislative sessions since 1819, and hand-drawn diagram explaining How a bill becomes law.

PROVIDER: AL Department of Archives and History
CONTACT: Tracey Berezansky
PHONE: (334) 242-4363, x274
EMAIL: dahtjb01@asnmail.asc.edu
URL: http://www.asc.edu/archives/legislat/legislat.html

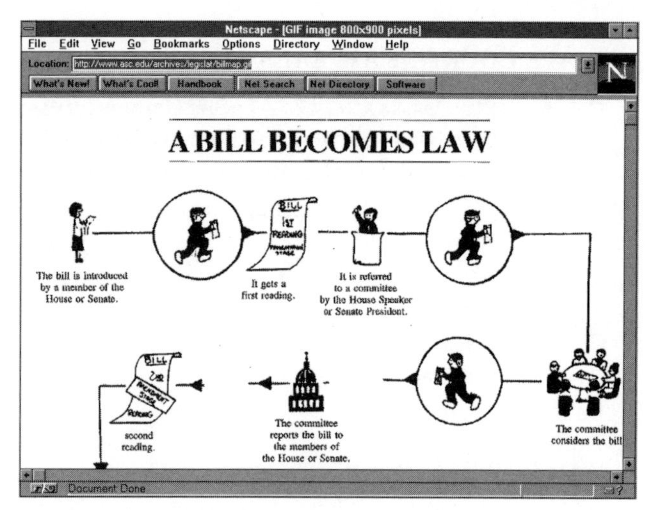

Figure D-4. http://www.asc.edu/archives/legislat/billmap.gif

The Alabama Department of Archives and History offers this explanation of how a bill becomes a law.

EXECUTIVE BRANCH

SECRETARY OF STATE

DESCRIPTION: The Alabama Secretary of State home page allows access to the Secretary of State's election, voter registration, and business regulation information. Visitors are able to write to the Secretary of State, access election results, and request a postcard voter registration application.

PROVIDER: Secretary of State's Office
CONTACT: Steve Prince, Assistant Director of the Public Information Division
EMAIL: Zackdawg@aol.com
URL: http://alsecst.jsu.edu:8000/

ALASKA

STATE HOME PAGE

DESCRIPTION: This is a word-searchable site. Links available here include:

- State of Alaska White Pages Lookup
- Alaska Seafood Cookbook
- Alaska Marine Highway Home Page
- Dept of Administration Home Page
- Legislature Home Page
- Dept of Labor Home Page
- Office of the Governor
- Dept of Natural Resources Home Page
- Dept of Environmental Conservation Home Page
- Dept of Fish and Game Image Gallery

URL: http://www.state.ak.us/

LEGISLATIVE BRANCH

ADMINISTRATIVE CODE

DESCRIPTION: All titles of the Alaska Administrative Code (state code) are searchable here.

PROVIDER: Touch N' Go Systems, Inc., and the Law Offices of James B. Gottstein
EMAIL: touchngo@touchngo.com
PHONE: (907) 274-6333
ADDRESS: 406 G Street, Suite 210, Anchorage, AK 99501
URL: http://www.touchngo.com/lglcntr/akstats/aac.htm

CONSTITUTION

DESCRIPTION: All sections of the state constitution (as amended to 1974) are searchable at this site.

PROVIDER: Touch N' Go Systems, Inc., and the Law Offices of James B. Gottstein
EMAIL: jimgott@touchngo.com
PHONE: (907) 274-6333
ADDRESS: 406 G Street, Suite 210, Anchorage, AK 99501
URL: http://info.alaska.edu:70/1s/Alaska/constitution

LEGISLATIVE MATERIAL

DESCRIPTION: Provides full-text access to:

- State Statutes Dating to 1993
- State Constitution
- State Executive Orders
- State Administrative Journal
- State Administrative Code
- Bill Tracking and Information from 1995
- Legislative Bills and Resolutions from 1983
- Legislature Committee Minutes from 1995
- Text of House and Senate Daily Journals from 1987
- Committee Minute Text from 1982
- Session Laws from 1981
- Legislative Uniform Rules
- Legislative Research Requests

PROVIDER: Juneau Legislative Information Office
ADDRESS: 130 Seward St, Suite 313, Juneau, AK 99801-2197

PHONE: (907) 465-4648
EMAIL: Lynn_Morley@Legis.state.ak.us
URL: http://www.legis.state.ak.us/

STATE STATUTES

DESCRIPTION: All titles of the Alaska Statutes (state code) are searchable here.

PROVIDER: Touch N' Go Systems, Inc., and the Law Offices of James B. Gottstein
EMAIL: touchngo@touchngo.com
PHONE: (907) 274-6333
ADDRESS: 406 G Street, Suite 210, Anchorage, AK 99501
URL: http://www.touchngo.com/lglcntr/akstats/Statutes.htm

JUDICIAL BRANCH

COURT SYSTEM HOME PAGE

DESCRIPTION:

- Recent Alaska Appellate Court Decisions
- Supreme Court Slip Opinions
- Court of Appeals Slip Opinions
- Court of Appeals Memorandum Opinions (MOJs)
- Alaska Rules of Appellate Procedure
- Alaska Rules of Civil Procedure
- Alaska Rules of Evidence with Commentary
- Recent Supreme Court Orders
- Changes and Additions to the Alaska Rules of Court
- Profile of the Alaska Court System
- Recent Court System Press Releases
- Alaska Bar Association Ethics Opinions from 1990

PROVIDER: Alaska Court Libraries
EMAIL: akctlib@alaska.net
URL: http://www.alaska.net/~akctlib/

STATE SUPREME COURT

DESCRIPTION: Alaska Supreme Court Opinions (general appeals) dating from 1991 are available in full text, as delivered from the courthouse. You can do a full-text search of the Alaska Supreme Court opinions or go to the recent opinions, or use the chronological or subject indices.

PROVIDER: Touch N' Go Systems, Inc., and the Law Offices of James B. Gottstein
EMAIL: jimgotts@touchngo.com
PHONE: (907) 274-6333
ADDRESS: 406 G Street, Suite 210, Anchorage, AK 99501
URL: http://touchngo.com/sp/sp.htm
URL: http://www.alaska.net/~akctlib/

STATE COURT OF APPEALS

DESCRIPTION: Alaska Court of Appeals Opinions (criminal appeals) dating from 1995 are available in full text, as delivered from the courthouse. You can do a full-text search of the Alaska Supreme Court opinions or go to the recent opinions, or use the chronological or subject indices.

PROVIDER: Touch N' Go Systems, Inc., and the Law Offices of James B. Gottstein
EMAIL: jimgotts@touchngo.com
PHONE: (907) 274-6333
ADDRESS: 406 G Street, Suite 210, Anchorage, AK 99501
URL: http://touchngo.com/ap/ap.htm
URL: http://www.alaska.net/~akctlib/

ARIZONA

STATE HOME PAGE

DESCRIPTION: Provides links to state agencies, and a searchable state agency phone directory.

URL: http://www.state.az.us/

LEGISLATIVE BRANCH

CONSTITUTION

DESCRIPTION: Article II (Declaration of Rights) of the 1912 Constitution of Arizona, as revised to January 1975.

PROVIDER: HarborNet
CONTACT: Dan Rubin
ADDRESS: 4810 Pt Fosdick Dr. NW, Gig Harbor, WA 98335
PHONE: (206) 858-8839
EMAIL: support@harbornet.com
URL: http://www.harbornet.com/rights/arizona.txt

LEGISLATIVE BILLS

DESCRIPTION: This site offers a searchable directory of legislative bills dating to 1994.

PROVIDER: Arizona Capitol Times and Arizona State University
CONTACT: Arizona Capitol Times
ADDRESS: 14 N. 18th Ave, Phoenix AZ 85007
EMAIL: pctp@asu.edu
URL: gopher://info.asu.edu/11/asu-cwis/pctp/legact

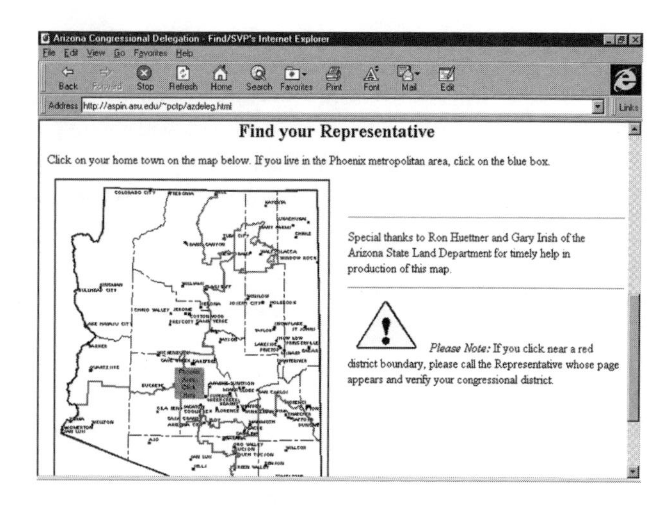

Figure D-5.
http://aspin.asu.edu/~pctp/azdeleg.html

Here's an excellent use of Web technology. By clicking on any Arizona town on this map, you can find the Congressional Representative for that town.

JUDICIAL BRANCH

COUNTY COURT

DESCRIPTION: The Pima County Consolidated Justice Courts server includes a "virtual court calendar," court forms, and links to the Maricopa County Court server.

ADDRESS: 115 N. Church Ave. Tucson, AZ 85701
EMAIL: Mik@pima.gov
PHONE: (520) 882-0044
URL: http://jp.pima.gov/

ARKANSAS

STATE HOME PAGE

DESCRIPTION: State government links are available here.

URL: http://www.state.ar.us:80/html/ark_govt.html

LEGISLATIVE BRANCH

CONSTITUTION

DESCRIPTION: This site provides article II (Arkansas Declaration of Rights) of the 1874 Constitution of Arkansas, as amended to 1975.

PROVIDER: HarborNet
CONTACT: Dan Rubin
ADDRESS: 4810 Pt Fosdick Dr. NW, Gig Harbor, WA 98335
PHONE: (206) 858-8839
EMAIL: support@harbornet.com
URL: http://www.harbornet.com/rights/arkansas.txt

LEGISLATIVE BILLS

DESCRIPTION: Search for acts from the recent General Assembly here.

PROVIDER: University of Arkansas, Fayetteville, AR
URL: http://www.uark.edu/~govninfo/PAGES/WAIS-SEARCH/acts.cgi

LEGISLATURE

DESCRIPTION: Searchable directory of state representatives. A clickable map of districts (click on your district to find your representative) is available here.

PROVIDER: University of Arkansas, Fayetteville, AR
URL: http://www.uark.edu/~govninfo/PAGES/LEGISLATIVE/index.html

STATE CODE

DESCRIPTION: Here you'll find Act 884 of 1977, as amended and codified as Arkansas Code Annotated (ACA), section 25, chapter 4 and related policies and guidelines under which state agencies acquire data processing and telecommunications equipment, software, and services.

PROVIDER: Arkansas Department of Computer Services
CONTACT: Penny Rubow
EMAIL: prubow@spd.state.ar.us
URL: http://w3spd.state.ar.us/contents.htm

JUDICIAL BRANCH

ARKANSAS JUDICIARY HOME PAGE

DESCRIPTION: This site includes info about the judiciary and opinions from the Arkansas Supreme Court and Arkansas Court of Appeals from January 1996.

URL: http://www.state.ar.us/supremecourt/

CALIFORNIA

STATE HOME PAGE

DESCRIPTION: There's all sorts of useful stuff available here. Perhaps the most useful is the topical/keyword/and agency index, which will help you find just about anything available online regarding California.

PROVIDER: Teale Data Center (California state agency)
EMAIL: WebMaster@teale.ca.gov
URL: http://www.ca.gov/gov/calhome.html

EXECUTIVE BRANCH

ENVIRONMENTAL INFO

DESCRIPTION: The California Environmental Resources Evaluation System (CERES) provides access to data describing California's rich and diverse resources, such as information about physical environments, living creatures and their habitats, and environmental impact reports and studies. Environmental information is searchable here by organization, geographic area and keyword. The site provides links to these resource-related agencies:

- California Coastal Commission
- Department of Boating and Waterways
- Department of Conservation
- Department of Fish and Game
- Department of Forestry and Fire Protection
- Department of Parks and Recreation
- Department of Water Resources
- California Conservation Corps
- California Tahoe Conservancy
- Colorado River Board of California
- California Energy Commission
- San Francisco Bay Conservation and Development Commission
- Santa Monica Mountains Conservancy
- State Coastal Conservancy
- California State Lands Commission
- State Reclamation Board
- CAL-FED Bay-Delta Program
- California Biodiversity Council
- California Rivers Assessment

PROVIDER: California Resources Agency
EMAIL: httpd@ceres.ca.gov
URL: http://www.ceres.ca.gov/

STATE AGENCIES

DESCRIPTION: Central site for connecting to state agencies, including:

- Contractors State License Board
- California Employment Development Department Server
- California Energy Commission Server
- California Department of Fish and Game Server
- California Franchise Tax Board
- California Department of General Services
- California Department of Department of Motor Vehicles
- California Governor's Office of Emergency Services
- California Resources Agency CERES System
- California Secretary of the State Elections
- California State Controller's Office
- California State Lands Commission
- California State Senate
- Legislative Analyst's Office
- California Department of Transportation
- California Department of Water Resources

PROVIDER: Teale Data Center (California state agency)
EMAIL: WebMaster@teale.ca.gov
URL: http://www.ca.gov/www.html
URL: http://www.ca.gov/gopher.html
URL: http://www.ganymede.org/agencies.html

STATE EMAIL DIRECTORY

DESCRIPTION: This site compiles all the available email addresses of federal and elected California officials. The list includes:

- Office of the President of the United States
- The United States Senate
- The United States House of Representatives
- Office of the Governor of California
- The California Senate
- The California Assembly
- California County and City Government Officials
- City of Berkeley
- City of Palo Alto
- City and County of San Francisco

PROVIDER: Cyberspace Today
EMAIL: vern@cybertoday.com
URL: http://www.cybertoday.com/ct/gov/

TAX FORMS

DESCRIPTION: This site provides state income tax forms, instructions and publications.

PROVIDER:	Franchise Tax Board
URL:	http://library.ca.gov/California/ftb/html/home.html
URL:	http://www.scubed.com/tax/state/1994/ca_forms/ca_index.html

LEGISLATIVE BRANCH

LEGISLATIVE INFORMATION

DESCRIPTION: This is simply the best state government site on the Internet. It's chock full of value. It's a wonder there are still legal publishers selling access to the material that the government of California is providing for free on the Net. The California Legislature mandated (via Assembly Bill 1624, chapter 1235/Statutes of 1993) that legislative materials be made available on the Internet. The law requires that for each current legislative session, the following information be made available on the Internet:

- The legislative calendar
- The schedule of legislative committee hearings
- A list of matters pending on the floors of both houses of the legislature
- A list of the committees of the legislature and their members
- The text of each bill introduced, including each amended, enrolled, and chaptered form of each bill
- The history of each bill introduced and amended
- The status of each bill introduced and amended
- All bill analyses prepared by legislative committees in connection with each bill
- All vote information concerning each bill
- Any veto message concerning a bill
- The California Code
- The California Constitution
- All statutes enacted on or after January 1, 1993

PROVIDER:	California Legislature, Sacramento, CA
EMAIL:	comments@leginfo.public.ca.gov
URL:	gopher://gopher.sen.ca.gov:70/
URL:	http://www.sen.ca.gov

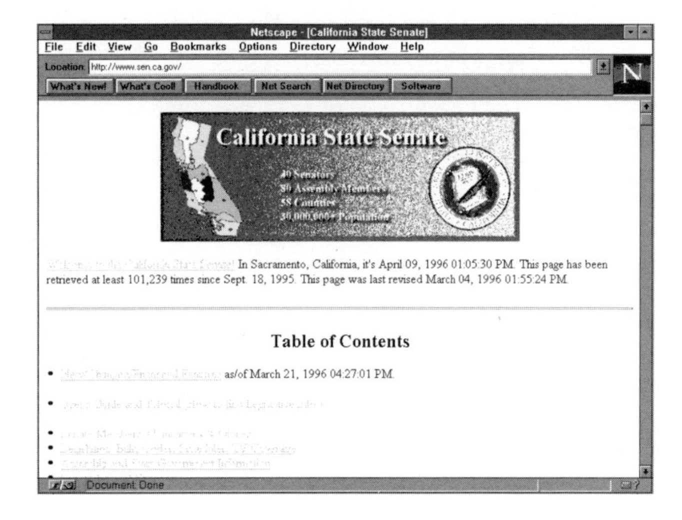

Figure D-6. http://www.sen.ca.gov

The best state government site on the Net.

STATUTES AND BILLS

DESCRIPTION: Searchable, full-text access to all 29 California Codes, bills dating to 1993 is available here; plus resolutions, and constitutional amendments, including status, history, votes, analyses, and veto messages, all dating back to 1993.

PROVIDER:	Legislative Counsel of California
URL:	http://www.leginfo.ca.gov/

BILL TRACKING SERVICE

DESCRIPTION: The California Senate offers a leading edge subscription service which sends email every time particular legislative bills (selectable by the subscriber) are amended, analyzed, or otherwise changed in any way (including status changes, such as vetos and votes).

PROVIDER:	California State Senate Rules Committee, Computer Services
URL:	Send email to: senatenews@sen.ca.gov In the body of the message, type: HELP

STATE ASSEMBLY

DESCRIPTION: Material available here includes a directory of assembly members, bill searching, legislative calendar, Daily File (session agenda), and an analysis of the state budget.

URL:	California State Assembly Computer Services
URL:	http://www.assembly.ca.gov

JUDICIAL BRANCH

DAILY COURT OPINIONS

DESCRIPTION: This is a cool site. It includes all cases from the past 30 days, arranged by subject from the U.S. Supreme Court, Ninth Circuit U.S. Court of Appeals, California Supreme and all California courts of appeal.

Today's opinions are presented separately. The service also features briefing papers by California law firms and classified job listings.

PROVIDER: The Recorder
EMAIL: recorder@callaw.com
URL: http://www.callaw.com/

CALIFORNIA JUDICIAL BRANCH

DESCRIPTION: Links include:

- California Court Web Sites—links to California court Web sites
- Opinions—opinions of the California Supreme Court and Courts of Appeal
- California Court System—graphic illustrating appellate and trial court system
- California Judicial System—constitutional authority, scope, budget
- Supreme Court—photograph and biographies of members, qualifications, jurisdiction
- Courts of Appeal—membership, jurisdiction
- Superior Courts—membership, jurisdiction
- Municipal Courts—membership, jurisdiction
- Judicial Council—membership, committees, activities
- Commission on Judicial Appointments—constitutional authority, function
- Commission on Judicial Performance—constitutional authority, function
- California Judges Association—functions
- State Bar of California—constitutional authority, admission, certification, judicial nominees
- Map of California Appellate Court Districts—counties included in each of the six districts

PROVIDER: Administrative Office of the Courts
URL: http://www.courtinfo.ca.gov

OTHER CALIFORNIA MATERIAL

STATE BAR ASSOCIATION

DESCRIPTION:

- Publications of the State Bar
- News Releases from the State Bar
- Sections of the State Bar
- Certified Lawyer Referral Services
- Consumer Information

PROVIDER: The State Bar of California
ADDRESS: 555 Franklin Street, San Francisco, CA 94102
PHONE: (415) 561-8200
EMAIL: comments@calbar.org
URL: http://www.calbar.org

CONSUMER ATTORNEYS OF CALIFORNIA (CAOC)

DESCRIPTION: The CAOC site contains information of interest to consumers, and to the plaintiff's bar.

URL: http://seamless.com/consumer

CALIFORNIA DIVORCE

DESCRIPTION: This site offers a consumer-oriented divorce tutorial. By filling out a form here, a completed Response and Confidential Counseling Statement will be prepared and mailed to you.

URL: http://www.legal.net/divorce.htm

CALIFORNIA CRIMINAL LAW

DESCRIPTION: This attorney-sponsored page offers some interesting insights into the state of criminal law in California, including:

- Information about California's "Three Strikes" law
- Download the United States Sentencing Commission, Guidelines Manual
- The consequences of a felony conviction in California
- A basic glossary of criminal law terms and jargon in California
- A traveler's guide to the courts of Silicon Valley and the judges who inhabit them

PROVIDER: The Law Offices of Jerome P. Mullins
URL: http://tsw.ingress.com/tsw/alawyer/criminal.html

LOS ANGELES HOME PAGE

DESCRIPTION: Includes links to city agencies, including:

- Office of the City Attorney
- Environmental Affairs Department
- Department of Building & Safety
- Los Angeles Police Department

PROVIDER: City of Los Angeles, Information Technology Agency
EMAIL: webmaster@www.ci.la.ca.us
URL: http://www.ci.la.ca.us/index.htm

COLORADO

STATE HOME PAGE

DESCRIPTION: Provides links to many state agencies.

URL: http://www.state.co.us

EXECUTIVE BRANCH

SECRETARY OF STATE

DESCRIPTION: Filing manual and forms

PROVIDER: iway hyperdocs ltd
CONTACT: James S. Bailey, President, Editor
EMAIL: jbailey@iway-hyperdocs.com
ADDRESS: 700 West Mississippi Avenue, Suite C-4, Denver, CO 80223
URL: http://www.aescon.com/crs95/sos/index.htm

LEGISLATIVE BRANCH

CONSTITUTION

DESCRIPTION: Full text of each article of the 1876 Constitution of Colorado is available here, as amended to 1980.

PROVIDER: iway hyperdocs ltd
CONTACT: James S. Bailey, President, Editor
EMAIL: jbailey@iway-hyperdocs.com
ADDRESS: 700 West Mississippi Avenue, Suite C-4, Denver, CO 80223
URL: http://www.aescon.com/crs95/colocons/index.htm

REVISED STATUTES

DESCRIPTION: The statutes are provided through an online collection of legal research resources compiled by Denver attorney Jeff McCarthy. The statutes at this site are the 1994 Colorado Revised Statutes, all 43 titles in hypertext format, published by iway hyperdocs ltd, a Colorado company. In order to use the iway hyperdocs Colorado Revised Statutes, you need to register online (no charge). The iway company may use the registration information to mail or fax to you information regarding the product and the Windows companion product.

PROVIDER: Jeff McCarthy
ADDRESS: 280 Detroit Street, Denver, CO 80206
PHONE: (303) 377-0765
FAX: (303) 321-8073
EMAIL: jeffmcc@usa.net
URL: http://usa.net/cololaw/research.htm
URL: http://www.aescon.com/iway/entry.htm

PROPOSED LEGISLATION

DESCRIPTION: The Colorado Alliance of Research Libraries (CARL) provides access to full text of bills before the Colorado General Assembly, status of bills, legislative calendar, and record of Assembly proceedings.

PROVIDER: Colorado Alliance of Research Libraries
ADDRESS: 3801 East Florida Street, Suite 300, Denver, CO 80210
PHONE: (303) 758-3030
FAX: (303) 758-0606
EMAIL: help@carl.org
URL: http://www.carl.org/carl.html
URL: telnet://carl.colorado.edu
then choose:
- PAC
- VT-100
- Other Library Systems
- Carl Systems Network Libraries - Western US
- Pikes Peak Library Systems
- Government Databases....
- Colorado Legislative Database

JUDICIAL BRANCH

COURT RULES

DESCRIPTION: Colorado Rules courtesy of iway hyperdocs:
- Rules of Civil Procedure
- Rules Governing the Practice of Law
- Rules Governing the Judiciary
- Rules of County Court Civil Procedure
- Rules of Procedure for Small Claims Courts
- Rules of Probate Procedure
- Rules of Juvenile Procedure
- Rules of Criminal Procedure
- Rules Governing the Public Defender Commission
- Rules for County Court Traffic Violations Bureaus
- Rules for Traffic Infractions
- Municipal Court Rules of Procedure
- Rules of Jury Selection and Service
- Appellate Rules
- Rules of Evidence
- Rules for Reapportionment Commission Proceedings
- Rules for Magistrates
- Uniform Local Rules for All State Water Court Divisions

PROVIDER: iway hyperdocs ltd.
CONTACT: James S. Bailey, President, Editor
EMAIL: jbailey@iway-hyperdocs.com
ADDRESS: 700 West Mississippi Avenue, Suite C-4, Denver, CO 80223
URL: http://www.aescon.com/crs95/rules/index.htm

OTHER COLORADO MATERIALS

COLORADO LEGAL ALLIANCE

DESCRIPTION: This is the central site for Colorado legal material. Examples of links available:

- Colorado Criminal Defense Bar
- Rocky Mountain Mineral Law Foundation
- Statutes - Cases - Rules - etc.
- Colorado Law By Practice Area
- Colorado Government
- Law related on-line systems in Colorado
- Colo-Law Listserv - Information about colo-law and list participants
- Directory - E-mail directory of Colorado lawyers
- Homepages - Colorado lawyers and firms
- Employment Postings - Lawyers and legal support

PROVIDER: Colorado Legal Alliance
EMAIL: jeffmcc@usa.net
URL: http://usa.net/cololaw/index.htm

COLORADO BAR ASSOCIATION

DESCRIPTION: This home page for the Colorado Bar Association, the first bar association to enter the Web, has information about itself, its newsletter, and public resources featuring such items as "How to Choose and Use a Lawyer," FAQS from Legal Lines, and educational materials available from the association.

URL: http://www.usa.net/cobar/index.htm

DOCUMENT CITATIONS

DESCRIPTION: The Colorado Alliance of Research Libraries (CARL.i.CARL;) maintains a network of databases including a searchable collection of Colorado state government publication titles. The publications listed come from all Colorado statutory government agencies including the General Assembly, Governor's Office, Supreme Court. This is essentially a citation database, searchable by title, series, or call number.

URL: telnet://pac.carl.org
then choose:

- PAC
- VT100
- Other Library Systems
- CARL Corp Network Libraries - Western US
- Colorado State Government Publications

CONNECTICUT

STATE HOME PAGE

DESCRIPTION: The Government and Law category includes the following links:

- Historical Information & Documents
- Connecticut Legislators' E-Mail Directory (Table version)
- Connecticut Legislative Guide
- Connecticut Towns, Cities, and Boroughs
- Connecticut Judicial Information
- Connecticut Public & Special Acts

PROVIDER: Connecticut State University
EMAIL: ctwww@www.ctstateu.edu.
URL: http://www.ctstateu.edu/state.html

LEGISLATIVE BRANCH

CONSTITUTION

DESCRIPTION: Use this site to retrieve full text of the 1876 State Constitution, as amended to 1992.

PROVIDER: Connecticut State University
EMAIL: ctwww@www.ctstateu.edu
URL: http://www.ctstateu.edu/state/historical/ct_const.html

LEGISLATIVE BILLS

DESCRIPTION: Summaries and full text of Public Acts from 1994 are available here.

PROVIDER: Connecticut State University
EMAIL: ctwww@www.ctstateu.edu.
URL: http://www.ctstateu.edu/state/public_acts/public_acts.html

CONNECTICUT STATE SENATE DEMOCRATS

DESCRIPTION: This site provides information on each of the Connecticut's 17 Democratic state senators: their current press releases, bios, and policy statements. Additionally, there is an interactive issues survey here that provides, information on legislative committees and procedure.

URL: http://www.senatedems.state.ct.us/

DELAWARE

STATE HOME PAGE

DESCRIPTION: The Government category provides contact directories for many state officials.

PROVIDER: Delaware Office of Information Systems
EMAIL: webmaster@ois.state.de.us
URL: http://www.state.de.us/

CONSTITUTION

DESCRIPTION: Article I (Bill of Rights) of the 1897 Constitution of Delaware, as amended to 1974 can be found here.

PROVIDER: HarborNet
CONTACT: Dan Rubin
ADDRESS: 4810 Pt Fosdick Dr. NW, Gig Harbor, WA 98335
PHONE: (206) 858-8839
EMAIL: support@harbornet.com
URL: http://www.harbornet.com/rights/delaware.txt

LEGISLATION

DESCRIPTION: Recent legislation signed by the governor.

PROVIDER: Delaware Office of Information Systems
EMAIL: webmaster@ois.state.de.us
URL: http://www.state.de.us/govern/governor/signed.htm

DISTRICT OF COLUMBIA

GOVERNMENT CENTER

DESCRIPTION: Information about the city is available at this site, including text and status of DC statehood legislation.

PROVIDER: The National Capital Area Public URL Network (CapURL is a nonprofit organization)
ADDRESS: 2002 G St. Street, N.W., Washington, DC 20052
PHONE: (202) 994-4245
FAX: (202) 994-2317
EMAIL: cap.gwu.org
URL: telnet://cap.gwu.edu
LOGIN: guest
PASSWORD: visitor
go dc

FLORIDA

STATE HOME PAGE

DESCRIPTION: The Florida Communities Network connects Florida for the purpose of economic development and government efficiency.

PROVIDER: Technology Resource Center in Tallahassee
EMAIL: ruddj@dms.state.fl.us
URL: http://fcn.state.fl.us
URL: http://www.state.fl.us

LEGISLATIVE BRANCH

CONSTITUTION

DESCRIPTION: The entire Constitution of Florida, as revised in 1968 and amended to 1975 is at this site.

PROVIDER: Florida State University
URL: http://garnet.acns.fsu.edu/~w870g003/flconst.html

LEGISLATIVE HOME PAGE

DESCRIPTION: Legislator directory, Hot Issues during upcoming legislative session, legislative committee membership, legislative calendar, bills, statutes, etc.

PROVIDER: Florida State University
URL: http://garnet.acns.fsu.edu/~w870g003/

LEGISLATIVE BILLS

DESCRIPTION: These are the (searchable) bills introduced in the Florida House and Senate during the last session.

PROVIDER: Florida State University
URL: http://garnet.acns.fsu.edu/~w870g003/bill.html
URL: http://www.scri.fsu.edu/fla-leg/bills/

LEGISLATIVE RULES

DESCRIPTION: This link provides House and Senate Rules of procedure.

PROVIDER: Florida State University
URL: http://garnet.acns.fsu.edu/~w870g003/documents.html

LOBBYISTS

DESCRIPTION: This site enables you to view, search, and download lists of registered lobbyists by name or affiliation.

PROVIDER: Florida State University
URL: http://garnet.acns.fsu.edu/~w870g003/lobby/lobby.html

STATUTES

DESCRIPTION: Searchable full text of statutes from 1993 are available here.

PROVIDER: Legislative Data Center, a division of the Joint Legislative Management Committee of the Florida Legislature
EMAIL: fla-leg@wane-leon-mail.scri.fsu.edu
URL: http://www.scri.fsu.edu/fla-leg/statutes/

JUDICIAL BRANCH

STATE SUPREME COURT

DESCRIPTION: The Judicial Online Super Highway User Access System (JOSHUA) is Florida's statewide judicial information system. It provides links to many judicial branch departments, and information sources, including:

- Legislation Affecting the Court System
- Administrative Home Page
- Family/Juvenile Courts Home Page
- Criminal Home Page
- Alternative Dispute Resolution
- District Courts of Appeal

PROVIDER: The Office of the State Courts Administrator at the Florida Supreme Court
URL: http://justice.courts.state.fl.us/

SUPREME COURT OPINIONS

DESCRIPTION: Here you will find full-text opinions since September 1995, searchable by party, month of decision and keyword.

PROVIDER: The University of Florida College of Law, in cooperation with the Supreme Court of Florida
URL: http://nersp.nerdc.ufl.edu/~lawinfo/flsupct/index.html

FLORIDA DEPARTMENT OF REVENUE

DESCRIPTION: Useful collection of information, including:

- The DOR Abbreviated Tax Guide
- Registering a Business in Florida
- Registering a Non-Profit Organization in Florida
- Avoid Top 5 Registration and Filing Errors

URL: http://fcn.state.fl.us/dor/revenue.html

EXECUTIVE BRANCH

ATTORNEY GENERAL OPINIONS

DESCRIPTION: The Florida Attorney General's office has launched a Web site that includes attorney general opinions, and frequently asked questions and answers.

URL: http://legal.firn.edu/agweb.html

OTHER FLORIDA MATERIAL

FLORIDA LAWYERS MAILING LIST

DESCRIPTION: This forum was established for Florida lawyers to exchange information about their areas of practice and availability for referrals. Subscribe by sending email to law@pd.net. In the body of your message type: subscribe fl-law, your name, your Florida Bar # or law school attended.

PROVIDER: George Little, Esq.
PHONE: (904) 526-5316
EMAIL: law@pd.net
URL: http://tally.gulfnet.com/user_pages/fl_law/fllawpg.htm

GEORGIA

STATE HOME PAGE

DESCRIPTION: Government agency links include:

- Georgia House of Representatives
- Department of Administrative Services
- Criminal Justice Technical Services

- Department of Archives and History
- Department of Audits
- Department of Corrections
- Department of Natural Resources

URL: http://www.state.ga.us/

CONSTITUTION

DESCRIPTION: This is a searchable version of the Constitution (effective as of 1983).

PROVIDER: Emory University School of Law
URL: http://www.law.emory.edu/GEORGIA/gaconst.html

HOUSE OF REPRESENTATIVES

DESCRIPTION: This link is to the House member directory.

URL: http://www.State.Ga.US/House/

HAWAII

STATE HOME PAGE

DESCRIPTION: This Web page provides information regarding the legal foundation for the restoration of Hawaiian independence, along with cultural perspectives from the people of Hawaii. The site also features links with other Hawaii, Sovereignty, and Indigenous resources.

PROVIDER: Executive Office Nation of Hawaii
ADDRESS: PO Box 80, Waimanalo, Hawaii
PHONE: (808) 259-5049 or (808) 259-7152
FAX: (808) 259-9542
EMAIL: exec@hawaii-nation.org
URL: http://www.aloha.net/nation/hawaii-nation.html
URL: http://www.hawaii.gov/

CONSTITUTION

DESCRIPTION: This site provides the preamble and article I (Bill of Rights) of the Constitution of Hawaii, as amended to 1968.

PROVIDER: HarborNet
CONTACT: Dan Rubin
ADDRESS: 4810 Pt Fosdick Dr. NW, Gig Harbor, WA 98335
PHONE: (206) 858-8839
EMAIL: support@harbornet.com
URL: http://www.harbornet.com/rights/hawaii.txt

DEPARTMENT OF TAXATION

DESCRIPTION: Links include:
- Tax Information Releases
- Hawaii Taxpayers Bill of Rights
- Outline of the Hawaii Tax System
- Tax Forms and Instructions

PROVIDER: Department of Taxation
ADDRESS: 830 Punchbowl Street, Room 22, Honolulu, HI 96813
URL: http://www.hawaii.gov/icsd/tax/tax.html

HAWAII RESOURCE LIBRARY

DESCRIPTION: Hawaiian history, culture, art, myths, legal documents, photos, ethnoarchaeology, genealogies, religion, biology, biographies, opinions, and much more.

PROVIDER: Hoo Mau Hala O Ku Inc.
ADDRESS: Pupukea Ahupua'a-O'ahu, Box 309, Haleiwa, ISNOH 96712, Kingdom of Hawai'i
EMAIL: monet@aloha.net
PHONE: (808) 638-8934
URL: http://hawaii-shopping.com./~sammonet/hrlhome.html

IDAHO

STATE HOME PAGE

DESCRIPTION: Links include:
- Executive Branch
- Secretary of State
- State Agencies
- State Rules & Regulations
- Judicial Branch
- Legislative Branch

PROVIDER: Information Technology Division of the Department of Administration
URL: http://www.state.id.us/

EXECUTIVE BRANCH

STATE AGENCIES

DESCRIPTION: Links to most state agencies.

URL: http://www.state.id.us/state.html

STATE AGENCY RULES AND REGS

DESCRIPTION: Idaho administrative bulletins, rules and regulations organized according to administrative agency.

PROVIDER: Division of Statewide Administrative Rules
CONTACT: Nick Powers
EMAIL: npowers@sco.state.id.us
PHONE: (208) 334-3577
URL: http://www.state.id.us/apa/apaindex.html

LEGISLATIVE BRANCH

CONSTITUTION

DESCRIPTION: Preamble and article I (Declaration of Rights) of the Constitution of Idaho, as amended to 1975.

PROVIDER: HarborNet
CONTACT: Dan Rubin
ADDRESS: 4810 Pt Fosdick Dr. NW, Gig Harbor, WA 98335
PHONE: (206) 858-8839
EMAIL: support@harbornet.com
URL: http://www.harbornet.com/rights/idaho.txt

LEGISLATIVE HOME PAGE

DESCRIPTION: Includes bill search, bill text & history, committee agendas, legislative calendars, member directory, procedural rules, etc.

URL: http://www.state.id.us/legislat/legislat.html

JUDICIAL BRANCH

JUDICIAL HOME PAGE

Links include:

- Idaho Court News Releases
- Idaho Supreme Court Opinions (searchable)
- Idaho Court of Appeals Opinions (searchable)
- State of Idaho Rules Amendments
- State of Idaho Judicial-Administrative Calendar of Events
- State of Idaho Mediator's List
- State of Idaho Judicial Staff Directory

PROVIDER: Idaho Supreme Court Technology Committee
CONTACT: Mary Fowler, Information Systems
ADDRESS: PO Box 83720, Boise, ID 83720-0101
PHONE: (208) 334-2850
URL: http://www.state.id.us/judicial/judicial.html

ILLINOIS

STATE HOME PAGE

DESCRIPTION: Links include: agencies, legislative info, capitol.

URL: http://www.state.il.us/

CONSTITUTION

DESCRIPTION: Preamble and article I (Declaration of Rights) of the Constitution of Illinois, as amended to 1970.

PROVIDER: HarborNet
CONTACT: Dan Rubin
ADDRESS: 4810 Pt Fosdick Dr. NW, Gig Harbor, WA 98335
PHONE: (206) 858-8839
EMAIL: support@harbornet.com
URL: http://www.harbornet.com/rights/illinois.txt

FREEDOM OF INFORMATION ACT

DESCRIPTION: The Illinois Legislature passed this law (ch. 116, par.201) in 1983.

PROVIDER: Office of the Secretary of State, Rhode Island State Archives
ADDRESS: 337 Westminster Street, Providence, RI
PHONE: (401) 277-2353
EMAIL: tslavin@archives.state.ri.us
URL: gopher://archives.state.ri.us:70/00/NAGARA/Records%20Laws/Illinois

NUCLEAR SAFETY LEGISLATION

DESCRIPTION: This directory contains Illinois Department of Nuclear Safety statutes and regulations.

URL: gopher://wiretap.spies.com:70/11/Gov/US-State/Illinois

ILLINOIS ENVIRONMENTAL PROTECTION AGENCY

URL: http://www.epa.state.il.us/

STATE TAX FORMS

DESCRIPTION: From this site you can download Illinois tax forms, instructions, informational bulletins and publications. In addition, the site provides info on sales and use tax, registration, and appeals.

PROVIDER: Illinois Department of Revenue and University of Chicago
URL: http://http.bsd.uchicago.edu/~idor/

INDIANA

STATE HOME PAGE

DESCRIPTION: Links include:

- Indiana Press Releases and Announcements
- Subject Index of Access Indiana Information Network
- Index by State Agencies and Commissions
- Community Networks across Indiana

URL: http://www.state.in.us/

STATE BAR ASSOCIATION

DESCRIPTION: This site includes an excellent centralized collection of Indiana law, including court opinions, statutes and regulations, and the Indiana Continuing Legal Education Forum.

PROVIDER: Indiana State Bar Association
ADDRESS: Indiana Bar Center, 230 E. Ohio St., Indianapolis, IN 46204-2119
PHONE: (317) 639-5465 or (800) 266-2581
EMAIL: isbaadmin@inbar.org
URL: http://www.iquest.net/isba/

COURT DECISIONS

DESCRIPTION: In cooperation with the Indiana Supreme Court, the Indiana University School of Law-Bloomington has announced the publication of all Indiana appellate opinions on the Internet. (This includes the Indiana Supreme Court, the Indiana Court of Appeals and the Indiana Tax Court.) Coverage began January 1, 1995. Indiana Supreme Court opinions are current; other courts should be current soon. Opinions are available in hypertext format, in ASCII and in the WordPerfect 6.0 format used by the courts. Biographical information about the current Supreme Court justices and historical information about the court is also provided.

URL: http://www.law.indiana.edu/law/incourts/incourts.html

CONSTITUTION

DESCRIPTION: Preamble and article I (Declaration of Rights) of the Constitution of Indiana, as amended to 1972.

PROVIDER: HarborNet
CONTACT: Dan Rubin
ADDRESS: 4810 Pt Fosdick Dr. NW, Gig Harbor, WA 98335
PHONE: (206) 858-8839
EMAIL: support@harbornet.com
URL: http://www.harbornet.com/rights/indiana.txt

STATE CODE

DESCRIPTION: This site links to the state code, state legislative bills, the state constitution, and the Indiana Uniform Fraudulent Transfer Act

PROVIDER: The Indiana University School of Law, Bloomington, IN
CONTACT: Will Sadler, Director of Electronic Legal Publishing
EMAIL: will@polecat.law.indiana.edu
URL: http://www.law.indiana.edu/law/in.html

IOWA

STATE HOME PAGE

DESCRIPTION: Links include:

- The Secretary of State's Home Page
- The Redbook: your Representatives, our Constitution and more!
- The State Library 'Gazebo' and a list of other State's Libraries
- Other Iowa Information Directories

URL: http://www.state.ia.us/

CONSTITUTION

DESCRIPTION: Preamble and article I (Bill of Rights) of the Constitution of Iowa.

PROVIDER: HarborNet
CONTACT: Dan Rubin
ADDRESS: 4810 Pt Fosdick Dr. NW, Gig Harbor, WA 98335
PHONE: (206) 858-8839

EMAIL: support@harbornet.com
URL: http://www.harbornet.com/rights/iowa.txt

LEGISLATION

DESCRIPTION: This legislative site, maintained by the Iowa Legislative News Service, contains legislative bills, General Assembly documents, and legal opinions from the Iowa Supreme Court and the Court of Appeals. Nice image of the State House!

URL: http://ialaw.giant.net/

LEGISLATURE

DESCRIPTION: This site links to current info from the Iowa Legislature, state budget, and state agencies.

URL: http://www/netins.net/showcase/IPTN/

KANSAS

CONSTITUTION

DESCRIPTION: Preamble and Bill of Rights of the Constitution of Kansas as amended to 1975.

PROVIDER: HarborNet
CONTACT: Dan Rubin
ADDRESS: 4810 Pt Fosdick Dr. NW, Gig Harbor, WA 98335
PHONE: (206) 858-8839
EMAIL: support@harbornet.com
URL: http://www.harbornet.com/rights/kansas.txt

STATE AGENCY AND LEGISLATIVE DATA

DESCRIPTION: The Information Network of Kansas (INK) provides access to Kansas' motor vehicle records, corporation database, a legislative bill tracking system, and several other substantive services. Note: INK is a fee-based service. A password is required for full access.

PROVIDER: Information Network of Kansas
PHONE: 800) 452-6727
URL: http://www.state.la.us/

KENTUCKY

STATE HOME PAGE

URL: http://www.state.ky.us/

LEGISLATURE

DESCRIPTION: Links include:

- The Legislative Process
- Schedules & Visitor Information
- Who's Who
- Organization & Administration
- LRC Services
- Legislation
- Other KY LRC & Gen. Assembly Resources

URL: http://www.lrc.state.ky.us/

CONSTITUTION

DESCRIPTION: The first URL, provides access to the preamble and Bill of Rights of the Constitution of Kentucky as amended to 1980. The second URL provides hypertext access to all 263 sections of the constitution.

PROVIDER: HarborNet
CONTACT: Dan Rubin
ADDRESS: 4810 Pt Fosdick Dr. NW, Gig Harbor, WA 98335
PHONE: (206) 858-8839
EMAIL: support@harbornet.com
URL: http://www.harbornet.com/rights/kentucky.txt
URL: http://www.lrc.state.ky.us/const/listsec1.htm

LOUISIANA

STATE HOME PAGE

PROVIDER: Division of Administration
CONTACT: Randy Walker
EMAIL: rwalker@doa.state.la.us
URL: http://www.state.la.us

CONSTITUTION

DESCRIPTION: Preamble and article I (Declaration of

Rights) of the Constitution of Louisiana as amended to 1975.

PROVIDER: HarborNet
CONTACT: Dan Rubin
ADDRESS: 4810 Pt Fosdick Dr. NW, Gig Harbor, WA 98335
PHONE: (206) 858-8839
EMAIL: support@harbornet.com
URL: http://www.harbornet.com/rights/louisana.txt

MAINE

STATE HOMEPAGE

DESCRIPTION: Maintained by the Office of Information Services, the Maine Page includes pointers to state and quasi-state agencies, resources of interest to tourists, and other Maine-based WWW sites. Of note, the site includes a gateway to the Web-servers of other states that allows users to navigate from state to state by selecting from a U.S. map.

URL: http://www.state.me.us

CONSTITUTION

DESCRIPTION: Preamble and Article I (Declaration of Rights) of the Constitution of Maine as amended to 1973.

PROVIDER: HarborNet
CONTACT: Dan Rubin
ADDRESS: 4810 Pt Fosdick Dr. NW, Gig Harbor, WA 98335
PHONE: (206) 858-8839
EMAIL: support@harbornet.com
URL: http://www.harbornet.com/rights/maine.txt

MARYLAND

STATE HOME PAGE

DESCRIPTION: Maryland has put a good deal of info on the Net. This site, known as the Maryland Electronic Capital offers:

- Governor's Office (press releases and other info from the governor)
- Maryland State Government links
- Maryland Counties and Cities links
- SAILOR, Legislative info

URL: http://www.mec.state.md.us/mec/

CONSTITUTION

DESCRIPTION: Declaration of Rights of the Constitution of Maryland of 1867.

PROVIDER: HarborNet
CONTACT: Dan Rubin
ADDRESS: 4810 Pt Fosdick Dr. NW, Gig Harbor, WA 98335
PHONE: (206) 858-8839
EMAIL: support@harbornet.com
URL: http://www.harbornet.com/rights/maryland.txt

MASSACHUSETTS

STATE HOME PAGE

DESCRIPTION: Includes access to many executive branch agencies.

URL: http://www.magnet.state.ma.us/

BANKRUPTCY DECISIONS

DESCRIPTION: This site enables searching of the full text of all published decisions of the United States Bankruptcy Court for the District of Massachusetts from January 1, 1995.

PROVIDER: Boston law firm of Craig and Macauley
EMAIL: cmpc@ultranet.com
ADDRESS: Federal Reserve Plaza, 600 Atlantic Avenue, Boston, MA 02210
PHONE: (617) 367-9500
URL: http://prospex.com/craig-macauley/bankruptcy.html

LEGISLATURE

DESCRIPTION: This site provides searchable access (via key word and bill number) to bill history information on legislation filed in the House and Senate. This information is updated weekly.

URL: http://www.magnet.state.ma.us/legis/ltsform.htm

CONSTITUTION

DESCRIPTION: Declaration of Rights of the Constitution of Massachusetts.

PROVIDER: HarborNet
CONTACT: Dan Rubin
ADDRESS: 4810 Pt Fosdick Dr. NW, Gig Harbor, WA 98335
PHONE: (206) 858-8839
EMAIL: support@harbornet.com
URL: http://www.harbornet.com/rights/massachu.txt
URL: http://www.magnet.state.ma.us/legis/const.htm

STATE TAX FORMS

DESCRIPTION: Forms are available in Adobe Acrobat format. Publications available include:

- A Guide to Estate Taxes
- A Guide to Withholding of Taxes on Wages
- Should You Be Paying Estimated Taxes?
- Taxpayer Advisory Bulletin, June 1995
- Taxpayer Advisory Bulletin, September 1995
- Taxpayer Advisory Bulletin, December 1995

URL: http://www.magnet.state.ma.us/dor/taxform.htm
URL: http://www.scubed.com/tax/state/1994/ma_forms/

MICHIGAN

STATE HOME PAGE

DESCRIPTION: Links include:

- Executive Branch
- Governor's Office
- First Lady's Office
- Secretary of State's Office
- Other Departments and Agencies
- The Legislative Branch
- House of Representatives
- Senate

URL: http://www.migov.state.mi.us/

STATE INFORMATION

DESCRIPTION: An assortment of state data are available at this site, including the roster of Michigan's congressional and state legislative personnel, county profiles, and gross state product data. Links include:

- Census Data for Michigan
- Federal Programs for Michigan
- Michigan Congressional Information
- Michigan County Profiles
- Michigan Governor's Office
- Michigan Legislature
- Michigan's Congressional Delegation

PROVIDER: University of Michigan
EMAIL: timothy@umich.edu
URL: gopher://una.hh.lib.umich.edu:70/11/socsci/poliscilaw/michres

CONSTITUTION

DESCRIPTION: Preamble and article I (Declaration of Rights) of the Constitution of Michigan as amended to 1972.

PROVIDER: HarborNet
CONTACT: Dan Rubin
ADDRESS: 4810 Pt Fosdick Dr. NW, Gig Harbor, WA 98335
PHONE: (206) 858-8839
EMAIL: support@harbornet.com
URL: http://www.harbornet.com/rights/michigan.txt

LEGAL UPDATE

DESCRIPTION: Recent updates in state law, amended court rules, etc. Links include:

- State of the Law 1995
- Supreme Court Orders
- Administrative Orders
- Highlights of Recent Legislation
- Focus on Michigan Practice

PROVIDER: State Bar of Michigan, Institute of Continuing Legal Education
ADDRESS: The Michael Franck Building, 306 Townsend St., Lansing, MI 48933
PHONE: (517) 372-9030
URL: http://www.umich.edu/~icle/

MINNESOTA

STATE HOME PAGE

DESCRIPTION: Known as North Star, this government site links to the various areas of government (executive, legislative and judicial).

PROVIDER: State government (various offices)
EMAIL: northstar@state.mn.us
URL: http://www.state.mn.us/

LEGISLATURE

DESCRIPTION: Links include:

- Minnesota House of Representatives
- Minnesota Senate
- Legislation and Bill Tracking
- Current Session Schedules
- Minnesota Statutes and Minnesota Session Laws
- Joint Legislative Departments and Commissions

PROVIDER: Minnesota Legislative Reference Library
EMAIL: www@library.leg.state.mn.us
URL: http://www.leg.state.mn.us/

CONSTITUTION

DESCRIPTION: Preamble and article I (Bill of Rights) of the Constitution of Minnesota as amended to 1974.

PROVIDER: HarborNet
CONTACT: Dan Rubin
ADDRESS: 4810 Pt Fosdick Dr. NW, Gig Harbor, WA 98335
PHONE: (206) 858-8839
EMAIL: support@harbornet.com
URL: http://www.harbornet.com/rights/minnesot.txt

TAX FORMS

DESCRIPTION: The Minnesota Department of Revenue, Communications Division is the source of this extensive collection of state tax forms and publications.

PROVIDER: Maxwell Laboratories
EMAIL: tax-help@scubed.com.
URL: http://www.scubed.com/tax/state/1994/mn_forms/mn_index.html

MISSISSIPPI

STATE HOME PAGE

DESCRIPTION: Links include:

- Department of Economic and Community Development
- Department of Human Services
- Department of Insurance
- Division of Medicaid
- Legislative PEER Committee
- Office of the State Auditor

PROVIDER: State Department of Information Technology Services
EMAIL: webmaster@its.state.ms.us
URL: http://www.state.ms.us/

CONSTITUTION

DESCRIPTION: DESCRIPTION: Preamble and article 3 (Bill of Rights) of the Constitution of Mississippi as adopted 1890.

PROVIDER: HarborNet
CONTACT: Dan Rubin
ADDRESS: 4810 Pt Fosdick Dr. NW, Gig Harbor, WA 98335
PHONE: (206) 858-8839
EMAIL: support@harbornet.com
URL: http://www.harbornet.com/rights/mississi.txt

MISSOURI

STATE GOVERNMENT HOME PAGE

DESCRIPTION: Links are provided to all areas of government from this site.

PROVIDER: Missouri Office of Administration
EMAIL: bkirk1@mail.state.mo.us
URL: http://www.state.mo.us/

SUPREME COURT

DESCRIPTION: Links are provided to dockets and opinions, the Missouri Court Automation Project, and a nice collection of other state judicial branches.

PROVIDER: Office of Communications Counsel
CONTACT: Elizabeth Ketcher
PHONE: (314) 751-4144
URL: http://www.state.mo.us/sca/mosupct.htm

LEGISLATURE

DESCRIPTION: Links to

- Bill Tracking Information
- House and Senate Joint Bill Tracking
- Missouri Revised Statutes
- Missouri House of Representatives
- Missouri Senate
- Legislative Joint Committees

PROVIDER: Missouri General Assembly
EMAIL: mohinfo@services.state.mo.us
URL: http://www.house.state.mo.us/

CONSTITUTION

DESCRIPTION: Preamble and article I (Bill of Rights) of the Constitution of Missouri as revised to 1974.

PROVIDER: HarborNet
CONTACT: Dan Rubin
ADDRESS: 4810 Pt Fosdick Dr. NW, Gig Harbor, WA 98335
PHONE: (206) 858-8839
EMAIL: support@harbornet.com
URL: http://www.harbornet.com/rights/missouri.txt

ST. LOUIS BAR ASSN

DESCRIPTION: Links to regional legal and political information are available here.

PROVIDER: Small Firm section of the City Bar Association
URL: http://www.abelaw.com/bamsl/sasfirm

MONTANA

CONSTITUTION

DESCRIPTION: Preamble and article II (Declaration of Rights) of the Constitution of Montana as ratified 1972.

PROVIDER: HarborNet
CONTACT: Dan Rubin
ADDRESS: 4810 Pt Fosdick Dr. NW, Gig Harbor, WA 98335
PHONE: (206) 858-8839
EMAIL: support@harbornet.com
URL: http://www.harbornet.com/rights/montana.txt

NEBRASKA

STATE GOVERNMENT HOMEPAGE

DESCRIPTION: Links include:

- Nebraska Unicameral Legislature
- State Agencies
- Nebraska State Government Directory
- Search for State Agency Personnel

EMAIL: webmaster@neon.nlc.state.ne.us
URL: http://www.state.ne.us/

LEGISLATURE

DESCRIPTION: Links include:

- Senators of the Unicameral
- Directory of Senators and Committee Assignments
- Nebraska Legislative Maps
- About the Unicameral Legislature
- Speaker's Office
- Bills and Other Current Legislative Documents
- Clerk of the Legislature
- Legislative Fiscal Office
- Legislative Ombudsman

EMAIL: webmaster@unicam3.lcs.state.ne.us
URL: http://unicam1.lcs.state.ne.us/

CONSTITUTION

DESCRIPTION: Preamble and article I (Bill of Rights) of the Constitution of Nebraska as of 1875.

PROVIDER: HarborNet
CONTACT: Dan Rubin
ADDRESS: 4810 Pt Fosdick Dr. NW, Gig Harbor, WA 98335
PHONE: (206) 858-8839
EMAIL: support@harbornet.com
URL: http://www.harbornet.com/rights/nebraska.txt

BUSINESS-RELATED STATUTES

DESCRIPTION: Full text of statutes, including corporate law, intellectual property law, and employment law.

PROVIDER: University of Nebraska Institute of Agriculture and Natural Resources, in cooperation with the University Department of Economic Development
CONTACT: Steve Williams
EMAIL: stevew@ded1.ded.state.ne.us
ADDRESS: 205 Miller Hall, Univ. of Nebraska, Lincoln, NE 65853
PHONE: (402) 472-5630
URL: gopher://liberty.uc.wlu.edu:70/11/gophers/other/United%20States%20-%20NE

- Nebraska STATUTES on ... Business Topics
  - Nebraska Business Corporation Laws
  - Nebraska Franchise Practices Act
  - Nebraska Wage and Hour Statutes
  - Nebraska Wage Payment Statutes
  - Employment Security Act
  - Employee Safety Statutes
  - Nebraska Sales and Use Tax Laws
  - Nebraska Product Liability Statutes
  - Uniform Partnership Act

- Cert. of Authority Foreign Corps/LimLiab
- Invention Development Services Disclosure Act
- Nebraska Tradename Registration Statutes
- Nebraska Trademark Registration Statutes
- Nebraska Trade Secret Statutes
- Nebraska Child Labor Laws
- Nebraska Quality Child Care Act

- Index of 'Acts' contained in Nebraska Statutes
- Index of 'Funds' identified in State Statutes

STATE BAR ASSOCIATION

DESCRIPTION: Links include:

- Search NSBA Membership Database
- Continuing Legal Education
- Ethics Opinions
- Publications
- About the NSBA
- Research
- District Court Rules

URL: http://www.nol.org/legal/nsba/index.html

LEGAL NET

DESCRIPTION: Most of these services involve a transaction fee (see description of Nebrask@online below). Links include:

- Nebraska State Bar Association
- Nebraska Workers' Compensation Court Services
- Nebraska Appellate Court Access
- Nebraska Secretary of State UCC Searches
- Nebraska Secretary of State Corporation and Business Entity Searches
- Nebraska Secretary of State EFS Searches
- Nebraska Drivers License Records from Division of Motor Vehicles
- Nebraska District Court Access
- Nebraska County Court Access

PROVIDER: Nebraska Library Commission
EMAIL: doug@nol.org
ADDRESS: 1221 'N' Street, Suite 303, Lincoln, NE 68508
PHONE: (402) 471-7810 or (800) 747-8177
URL: http://www.nol.org/legal/index.html

NEBRASK@ ONLINE

DESCRIPTION: Nebrask@ Online is an information and communication network of the State of Nebraska. A subscription is required for access, at the rate of $50 per year, plus a uniform connect time fee of $0.12 per minute (no connect time fee if you access through the Internet). In addition, for certain state records, a transaction or record search fee is made. These include such items as drivers license records, UCC records and corporate records to provide equal electronic access to state, county, local, association and other public information to the citizens and businesses of Nebraska and the United States. Links include:

- Bank Net
- Legal Net
- Insurance Net
- Library Net
- State Net
- Community Net

PROVIDER: Nebraska Library Commission
EMAIL: doug@nol.org
ADDRESS: 1221 'N' Street, Suite 303, Lincoln, NE 68508
PHONE: (402) 471-7810 or (800) 747-8177
URL: http://www.nol.org/

NEVADA

CONSTITUTION

DESCRIPTION: Preamble and article I of the Constitution of Nevada as amended to 1974.

PROVIDER: HarborNet
CONTACT: Dan Rubin
ADDRESS: 4810 Pt Fosdick Dr. NW, Gig Harbor, WA 98335
PHONE: (206) 858-8839
EMAIL: support@harbornet.com
URL: http://www.harbornet.com/rights/nevada.txt

NEW HAMPSHIRE

STATE HOMEPAGE

DESCRIPTION: Links include:

- State Government Locator
- New Hampshire General Court (New Hampshire's legislative branch)
- Judicial Branch
- Local Government Resources
- Information about New Hampshire's Congressional Delegation

PROVIDER: New Hampshire State Library
URL: http://www.state.nh.us/

SUPREME COURT

DESCRIPTION: This site contains information including slip opinions, case lists, and oral argument calendars.

URL: http://www.state.nh.us/courts/supreme.htm

CONSTITUTION

DESCRIPTION: Part First (Bill of Rights) of the Constitution of New Hampshire as amended to 1980.

PROVIDER: HarborNet
CONTACT: Dan Rubin
ADDRESS: 4810 Pt Fosdick Dr. NW, Gig Harbor, WA 98335
PHONE: (206) 858-8839
EMAIL: support@harbornet.com
URL: http://www.harbornet.com/rights/newhamp.txt

STATE BAR ASSOCIATION

DESCRIPTION: Provides info about lawyer referral.

URL: http://www.nh.com/legal/nhbar/

NEW JERSEY

STATE HOME PAGE

DESCRIPTION: Links include:

- Office of the Governor
- State Departments and Agencies
- The New Jersey Legislature
- The Judiciary
- County and Municipal Government

PROVIDER: State Department of Treasury, the Office of Telecommunications and Information Systems
EMAIL: cfoley@state.nj.us
URL: http://www.state.nj.us/

CONSTITUTION

DESCRIPTION: Preamble and article I (Rights and Privileges) of the Constitution of New Jersey as amended to 1975.

PROVIDER: HarborNet
CONTACT: Dan Rubin
ADDRESS: 4810 Pt Fosdick Dr. NW, Gig Harbor, WA 98335
PHONE: (206) 858-8839
EMAIL: support@harbornet.com
URL: http://www.harbornet.com/rights/newjersy.txt

NEW MEXICO

STATE HOME PAGE

DESCRIPTION: Links include:

- Legislative Bill Locator
- Information Resources by Agency
- State Agency Phone List
- Office of the Governor
- State Legislators

CONTACT: Phyllis Vigil
EMAIL: pvigil@isd.state.nm.us
PHONE: (505)827-2943
URL: http://www.state.nm.us/

CONSTITUTION

DESCRIPTION: Preamble and article II (Bill of Rights) of the Constitution of New Mexico as adopted 1911 and amended to 1974.

PROVIDER: HarborNet
CONTACT: Dan Rubin
ADDRESS: 4810 Pt Fosdick Dr. NW, Gig Harbor, WA 98335
PHONE: (206) 858-8839
EMAIL: support@harbornet.com
URL: http://www.harbornet.com/rights/newmexio.txt

LEGALNET

DESCRIPTION: LegalNet is one of the systems that comprise TechNet, a fiber-optic network that connects state resources such as universities, government agencies and military installations. Legal resources available include URL to state motor vehicle and corporation databases, state regulations, court dockets, opinions, rules and forms, border trade information, and county and city data (tax data, county codes). The system has a nice looking (text-based) interface screen. Some of the function keys may not be mapped correctly for your keyboard. Contact customer service (see email address below) for help.
Costs: A subscription account is required to URL Legal-Net. You can subscribe as an individual or as a member of an affiliated organization (such as the New Mexico Bar Association). An individual subscription costs $50 per year, plus usage charges averaging about 40 cents per minute. Certain services entail additional charges. For example, it costs $2.50 to obtain a vehicle registration file through LegalNet.

PROVIDER: Technet
EMAIL: inettgen@technet.nm.org

PHONE: (505) 345-6555
URL: telnet://technet.nm.org

TAX FORMS

DESCRIPTION: David Carter of Los Alamos National Laboratory is the source of this collection of state personal income tax forms.

PROVIDER: Maxwell Laboratories
EMAIL: tax-help@scubed.com.
URL: http://www.scubed.com/tax/state/1994/nm_forms/nm_index.html

NEW YORK

STATE HOME PAGE

DESCRIPTION: Links to the three primary branches of state government.

PROVIDER: New York State Information Locator
ADDRESS: Room 9C71 CEC, Albany, NY 12230
EMAIL: ilsadmin@unix2.nysed.gov
URL: http://unix2.nysed.gov/ils/
URL: gopher://unix2.nysed.gov:71/11/agencies then choose:
- New York State Executive Branch/
- New York State Judicial Branch/
- New York State Legislative Branch/

LEGISLATIVE BRANCH

STATE STATUTES

DESCRIPTION: The N.Y. State Legislature provides direct telnet URL to the State Code (both consolidated and unconsolidated laws - see New York State Laws option on menu. You can read the full text of legislative bills (although note that you must know the bill number), check current bill status, and browse the sponsor's Memorandum in Support. You can also review assembly committee and floor calendars, and find out when and where public hearings are being held. The menu options are:
- Bill Information
- Assembly Calendar
- Hearing Schedule
- Committee Agenda
- New York State Laws

URL: telnet://assembly.state.ny.us
USERID: guest
PASSWORD: pw
URL: gopher://lbdc.senate.state.ny.us:70/11/.laws
URL: gopher://assembly.state.ny.us/1

LEGISLATIVE BILL AND SENATE INFORMATION

DESCRIPTION: New York has legislated (Legislative Resolution J4283, passed in July 1994) that specific information will be provided over the Internet: bills, bill memorandum, and resolutions; status of all bills; vote information; public hearing notices; consolidated and unconsolidated laws of the state; the constitution; and "other information" deemed appropriate. This site also contains basic information about the Senate, its members, and the legislative process. Here are the menu headings at this site:
- Senate member directory
- Senate legislative schedule
- Senate rules
- Senate committee membership and schedule
- Legislative public hearings
- Legislative bill information

URL: gopher://gopher.senate.state.ny.us:70/11/

CONSTITUTION

DESCRIPTION: Preamble and article I (Bill of Rights) of the Constitution of New York as amended to 1985.

PROVIDER: HarborNet
CONTACT: Dan Rubin
ADDRESS: 4810 Pt Fosdick Dr. NW, Gig Harbor, WA 98335
PHONE: (206) 858-8839
EMAIL: support@harbornet.com
URL: http://www.harbornet.com/rights/newyork.txt

JUDICIAL BRANCH

STATE COURTS

DESCRIPTION: Links include:
- New York State Court of Appeals
- New York State Court of Claims
- New York State Supreme Court
- Office of Court Administration
- Directory of Superior, Lower and Family Courts in New York State

PROVIDER: New York State Library
ADDRESS: Cultural Education Center, Empire State Plaza, Albany, NY 12230
CONTACT: Robert Trombly
PHONE: (518) 473-6841

EMAIL: rtrombly%sedofis@vm1.nysed.gov
URL: gopher://unix2.nysed.gov:71/1/agencies/judicial

STATE COURT OF APPEALS

DESCRIPTION: Decisions from New York's highest court. The Cornell URL site offers decisions dating from January 1993. Cornell has done a nice job of indexing by topic, by party name, and by year.

PROVIDER: Cornell Law School
URL: http://www.law.cornell.edu:80/ny/ctap/overview.html

STATUTES GOVERNING JURISDICTION OF THE COURT

DESCRIPTION: Article 56 of the New York Civil Practice Law & Rules is titled Appeals to the Court of Appeals. This site offers full text of the statute.

PROVIDER: Cornell Law School
URL: http://www.law.cornell.edu:80/ny/ctap/overview.html

MISCELLANEOUS

NYSDOC

DESCRIPTION: NYSDOC is a mailing list for New York State government documentsand information issues.

CONTACT: David Gosda, New York State Library
EMAIL: david@unix2.nysed.gov
PHONE: (518) 473-6297
URL: To subscribe, send a message to listproc@unix2.nysed.gov with message "subscribe NYSDOC firstname lastname". To post messages, send to nysdoc@unix2.nysed.gov

STATE BAR ASSOCIATION

PROVIDER: State bar
EMAIL: garys@nysba.org
URL: http://www.nysba.org/

NEW YORK TRIAL LAWYERS

DESCRIPTION: This site provides brief descriptions of publications and services it offers.

URL: http://www.nystla.org

NORTH CAROLINA

STATE HOME PAGE

DESCRIPTION: Extensive collection of links to state government sites, including bill status information from the North Carolina General Assembly.

EMAIL: www@sips.state.nc.us
URL: http://www.sips.state.nc.us/

CENTRAL NORTH CAROLINA SITE

DESCRIPTION: This site provides URL to the resources of the Institute of Government, the largest and most diversified of the university-based governmental training and research organizations in the United States. NCINFO was developed in partnership with the North Carolina Association of County Commissioners and the North Carolina League of Municipalities. From here, you can connect to many useful local, state, and federal government information resources.

PROVIDER: The Institute of Government
ADDRESS: CB # 3330 Knapp Building, The University of North Carolina, Chapel Hill, NC 27599-3330
CONTACT: Pat Langelier
EMAIL: pal.iog@mhs.unc.edu, gophermaster@ncinfo.iog.unc.edu
URL: http://ncinfo.iog.unc.edu

EXECUTIVE BRANCH

STATE AGENCIES

DESCRIPTION: This site provides links to the following state agencies:

- Center for Geographic Information and Analysis (CGIA)
- Department of Agriculture
- Department of Commerce
- Department of Insurance (DOI)
- Department of Public Instruction (DPI)
- Employment Security Commission (ESC)
- North Carolina General Assembly
- Information Resource Management Commission (IRMC)
- North Carolina Information Highway (NCIH)
- Office of State Budget and Management (OSBM)
- Office of State Personnel Job Vacancies
- State Information Processing Services (SIPS)
- State Library

URL: http://www.sips.state.nc.us/nchome.html

LEGISLATIVE BRANCH

LEGISLATIVE BILLS

DESCRIPTION: Bills in the North Carolina General Assembly are drafted using a word processing format called MASS11. The documents at this site are in the MASS11 format. Therefore, to read these bills, you will need to convert the text into a format readable by your word processor. Available documents include text of bills, and bill history reports.

PROVIDER: North Carolina State Legislature
EMAIL: leginfo@ftp.legislature.state.nc.us
CONTACT: Nassib Nassar
PHONE: (919) 248-9209
EMAIL: mikev@mcnc.org
URL: gopher://ftp.legislature.state.nc.us/

CONSTITUTION

DESCRIPTION: Preamble and article I (Declaration of Rights) of the Constitution of North Carolina as amended to 1975.

PROVIDER: HarborNet
CONTACT: Dan Rubin
ADDRESS: 4810 Pt Fosdick Dr. NW, Gig Harbor, WA 98335
PHONE: (206) 858-8839
EMAIL: support@harbornet.com
URL: http://www.harbornet.com/rights/no-carol.txt

JUDICIAL BRANCH

COURT OF APPEALS DECISIONS

DESCRIPTION: Full text of opinions dating back to November 1994.

PROVIDER: North Carolina Government News Service
URL: http://www.nando.net/insider/appeals/appeals.html

NC SUPREME COURT OPINIONS

DESCRIPTION: Full text of opinions dating back to November 1994.

PROVIDER: North Carolina Government News Service
URL: http://www.nando.net/insider/supreme/supco.html
URL: ftp://SunSite.unc.edu/pub/Politics/nc-supreme-court

NORTH DAKOTA

STATE HOME PAGE

DESCRIPTION: Includes links to government agencies.

EMAIL: rutherfo@pioneer.state.nd.us
URL: http://www.state.nd.us/

LEGISLATIVE BILLS

DESCRIPTION: Summaries and full text of current bills, and legislative committee hearing schedules.

PROVIDER: North Dakota State University
CONTACT: Marty Hoag, NDSU ITS
PHONE: (701) 231-8639 or (701) 231-868
EMAIL: hoag@VM1.NoDak.EDU
URL: http://rrnet.com:80/ndgovt/

CONSTITUTION

DESCRIPTION: Preamble and article I (Declaration of Rights) of the Constitution of North Dakota as amended to 1973.

PROVIDER: HarborNet
CONTACT: Dan Rubin
ADDRESS: 4810 Pt Fosdick Dr. NW, Gig Harbor, WA 98335
PHONE: (206) 858-8839
EMAIL: support@harbornet.com
URL: http://www.harbornet.com/rights/nodakota.txt

OHIO

STATE GOVERNMENT HOME PAGE

DESCRIPTION: This site offers government news stories from The Daily Reporter, and includes the following links:

- State Library of Ohio
- General Services Administration
- Ohio Environmental Protection Agency
- Public Utilities Commission of Ohio
- Ohio Accountancy Board
- Ohio Online Export Directory
- Search the State of Ohio Employee Telephone Directory

URL: http://sddtsun.sddt.com/~columbus/Pages/govtop.html

OHIO LEGAL LINKS

DESCRIPTION: Links include:
- Central Ohio Legal News
- The Daily Reporter legal news library
- Special Series - Tort Reform: Is the System Broken?
- Bar Briefs - December/January edition online
- Legal Briefs - law-related briefs
- Columbus Bar Association
- Complete text: State of the Judiciary speech

PROVIDER: Columbus Daily Reporter
URL: http://www.sddt.com/~columbus/Pages/lawtop.html

CONSTITUTION

DESCRIPTION: Preamble and article I (Bill of Rights) of the Constitution of Ohio as amended to 1974.

PROVIDER: HarborNet
CONTACT: Dan Rubin
ADDRESS: 4810 Pt Fosdick Dr. NW, Gig Harbor, WA 98335
PHONE: (206) 858-8839
EMAIL: support@harbornet.com
URL: http://www.harbornet.com/rights/ohio.txt

LEGISLATIVE BRANCH

OHIO LEGISLATIVE AND GOVERNMENT INFORMATION

DESCRIPTION: This server contains the current Ohio Legislative and Government Directory. Links include:
- About the Legislative Directory
- Current Ohio State Government Directories (compiled by East Knox H.S.)
- Ohio House of Rep - pre 1994 election
- Ohio Senate - pre 1994 election
- State Officials

URL: gopher://gopher.osc.edu:70/11/Ohio%20Legislative%20Information/Legislative%20Information%20%26%20Directories

JUDICIAL BRANCH

CENTRAL OHIO COURTS

DESCRIPTION: Links include:
- Franklin County Common Pleas Court Trial Assignments
- Franklin County Judges Bios
- Ohio Supreme Court Justices Bios

PROVIDER: Columbus Daily Reporter
URL: http://www.sddt.com/~columbus/Pages/lawtop.html

SUPREME COURT

DESCRIPTION: Opinions and announcements provided in ASCII and Word 6.0 format. The second URL here provides searchable access to Ohio Supreme Court opinions.

URL: ftp://ftp.sconet.ohio.gov/ftp/
URL: http://winslo.ohio.gov/stgvjud.html

OHIO COURT OPINIONS

DESCRIPTION: URL to Ohio State Supreme Court opinions and Ohio 8th District Court opinions.

PROVIDER: Youngstown University Free-net
URL: telnet://yfn2.ysu.edu
LOGIN: visitor
then choose: The Courthouse
then choose: Ohio State Supreme Court Opinions
then choose: Ohio 8th District Court Opinions

MISCELLANEOUS

STATE LIBRARY

DESCRIPTION: This home page contains links to all state agency Web servers as well as publications and the catalog of the State Library.

URL: http://winslo.ohio.gov

COLUMBUS OHIO BAR ASSN

URL: http://www.smartpages.com/cba/index.html

OKLAHOMA

STATE GOVERNMENT HOME PAGE

DESCRIPTION: Links include:
- Oklahoma House of Representatives
- Oklahoma State Senate
- Oklahoma Court of Criminal Appeals

- Oklahoma's Congressional Delegation
- Oklahoma Tax Commission
- Oklahoma State Agencies

URL: http://www.oklaosf.state.ok.us/

OKLAHOMA DECISIONS

DESCRIPTION: Contains weekly updated Oklahoma Supreme Court, Court of Criminal Appeals, Court of Appeals and Attorney General Opinions. Also, the Oklahoma Administrative Code titles are on site.

PROVIDER: University of Oklahoma
EMAIL: pdq@mail.uoknor.edu
URL: http://www.uoknor.edu/okgov

CONSTITUTION

DESCRIPTION: Article II (Bill of Rights) of the Constitution of Oklahoma as adopted in 1907 and as amended to 1975.

PROVIDER: HarborNet
CONTACT: Dan Rubin
ADDRESS: 4810 Pt Fosdick Dr. NW, Gig Harbor, WA 98335
PHONE: (206) 858-8839
EMAIL: support@harbornet.com
URL: http://www.harbornet.com/rights/oklahoma.txt

TULSA COUNTY SHERIFF

DESCRIPTION: Provides crime-related information, including mug shots of most wanted criminals, Tulsa County crime statistics, info on the local Gangs Task Force.

PROVIDER: Tulsa County Sheriff's Office, Tulsa, Oklahoma
EMAIL: tcso@galstar.com
CONTACT: Josh McCormick
PHONE: (918) 8353655
EMAIL: jmccorm@galaxy.galstar.com
URL: gopher://gopher.galaxy.galstar.com/1/tcso

UNIVERSITY OF OKLAHOMA LAW CENTER

DESCRIPTION: This site contains information about the Law Center and library, pointers to Oklahoma resources, and a section on Native American Legal Resources.

URL: http://www.law.uoknor.edu

OREGON

STATE GOVERNMENT HOME PAGE

DESCRIPTION: Many state agency links are available here, including:
- Oregon Department of Revenue
- Oregon Secretary of State
- Criminal Justice Services Division

URL: http://www.state.or.us/governme.htm

LEGISLATURE

DESCRIPTION: Links include:
- Who's Who in the Capitol
- Legislative Measures
- Committee Information
- Information on the Legislative Process

URL: gopher://gopher.leg.state.or.us/

SELECTED LEGISLATION

DESCRIPTION: Legislation introduced by Senator Jeannette Hamby in the Sixty-Eighth Legislative Assembly.

URL: http://www.teleport.com/~senhamby/legislation.html

LEGISLATIVE BILLS

DESCRIPTION: This appears to be a selective, rather than comprehensive collection of state bills.

PROVIDER: Oregon State University
URL: gopher://gaia.ucs.orst.edu:70/11/osu-i+s/OLIS

LEGISLATIVE COMMITTEE MINUTES

DESCRIPTION: This is an experimental service providing full-text searching of the minutes of committees of the 1991 and 1993 Oregon Legislature.

PROVIDER: State Archives
URL: http://159.121.28.251/minutes.html

CONSTITUTION

DESCRIPTION: Preamble and article I (Bill of Rights) of the Constitution of Oregon.

PROVIDER: HarborNet
CONTACT: Dan Rubin
ADDRESS: 4810 Pt Fosdick Dr. NW, Gig Harbor, WA 98335
PHONE: (206) 858-8839
EMAIL: support@harbornet.com
URL: http://www.harbornet.com/rights/oregon.txt

TAX FORMS

DESCRIPTION: Information, publications, and state personal income tax forms from the state treasury department.

PROVIDER: Oregon Department of the Treasury
URL: http://www.dor.state.or.us/

PENNSYLVANIA

STATE GOVERNMENT HOME PAGE

DESCRIPTION: Links provided here to each branch of government.

EMAIL: webmaster@state.pa.us
URL: http://www.state.pa.us/government.html

EXECUTIVE BRANCH

STATE DATA CENTER

DESCRIPTION: Official source of demographic and economic information.

PROVIDER: The Pennsylvania State Data Center
ADDRESS: Penn State Harrisburg, 777 West Harrisburg Pike, Middletown, PA 17057
PHONE: (717) 948-6336
EMAIL: CMG11@psuvm.psu.edu
URL: http://howard.hbg.psu.edu/psdc/psdchome1.1.html

DEPARTMENT OF ENVIRONMENTAL RESOURCES

DESCRIPTION: Various environmental resources a vailable here.

PROVIDER: State environmental agency
EMAIL: webmaster@a1.dep.state.pa.us
URL: http://www.dep.state.pa.us/

LEGISLATIVE BRANCH

CONSTITUTION

DESCRIPTION: Full text of the Constitution of Pennsylvania.

PROVIDER: State of Pennsylvania
EMAIL: support@harbornet.com
URL: http://www.state.pa.us/PA_Constitution.html

JUDICIAL BRANCH

STATE LEGAL RESOURCES

DESCRIPTION: Links include local rules of court and pointers to Pennsylvania legislators and law firms.

PROVIDER: ERIENET, an Internet service provider in Erie, Pennsylvania
CONTACT: Dan Pastore, a partner at The McDonald Group
EMAIL: dan@erie.net
URL: http://moose.erie.net/~lawweb/

MISCELLANEOUS RESOURCES

PHILADELPHIA DIRECTORY

DESCRIPTION: This site provides an email directory for lawyers, law firms, legal associations, courts and law schools in the Philadelphia area. Since it has just debuted, current listings are thin.

URL: http://www.pond.com/~alexion/pleed.htm

RHODE ISLAND

STATE GOVERNMENT HOME PAGE

DESCRIPTION: Links to the secretary of state's and governor's online offices.

URL: http://www.ids.net/ri/gov.html

LEGISLATIVE BRANCH

ENACTED LEGISLATION

DESCRIPTION: Summaries of state laws.

URL: http://www.sec.state.ri.us/wwwenact.htm

LEGISLATIVE BILLS

DESCRIPTION: Summaries of state House and Senate bills.

URL: http://www.sec.state.ri.us/sorbills.htm

CONSTITUTION

DESCRIPTION: Preamble and article I (Declaration of Rights) of the Constitution of Rhode Island.

PROVIDER: HarborNet
CONTACT: Dan Rubin
ADDRESS: 4810 Pt Fosdick Dr. NW, Gig Harbor, WA 98335
PHONE: (206) 858-8839
EMAIL: support@harbornet.com
URL: http://www.harbornet.com/rights/r-island.txt

SELECT STATE LAWS

DESCRIPTION: The RI State Archives hold records dating from 1638 to the present. This site offers historical records, including Civil War documents, and the text of a few state laws.

PROVIDER: Office of the Secretary of State, Rhode Island State Archives
ADDRESS: 337 Westminster Street, Providence, RI
PHONE: (401) 277-2353
EMAIL: tslavin@archives.state.ri.us
URL: gopher://archives.state.ri.us

SOUTH CAROLINA

STATE GOVERNMENT HOME PAGE

DESCRIPTION: Links include:

- Governor's Office
- State Treasurer's Office
- Legislature
- State Agencies

URL: http://www.state.sc.us:80/gov.html

EXECUTIVE BRANCH

PENDING REGULATIONS

DESCRIPTION: Links include:

- Search by Regulation Document Number
- Search by Regulation Subject Matter
- Search by Promulgating Agency

URL: http://www.lpitr.state.sc.us/regs.htm

LEGISLATIVE BRANCH

LEGISLATURE HOME PAGE

DESCRIPTION: Links to statutes, bills and regulations and legislative databases.

URL: http://www.state.sc.us:80/legislature.html

NEW LAWS

DESCRIPTION: Full text of acts passed in the most recent legislative session. Following each act number are the ratification number (preceded by an "R"), the bill number (preceded by an "H" for House or an "S: for Senate), a brief description and the date the act became effective. An act will not be added to this page until it has been assigned an act number. To see the full text of an act, select the highlighted Act number.

URL: http://www.lpitr.state.sc.us/newlaws.htm

BILLS AND RESOLUTIONS

DESCRIPTION: Links include:

- Search by Bill Number
- Search by Subject Matter
- Search by Primary Sponsor
- The General Appropriations Page
- Introduced Bills - Tear Sheets

URL: http://www.lpitr.state.sc.us/legbe4.htm

CONSTITUTION

DESCRIPTION: Article I (Declaration of Rights) of the Constitution of South Carolina as revised to 1981.

PROVIDER: HarborNet
CONTACT: Dan Rubin
ADDRESS: 4810 Pt Fosdick Dr. NW, Gig Harbor, WA 98335
PHONE: (206) 858-8839
EMAIL: support@harbornet.com
URL: http://www.harbornet.com/rights/s-carol.txt

PUBLIC RECORDS ACT

DESCRIPTION: The South Carolina Governor signed into law major amendments to the state's Public Records Act in 1990.

PROVIDER: Office of the Secretary of State, Rhode Island State Archives
ADDRESS: 337 Westminster Street, Providence, RI
PHONE: (401) 277-2353
EMAIL: tslavin@archives.state.ri.us
URL: gopher://archives.state.ri.us:70/00/NAGARA/Records%20Laws/South%20Carolina

SOUTH DAKOTA

STATE GOVERNMENT HOME PAGE

DESCRIPTION: Links include:
- State Government Agencies
- Legislative Information
- Agencies Connected to Internet
- Home Pages for State Employees
- Governor's Office

URL: http://www.state.sd.us/state/overview.html

CONSTITUTION

DESCRIPTION: Preamble and article VI (Bill of Rights) of the Constitution of South Carolina as amended to 1975.

PROVIDER: HarborNet
CONTACT: Dan Rubin
ADDRESS: 4810 Pt Fosdick Dr. NW, Gig Harbor, WA 98335
PHONE: (206) 858-8839
EMAIL: support@harbornet.com
URL: http://www.harbornet.com/rights/s-dakota.txt

TENNESSEE

STATE HOMEPAGE

DESCRIPTION: Links include:
- Department of Employment Security
- Tennessee Supreme Court
- Department of Financial Institutions
- Secretary of State

PROVIDER: State Telecommunications Department
EMAIL: webmaster@mail.state.tn.us
URL: http://www.state.tn.us

SUPREME COURT

DESCRIPTION: This site provides: general information about the courts of Tennessee, and associated support agencies, commissions, and boards, listings of currently available opinions, including Court of Appeals, Court of Criminal Appeals, and Tennessee Supreme Court Opinions.

EMAIL: IB271T2@mailaoc.state.tn.us
URL: http://www.tsc.state.tn.us/

CONSTITUTION

DESCRIPTION: Article I (Declaration of Rights) of the Constitution of Tennessee.

PROVIDER: HarborNet
CONTACT: Dan Rubin
ADDRESS: 4810 Pt Fosdick Dr. NW, Gig Harbor, WA 98335
PHONE: (206) 858-8839
EMAIL: support@harbornet.com
URL: http://www.harbornet.com/rights/tennesse.txt

STATE BAR ASSOCIATION

DESCRIPTION: Several interesting sounding links here, but they're mostly limited to bar association members.

PROVIDER: Tennessee Bar Association
ADDRESS: 3622 West End Ave, Nashville, TN 37205
PHONE: (615) 383-7421
EMAIL: Info@tba.org
URL: http://www.tba.org/

TEXAS

STATE GOVERNMENT HOME PAGE

DESCRIPTION: Links include:
- Government Agencies
- Legislative Information and Legislative Server
- County and City Information and other local government
- Government Documents
- Texas Administrative Code
- General Appropriations Act
- Information for Texas State Agencies (policies, standards, resources)

PROVIDER: Texas Department of Information Services
EMAIL: webmaster@www.state.tx.us
URL: http://www.texas.gov/

EXECUTIVE BRANCH

TEXAS ADMINISTRATIVE CODE

DESCRIPTION: The Texas Secretary of State's office maintains a very current version of the complete code at this site.

PROVIDER: Secretary of State's Office
URL: http://register.sos.texas.gov:80/tac/

LEGISLATIVE BRANCH

LEGISLATURE

DESCRIPTION: This site has been created so that the public can obtain information about the Texas Legislature. Links include:

- Texas Legislation and Legislative Information
- The Texas Senate
- The Texas House of Representatives
- The Legislative Branch of Government
- Legislative Districts
- Texas Capitol Information
- Texas Constitution

PROVIDER: The Texas Legislative Council Information Systems Division
URL: gopher://capitol.tlc.texas.gov

CONSTITUTION

DESCRIPTION: The first URL will take you to the preamble and article I (Bill of Rights) of the Constitution of Texas as amended to 1969. The second URL provides access to a hypertextual version of the entire constitution, as provided by the University of Texas at Austin School of Law.

PROVIDER: HarborNet
CONTACT: Dan Rubin
ADDRESS: 4810 Pt Fosdick Dr. NW, Gig Harbor, WA 98335
PHONE: (206) 858-8839
EMAIL: support@harbornet.com
URL: http://www.harbornet.com/rights/texas.txt
URL: http://www.law.utexas.edu/library/netref/txconst/intro.html

JUDICIAL BRANCH

RULES OF CRIMINAL AND CIVIL EVIDENCE

DESCRIPTION: The Texas Rules of Criminal and Civil Evidence are available in a hypertext format.

PROVIDER: University of Texas at Austin School of Law
URL: http://www.law.utexas.edu/library/netref/texas.html

MISCELLANEOUS RESOURCES

TEXAS LAWYERS MAILING LIST

DESCRIPTION: This list has been created by research attorney Clint Sare of the Seventh Court of Appeals of Texas. It is restricted to lawyers who practice in Texas. It is requested that you include an introduction in your subscription request so that it can be distributed to therest of the list.

URL: Send the following message in the subject line to sare@arn.net: SUBSCRIBE TX-LAW

HOUSTON AREA LAW LIBRARIANS (HALL)

DESCRIPTION: The HALL home page includes a list of pointers to current officers, membership information, and news about meetings and special activities. Pointers to Texas information resources, federal information, resource finding aids, and other law-related resources on the Internet have been added.

URL: http://www.law.uh.edu/hall/

UTAH

STATE GOVERNMENT HOME PAGE

DESCRIPTION: Links include:

- Courts
- Elections
- State Agencies
- Public Education
- Higher Education
- Cities & Towns
- Counties

URL: http://www.state.ut.us/

LEGISLATIVE BRANCH

CONSTITUTION

DESCRIPTION: Preamble and article I (Declaration of Rights) of the Constitution of Utah, as amended to 1973.

PROVIDER: HarborNet
CONTACT: Dan Rubin
ADDRESS: 4810 Pt Fosdick Dr. NW, Gig Harbor, WA 98335
PHONE: (206) 858-8839
EMAIL: support@harbornet.com
URL: http://www.harbornet.com/rights/utah.txt

LEGISLATIVE BILLS

DESCRIPTION: Links from the current legislative session include:

- Bill Text Files
- Bill Status Files
- Journal Files
- Agendas
- House and Senate Schedules
- Bill Indexes

PROVIDER: Legislative Research & General Counsel
ADDRESS: 436 State Capitol, Salt Lake City, UT 84114
(801) 538-1032
EMAIL: legisweb@state.ut.us
URL: http://www.le.state.ut.us/1996/1996.HTM

STATUTES AND BILLS

DESCRIPTION: This site provides access to the unannotated, searchable Utah Code, Advance Reports, legislative bills, and info from state government agencies.

PROVIDER: University of Utah Law Library
URL: http://info.law.utah.edu/utahlink.html

JUDICIAL BRANCH

UTAH STATE COURT SYSTEM

DESCRIPTION: Links include:

- The Supreme Court
- The Court of Appeals
- District Courts
- Court Statistics
- Proposed Rule Changes
- Court Forms

EMAIL: barbaram@courtlink.utcourts.gov
URL: http://courtlink.utcourts.gov/

VERMONT

STATE HOME PAGE

URL: http://www.cit.state.vt.us/

GOVERNMENT DATA

DESCRIPTION: Search through Vermont Supreme Court opinions, session laws and current bills, Environmental Law Division decisions.

PROVIDER: Middlebury College Library
URL: http://www.middlebury.edu

STATE SUPREME COURT DECISIONS

DESCRIPTION: Full-text, searchable opinions dating to 1991 (not comprehensive) are available here.

URL: gopher://dol.state.vt.us:70/11GOPHER_ROOT3%3A%5BSUPCT%5D

CONSTITUTION

DESCRIPTION: Article 1-21 (A Declaration Of The Rights Of The Inhabitants Of The State Of Vermont) of the Constitution of Vermont.

PROVIDER: HarborNet
CONTACT: Dan Rubin
4810 Pt Fosdick Dr. NW, Gig Harbor, WA 98335
PHONE: (206) 858-8839
EMAIL: support@harbornet.com
URL: http://www.harbornet.com/rights/vermont.txt

VIRGINIA

STATE GOVERNMENT HOME PAGE

DESCRIPTION: Links include:

- Virginia state government
- Local government links of interest
- Virginia General Assembly

PROVIDER: Commonwealth of Virginia
EMAIL: aphaup.dit@state.va.us
URL: http://www.state.va.us/home/governmt.html

VIRGINIA GENERAL ASSEMBLY PAGE

DESCRIPTION: Links to legislative agencies, bills and resolutions.

URL: http://www.state.va.us/dlas/welcome.htm

LEGISLATIVE BILLS AND RESOLUTIONS

DESCRIPTION: Links include:

- Numerical Bill List
- Bill Subject Index
- General Assembly Members
- Standing Committees

URL: http://www.state.va.us/dlas/br.htm

CONSTITUTION

DESCRIPTION: Article I (Bill of Rights) of the Constitution of Virginia.

PROVIDER: HarborNet
CONTACT: Dan Rubin
ADDRESS: 4810 Pt Fosdick Dr. NW, Gig Harbor, WA 98335
PHONE: (206) 858-8839
EMAIL: support@harbornet.com
URL: http://www.harbornet.com/rights/virginia.txt

PRIVACY LAW

DESCRIPTION: This file represents various chapters of Virginia law concerned with privacy, including the Privacy Protection Act of 1976.

PROVIDER: Computer Professionals for Social Responsibility
ADDRESS: PO Box 717, Palo Alto, CA 94301
PHONE: (415) 322-3778
EMAIL: cpsr@csli.stanford.edu
URL: http://snyside.sunnyside.com/cpsr/privcy/law/va_privacy_law.txt

VIRGINIA DECLARATION OF RIGHTS

PROVIDER: The Internet Wiretap, Cupertino, CA
EMAIL: gopher@wiretap.spies.com
URL: http://wiretap.spies.com/Gopher/Gov/US-History/virginia.dec

WASHINGTON

STATE HOME PAGE

DESCRIPTION: Links include:

- Office of the Governor
- Washington State Legislature
- Washington State Courts
- Washington State Government Index
- Local and Regional Government Index

PROVIDER: State Department of Information Services
URL: http://www.wa.gov/wahome.html

LEGISLATIVE BILLS AND STATE CODE

DESCRIPTION: Via this site, the state legislature provides URL to legislative information found in bills (all versions, including session laws), amendments, bill reports, bill digests (including veto messages), bill histories, sponsor reports, roll calls on bills, legislative and committee schedules, the Revised Code of Washington (RCW), the Washington Constitution, and online informational files. The provider will update the information once daily while the legislature is in session.

PROVIDER: Legislative Service Center
ADDRESS: 2404 Chandler Court SW, Olympia, WA 985026034
EMAIL: support@leg.wa.gov
PHONE: (206) 7867725
URL: http://leginfo.leg.wa.gov

STATE COURT PAGE

DESCRIPTION: Links include:

- Washington Court Directory
- A directory of courts and addresses
- Discover how to obtain on-line access to court information in Washington State
- Court News
- Press releases and reports
- Court Forms and Instructions

PROVIDER: The Office of the Administrator for the Courts
ADDRESS: 1206 S. Quince, PO Box 41170, Olympia, WA 98504
PHONE: (360) 753-3365
URL: http://www.wa.gov/courts/home.htm

WEST VIRGINIA

CONSTITUTION

DESCRIPTION: Article III (Bill of Rights) of the Constitution of West Virginia.

PROVIDER: HarborNet
CONTACT: Dan Rubin
ADDRESS: 4810 Pt Fosdick Dr. NW, Gig Harbor, WA 98335
PHONE: (206) 858-8839
EMAIL: support@harbornet.com
URL: http://www.harbornet.com/rights/w-virgin.txt

WISCONSIN

STATE HOMEPAGE

DESCRIPTION: Links to state agencies, and local government sites.

EMAIL: wisc-web@badger.state.wi.us
URL: http://badger.state.wi.us/

CONSTITUTION

DESCRIPTION: Preamble and article I (Declaration of Rights) of the Constitution of Wisconsin as amended to 1975.

PROVIDER: HarborNet
CONTACT: Dan Rubin
ADDRESS: 4810 Pt Fosdick Dr. NW, Gig Harbor, WA 98335
PHONE: (206) 858-8839
EMAIL: support@harbornet.com
URL: http://www.harbornet.com/rights/wisconsi.txt

STATE BAR ASSOCIATION

DESCRIPTION: Links include:

- Legal Resources
- Discussion Groups
- State Bar Information
- State Bar CLE
- Legal Directories

EMAIL: webmaster@wisbar.org
URL: http://wwwdev.binc.net:470/
URL: http://www.wisbar.org

WYOMING

STATE GOVERNMENT HOME PAGE

DESCRIPTION: Links include:

- Wyoming State Government
- Wyoming State Statutes
- Proposed Bills

URL: gopher://ferret.state.wy.us/1

EXECUTIVE BRANCH

ADMINISTRATIVE RULES AND REGULATIONS

DESCRIPTION: Searchable full-text access.

URL: gopher://ferret.state.wy.us:70/11/wgov/eb/sos/arr

LEGISLATIVE BRANCH

STATE STATUTES

DESCRIPTION: Searchable access to statutes.

PROVIDER: Wyoming Department of Administration & Information
CONTACT: John Baker
PHONE: (307) 777-5083
EMAIL: gopher-h@ferret.state.wy.us
URL: gopher://ferret.state.wy.us:70/11/wgov/lb/statutes

CONSTITUTION

DESCRIPTION: Preamble and article I (Declaration of Rights) of the Constitution of Wyoming.

PROVIDER: HarborNet
CONTACT: Dan Rubin
ADDRESS: 4810 Pt Fosdick Dr. NW, Gig Harbor, WA 98335
PHONE: (206) 858-8839
EMAIL: support@harbornet.com
URL: http://www.harbornet.com/rights/wyoming.txt

LEGAL RESOURCES FOR ALL STATES

EXECUTIVE BRANCH

ENVIRONMENTAL REGULATIONS

DESCRIPTION: This fee-based site provides access to most state environmental and safety regulations.

PROVIDER: Counterpoint Publishing
EMAIL: info@counterpoint.com
URL: http://cfr.counterpoint.com/

TAX LAW COMPENDIUM

DESCRIPTION: The Villanova Center for Information Law and Policy has compiled student tax papers on this gopher server.

URL: http://ming.law.vill.edu/vill.tax.1.compen/files/student_papers/nonresat.htm

LEGISLATIVE BRANCH

NATIONAL CONFERENCE OF STATE LEGISLATURES

DESCRIPTION: This is the Web site of NCSLnet, National Conference of State Legislatures. It includes links to NCSL publications and databases.

PROVIDER: National Conference of State Legislatures
CONTACT: Doug Sacarto, NCSLnet Administrator
ADDRESS: 1560 Broadway, Suite 700, Denver, CO 80202
EMAIL: Doug.Sacarto@ncsl.org
URL: http://www.ncsl.org/

STATE CONSTITUTIONS

DESCRIPTION: The "bill of rights" portions of all constitutions are available at these sites.

PROVIDER: HarborNet
CONTACT: Dan Rubin
ADDRESS: 4810 Pt Fosdick Dr. NW, Gig Harbor, WA 98335
PHONE: (206) 858-8839
EMAIL: support@harbornet.com
URL: http://www.harbornet.com/rights/
URL: http://www.harbornet.com/rights/states.html

TELECOM LEGISLATION

DESCRIPTION: This is a list of selected 1993 state telecommunications legislation. Additionally, this site offers model resolutions for four electronic legislative issues.

PROVIDER: Center for Civic Networking (CCN)
URL: ftp://ftp.std.com/associations/civicnet

JUDICIAL BRANCH

NATIONAL CENTER FOR STATE COURTS (NCSC)

DESCRIPTION: The NCSC is an independent, nonprofit organization dedicated to the improvement of justice. Following are the headings on this home page:

- Court Technology Programs
- Research
- Institute for Court Management
- Court Services Division
- International
- Office of Government Relations
- Staff E-Mail Adresses

PROVIDER: National Center for State Courts
ADDRESS: 300 Newport Avenue, Williamsburg, VA 23185
CONTACT: webmaster@ncsc.dni.us!
URL: http://www.ncsc.dni.us/

CITATION STANDARDS

DESCRIPTION: A statebystate guide to citation styles required by the appellate courts of each state.

PROVIDER: Cornell University
URL: gopher://gopher.law.cornell.edu:70/00/other/jurisdiction/Citation%20Standards

STATE LAW COLLECTIONS

CENTRALIZED STATE LAW

DESCRIPTION: This Web site offers many legal resources for each state, in one central Internet location.

PROVIDER: Washburn University Law School, Topeka, KS 66621
CONTACT: Lloyd Herrera, Computer Services Technician
PHONE: (913)-231-1010 x1782
EMAIL: zzherr@acc.wuacc.edu.
URL: http://law.wuacc.edu/washlaw/uslaw/statelaw.html

STATE GOVERNMENT GOPHERS

DESCRIPTION: Offers one-stop access to a many state gophers.

PROVIDER: University of Southern California
CONTACT: Mark Brown
EMAIL: cwis-wizs@usc.edu
PHONE: (213) 740-2957
URL: gopher://cwis.usc.edu:70/11/Other_Gophers_and_Information_Resources/Gophers_by_Subject/Gopher_Jewels/government/states
PROVIDER: Cornell Law School
URL: gopher://marvel.loc.gov:70/11/federal/state.local

STATESEARCH

DESCRIPTION: StateSearch is a service of the National Association of State Information Resource Executives and is designed to serve as a topical clearinghouse to state government information on the Internet. There are 23 categories of information including: Regulation and Licensing, State Legislatures, and Government Agencies.

URL: http://www.state.ky.us/nasire/NASIREhome.html

INTERNATIONAL
(by country)

AUSTRALIA

COURTS

AUSTRALIA CASE LAW

DESCRIPTION: This searchable database provides Victorian Magistrates Court opinions 1992-1994 and all judgments from the High Court of Australia for 1995.

URL: http://www.lawnet.com.au

AUSTRALIAN FOUNDATION

DESCRIPTION:

- Family Court of Australia judgments
- Land and Environment Court of NSW judgments
- Administrative Appeals Tribunal
- Supreme Court of Tasmania judgments
- Industrial Court of Australia judgments
- High Court of Australia judgments

PROVIDER: The Law Foundation of New South Wales
URL: http://www.fl.asn.a

VETNET AUSTRALIA

DESCRIPTION: This site contains veterans' cases from Veterans' Review Board, Administrative Appeals Tribunal, Federal Court of Australia and High Court of Australia. It also has medical information on diseases and disabilities, with special reference to war and defenSes causes. Contains whole body assessment publication GARP.

URL: http://www.onthenet.com.au/~gmylne/Welcome.html

NATIVE TITLE CASES ARCHIVE

DESCRIPTION: This is a collection of legal authorities and documents relating to the Mabo decision and the Federal Native Title Act. It includes decisions and determinations rendered in land dispute cases, jurisdictional authority cases, and others.

PROVIDER: Department of Anthropology at the University of Western Australia
URL: http://www.arts.uwa.edu.au/AnthropWWW/ntcases.htm

WEEKLY CASE SUMMARIES

DESCRIPTION: This company offers weekly judgment summaries handed down by various courts, transcripts of the radio program The Law Report, and the LBC Internet Law Journal featuring short articles on a variety of legal topics.

PROVIDER: Law Book Company Information Services
EMAIL: LBCCUSTOMER@lbc.com.au
URL: http://www.ozemail.com.au:80/~lawbook/

LEGISLATION

AUSTRALIAN LAW

DESCRIPTION: Searchable access to a comprehensive (over 1000 Australian laws) collection of statutes.

PROVIDER: Australasian Legal Information Institute
URL: http://austlii.law.uts.edu.au/cth_legis/cth-acts-toc.html

ENVIRONMENTAL LEGISLATION

DESCRIPTION: This site offers a searchable database of full-text Australian environmental laws, including intercountry agreements provided via the Environmental Resources Information Network (ERIN).

PROVIDER: Australian National Parks and Wildlife Service
ADDRESS: Nature Conservation House, 153 Emu Bank Belconnen ACT, GPO Box 636, Canberra ACT 2601, Australia
CONTACT: Wayne Slater
PHONE: 61 6 250 0383
EMAIL: wayne@erin.gov.au, gopher@erin.gov.au
URL: http://kaos.erin.gov.au

MOTORCYCLE REGULATIONS

PROVIDER: Cameron Simpson
EMAIL: cameron@dap.csiro.au
URL: http://www.dap.csiro.au/~cameron/moto/licencing.html

GOVERNMENT SITES

AUSTRALIAN GOVERNMENT HOME PAGE

DESCRIPTION: This site is the gateway to Australian

governmental resources. It includes links to Australian departments and agencies, Australian state government sites, pointers to the Australian Parliament Home Page and the National Library of Australia, and other places. All their materials are keyword searchable. A good place to start, if you want to browse Australian government sites.

PROVIDER: Australian Office of Government Information and Advertising
URL: http://gov.info.au/

PARLIAMENT

DESCRIPTION: This site includes links to the Department of the Senate, the Department of House of Representatives, and parliamentary information. It includes texts of the week- ly Hansard, daily programs and Order of Business of the two houses, bulletins of votes, proceedings, and events in the parliament, official business on the agenda, biographical information on members and senators, 1995-96 budget papers, and more. Keyword searching of the Hansards, Notice Papers, Senate Journals, and the House of Representatives Votes and Proceedings is available.

PROVIDER: Parliamentary Library and the Australian National University
URL: http://www.aph.gov.au/

NATIONAL LIBRARY OF AUSTRALIA (NLA)

DESCRIPTION: The NLA also has a number of pointers to federal, state, and local government resources. They also make available an archive of policy documents related to the response of Australian governments to the global communications infrastructure.

URL: http://www.nla.gov.au/oz/gov/

COLLECTIONS

AUSTRALIAN RESOURCE COLLECTION

DESCRIPTION: The solicitors of Price Brent in Melbourne have a long, if fairly disorganized, list of legal resources, products, and services in the Australia/Oceania region, interspersed with some popular U.S. sites. Most of the materials and pointers relate to telecommunications, multimedia, and business law. Turn off the images on your browser before connecting, unless you like to wait.

PROVIDER: Price Brent (law firm), Melbourne
URL: http://technoculture.mira.net.au/pbclick.htm

AUSTRALIAN LEGAL RESOURCE COLLECTION

DESCRIPTION: This is an excellent, extensive collection of Australian law, and other legal material, including links to Australian legal organizations (including law firms), and Australian legal events. Very impressive site.

PROVIDER: Daniel Austin, Undergraduate, Australian National University
EMAIL: dan@spirit.net.au.
URL: http://spirit.com.au/~dan/law/

VARIOUS LEGAL MATERIALS

DESCRIPTION: This gopher contains pointers to law directories, bibliographies, electronic lists, electronic journals (including E Law, from Murdoch University), ftp archives, law library catalogs, and more. The overwhelming majority of pointers are to U.S. and international legal resources, but a few Australian resources can be found.

PROVIDER: Murdoch University Law Library
URL: gopher://infolib.murdoch.edu.au/11/.ftp/pub/subj/law

MISCELLANEOUS

ABORIGINAL STUDIES ARCHIVES

DESCRIPTION: This site offers a number of legal, historical, and economic documents relating to native populations of Australia and Oceania. The electronic archive includes numerous land claim transcripts and findings of the Royal Commission into Aboriginal Deaths in Custody.

PROVIDER: Australian National University
URL: http://coombs.anu.edu.au/SpecialProj/ASEDA/ASEDA.html

AUSTRALIAN FOI

DESCRIPTION: This site is devoted to freedom of information issues and a newsletter called the FOI Review.

PROVIDER: Public Interest Advocacy Centre, Sydney, NSW
URL: http://www.its.newnham.utas.edu.au:80/dept/comlaw/law/foi/

AUSTRALIAN LAW SCHOOLS

DESCRIPTION: Links to most Australian law schools.

PROVIDER: Australian National University
EMAIL: eo.law@uniserve.edu.au
URL: http://uniserve.edu.au/law/pub/edinst

PATENT AND TRADEMARK FILING REQUIREMENTS

DESCRIPTION: This law firm offers a list of Australian intellectual property (patent and trademark) registration filing requirements.

PROVIDER: Fisher and Kelly (law firm)
EMAIL: fisher-kelly@mailbox.uq.oz.au
PHONE: +617 38700600
FAX: +617 38700525
URL: http://www.uq.oz.au/~zzfisher/index.html

WEBCOMNET BUSINESS NFORMATION DIRECTORY

DESCRIPTION: This company hosts a searchable business information directory with Australian and worldwide commercial information covering many business areas, including accounting, advertising, banking, finance, law and marketing. It also includes an index of annotated links to many professional firms

URL: http://www.camtech.com.au/webcomnet/

AUSTRIA

ENVIRONMENTAL INFORMATION ACT

DESCRIPTION: This law concerns access to information on the environment.

PROVIDER: Central European Environmental Data Request Facility, which is administered by the International Society for Environmental Protection through a contract with the Austrian Federal Ministry for Environment, Youth and Family
ADDRESS: Marxergasse 3/20, A-1030, Vienna, Austria
CONTACT: Joerg Fineisen
PHONE: 43 1 715 58 79
FAX: 43 1 715 28 29
EMAIL: system-info@cedar.univie.ac.at
URL: html://pan.cedar.univie.ac.at/gopher_ref/BMUJF/bmujf.html

BRUNEI

BACKGROUND ON BRUNEI

DESCRIPTION: 1994 U.S. State Department Report on Human Rights, CIA World Factobook Info, travel info.

PROVIDER: Asian Institute of Technology, Thailand
CONTACT: J. Brubaker
EMAIL: staff@EMAILhost.ait.ac.th
URL: http://EMAILhost.ait.ac.th/Asia/infobr.html

CANADA

COURTS

SUPREME COURT OF CANADA DECISIONS

DESCRIPTION: This site provides a searchable decision index, and Court rulings and bulletins starting from 1993. Decisions are available in English and French, in three formats: Macintosh MS-Word 4.0, PC WordPerfect 5.1 and ASCII text.

PROVIDER: University of Montreal
CONTACT: Pablo Fuentes
EMAIL: fuentesp@droit.UMontreal.ca
ADDRESS: C.P. 6128, succursale A, Montreal, Quebec, Canada H3C 3J7
PHONE: (514) 343-2142
URL: http://www.droit.umontreal.ca/Droit/CSC/SCC.html

SUPREME COURT SUMMARIES

DESCRIPTION: This site, provides summaries of recent decisions by the Supreme Court and higher provincial courts on selected cases of interest. Also available in French.

PROVIDER: QuickLaw
URL: http://www.qlsys.ca/whatshot.html

LEGISLATION

CONSTITUTION

DESCRIPTION: Includes the Canada Constitution Acts of 1867 and 1982, the Canada Lake Meech Accord of 1987, and the Charlottetown Constitutional Agreement.

URL: http://wiretap.spies.com/Gopher/Gov/World/canada.con

CHARTER OF RIGHTS AND FREEDOMS

DESCRIPTION: Full-text, excerpted from the Constitution Act 1982.

PROVIDER: Electronic Frontier Canada
CONTACT: Carl Jorgensen
PHONE: (514) 398-7416
EMAIL: efc@graceland.uwaterloo.ca or efc-gopher@cim.mcgill.ca
URL: gopher://insight.mcmaster.ca/70/00/org/efc/canada.charter

CRIMINAL CODE OF CANADA

DESCRIPTION: Complete text, with hyperlinks.

URL: http://insight.mcmaster.ca/org/efc/pages/law/cc/cc.html

ONTARIO FAMILY LAW BULLETIN

DESCRIPTION: This monthly bulletin deals with the latest cases, and changes in statutes and rules that affect family law in Ontario.

PROVIDER: Contributors are lawyers Malcolm C. Kronby and Jeffery Wilson, who presently edit the Ontario Family Law Reporter, and Andrew Freedman of Cole Valuation Partners Limited
EMAIL: Malcolm C. Kronby 73744.445@compuserve.com, or mckronby@inforamp.net
Jeffery Wilson 76132.516@compuserve.com
Andrew Freedman 102033.624@compuserve.com
ACCESS: misc.legal.moderated (newsgroup)

ONTARIO STATUTES

DESCRIPTION: The site also has some employment-related, full text and Ontario statutes, including Employment Standards Act, Human Rights Code, Occupational Health and Safety Act, and the Workers Compensation Act.

PROVIDER: Aurora Professional Press, located in Aurora, Ontario, Canada, is a division of Canada Law Book Inc.
URL: http://www.io.org/~aurora/APP/

QUEBEC CIVIL CODE

DESCRIPTION: Provides search-access to the code in French.

PROVIDER: University of Montreal
ADMINISTRATOR: Pablo Fuentes
ADDRESS: C.P. 6128, succursale A, Montreal, Quebec, Canada H3C 3J7
PHONE: (514) 343-2142
EMAIL: fuentesp@droit.UMontreal.ca
URL: http://www.droit.umontreal.ca/cgibin/ecfTDM

GOVERNMENT SITES

CANADIAN FOREIGN AFFAIRS

DESCRIPTION: Information concerning Canadian foreign policy, international trade issues, and international law.

PROVIDER: The Canadian Department of Foreign Affairs and International Trade
URL: http://www.dfait-maeci.gc.ca

DEPARTMENT OF JUSTICE

DESCRIPTION: This is a slick page that includes some Canadian laws and bills, publications and info about the DOJ.

PROVIDER: Department of Justice of Canada
URL: http://canada.justice.gc.ca/index_en.html

GOVERNMENT COLLECTION

DESCRIPTION: Michael O'Reilly, a freelance journalist in Canada, has created a Web page with pointers to Canadian government information sources of interest to journalists. He includes pointers to Statistics Canada, the Canadian Parliamentary Channel, and the Canadian Radio and Telecommunications Commission.

URL: http://www.empath.on.ca:80/helplink/mo/Cangvt.html

HOUSE OF COMMONS

DESCRIPTION: The House of Commons site is still relatively undeveloped; it provides brief information about what the House of Commons is, and links to lists of members, as well as contact information for them.

URL: http://info.ic.gc.ca/opengov/commons/commons.html

NATIONAL LIBRARY OF CANADA

DESCRIPTION: This gopher server offers a broad range of materials and links to Canadian government information, at the federal/ state, and departmental level. Many of their documents are searchable. There is too much there to even begin to adequately list here, but it is a good starting point toward finding hard-to-find Canadian legal materials. Available in French and English.

URL: gopher://gopher.nlc-bnc.ca/

SECURITIES COMMISSION

DESCRIPTION: This site offers a database of over 500,000 Canadian official documents filed with the Ontario Securities Commission from 1986 to June 1995. In addition, it offers access to the most current issue of the OSC Bulletin from the Ontario Securities Commission, CanCorp Guide to Corporate Reports, and other material.

URL: http://www.mmltd.com/files/prod_serv/corp_inf/corpinf.html

COLLECTIONS

CANADIAN LEGAL NETWORK

DESCRIPTION: This site has been developed to provide public access to the various resources of the Canadian legal system and its services. Users of CanLaw will have access to information such as a directory of law firms for each province; Canadian courts; legal research resources; Canadian government Internet resources; law practices support services and legal newsgroups. The primary purpose of CanLaw is to provide the Canadian lawyer a vehicle for communicating with their clients, their peers, and the global legal community. A very comprehensive resource.

URL: http://www.canlaw.net/canlaw/

CANADIAN RESOURCES

DESCRIPTION: The May 29, 1995 issue of the electronic newsletter LAIR focuses on Canadian Legal Resources. It is an overview look at the variety of materials available through WWW, gopher, and listserv resources relating to Canadian legal materials.

PROVIDER: University of Texas
URL: http://www.law.utexas.edu/lair/vol-1/sum95-16.html

LEGAL RESOURCE COLLECTION

DESCRIPTION: This collection is organized under the topics Legal Information, Tax and Accounting, Universities and Colleges, Lawyers and Law Firms, Canadian Federal Government, Canadian Provincial Governments, Legal Publishers and Commercial Sites, Newsgroups, and Free Speech on the Information Highway.

PROVIDER: Peter Sim, a barrister and solicitor in Winnipeg
URL: http://www.mbnet.mb.ca/~psim/can_law.html

LEGAL RESOURCE COLLECTION

DESCRIPTION: This site gathers together Canadian legal online services, Canadian lawyers and law firms on the Internet, legal mailing lists, legal organizations and associations, and legal publishers.

PROVIDER: Alan M. Ghatan (barrister and solicitor)
URL: http://www.io.org/~agahtan/master.htm#TOP

LEGAL RESOURCE COLLECTION

DESCRIPTION: This page has been created to provide Canadian lawyers, particularly government lawyers, with links of interest. Contains an excellent and up-to-date collection of links to Canadian resources, U.S. resources, and international legal resources. Of particular note are her links to aboriginal legal resources, women and the law, the DIANA Human Rights database, and Simpson trial transcripts.

PROVIDER: Judith Bowers
URL: http://www.law.ubc.ca/guests/bowers.html

CANADIAN OPEN GOVERNMENT PILOT PROJECT

DESCRIPTION: This project, sponsored by Industry Canada, aims to provide wider access to Canadian government information through computer networks. So far, it contains pointers to the Senate, the House of Commons, political party home pages, the Supreme Court, federal and provincial budgets, federal departments, and provincial information.

URL: http://info.ic.gc.ca/opengov/

MISCELLANEOUS

CANADIAN BAR ASSOCIATION (CBA)

DESCRIPTION: The CBA and the Canadian Bar Association Ontario (CBAO) are professional organizations comprised of Canadian lawyers. The purpose of this gopher site is to disseminate information to members of the CBA and CBAO as well as to the public. Contains legal documents and information about Canadian immigration and citizenship.

URL: http://www.algonquinc.on.ca:80/cba/
URL: gopher://inforamp.net:70/11/society/law/cba

CANADIAN LEGAL SEARCH

DESCRIPTION: This is an HTML interface Harvest search engine for locating Canadian legal Information or Canadian government information on the Internet, be it on the WWW, on gophers, or on ftp archives. The engine allows you to see where, and how many times, your search terms occur in the document, prior to actually viewing the source. Part of the Canadian Open Government Pilot Project. Available also in French.

URL: http://info.ic.gc.ca/champlain/champlain.html

DIRECTORY OF CANADIAN LAWYERS AND LAW FIRMS

DESCRIPTION: A growing listing of almost 1000 Canadian lawyers and law firms with Internet accessible email. The first and most comprehensive index to Canadian lawyers and law firms with Internet email addresses. Makes extensive use of graphics.

URL: http://www.carswell.com:80/LawDir/

IMMIGRATION SITE

DESCRIPTION: This site contains information about temporary and permanent U.S. immigration work permits for Canadian businesses and professionals. It is designed primarily for Canadian companies doing business with the U.S., U.S. companies hiring Canadians, human resource/relocation managers, lawyers and accountants. It also provides generous portions of key sections from the Canada-U.S. Business Immigration Handbook, published by Carswell.

PROVIDER: Joseph C. Grasmick
URL: http://www.netoffice.com/~grasmick/

JOURNAL: GOVERNMENT INFORMATION IN CANADA

DESCRIPTION: This site provides access to a quarterly electronic journal for discussion and study of Canadian federal, provincial/territorial, and local government information. Available in both English and French. There are currently four issues published.

URL: http://www.usask.ca/library/gic/index.html

CHILE

CHILEAN STATUTES

DESCRIPTION: Both this site and the Chilean Legislation site below provide laws and other information about Chile.

URL: http://nexus.chilenet.cl/index/
URL: http://sunsite.dcc.uchile.cl/chile/list.html

CHILEAN LEGISLATION (IN SPANISH)

2. Instrucciones y manuales de este servidor/
3. Descripcion de CONICYT About CONICYT/
4. Concursos, becas y programas de CONICYT/
5. Concursos de otras instituciones/
6. Bases de datos sobre proyectos de investigacion en Chile/
7. Servicios de informacion de CONICYT/
8. Bases de datos bibliograficas y referenciales de CONICYT/
9. Bases de datos bibliograficas de otras instituciones/
10. Revistas, publicaciones y comunicados de CONICYT/
11. Estadisticas en ciencia y tecnologia/
12. Legislacion chilena/
13. Investigadores chilenos en el extranjero/
14. Conexion a otros Gopher y servicios de informacion/
15. Conexion a REUNA e Internet (maquina huelen)/

URL: http://daniel.conicyt.cl/

CHILEAN HOUSE OF REPRESENTATIVES

DESCRIPTION: Contains the Constitution of Chile, organic structure, Deputees and Senators, several specific Laws of the Republic.

PROVIDER: Congress of the Republic of Chile
URL: http://ami.congreso.cl/

CHINA

ARMY AREA HANDBOOK

DESCRIPTION: This monograph provides an overview of China's legal system, culture, history, economy, people, geography, and current international relationships, as well as a wealth of other information. This document was extracted from the Department of Commerce, Economics and Statistics Division's National Trade Data Bank (NTDB) CD-ROM.

PROVIDER: University of Minnesota - St. Louis
URL: gopher://UMSLVMA.UMSL.EDU:70/11/LIBRARY/GOVDOCS/ARMYAHBS/AAHB9

CONSTITUTION OF THE PEOPLE'S REPUBLIC OF CHINA

DESCRIPTION: Adopted on December 4, 1982.

PROVIDER: The Internet Wiretap retrieved this document from the CPSR Privacy/Information Archive
URL: http://wiretap.spies.com/Gopher/Gov/World/china.con

CRIMINAL JUSTICE SYSTEM IN CHINA

DESCRIPTION: This document broadly describes the administration of criminal justice in the People's Republic of China.

PROVIDER: Asian Institute of Technology, Thailand
CONTACT: J. Brubaker
EMAIL: staff@EMAILhost.ait.ac.th
URL: gopher://emailhost.ait.ac.th:70/00/AsiaInfo/CountryInfo/China%20%28P.R.C.%29/Criminal%20Justice%20System%20In%20China

CUBA

CUBA RESOURCES

DESCRIPTION: Expansive collection of Cuban material, including Constitutions, Castro Speech Database, CubaNet Archive.

URL: http://ix.urz.Uni-Heidelberg.de/~pklee/Cuba

CUBA

DESCRIPTION: This collection includes national economic information, maps, and links to many other Cuban sites.

URL: http://www.unipr.it/~davide/cuba/home.html

CZECH REPUBLIC

CZECH LEGAL RESOURCES

DESCRIPTION: Information concerning Czech government and law (in English and Czech).

URL: gopher://fenrir.psp.cz/1

EGYPT

ARMY AREA HANDBOOK

DESCRIPTION: This monograph provides an overview of Egypt's legal system, culture, history, economy, people, geography, and current international relationships, as well as a wealth of other information. This document was extracted from the Department of Commerce, Economics and Statistics Division's National. Trade Data Bank (NTDB) CD-ROM.

PROVIDER: University of Minnesota - St. Louis
URL: gopher://UMSLVMA.UMSL.EDU:70/11/LIBRARY/GOVDOCS/ARMYAHBS/AAHB7

ESTONIA

CONSTITUTION

DESCRIPTION: This full-text document is 96 pages. The version at the University of Kansas is identified as the Estonian Constitution, while the version at the Internet Wiretap and the CPSR site are identified as "Draft" Constitution.

PROVIDER: University of Kansas
CONTACT: Wayne Chander
EMAIL: waynec@kuhub.cc.ukans.edu
URL: http://wiretap.spies.com/Gopher/Gov/World/estonia.con

EUROPEAN COMMUNITY

EUROPEAN ENVIRONMENTAL CONVENTIONS

DESCRIPTION: This site provides access to many European environmental resources in addition to full-text versions of various European environmental conventions and protocols, including:

- Action Plan for the Human Environment (Stockholm, 1972).
- The Control of Transboundary Movements of Hazardous Wastes
- Bonn Convention on the Conservation of Migratory Species

- Convention on Environmental Impact Assessment
- Convention on the International Trade in Endangered Species
- LongRange Transboundary Air Pollution (13 Nov 79)
- The Protection of the World Cultural and Natural Heritage
- UNCED: Convention on Biological Diversity
- Vienna Convention for the Protection of the Ozone Layer (1985) - Wetlands of International Importance

PROVIDER: Central European Environmental Data Request Facility, which is administered by the International Society for Environmental Protection through a contract with the Austrian Federal Ministry for Environment, Youth and Family
ADDRESS: Marxergasse 3/20, A-1030, Vienna, Austria
CONTACT: Joerg Fineisen
PHONE: 43 1 715 58 79
FAX: 43 1 715 28 29
EMAIL: system-info@cedar.univie.ac.at
URL: http://pan.cedar.univie.ac.at/convention

EUROPEAN LEGAL CENTER

DESCRIPTION: The Faculty of Law, University of Leeds (including the Centre for Criminal Justice Studies and the Centre for the Study of Law in Europe) is also on line.

URL: http://www.leeds.ac.uk/
URL: http://www.bris.ac.uk/Depts/Law/

EUROPEAN UNION BASICS

DESCRIPTION: This file contains a list of frequently asked questions (FAQ) and answers about the European Union. Topics include the European Court of Justice, European Parliament, European Council, and the North American Free Trade Agreement.

PROVIDER: Allmansland/De Schutter Digital Media
CONTACT: Roland Siebelink
EMAIL: eubasics@allmansland.com
URL: http://eubasics.allmansland.com/index.html

EUROPEAN PATENT OFFICE

DESCRIPTION: The Vienna branch of the European Patent Office is now on line. This local branch specializes in supplying technical and legal information contained in patent documents. You will find details of how to apply for and submit patents, how to purchase copies of patents, plus details of the office and the work they do.

URL: http://www.epo.co.at/epo/

DIRECTIVE ON COPYRIGHT

DESCRIPTION: This Council Directive of May 14, 1991 concerns the legal protection of computer programs. This document is from the Official Journal of the European Communities, May 17, 1991, No. L 122/42.

URL: http://wiretap.spies.com/Gopher/Gov/Other/copyrigh.ec

RESOLUTION ON TIBET

DESCRIPTION: This is the complete text of a resolution on Tibet that was adopted by the European Parliament on December 15, 1992.

URL: http://wiretap.spies.com/Gopher/Gov/Other/tibet.ec

ROMAN LAW (IN LATIN)

DESCRIPTION: The compilers of this collection of ancient Roman text (Corpus Iuris Iustiniani) state their objectives this way: "The traditions of Roman Law ... play a significant role in the creation of the private law for the European community. It is therefore necessary that the texts representing this tradition be ...available." The texts include medieval commentary, and biographies of ancient lawyers. All texts in this collection are in Latin.

PROVIDER: Thomas Rifner
EMAIL: zxmog07@studserv.zdv.uni-tuebingen.de
URL: http://www.jura.unisb.de/Rechtsgeschichte/Ius. Romanum/origo.html

FINLAND

VARIOUS LAWS (IN FINNISH)

DESCRIPTION: The materials provided here are courtesy of a student organization, which does not guarantee the accuracy of the texts.

PROVIDER: Lysator, a students computer society, Linkoping Univeristy, Sweden
CONTACT: Tommy Persson
EMAIL: gopher@lysator.liu.se
ADDRESS: Lysator Computer Club, c/o Dept. of EE, Linkoping Univeristy, S-581 83 Linkoping, Sweden
URL: gopher://gopher.lysator.liu.se:70/11/project-runeberg/txt/finnlaw/lait

FRANCE

COLLECTION

DESCRIPTION:
- French Law Dictionary
- Consumery Code ("le Code de la Consommation")
- Constitution ("la Constitution de la Republique francaise")
- French Declaration of Human Right ("la Declaration des Droits de l'Homme,")
- Constitutional Council ("le Conseil Constitutionnel")

URL: http://www.ensmp.fr:80/%7escherer/adminet/min/jus/

COLLECTION

DESCRIPTION:
- French Code on Judicature ("Code de l'Organisation judiciaire")
- Law on compensation in case of car accidents ("loi sur l'indemnisation des victimes d'accidents de la circulation"
- Code of Intellectual Property ("Code de la Propriete intellectuelle")
- Law on Computating and Liberty ("loi Informatique et liberte")
- Law about nonprofit Companies ("loi du 1er juillet 1901 sur les Associations")

URL: http://www.fdn.fr/~rabenou/

FRENCH LAW LIST

DESCRIPTION: Law-France is an open but moderated mailing list for the exchange of information about the practice of law in France. Postings from members (in French and English) are sent out in digest form on at most a once-a-day basis. Send email to law-france request@ amgot.org with "subscribe" in the subject line. An infopage will be sent to you giving instructions on how to use the service.

GERMANY

CONSTITUTIONAL COURT DECISIONS

DESCRIPTION: This site contains decisions of the federal constitutional court as well as hyperlinks to other law related Web services in Germany.

PROVIDER: German University of Passau
URL: http://www.uni-passau.de/jurf/

CONSTITUTION

DESCRIPTION: The Basic Law for the Federal Republic of Germany (the Constitution) was promulgated by the Parliamentary Council on May 23, 1949, and amended by the Unification Treaty of August 31, 1990 and Federal Statute of September 23, 1990. The English version of the Basic Law available at both URLs indicated here is preceded by a letter from President Richard von Weizsaecker. It is not part of the Basic Law, but provides some history and perspective. This document is available in both English and German.

PROVIDER: The english version of the Basic Law is provided courtesy of General Electric's Germany & Europe Roundtable. For information contact the G&E RT sysop Tony Kendall at: usa.germany@genie.geis.com. The German version is provided by Saarbruecken University.
CONTACT: Studly Gopher Admin
PHONE: (612) 338-3970
EMAIL: gopher@turnip.com
URL: http://wiretap.spies.com/Gopher/Gov/World/germany.con

HAITI

UNOFFICIAL HAITI HOME PAGE

PROVIDER: Ralph Reed
EMAIL: RafReid@primenet.com
URL: http://www.primenet.com/~rafreid/

HONG KONG

BASIC LAW OF HONG KONG

DESCRIPTION: Full title of this document is "The Basic Law of the Hong Kong Special Administrative Region of the People's Republic of China." It was adopted on April 4, 1990 by the Seventh National People's Congress of the People's Republic of China.

URL: http://wiretap.spies.com/Gopher/Gov/World/hongkong.con

BILL OF RIGHTS ORDINANCE

DESCRIPTION: This document notes that it may contain spelling errors and omissions.

URL: http://wiretap.spies.com/Gopher/Gov/World/rights91.hk

HUNGARY

CONSTITUTION OF THE REPUBLIC OF HUNGARY

URL: http://wiretap.spies.com/Gopher/Gov/World/hungary.con

INDONESIA

BACKGROUND

DESCRIPTION: Various documents describing the country, including the criminal justice system, economic policy and trade practices.

PROVIDER: Asian Institute of Technology, Thailand
CONTACT: J. Brubaker
EMAIL: staff@EMAILhost.ait.ac.th
URL: http://www.ait.ac.th/Asia/infoid.html

ARMY AREA HANDBOOK

DESCRIPTION: This monograph provides an overview of Indonesia's legal system, culture, history, economy, people, geography, and current international relationships, as well as a wealth of other information. This document was extracted from the Department of Commerce, Economics and Statistics Division's National Trade Data Bank (NTDB) CD-ROM.

PROVIDER: University of Minnesota - St. Louis
URL: gopher://UMSLVMA.UMSL.EDU:70/11/LIBRARY/GOVDOCS/ARMYAHBS/AAHB8

ISRAEL

COURTS

LEGAL ISSUES AND RULINGS

DESCRIPTION: The Israeli Foreign Ministry provides access to an English-language collection of government documents and court decisions on notable issues. Following are examples of the available documents:

- Expulsions and the Fourth Geneva Convention
- Temporary Exclusion Orders - Legal Aspects
- Israel Supreme Court on Temporary Expulsion HAMAS
- Israel's Interrogation Policies and Practices
- Justice Minister Liba'i on Demjanjuk Appeal Decision
- The Demjanjuk Appeal-Summary Supreme Court Ruling
- Decision Israel Supreme Court on Demjanjuk Petition
- Memorandum Regarding Vanunu-Justice Ministry
- Attorney Generals Opinion on Kach and Kahane Chai
- Cabinet Decision Outlawing Kach and Kahane Chai
- Commission of Inquiry Report - Hebron Massacre

PROVIDER: Israel Foreign Ministry, Information Division, Jerusalem
EMAIL: ask@israel-info.gov.il
CONTACT: Julie Greenblatt, Israel Information Service Info Officer
URL: gopher://israel-info.gov.il/leg

LEGISLATION

BASIC LAW

DESCRIPTION: The Israel Information Service provides English full-text versions of the Israeli Basic Law as follows:

- Basic Law: The Government (new law)
- Basic Law: The Government (old law)
- Basic Law: The President of the State
- Basic Law: (The Knesset)
- Basic Law: Judicature
- Basic Law: Israel lands
- Basic Law: The State Economy
- Basic Law: The Army
- Basic Law: Jerusalem
- Basic Law: The State Comptroller
- Basic Law: Freedom of Occupation (1992, 1994)
- Basic Law: Human Dignity and Liberty
- The Prevention of Terrorism Ordinance, 5708-1948
- Law of Return, 5710-1950
- Nazi and Nazi collaborators (Punishment) law, 5710-1950
- The Golan Heights law - Dec. 14, 1981
- Protection of Holy Places Law, 1967

PROVIDER: Israel Foreign Ministry, Jerusalem
EMAIL: ask@israel-info.gov.il
CONTACT: Julie Greenblatt, Israel Information Service Info Officer

URL: gopher://israel-info.gov.il/constit

DECLARATION OF INDEPENDENCE

DESCRIPTION: Issued at Tel Aviv on May 14, 1948.

URL: http://wiretap.spies.com/Gopher/Gov/Other/israel.dec

MISCELLANEOUS

ISRAEL INFORMATION SERVICE

DESCRIPTION: The Israeli government, through its Foreign Ministry offers access to a variety of documents on various subjects, including:

- The Israeli Government - Functions, Names, and Addresses
- Israeli-Arab Relations - Basic Reference Documents
- The Israeli-Arab Peace Process
- Policy Speeches, Interviews
- Basic Laws and Legal Issues in Israel
- Israel's Diplomatic Relations
- The Environment
- Anti-Semitism and the Holocaust

PROVIDER: Israel Foreign Ministry, Information Division, Jerusalem
EMAIL: ask@israel-info.gov.il
CONTACT: Julie Greenblatt, Israel Information Service Info Officer
URL: gopher://israel-info.gov.il/

ARMY AREA HANDBOOK

DESCRIPTION: This monograph provides an overview of Israel's legal system, culture, history, economy, people, geography, and current international relationships, as well as a wealth of other information. This document was extracted from the Department of Commerce, Economics and Statistics Division's National Trade Data Bank (NTDB) CD-ROM.

PROVIDER: University of Minnesota - St. Louis
URL: gopher://UMSLVMA.UMSL.EDU:70/11/LIBRARY/GOVDOCS/ARMYAHBS/AAHB6

ITALY

LEGISLATION

CONSTITUTION (IN ITALIAN)

PROVIDER: The Internet Wiretap retrieved this document from the newsgroup: soc.culture.italian. It had apparently been placed there by Luigi Semenzato of the University of California, Berkeley.
URL: http://wiretap.spies.com/Gopher/Gov/World/italy.con

FAIR TRADING ACT

DESCRIPTION: The Italian Competition Authority site includes an English translation of the Competition and Fair Trading Act.

PROVIDER: The Italian Competition Authority
EMAIL: antitrust@agcm.it
URL: http://www.agcm.it/

MISCELLANEOUS

ITALIAN LAW COLLECTION

PROVIDER: School of Advanced Comparative Legal Studies, Faculty of Law, Univ. of Torino
CONTACT: P.G.Monateri School of Advanced Computer Legal Studies
URL: http://www.gelso.unitn.it/card-adm/it_law.htm

SELECTION OF LEGAL DATABASES

DESCRIPTION: The following databases are available:

- DOGI Abstracts of Italian Law Journals
- STOP Abstracts of Legal Info published in the Italian Press
- BIGA Italian Legal Bibliography on the Environment
- DARC State of Implementation in Italy of EC Directives on the Environment
- VIPD Independent Life of People with Disabilities
- ATTI Acts of Public Administration (experimental)
- ATEX Acts (Full Text) of Public Administration (experimental)
- CORI Collective Agreements of Employers in the Research Sector

PROVIDER: Instituto per la Documentazione Giuridica (IDG) of the National Research Council (CNR) of Florence (Italy)
CONTACT: Giuseppina Sabato
EMAIL: sabato@idg.fi.cnr.it
ADDRESS: IDG Servizio Elaborazione Dati, Via V. de Gama, 223 50134, Florence, Italy
PHONE: +3955410977
FAX: +395541064
URL: gopher://risc.idg.fi.cnr.it:70/00/BANCHEI/banchei

JAPAN

CONSTITUTION

DESCRIPTION: The text of the 1946 constitution of Japan in English.

URL: http://wiretap.spies.com/Gopher/Gov/World/japan.con

PATENT RIGHTS IN JAPAN

DESCRIPTION: Report of the U.S. General Accounting Office concerning experiences of U.S. companies regarding patent rights in Japan, dated July 1993.

PROVIDER: University of Washington, Technical Japanese Program, Seattle, Washington
EMAIL: jonwd@u.washington.edu
URL: ftp://ftp.uwtc.washington.edu/pub/Japanese/Misc/GAOonPatentinginJapan

ARMY AREA HANDBOOK

DESCRIPTION: This monograph provides an overview of Japan's legal system, culture, history, economy, people, geography, and current international relationships, as well as a wealth of other information. This document was extracted from the Department of Commerce, Economics and Statistics Division's National Trade Data Bank (NTDB) CD-ROM.

PROVIDER: University of Minnesota - St. Louis
URL: gopher://UMSLVMA.UMSL.EDU:70/11/LIBRARY/GOVDOCS/ARMYAHBS/ARMANTOC

LAOS

POLITICAL CLIMATE

DESCRIPTION: Various documents provide background on the country's political climate including the human rights situation.

PROVIDER: Asian Institute of Technology, Thailand
CONTACT: J. Brubaker
EMAIL: staff@EMAILhost.ait.ac.th
URL: http://www.ait.ac.th/Asia/infols.html

LATIN AMERICA

LEGISLATIVE AND LEGAL DATABASE

DESCRIPTION: The Index to Latin American Legislation (also named the International Legal Database (LAWL)) contains abstracts of legislation of 22 Latin and Central American countries. The database has recently been expanded to include Portuguese legislative material. This file can be searched by subject or country.

PROVIDER: The Hispanic Division of the United States Law Library of Congress acquires approximately 50,000 issues of the legal gazettes published by the various Latin and Central American countries. These gazettes are the primary legal source material for this database.

AVAILIBILITY: Searching hours (U.S. Eastern time) are:
Monday through Friday from 6:30 a.m. to 9:30 p.m.
Saturday from 8:00 a.m. to 5:00 p.m.
Sunday from 1:00 p.m. to 5:00 p.m.
Closed on national holidays

URL: http://lcweb.loc.gov/homepage/online.html

then choose: Connect to LOCIS (Public Users ...) <TEL>
press Enter
then choose: Foreign Law

MACEDONIA

CONSTITUTION OF THE REPUBLIC OF MACEDONIA

DESCRIPTION: This constitution was adopted by the Assembly of the Republic of Macedonia.

URL: http://wiretap.spies.com/Gopher/Gov/World/macedonia.con

MALAWI

DRAFT CONSTITUTION

URL: http://wiretap.spies.com/Gopher/Gov/World/malawi.con

MALAYSIA

POLITICAL CLIMATE

DESCRIPTION: Various documents provide background on the country's political climate including the criminal justice system.

PROVIDER: Asian Institute of Technology, Thailand
CONTACT: J. Brubaker
EMAIL: staff@EMAILhost.ait.ac.th
URL: http://www.ait.ac.th/Asia/infomy.html

MALAYSIA ENVIRONMENTAL MATERIAL

DESCRIPTION: This site is maintained by the Malaysian Department of Environment.

URL: http://pop.jaring.my/jas/start.html

MEXICO

CONSTITUTIONS (IN SPANISH)

URL: http://wiretap.spies.com/Gopher/Gov/World/mex1836.con
http://wiretap.spies.com/Gopher/Gov/World/mex1857.con

LEGISLATION (IN SPANISH)

DESCRIPTION: This site provides legal information about Mexico, research areas, and projects under development. The site contains Constitutions of Mexico, information about the Institute and the activities of its faculty, and links to other Mexican sites of interest. They also provides telnet access to UNAM JURE-II, a database of Mexican legislative information from 1962 to the present (you must have a password to access information before January of the current year). In Spanish.

PROVIDER: Institute of Legal Research, National University of Mexico
URL: http://info.juridicas.unam.mx/

MONGOLIA

CONSTITUTION

URL: http://www.bluemarble.net/~mitch/mong/consttn.html

MYANMAR (BURMA)

POLITICAL CLIMATE

DESCRIPTION: Various documents provide background on the country's political climate including the human rights situation.

PROVIDER: Asian Institute of Technology, Thailand
CONTACT: J. Brubaker
EMAIL: staff@EMAILhost.ait.ac.th
URL: http://www.ait.ac.th/Asia/infobm.html

NETHERLANDS

CONSTITUTION

DESCRIPTION: The first URL below provides the Constitution in Dutch. The second site provide the English version, and the third the Spanish.

URL: http://www.eur.nl/frg/grondwet.html (Dutch version)
URL: http://www.law.cornell.edu/law/index.html (English version)
URL: gopher://ulima.edu.pe:70/00/ccpp/seccion1/cextr/europa/holanda.txt (Spanish version)

NATIONAL ACTION PROGRAM ELECTRONIC HIGHWAY

URL: http://www.nic.surfnet.nl/nap/home.html (Dutch version)
URL: http://www.nic.surfnet.nl/nap/nap-en.html (English version)

LOKET PARLEMENT, INFORMATION ON THRONE AND PARLIAMENT

DESCRIPTION: Document appears to be in Dutch.

URL: http://www.dds.nl/overheid/pdc

NEW ZEALAND

NEW ZEALAND STATUTES

DESCRIPTION: NZ statutes are now available on a new database called the Knowledge Basket.

URL: http://io.kete.co.nz/

GOVERNMENT PAGE

DESCRIPTION: This page offers information concerning the parliamentary system, government press releases, party documents, documents from Ministries: Bills, budgets, reports, and papers. The following are selected items from the site as collected on another Web page provided by the University of Waikato School of Law in New Zealand:

- Treaty of Waitangi
- New Zealand Bill of Rights
- Members of the House of Representatives
- How to make a submission to a Parliamentary Select Committee
- MMP vs FPP
- A List of New Zealand Lawyers on Email
- Auckland Law School
- The Maori Law Review - a monthly review of law affecting the Maori

PROVIDER: Victoria University, Wellington
ADDRESS: PO Box 600, Wellington, New Zealand
PHONE: 64 4 472 1000
CONTACT: Matthew.Sheppard@vuw.ac.nz
URL: http://www.govt.nz/
URL: http://www2.waikato.ac.nz/law/library/nz.html

PERU

CONSTITUTION OF PERU

DESCRIPTION: This document is available at these sites only in Spanish.

PROVIDER: La Red Cientifica Peruana, a nonprofit organization in Peru, connected that country to the NSF backbone in February 1994
URL: gopher://gopher.rcp.net.pe:70/11/adperu/Constitucion
PROVIDER: The Internet Wiretap
URL: gopher://wiretap.spies.com:70/00/Gov/World/peru.con

PHILIPPINES

POLITICAL CLIMATE

DESCRIPTION: Various documents provide background on the country's political climate including the criminal justice system.

PROVIDER: Asian Institute of Technology, Thailand
CONTACT: J. Brubaker
EMAIL: staff@EMAILhost.ait.ac.th
URL: http://www.ait.ac.th/Asia/infoph.html

ARMY AREA HANDBOOK

DESCRIPTION: This monograph provides an overview of Philippine's legal system, culture, history, economy, people, geography, and current international relationships, as well as a wealth of other information. This document was extracted from the Department of Commerce, Economics and Statistics Division's National Trade Data Bank (NTDB) CD-ROM.

PROVIDER: University of Minnesota - St. Louis
URL: gopher://UMSLVMA.UMSL.EDU:70/11/LIBRARY/GOVDOCS/ARMYAHBS/AAHB4

POLAND

GOVERNMENT SITE

DESCRIPTION: The Polish government server provides info and documents from various agencies in Polish.

URL: http://www.urm.gov.pl/welcome.html

CONSTITUTION

URL: http://www.econ.uni-hamburg.de/law/pl__indx.html

ROMANIA

DRAFT CONSTITUTION

PROVIDER: The Internet Wiretap
URL: http://wiretap.spies.com/Gopher/Gov/World/romania.con

RUSSIA

LEGISLATION

CONSTITUTION

DESCRIPTION: Complete Englishlanguage translation (83 screens) of the new Constitution of the Russian Federation as approved by RF President Boris Yeltsin and submitted to national referendum in December 1993.

PROVIDER: Washburn University, School of Law Library
ADDRESS: 1700 College, Topeka, KS 66621
PHONE: (913) 231-1010
FAX: (913) 232-8087
CONTACT: Mark Folmsbee
EMAIL: zzfolm@acc.wuacc.edu
URL: http://law.wuacc.edu/washlaw/forint/europe/russia.html

LAW COLLECTION

DESCRIPTION: This site offers a collection of laws and government decrees.

PROVIDER: European Law Students Association
CONTACT: Myroslav J. Muenzer
ADDRESS: Jean-Paul-Str. 18, D-95444 Bayreuth, Germany
EMAIL: MyM@uni-bayreuth.de
PHONE: ++49-921-515778
URL: http://www.unibayreuth.de/students/elsa/jura/geo/jurweb-russland.html

LAW COLLECTION

DESCRIPTION: The purpose of this server is to provide access to legal and related information concerning the Russian Federation (and the United States, to a lesser extent) in order to promote mutual understanding and to facilitate international business. Features include: Russian laws, tutorial on Russian legal research, and legal and business memoranda and commentaries.

URL: http://solar.rtd.utk.edu/~sanor/main.html

MISCELLANEOUS

DOING BUSINESS INFO

DESCRIPTION: This is the home page for the Department of Commerce's Business Information Service for the Newly Independent States (BISNIS), the U.S. government's one-stop shop for doing business in Russia and the other states of the former Soviet Union.

URL: http://www.itaiep.doc.gov/bisnis/bisnis.html

BUSINESS LAW JOURNAL

DESCRIPTION: The journal Rules and Regulations in Russia featured articles on local business regulations. However, the journal is no longer in print. The URL indicated here archives issues three and four from 1994. Issue three offers the full text in English of the Russian Copyright Law, while issue four discusses import/export tariffs.

PROVIDER: NEVAlink Company, 4 Asaf'eva St., St. Petersburg, Russia
PHONE: +7 812 592 3737 or +7 812 592 2237
FAX: +7 812 592 2236
CONTACT: Nicholai Gluzdov
EMAIL: ng@sppress.spb.su
URL: http://www.spb.su/rulesreg/index.html

RUSSIAN AND EAST EUROPEAN STUDIES

DESCRIPTION: The Russian and East European studies home pages are a comprehensivehypertext guide to the worldwide networkaccessible resources available to scholars in the interdisciplinary study of Russia and Eastern Europe. Resources are subdivided into separate pages by discipline, including government and public affairs.

PROVIDER: University of Pittsburgh Center for Russian and East European Studies and the University of Pittsburgh Library System, Networked Information Services Group
CONTACT: Casey Palowitch
EMAIL: cjp@acid.library.pitt.edu.
URL: http://www.pitt.edu/~cjp/rees.html

SINGAPORE

POLITICAL CLIMATE

DESCRIPTION: Various documents provide background on the country's political climate including the criminal justice system.

PROVIDER: Asian Institute of Technology, Thailand
CONTACT: J. Brubaker
EMAIL: staff@EMAILhost.ait.ac.th
URL: http://www.ait.ac.th/Asia/infosg.html

LEGAL PROFESSION ACT

URL: gopher://gopher.technet.sg:2100/00/PIPS/prof/pr7.txt

ARMY AREA HANDBOOK

DESCRIPTION: This monograph provides an overview of Singapore's legal system, culture, history, economy, people, geography, and current international relationships, as well as a wealth of other information. This document was extracted from the Department of Commerce, Economics and Statistics Division's National Trade Data Bank (NTDB) CD-ROM.

PROVIDER: University of Minnesota - St. Louis
URL: gopher://UMSLVMA.UMSL.EDU:70/11/LIBRARY/GOVDOCS/ARMYAHBS/AAHB5

SLOVAKIA

CONSTITUTION

DESCRIPTION: Passed by the Slovak National Council on September 1, 1991, this site provides additional information about Slovakia including its political climate.

URL: gopher://gopher.GsuEDU:70/11/Departments/rgc/FACULTY/ECA/Slovakia

SOUTH AFRICA

COURTS

SOUTH AFRICAN CONSTITUTIONAL COURT

DESCRIPTION: The Law School Constitutional Repository at the University of the Witwatersrand in Johannesburg, South Africa provides South African Constitutional Court Opinions, Constitutional Documents, and info about the Court and its Judges.

URL: http://www.law.wits.ac.za/lawreps.html

OTHER

CONSTITUTION

DESCRIPTION: Here are two English-language versions of the same document. The Rhodes University site is easiest to access, and provides the constitution by separate chapter and schedule, as well as combined in one document. The German site offers the entire document in one file, although in compressed version. However, the German server can uncompress on the fly (meaning, it can uncompress as it transfers the file to your home directory). To get the uncompressed version, just leave (.gz) ending off the file name when you execute the transfer. That is, once you have entered the directory (see below), to receive the constitution uncompressed, type: get South-Africa-Constitution

PROVIDER: Rhodes University
ADMINISTRATOR: Computer Centre
PHONE: 27 461 318284
EMAIL: postmaster@ru.ac.za
URL: gopher://gopher.ru.ac.za:70/11/politics/const
PROVIDER: University of Stuttgart, Computational Center, Germany
EMAIL: admin@ftp.uni-stuttgart.de

GOVERNMENT SITE

DESCRIPTION: Constitution, legislation and policy of all aspects of public life in South Africa.

CONTACT: webmaster@polity.org.za
URL: http://www.polity.org.za/gnuindex.html

AFRICAN NATIONAL CONGRESS (ANC)

DESCRIPTION: Provides access to a rich assortment of ANC documents. Here are the available directories with examples of available files:

ANC Historical Documents
- ANC Policy Guidelines 1992
- ANC and the Bill of Rights 19231993
- Constitution of the ANC 1991
- Freedom Charter (1955)
- Harare Declaration (1989)
- Manifesto of Umkhonto we Sizwe (1961)
- Minutes & Accords with SA Govt (19901991)
- Nelson Mandela's speech on release from prison (1990)

ANC Policy Documents
- A Bill of Rights for the New South Africa
- ANC Foreign Policy
- ANC constitutional principles
- Policing in the transition
- Principles of environmental policy
- Restitution of Land Rights
- Women's Charter for Effective Equality

ANC Press Statements

Daily News Briefings

Miscellaneous Documents
- Code of Conduct for Elected Members of the ANC
- National Peace Accord 1991
- Nelson Mandela biographical details
- Nelson Mandela Various Addresses
- Telephone numbers of cabinet ministers

PROVIDER: African National Congress, Dept Information & Publicity
ADDRESS: PO Box 61884, Marshalltown, 2107 Johannesburg, RSA

PHONE: 27 11 330 7096
FAX: 27 11 333 8870
EMAIL: ancdip@wn.apc.org
CONTACT: SANGONeT Support
PHONE: 27 11 838 6943
EMAIL: support@wn.apc.org
URL: gopher://gopher.wn.apc.org

SOMALIA

ARMY AREA HANDBOOK

DESCRIPTION: This monograph provides an overview of Somalia's legal system, culture, history, economy, people, geography, and current international relationships, as well as a wealth of other information. This document was extracted from the Department of Commerce, Economics and Statistics Division's National Trade Data Bank (NTDB) CD-ROM.

PROVIDER: University of Minnesota - St. Louis
URL: gopher://UMSLVMA.UMSL.EDU:70/11/LIBRARY/GOVDOCS/ARMYAHBS/AAHB3

SOUTH KOREA

CONSTITUTION

PROVIDER: Seoul National University College of Law
EMAIL: remus@plaza.snu.ac.kr or hryoo@siu.edu
URL: http://plaza.snu.ac.kr/~remus/constit.htm

COURT ORGANIZATION ACT

PROVIDER: Seoul National University College of Law
EMAIL: remus@plaza.snu.ac.kr or hryoo@siu.edu
URL: http://plaza.snu.ac.kr/~remus/court.htm

ARMY AREA HANDBOOK

DESCRIPTION: This monograph provides an overview of South Korea's legal system, culture, history, economy, people, geography, and current international relationships, as well as a wealth of other information. This document was extracted from the Department of Commerce, Economics and Statistics Division's National Trade Data Bank (NTDB) CD-ROM.
PROVIDER: University of Minnesota - St. Louis
URL: gopher://UMSLVMA.UMSL.EDU:70/11/LIBRARY/GOVDOCS/ARMYAHBS/AAHB1

SOVIET UNION

CONSTITUTION

DESCRIPTION: This document is also known as the Fundamental Law of the USSR. It was adopted at the Seventh Session of the Supreme Soviet on October 7, 1977.

URL: http://wiretap.spies.com/Gopher/Gov/World/ussr77.con

EX-USSR DATABASE

DESCRIPTION: The EXUSSR database has information about the 15 republics of the exSoviet Union such as list of top government officials in Russia, Turkmenistan, Tajikistan, Tatarstan, Uzbekistan, Kazakhstan, Belarus, & Kyrgyzstan, a "Who's Who" of leaders in the republics, lists of Internet listservs, usenet newsgroups, ftp sites, news boards and news services about Russia and Eastern Europe, email and snail mail/postal addresses of institutions and organizations in the exUSSR.

PROVIDER: University of Kansas
CONTACT: Wayne Chander
EMAIL: waynec@kuhub.cc.ukans.edu
URL: http://telnet ukanaix.cc.ukans.edu/
LOGIN: ex-ussr

COMMUNIST MANIFESTO

DESCRIPTION: Written by Karl Marx and Frederick Engels. This version is reprinted in its entirety with the exception of part III, a short polemic against certain political groups of their time (1847) with whom Marx and Engels disagreed.

URL: http://wiretap.spies.com/Gopher/Gov/Other/commun.mf

POSTSOVIET STUDY RESOURCES ON THE INTERNET

DESCRIPTION: This paper is a summary of the Internet sources uncovered in the author's search for "alternatives to the mainstream media sources concerning Eastern Eurpe and the former Soviet Union." The findings are divided into two categories: contemporary news and discussion sources and archived documents, directories and bibliographies.

PROVIDER: Document is compiled, edited and with commentary by Ian Kallen. Gopher server provided by the Vienna University of Economics and Business Administration
EMAIL: gopher-adm@wu-wien.ac.at
PROVIDER: CERRO, the Central European Regional Research Organization is a joint initiative of several institutions, including Vienna University, Slovak Academy of Sciences, Bratislava, CSFR, and the University of North Carolina, Chapel Hill, North Carolina, USA.
ADDRESS: Interdisciplinary Institute for Urban & Regional Studies, University of Economics and Business Administration, Augasse 2-6, A-1090 Vienna, Austria
EMAIL: cerro@nestroy.wu-wien.ac.at
URL: http://osiris.wu-wien.ac.at/

SPAIN

CONSTITUTION

DESCRIPTION: This is the Spanish Constitution, in Spanish language.

PROVIDER: University of Granada
URL: http://www.ugr.es/~amunoz/Welcome.html

SWEDEN

VARIOUS LAWS

DESCRIPTION: Provides access to various laws (in Swedish), including the Swedish Data Privacy Act.i.Sweden: Data Privacy Act;.i.Data Privacy Act: Swedish;. A note on this server cautions that these materials are not guaranteed to be accurate.

PROVIDER: Lysator, a students computer society, Linkoping Univeristy, Sweden
CONTACT: Tommy Persson
EMAIL: gopher@lysator.liu.se
URL: gopher://gopher.lysator.liu.se:70/11/project-runeberg/txt/swedhack

THAILAND

POLITICAL CLIMATE

DESCRIPTION: Various documents provide background on the country's political climate including the criminal justice system, and the human rights situation.

PROVIDER: Asian Institute of Technology, Thailand
CONTACT: J. Brubaker
EMAIL: staff@EMAILhost.ait.ac.th
URL: http://www.ait.ac.th/Asia/infoth.html

UKRAINE

UKRAINIAN LAW OUTLINE

DESCRIPTION: Provides synopsis, in outline format, of several topics of Ukrainian law.

URL: http://www.bcpl.lib.md.us/~jbyrley/hompage.html

UNITED KINGDOM

ANCIENT LAW

BILL OF RIGHTS, 1689

DESCRIPTION: Subtitled: An Act Declaring the Rights and Liberties of the Subject and Settling the Succession of the Crown.

URL: http://wiretap.spies.com/Gopher/Gov/World/england.bil

MAGNA CARTA

DESCRIPTION: The original of this document is in Latin, but this version is English.

PROVIDER: Posted by the Internet Wiretap, this document was prepared by the Cleveland Free-Net, and distributed by the National Public Telecomputing Network
URL: http://wiretap.spies.com/Gopher/Gov/World/magna.txt

LAWS OF WILLIAM THE CONQUEROR

DESCRIPTION: Normans conquered England in 1066. Willaim died 1087.

URL: http://wiretap.spies.com/Gopher/Gov/Other/william.law

MISCELLANEOUS

U.K. PUBLIC RECORDS

DESCRIPTION: The Public Record Office (PRO) is the repository of the national archives for England and Wales. For the most part, this site merely provides information about the office.

URL: http://www.open.gov.uk/pro/prohome.htm

REPORT ON CIVIL JUSTICE

DESCRIPTION: "Access to Justice - The report on the administration of civil justice in England & Wales", is also known as the Woolf Report.

PROVIDER: CTI Centre for Law based at the Law School at the University of Warwick
URL: http://ltc.law.warwick.ac.uk/woolf/woolf.html

LAW COLLECTION

DESCRIPTION: The Law Technology Centre provides access to some unique materials (The Law Technology Journal) and otherwise provides a wide-ranging collection of varied legal materials.

PROVIDER: Warwick University
CONTACT: Colin Shaw
ADDRESS: Law Technology Centre, University of Warwick, Coventry, CV4 7AL England
EMAIL: CTILaw@warwick.ac.uk
PHONE: 44 203523097
FAX: 44 203524105
URL: http://ltc.law.warwick.ac.uk/

THE LAW SOCIETY OF ENGLAND AND WALES

DESCRIPTION: This project of the Law Society of England and Wales provides services and information to solicitors and legal practitioners throughout the United Kingdom and worldwide.

URL: http://www.lawsoc.org.uk/

YUGOSLAVIA

ARMY AREA HANDBOOK

DESCRIPTION: This monograph provides an overview of Yugoslavia's legal system, culture, history, economy, people, geography, and current international relationships, as well as a wealth of other information. This document was extracted from the Department of Commerce, Economics and Statistics Division's National Trade Data Bank (NTDB) CD-ROM.

PROVIDER: University of Minnesota - St. Louis
URL: gopher://UMSLVMA.UMSL.EDU:70/11/LIBRARY/GOVDOCS/ARMYAHBS/AAHB2

INTERNATIONAL
(other resources)

TREATIES

TRADE LAW TREATIES

DESCRIPTION: This site provides access to international trade conventions and other relevant trade instruments, from 1891 - today. Documents are arranged in menus according to date, from the pre-1920s, through each decade to the present. However, documents are only retrievable from certain of the menus. It is unclear if this is because some documents are unavailable, or if retrieval is based on date of each document's revision (as opposed to document's orgination date). Available documents in full text include:

1950s

- Convention on the Contract for the International Carriage of Goods by Road, Geneva 1978

1960s

- Paris Convention for the Protection of Industrial Property of 1883 (amended through 1967)
- EEC Convention on Jurisdiction and the Enforcement of Judgments in Civil and Commercial Matters (Full Faith and Credit Convention)
- International Convention for the Protection of Industrial Property 1967 revision (originally 1883)

1970s

- The York-Antwerp Rules 1974
- The Hamburg Rules: United Nations Convention on the Carriage of Goods by Sea (1979)
- The Hague-Visby Rules as implemented by the Carriage of Goods by Sea Act 1971
- Universal Copyright Convention (Paris 1971 revision)
- Patent Co-operation Treaty (amended in 1979 and modified in 1984)
- Convention on the Means of Prohibiting and Preventing the Illicit Import, Export and Transfer of Ownership of Cultural Property
- Berne Convention for the Protection of Literary and Artistic Works (1896, amended through 1979)
- Hague Convention on the Law Applicable to Agency

1980s

- Convention on the Law Applicable to Contracts for the International Sale of Goods
- UN Convention on International Bills of Exchange
- UNCTAD Model Clauses on Marine Cargo Insurance
- EEC Convention on the Law Applicable to Contractual Obligations

1990s

- General Agreement on Tariffs and Trade 1994
- North American Free Trade Agreement NAFTA
- EEC Maastricht Treaty

PROVIDER: University of Tromsx, Institutt for Rettsvitenskap (IRV)
ADDRESS: Breivika, N-9037, Tromsx, Norway
PHONE: 47 776 44197
FAX: 47 776 44775
EMAIL: ananse@irv.uit.no
URL: http://ananse.irv.uit.no/trade_law/nav/conventions.html

ENVIRONMENTAL TREATIES

DESCRIPTION: There are two menu options here providing access to hundreds of international environmental agreements. One provides full-text access to a collection of treaties, and one provides summaries of a different collection of treaties and agreements.

The full-text international treaty and agreement texts are from the publication World Treaties for the Protection of the Environment edited by Tullio Scovazzi and Tullio Treves, published (1992) by the Istituto per L'Ambiente, a research institution based in Milan, Italy that promotes interdisciplinary studies on the environment.

The summarized agreements are derived from the United Nations Environment Programme's Register of International Treaties and Other Agreements in the Field of the Environment, May 1991 edition. Aside from the introduction and index, each file is a summary of an individual agreement, including:

- objectives
- provisions
- date of adoption
- place of adoption
- date of entry into force
- official languages
- lists of signatories, dates of entry into force and/or withdrawal of each

PROVIDER: Consortium for International Earth Science Information Network (CIESIN, pronounced "season"), a corporation formed to respond to the creation of the CIESIN initiative the U.S. Congress
ADDRESS: CIESIN User Services, 2250 Pierce Road, University Center, MI 48710
PHONE: (517) 797-2727
FAX: (517) 797-2622
EMAIL: ciesin.info@ciesin.org
CONTACT: Sharlyn Thomas
PHONE: (517) 797-2646
EMAIL: sthomas@ciesin.org
URL: gopher infoserver.ciesin.org

GENERAL AGREEMENT ON TARIFFS AND TAXES (GATT)

DESCRIPTION: GATT is a multilateral treaty subscribed by 103 governments, called the "Contracting Parties." It entered into force in January 1948. GATT is both a set of rules and a forum in which countries can participate in discussions to overcome their trade problems and negotiate to enlarge world trading opportunities. The full text of GATT is available at the USDA site below. A list of member countries, and other info about GATT is available from the UN, as indicated below.

PROVIDER: United Nations
URL: gopher://gopher.undp.org:70/11/unearth/organizations/gatt

TREATY COLLECTIONS

VARIOUS TREATIES

PROVIDER: The Internet Wiretap
URL: http://wiretap.spies.com/Gopher/Gov/Treaties

- Geneva Conventions.i.Geneva Conventions;/
- Hague Conventions.i.Hague Conventions;/
- League of Nations.i.League of Nations;/
- The Law of the Sea;The Law of the Sea (1982)/
- Various Treaties/
- then choose from the following:

- Charter of the United Nations Charter
- Conference on the Protection of Cultural Property in Conflict
- Convention Against Torture and Cruel Punishment
- Convention for Protection of World Cultural & Natural Heritage
- Convention for the Prevention of Marine Pollution
- Convention on Discrimination Against Women
- Convention on Fishing and High Seas Resources 1958
- Convention on Hostile Use of Environmental Modification Techniques
- Convention on International Trade in Endangered Species
- Convention on Wetlands of International Importance
- Convention on the Continental Shelf 1958
- Convention on the .High Seas 1958
- Convention on the Prevention and Punishment of Genocide
- Convention on the Rights of the Child
- Convention on the Territorial Sea 1958
- Convention to Prohibit Import and Export of Cultural Property
- International Convention for the Regulation of Whaling 1946
- International Convention on the Elimination of Racial Discrimination
- International Covenant on Civil and Political Rights
- International Covenant on Economic, Social, Cultural Rights
- Montreal Protocol on Substances that Deplete the Ozone Layer
- North Atlantic Treaty 1949
- Paris Convention for Protection of Industrial Property 1967
- Patent Cooperation Treaty 1970
- Patent Cooperation Treaty Regulations 1970
- Prohibition of Bacteriological and Toxin Weapons 1972
- Protocol I Relating to the Status of Refugees, New York 1967
- Protocol for Prohibition of Poisonous Gases 1928
- Roerich Pact: Institutions and Monuments in the Americas
- Statute of the International Court of Justice
- Treaty on the Nonproliferation of Nuclear Weapons 1968
- Universal Copyright Convention as Revised at Paris 1971
- Unlawful Acts Against Civil Aviation 1971
- Vienna Convention for the Protection of the Ozone Layer 1985
- Vienna Convention on Consular Relations (with Protocols)
- Vienna Convention on Diplomatic Relations (with Protocols).
- Vienna Convention on the Law of Treaties 1969.

MAASTRICHT TREATY OF EUROPEAN UNION

DESCRIPTION: This directory contains the latest addition to the Treaty on European Union signed at Maastricht on February 7, 1992.

PROVIDER: Cornell Law School
URL: gopher://gopher.law.cornell.edu:70/77/foreign/.mass_index/maastricht

MULTILATERAL TREATIES

DESCRIPTION: The Multilaterals Project is an experimental program begun at the Fletcher School of Law and Diplomacy in Medford, Mass. to make available to the Internet community the text of a wide variety of multilateral conventions. Although most of these treaties are now in force, a fair number, including the U.N. Convention on the Law of the Sea signed in 1982, have not yet achieved the necessary number of ratifications. Almost all are available in print form, although it is expected in the future that this project will post conventions that have been signed only very recently.

Although the primary focus has been on international environmental instruments, conventions dealing with human rights, the laws of war, and other fields are also included. Following is a partial list of available documents (note that many of the titles have been abridged for the sake of brevity).

- Action Plan for the Human Environment (Stockholm, 1972)
- Agreement Governing the Activities of States on the Moon
- Agreement on the Rescue of Astronauts, the Return of Astronauts - Basel Convention on the Control of Transboundary Movement
- Berne Conv. for the Protection of Literary & Artistic Works
- Charter of the United Nations (1945)
- Conv. on Fishing & Conserv. of Living Res. of the High Seas
- Conv. on the Territorial Sea & the Contiguous Zone (1958)
- Convention for the Protection of the Mediterranean Sea
- Convention for the Protection of the World Cultural
- Convention for the Suppression of Unlawful Acts
- Convention on Environmental Impact Assessment
- Convention on the Continental Shelf (1958)
- Convention on the Elimination of All Forms of Discrimination

- Convention on the High Seas (1958)
- Convention on the Means of Prohibiting and Preventing Illicit
- Convention on the Prevention and Punishment of Genocide (1948)
- Convention on the Prohibition of Military or any Other Hostile - Convention on the Prohibition of the Development, Production
- Convention on the Rights of the Child (1989)
- Declaration of the United Nations Conference on the Human
- International Convention for the Regulation of Whaling (1946)
- International Covenant on Civil and Political Rights (1966)
- International Covenant on Economic, Social, and Cultural Rights - International Tropical Timber Agreement (1983)
- Montreal Protocol on Substances that Deplete the Ozone Layer
- Optional Protocol to the International Covenant on Civil
- Paris Conv. for the Protection of Indus. Property (rev.1967)
- Patent Cooperation Treaty; with Regulations (1970)
- Protocol Additional to the Geneva Conventions
- Protocol for the Prohibition of the Use in War of Asphyxiating
- Protocol relating to the Status of Refugees (1967)
- Regional Convention for the Conservation of the Red Sea & Gulf
- Statute of the International Court of Justice (1945)
- The General Agreement on Tariffs and Trade (1947)
- Treaty on Principles Governing the Activities of States
- Treaty on the NonProliferation of Nuclear Weapons (1968)
- Universal Copyright Convention as revised at Paris, 1971
- Universal Declaration of Human Rights
- Vienna Convention for the Protection of the Ozone Layer (1985)
- Vienna Convention on Consular Relations and Protocols (1963)
- Vienna Convention on Diplomatic Relations & Protocols (1961)
- Vienna Convention on the Law of Treaties (1969)
- World Charter for Nature (1982)

PROVIDER: Fletcher School of Law & Diplomacy, Multilaterals Project
CONTACT: Peter Stott, director
EMAIL: pstott@pearl.tufts.edu
pstott@igc.apc.org
URL: ftp://ftp.fletcher.tufts.edu/pub/diplomacy
PROVIDER: Cornell Law School
URL: gopher://gopher.law.cornell.edu:70/11/foreign/fletcher

UNITED NATIONS

UNITED NATIONS RESOLUTIONS

DESCRIPTION: This is the home site for U.N. information. Resolutions are available in full text, dating back over 10 years. Menu options include:

- The United Nations, what it is and what it does/
  - Charter of the United Nations
  - Statute of the International Court of Justice
  - Universal Declaration of Human Rights
  - United Nations Peace-Keeping Operations/
- United Nations Current Information
  - United Nations Daily Journal/
  - Security Council Resolutions/ (Back to 1974)
  - Secretary General Reports and other Security Council Docs/
- United Nations Documents
  - General Assembly Conventions/
  - General Assembly Resolutions/ (Back to 1981)
  - Economic and Social Council Resolutions/
- Environment Related Information

PROVIDER: United Nations
CONTACT: Malcolm Chapman
PHONE: (212) 906-6585
EMAIL: Root@undp.org
URL: gopher://gopher.undp.org

UNITED NATIONS JUSTICE NETWORK (UNCJIN)

DESCRIPTION: The UNCJIN was established in 1989 to implement a worldwide network to enhance dissemination and the exchange of information concerning criminal justice and crime prevention issues. UNCJIN is funded, in part, by the United States Bureau of Justice Statistics (a division of the U.S. Department of Justice). Other supporters are the United Nations Criminal Justice and Crime Prevention Branch in Vienna, the State University of New York at Albany, and the Research Foundation of the State University of New York. UNCJIN options (described below) include:

- United Nations Rules
- UN Criminal Justice Country Profiles
- United Nations Development Program
- World Criminal Justice Library Network

PROVIDER: United Nations Justice Network
ADDRESS: 423 State Street. Albany, NY 12203
CONTACT: Adam Bouloukos, Systems Operator

EMAIL: ab5202@uacsc1.albany.edu
URL: gopher://UACSC2.ALBANY.EDU:70/ /11newman

UNITED NATIONS RULES

DESCRIPTION: Standards, guidelines and international instruments promulgated by the United Nations. Options include:

- Standard Minimum Rules for the Treatment of Prisoners
- Declaration against Torture and other Cruel, Inhuman or Degrading Treatment or Punishment
- Code of Conduct for Law Enforcement Officials
- Safeguards Guaranteeing Protection of the Rights of those Facing the Death Penalty
- The Milan Plan of Action
- Guiding Principles for Crime Prevention and Criminal Justice in the Context of Development and a New Economic Order
- Basic Principles on the Independence of the Judiciary
- Model Agreement on the Transfer of Foreign Prisoners and Recommendations on the Treatment of Foreign Prisoners
- Standard Minimum Rules for the Administration of Juvenile Justice
- Declaration of Basic Principles of Justice for Victims of Crime and the Abuse of Power
- Standard Minimum Rules for NonCustodial Measures
- Guidelines for the Prevention of Juvenile Delinquency
- Rules for the Protection of Juveniles Deprived of their Liberty
- Basic Principles on the Use of Force and Firearms by Low Enforcement Officials
- Basic Principles on the Role of Lawyers
- Guidelines on the Role of Prosecutors
- Model Treaty on Extradition
- Model Treaty on Mutual Assistance in Criminal Matters
- Model Treaty on the Transfer of Proceedings in Criminal Matters
- Model Treaty on the Transfer of Supervision of Offenders Conditionally Sentenced or Conditionally Released
- Model Treaty for the Prevention of Crimes that Infringe on the Cultural Heritage of Peoples in the Form of Movable Property
- Annex to Resolution on Measures Against International Terrorism

PROVIDER: United Nations Justice Network
ADDRESS: 423 State Street. Albany, NY 12203
CONTACT: Adam Bouloukos, Systems Operator
EMAIL: ab5202@uacsc1.albany.edu
URL: gopher://UACSC2.ALBANY.EDU:70/ /11newman/crjrules

UN CRIMINAL JUSTICE COUNTRY PROFILES

DESCRIPTION: World crime surveys of 113 countries, including (depending on the country) descriptions of each country's criminal justice system, numbers of recorded crimes (broken down by type of crime by year 1980 - 1986).

PROVIDER: Surveys were conducted by the Crime Prevention and Criminal Justice Branch, Centre for Social Development and Humanitarian Affairs (CSDHA), United Nations Office in Vienna. Availability by the UNCJIN (see description above).
URL: gopher://UACSC2.ALBANY.EDU:70/ /11newman/crjrules

HUMAN RIGHTS MATERIALS

FOURTH WORLD DOCUMENTATION PROJECT (FWDP)

DESCRIPTION: The purpose of the FWDP is to gather documents written by or about Fourth World Nations and distribute them to tribal governments, researchers, and interested individuals. Files concern aboriginal, indigenous and other native people.

PROVIDER: The Center for World Indigenous Studies
ADDRESS: c/o The Fourth World Documentation Project, PO Box 2574, Olympia, WA 98507-2574
CONTACT: John Burrows
PHONE: (206) 786-9629
EMAIL: jburrows@halcyon.com
URL: ftp://ftp.halcyon.com/pub/FWDP/

HUMANITARIAN LAW COLLECTION

DESCRIPTION: Options at this site include:

- Basic rules of Humanitarian law in armed conflicts
- International Humanitarian Law Full texts of the Geneva Conventions
- States party to the Geneva Conventions and their Additional Protocols
- Humanitarian law issues
- Information for defence and military staff

PROVIDER: International Committee of the Red Cross
URL: http://www.icrc.ch/icrcnews/22f2.ht

HUMAN RIGHTS REPORTS

DESCRIPTION: The U.S. State Department Human Rights Country Reports are transmitted annually by the U.S. Department of State to the Congress. As mandated by the Foreign Assistance Act of 1961 (FAA), the reports are "a full and complete report regarding the status of internationally recognized human rights in countries that received assistance under the FAA, and in all other foreign countries which are members of the United Nations and which are not otherwise the subject of a human rights report under the Act."

The reports cover internationally recognized individual, political, civil, and worker rights, as set forth in the Universal Declaration of Human rights. They identify where there is armed conflict, torture, discrimination, etc.

PROVIDER: Voice of America Computer Services Division
PHONE: (202) 619-2020
EMAIL: postmaster@voa.gov
URL: gopher://gopher.VOA.GOV:70/11/pub/documents/human_rights_94

INSTITUTE FOR GLOBAL COMMUNICATION LAW

DESCRIPTION: The Institute for Global Communications (IGC) Networks includes PeaceNet, EcoNet, ConflictNet, and LaborNet. These networks host conferences on human rights, conflict resolution, environmental law, women, labor, etc.

The IGC gophers are free, and offer a variety of legal documents concerning the environment, human rights, labor and conflict resolution. Full participation in the IGC communication networks requires network membership (and associated fees).

PROVIDER: Institute for Global Communications (U.S. member of the Association for Progressive Communications, a 16-country association of computer networks working for peace, human rights, environmental protection, social justice and sustainability)
ADDRESS: 18 De Boom Street, San Francisco, CA 94107
PHONE: (415) 442-0220
FAX: (415) 546-1794
EMAIL: igc-info@igc.apc.org
URL: gopher://gopher.igc.apc.org

WOMEN'S RIGHTS

DESCRIPTION: "Women of the World: Formal Laws and Policies Affecting Their Reproductive Lives." This is a report analyzing women's legal status in Brazil, China, Germany, India, Nigeria, and the United States with regard to health, population and family planning, contraception and contraceptive technology, abortion, sterilization, STDs and HIV/AIDS, safe motherhood, rape, and patients' rights.

PROVIDER: The Center for Reproductive Law and Policy
URL: http://www.echonyc.com/~jmkm/wotw/

INTERNATIONAL TRADE LAW

INTERNATIONAL TRADE LAW COLLECTION

DESCRIPTION: The stated objective of the International Trade Law Project is: "To investigate the potential of W3 as an information resource, with regard to legal research and education. This we plan to do taking a practical example, - focusing on international trade law as a limited and vitally important area of law that is of international interest." The site includes a lot of substantive material, including international trade treaties, conventions, model laws, rules and other relevant trade instruments.

PROVIDER: University of Tromsø (Norway) Law Faculty
URL: http://ra.irv.uit.no/trade_law/itlp.html

U.S. INTERNATIONAL TRADE COMMISSION (USITC)

DESCRIPTION: Full text of the Harmonized Tariff Schedule, rules, news releases and other documents from the USITC are available here.

URL: http://www.usitc.gov

OTHER SOURCES OF INTERNATIONAL LEGAL INFORMATION

CIA WORLD FACTBOOK

DESCRIPTION: The World Factbook is produced annually by the Central Intelligence Agency for the use of U. S. government officials. The book contains information on over 247 nations and entities, as well as the United

Nations, and other international organizations. It also provides an international weights and measures cross-reference file. For each country, the book discusses the legal system, political climate, physical aspects (climate, terrain, land use, environment, people, national holidays, etc.). The Factbook is available at many sites. The University of Missouri site has the most current version in browsable form (arranged by country), while the University of North Carolina offers a searchable version.

PROVIDER: University of North Carolina - Chapel Hill
EMAIL: gophermaster@sunsite.unc.edu
URL: http://sunsite.unc.edu

CONSTITUTIONS OF THE WORLD

DESCRIPTION: Updated regularly, these sites contain English versions of several world constitutions, including those from Canada, France, Japan, Mexico, and the United States.

URL: http://info.ic.gc.ca/~will/Other/Legal/pointers.html
URL: http://www.law.cornell.edu/law/index.html

CRIMINAL JUSTICE

DESCRIPTION: International criminal justice Web sites are centrally linked here.

PROVIDER: U.S. Department of Justice
URL: http://www.usdoj.gov/ojp/rol/docs/home.html

EASTERN EUROPE

DESCRIPTION: Country home pages including legal material: Estonia, Latvia, Hungary, Lithuania, Poland, Romania, Slovakia. Slovenia, Croatia, Czech Republic, Bulgaria.

URL: http://www.itaiep.doc.gov/eebic/cdceec.html

INTERNATIONAL LAW LIST FAQ

DESCRIPTION: In answer to the many questions that arise concerning the INT-LAW list, Lyonette Louis-Jacques maintains a document that answers frequently asked questions (FAQ). The most recent version is 15K (about 5-6 pages long) and is dated April 22, 1995. This version answers general questions about INT-LAW including how to unsubscribe and how to subscribe.

URL: http://www.lib.uchicago.edu/~llou/intlawfaq.html

NORTH ATLANTIC TREATY ORGANIZATION (NATO)

DESCRIPTION: The (NATO) Internet site provides a library of current and historical documents, including conventions, declarations and protocols. The NATO Handbook offers insight into how NATO works, as well as the North Atlantic Treaty. Following are the menu options at the NATO site:

- NATO CONTACT Points/
- NATO Basic Texts/
- NATO Communiques, Speeches and Press Releases/
- NATO Military Committee Press Releases/
- NATO Handbook Edition 1992/
- NATO Factsheets/
- NATO Review/
- NATO Seminars, Workshops and Colloquia/
- NATO Focus (Biographies)/
- NATO Academic Fellowships/
- NATO Agencies and Military Commands/
- NATO Scientific and Environmental Affairs/
- NACC and Partnership for Peace Country Documents/
- NATO Binary Files (Images)/
- NATO Miscellaneous/

PROVIDER: North Atlantic Treaty Organization Integrated Data Service
CONTACT: Mr. Chris Scheurweghs
ADDRESS: Boulevard Leopold III, 1110 Brussels, Belgium
PHONE: 32 2 728 4599
FAX: 32 2 728 5229
EMAIL: gopher@stc.nato.int
scheurwe@hq.nato.int
Chris.Scheurweghs@eurokom.ie
URL: gopher://marvin.stc.nato.int:70/11/natodata

SPANISH SPEAKING COUNTRIES

DESCRIPTION: This page provides links to collections of sites in various countries.

URL: http://edb518ea.edb.utexas.edu/html/latinamerica.html

WORLD BANK

DESCRIPTION: The World Bank Public Information Service provides access to World Bank policy papers, environmental reports, project information documents, country economic reports and publications catalogs.

PROVIDER: The World Bank
ADDRESS: 1818 H Street, N.W., Washington, DC 20433
EMAIL: webmaster@www.worldbank.org
URL: gopher://gopher.worldbank.org

Mailing Lists

AALSMIN-L

DESCRIPTION: A discussion group for people who are members of the Association of American Law Schools' Section on Minority Groups. The Association of American Law Schools is not the owner of the list, however; the listowner is Odeana R. Neal, Assistant Professor at the University of Baltimore School of Law. Only members of the AALS Section on Minority Groups will be permitted to join AALSMIN-L. The list management reserves the right to remove anyone who is ineligible or who abuses their list privileges.

SUBSCRIPTION ADDRESS: listserv@ube.UBALT.edu
MAIL ADDRESS: AALSMIN-L@ube.ubalt.edu
ARCHIVE: Monthly archives of AALSMIN-L may also be obtained via gopher at gopher.ube.ubalt.edu, located under Campus-Wide Information/Academic Computing Center/Files on FILESERV

ABA-UNIX-LIST

DESCRIPTION: American Bar Association UNIX list.

SUBSCRIPTION ADDRESS: listserv@austin.onu.edu
MAIL ADDRESS: aba-unix-list@austin.onu.edu

ACALI-L

DESCRIPTION: Innovative methods of teaching law, particularly using technology; mostly Australian/New Zealand subscribers.

SUBSCRIPTION ADDRESS: listserv@sulaw.law.su.oz.au
MAIL ADDRESS: ACALI-L@sulaw.law.su.oz.au

ADA-LAW

DESCRIPTION: Americans with Disabilities Act discussion list. This is a high traffic list.

SUBSCRIPTION ADDRESS: listserv@vm1.nodak.edu or
listserv@ndsuvm1.bitnet
MAIL ADDRESS: ada-law@vm1.nodak.edu

ADMINLAW

DESCRIPTION: Administrative Law list (moderated).

SUBSCRIPTION ADDRESS: listserv@cali.kentlaw.edu
MAIL ADDRESS: adminlaw@cali.kentlaw.edu

AGLAW-L

DESCRIPTION: Agricultural Law list.

SUBSCRIPTION ADDRESS: listserv@lawlib.wuacc.edu
subscribe aglaw-l <Your Name>
MAIL ADDRESS: agalaw-l@lawlib.wuacc.edu

AI-L

DESCRIPTION: The Artificial Intelligence and Law Discussion list is not moderated, so anything you send to the list will be distributed to all subscribers.

SUBSCRIPTION ADDRESS: listserv@austin.onu.edu
MAIL ADDRESS: ai-l@austin.onu.edu
ARCHIVE: The two commands relevant to the archives are "index" and "get". A message to the listserv, the body of which consists of the command: index ail-l will retrieve the index for the AI-L archive. A message, the body of which consists of the command: get ail-l 10-91 will get the archive for the list for October 1991. AI-L messages are also browsable at the Cornell Law School gopher as follows:
gopher.law.cornell.edu
then choose: Discussions and Listserv archives

ALMANAC

DESCRIPTION: This list distributes White House press releases and position papers.

SUBSCRIPTION ADDRESS: almanac@esusda.gov
SUBSCRIPTION INSTRUCTIONS: Sending the command: SUBSCRIBE WH-SUMMARY will provide instructions for accessing other documents and a daily summary of press conferences

AMEND1-L

DESCRIPTION: Discussion list for free speech issues in the U.S. and elsewhere; freedom of expression, privacy, censorship, etc. Postings to this list can be quite lengthy.

SUBSCRIPTION ADDRESS: listserv@uafsysb.uark.edu
subscribe amed1-l <Your Name>
MAIL ADDRESS: amend-l@uafsysb.uark.edu

AMEND2

DESCRIPTION: Colorado Constitutional Amendment 2 list; discussions of the amendment banning legislation providing civil rights protection for homosexuals.

SUBSCRIPTION ADDRESS: (1) Send the following message to majordomo@cs.colorado.edu:
subscribe amend2-discuss (omit your name);
(2) Send "subscribe amend2-discuss Your Name" to amend2-discuss-request@cs.colorado.edu

ANZ-LAW-LIBRARIANS-ONE

DESCRIPTION: Australia and New Zealand law librarians open list.

SUBSCRIPTION ADDRESS: majordomo@uow.edu.au
subscribe anz-law-librarians-one
To unsubscribe send the following text in the body of the message to majordomo@wyrm.cc.ouw.edu.au:
unsubscribe anz-law-librarians-one <Your Name>
MAIL ADDRESS: anz-law-librarians-one@uow.edu.au

APDA

DESCRIPTION: American Parliamentary Debate Association discussion list.

SUBSCRIPTION ADDRESS: listserv@pucc.bitnet
MAIL ADDRESS: apda@pucc.bitnet

ARIZONA

DESCRIPTION: Arizona State Public Information Network.

SUBSCRIPTION ADDRESS: listserv@asuvm.inre.asu.edu or listserv@asucad.bitnet
MAIL ADDRESS: arizona@asuvm.inre.asu.edu or arizona@asucad.bitnet

ASILIELG

DESCRIPTION: A discussion group for persons practicing and teaching international economic law who are members of the American Society of International Law's International Economic Law Interest Group. The list management reserves the right to remove anyone who is ineligible or who abuses their list privileges. Topics discussed on this list include anything connected with international economic law. Tell about new cases, ask about new EC directives, editorialize, criticize, review books, make requests for assistance with research, make requests for assistance with pedagogical tools. List management would like to encourage erudite discussions of international economic law topics, they would also love for this to be a clearing house for requests about anything that can make our professional lives easier and more interesting. Make personal replies when they are appropriate.

SUBSCRIPTION INFO: Send a subscription message to "listserver@cali.kentlaw.edu" with the following message text: "SUBSCRIBE ASILIELG <Your name and position and institution here>".
For example: "SUBSCRIBE ASILIELG John Doe, Professor of Law, Univ. of GATT".
MAIL ADDRESS: ASILIELG@cali.kentlaw.edu

ASP-L

DESCRIPTION: Academic Support Program Directors discussion list. ASP-L was created by Julie Fenton, Assistant Dean of Students, Chicago-Kent College of Law, for people supervising, developing, and teaching in academic support programs at law schools. It is closed to all other persons. If you have any technical questions concerning ASP-L, list management suggests contacting Larry Donahue, <ldonahue@chicagokent.kentlaw.edu>, who will be glad to answer any specific questions you may have.

SUBSCRIPTION INFO: Send the following email message to listserver@chicagokent.kentlaw.edu
subscribe ASP-L Your full name, Your position
MAIL ADDRESS: asp-l@chicagokent.kentlaw.edu

BANKRLAW

DESCRIPTION: Internet discussion group that focuses on all aspects of bankruptcy. This includes business and financial aspects, legal aspects, teaching aspects as well as practical aspects.

SUBSCRIPTION ADDRESS: listserv@polecat.law.indiana.edu
subscribe bankrlaw <Your Name>
MAIL ADDRESS: bankrlaw@polecat.law.indiana.edu
ARCHIVE: http://www.kentlaw.edu/lawnet/lawnet.html

BAYOUDOC

DESCRIPTION: Bayou Area Government Documents Discussion Group.

SUBSCRIPTION ADDRESS: listserv@vm.cc.latech.edu
MAIL ADDRESS: bayoudoc@vm.latech.edu

BIOETHICSLAW-L

DESCRIPTION: Bioethics Law list.

SUBSCRIPTION ADDRESS: listserv@lawlib.wuacc.edu
subscribe bioethicslaw-l
MAIL ADDRESS: bioethicslaw-l@lawlib.wuacc.edu

BIZLAW-L

DESCRIPTION: This list is a forum for members (and friends) of the AALS Section on Business Associations who are interested in the academics of business law. It is a forum for discussing legal issues related to business associations, for gathering and sharing information concerning works in progress, conferences and workshops.

SUBSCRIPTION ADDRESS: listserv@umab.umd.edu
SUBSCRIPTION COMMAND: sub bizlaw-l <your name>
MAIL ADDRESS: bizlaw-l@umab.umd.edu

BUSLIB-L

DESCRIPTION: Includes discussions of general and international business resources. Foreign exchange rates on the Internet, foreign company, export, import, etc. info and other useful resources announced.

SUBSCRIPTION ADDRESS: listserv@idbsu.idbsu.edu or listserv@idbsu.bitnet
SUBSCRIPTION COMMAND: Send the following message: subscribe BUSLIB-L <Your Name>
MAIL ADDRESS: buslib-l@idbsu.idbsu.edu or buslib-l@idbsu.bitnet

CALDOC-L

DESCRIPTION: The California Documents list is for California documents librarians to exchange information regarding California and federal documents issues and to better communicate with the State Library and the California Regional Library in Sacramento. The list is unmoderated and open to the public. Principal Contact is Carol Bednar (cbednar@fullerton.edu).

SUBSCRIPTION ADDRESS: listserv@fullerton.edu
MAIL ADDRESS: caldoc-l@fullerton.edu

CALGOVINFO

DESCRIPTION: Discussion list for the issue of putting California government information on-line.

SUBSCRIPTION ADDRESS: listserv@cpsr.org
MAIL ADDRESS: calgovinfo@cpsr.org
ARCHIVE: gopher://gopher.cpsr.org
http://cpsr.org/lomepage

CALI-L

DESCRIPTION: The list sponsored by the Center for Computer-Assisted Legal Instruction (CALI), focuses on the use of computers and computer-based training in law schools, technical and support issues relating to CALI's products, authoring CALI lessons, the CALI Conference for Law School Computing Professionals, and just about anything else along those lines. Subscribers include law professors, students, CALI people (staff, board members, school reps, authors, potential authors, etc.) and anyone else who is interested in participating. If you have any questions or problems, send a message to the list moderator, David Kiefer, CALI/LEAP Programming Director, at dkiefer@mail.kentlaw.edu, or call (312) 906-5303.

SUBSCRIPTION ADDRESS: listserv@cali.kentlaw.edu
MAIL ADDRESS: cali-l@cali.kentlaw.edu

CALIBD-L

DESCRIPTION: Center for Computer-Assisted Legal Instruction (CALI) Board of Directors list.

SUBSCRIPTION ADDRESS: listserv@cali.kentlaw.edu
MAIL ADDRESS: calibd-l@cali.kentlaw.edu

CALL-L

DESCRIPTION: Canadian Academic Law Libraries list.

SUBSCRIPTION ADDRESS: listserv@unbvm1.bitnet
MAIL ADDRESS: call-l@unbvm1.bitnet

CASEBASE-L

DESCRIPTION: CaseBase user discussion list.

SUBSCRIPTION ADDRESS: listserv@lawlib.wuacc.edu
subscribe casebase-l <Your Name>
MAIL ADDRESS: casebase-l@lawlib.wuacc.edu

CIVIL-JUSTICE

DESCRIPTION: The civil-justice list will provide information on legislation, studies, policy papers, and campaigns aimed at restricting victims' rights and weakening liability laws. This is a low-volume list with all messages originating from the listowner (like a newsletter rather than a discussion list). However, submissions are readily accepted.

SUBSCRIPTION INFO: Send email to listproc@essential.org. In the body of the message write: subscribe civil-justice <First Name, Last Name>
MAIL ADDRESS: civil-justice@essential.org

CIVILRTS

DESCRIPTION: This list is a discussion group for law professors and others writing, teaching and working in civil rights and civil liberties and related areas in federal courts and constitutional law.

SUBSCRIPTION ADDRESS: listserv@chicagokent.kentlaw.edu
MAIL ADDRESS: civilrts@chicagokent.kentlaw.edu

CJUST-L

DESCRIPTION: This is the Criminal Justice discussion list.

SUBSCRIPTION ADDRESS: Send the following message to
listserv@iubvm.ucs.indiana.edu or
listserv@cunyvm.cuny.edu
subscribe cjust-l <Your Name>
MAIL ADDRESS: cjust-l@cunyvm.cuny.edu

CLIPPER

DESCRIPTION: This is a news and announcement-type mailing list for Clipper chip issues and encryption/electronic privacy issues in general.

SUBSCRIPTION ADDRESS: majordomo@vector.casti.com
SUBSCRIPTION COMMAND: subscribe CLIPPER
MAIL ADDRESS: clipper@vector.casti.com.

CNI-COPYRIGHT

DESCRIPTION: The Copyright and Intellectual Property Forum of the Coalition for Networked Information was organized to give those who ask, answer, and discuss copyright questions of any type a forum for discussion. Discussion is not limited to any one area such as copyright for electronic materials.

All questions regarding the substance of, or policies related to the discussions on this moderated forum, and queries regarding difficulties with mail or requests for technical assistance should be sent to the Coalition's Systems Coordinator, Craig A. Summerhill (craig@cni.org). Questions regarding the content of the forum should be directed to: mjensen@charlie.usd.edu or cjg@stubbs.ucop.edu

To see a list of suggested issues to be addressed on this forum, send the following command in the body of a message to
listserv@cni.org: Information CNI-COPYRIGHT

SUBSCRIPTION ADDRESS: listserv@cni.org
MAIL ADDRESS: cni-copyright@cni.org.
ARCHIVE: The Coalition operates these network services:
BRS/SEARCH databases: telnet cni.org login: brsuser
CNI WEB SERVER: http://www.cni.org/CNI.homepage.html

CNI-LEGISLATION

DESCRIPTION: This moderated list is the Coalition for Networked Information's Working Group on Legislation, Codes, Policies, and Practices. The list is intended to provide a forum for the discussion of matters related to policies, positions, principles, codes, statutes, etc., whether federal, state, local, or institutional, pertaining to networked information, and to share information about the Coalition's Legislation, Codes, Policies, and Practices Working Group.

SUBSCRIPTION ADDRESS: listserv@cni.org
MAIL ADDRESS: cni-legislation@cni.org
ARCHIVE: The Coalition operates these network services:
BRS/SEARCH databases: telnet cni.org login: brsuser
CNI WEB SERVER: http://www.cni.org/CNI.homepage.html

CNI-PUBINFO

DESCRIPTION: This moderated list is the Coalition for Networked Information's to Public Information Working Group. The list is intended to provide a forum for the discussion of matters related to the provision of public information, especially that information collected by the United States government, via electronic networks, and to share information about the Coalition's to Public Information Working Group.

SUBSCRIPTION ADDRESS: listserv@cni.org
MAIL ADDRESS: cni-pubinfo@cni.org
ARCHIVE: The Coalition operates these network services:
BRS/SEARCH databases: telnet cni.org login: brsuser
CNI WEB SERVER: http://www.cni.org/CNI.
homepage.html

COGOPUB-L

DESCRIPTION: Colorado Government and Public Information.

SUBSCRIPTION ADDRESS: listproc@lists.colorado.edu
MAIL ADDRESS: cogopub-l@lists.colorado.edu

COMLAW-L

DESCRIPTION: This list focuses on computers and legal education.

Subscription Address: listserv@vm.ucs.ualberta.ca or
listserv@ualtavm.bitnet
Mail Address: listserv@vm.ucs.ualberta.ca or
comlaw-l@ualtavm.bitnet

COMLAW-L

Description: Washburn Communications Law Society list; TELEJURIST e-journal distributed herein.

Subscription Address: listserv@lawlib.wuacc.edu
Mail Address: COMLAW-L@lawlib.wuacc.edu

COMPCONS

Description: A list for the exchange of ideas and information on constitutions, constitutional law, and constitutionalism around the world. It is sponsored by the Center for the Study of Constitutionalism in Eastern Europe at the University of Chicago Law School and the University of Richmond School of Law.

Subscription Info: To join the list, address your message to:
listserve@UofRLaw.URich.edu
and send this text: subscribe CompCons <Your Name>
This message will also prompt from CompCons a reply that will include additional information about the operation of the list.
Mail Address: compcons@UofRLaw.URich.edu

CONTRACTS

Description: This list is for those involved or interested in the teaching of contract law. According to the list's management, the list should not be used as "a vehicle to provide advice...for an individuals problems...." The list is unmoderated but limited moderation may be imposed if postings stray beyond the list's purpose.

Subscription Address: listserv@austin.onu.edu
Mail Address: contracts@austin.onu.edu.

COSELL-L

Description: This is the Consortium of Southeastern Law Libraries (COSELL) bulletin board.

Subscription Address: listserv@alpha.acast.nova.edu
Mail Address: cosell-l@alpha.acast.nova.edu

COUNTERSERVE

Description: This list is sponsored by Counterpoint Publishing, a company that provides the following services on the Internet:

- The Daily Federal Register
- The Code of Federal Regulations
- The Commerce Business Daily
- Various NRC and DOE Regs and Documents

Subscription Address: majordomo@counterpoint.com
Mail Address: counterserve@counterpoint.com

CPSR-ANNOUNCE

Description: Computer Professionals for Social Responsibility e-journal.

Subscription Address: listserv@cpsr.org or
listserv@sunnyside.com
Subscription Info: In the body of your subscription request, enter:
subscribe cpsr-announce <Your Name>
Mail Address: cpsr-announce@cpsr.org
CPSR WEB SERVER: http://cpsr.org/homepage

CPSR-GLOBAL

Description: The Computer Professionals for Social Responsibility's Global Issues list unites people all over the world who want to talk about decisions the U.S.A. will make on the information infrastructure, or NII, that will affect the rest of the world. List management wants the NII to be a positive force for a GII (global information infrastructure); issues of national identity, "cultural pollution," and international communication and the GII; the new emerging GII world culture; international issues of security and privacy and computer law; international issues of computer development (keyboards, safety); issues of design; language; and whatever other global issues you want to discuss. You don't have to belong to CPSR to join the discussion!!!

Subscription Address: listserv@cpsr.org or
listserv@sunnyside.com
Subscription Info: In the body of your subscription request, enter:
subscribe cpsr-global <Your Name>
Mail Address: cpsr-global@cpsr.org
CPSR WEB SERVER: http://cpsr.org/homepage

CRIM-L

Description: Australian Criminal Justice and Criminology Mailing List.

Subscription Address: listserv@sulaw.law.su.oz.au
Mail Address: crim-l@sulaw.law.su.oz.au

CRIMPROF

DESCRIPTION: A "closed" list limited to law professors who teach or write in the areas of criminal law or criminal procedure. Although this list is mainly intended for those who teach in law schools, those who teach in undergraduate colleges can subscribe, so long as they teach criminal law or criminal procedure at their institution.

SUBSCRIPTION ADDRESS: To subscribe, send a message to listserv@chicagokent.kentlaw.edu
SUBSCRIPTION INSTRUCTIONS: send the following text in the body of the message
subscribe crimprof <Your Name>, <Your Title>, <Your Institution>
e.g. subscribe CRIMPROF John Doe, Assoc. Prof. of law, State University
Subscriptions are not automatic, but will be forwarded to Prof. Stephen D. Sowle (ssowle@kentlaw.edu).

CRYONICS

DESCRIPTION: This list focuses on cryonics including legal issues.

SUBSCRIPTION ADDRESS: According to the list administrator, the best way to subscribe or unsubscribe is to just send email to kqb@whscad1.att.com with a request to subscribe or unsubscribe
MAIL ADDRESS: kqb@whscad1.att.com
The list requires that you include a subject heading to post a message.

CTI-LAW

DESCRIPTION: A discussion group for lawyers, especially those interested in the use of information technology within legal teaching. You will also receive mail directed to this list's super-list CTI-ALL.

SUBSCRIPTION ADDRESS: mailbase@mailbase.ac.uk
SUBSCRIPTION COMMAND: join cti-law <Your Name>
MAIL ADDRESS: cti-law@mailbase.ac.uk

CYBERIA-L

DESCRIPTION: The Law and Policy of Computer Networks. This is a moderated list.

SUBSCRIPTION ADDRESS: listserv@eagle.birds.wm.edu
MAIL ADDRESS: cyberia-l@birds.wm.edu
ARCHIVE: Archived CYBERIA-L messages are browsable at the Cornell Law School gopher

DATA-PROTECTION

DESCRIPTION: U.K. Data Protection Law discussion list.

SUBSCRIPTION ADDRESS: mailbase@mailbase.ac.uk
SUBSCRIPTION COMMAND: join data-protection <Your Name>
MAIL ADDRESS: data-protection@mailbase.ac.uk

DISC-EVIDENCE

DESCRIPTION: Evidence Law list.

SUBSCRIPTION ADDRESS: disc-evidencerequest@mail.unet.umn.edu
MAIL ADDRESS: DISC-EVIDENCE@mail.unet.umn.edu

DISPUTE-RES

DESCRIPTION: This is a list designed to promote communication among those teaching about dispute resolution and working in projects involving alternative forms of conflict resolution. It provides an opportunity to raise issues and share concerns related to the use of nonadversarial models of dispute resolution in many different contexts.

SUBSCRIPTION ADDRESS: listserv@fatty.law.cornell.edu
MAIL ADDRESS: dispute-res@listserv.law.cornell.edu
ARCHIVE: Archived DISPUTE-RES messages are browsable at the University of Massachusetts Amherst Campus-Wide Information System
ARCHIVE URL: gopher://gopher.umass.edu:70/11/academic/law/disputearchs

DNSLIST

DESCRIPTION: A listserv for associate and assistant deans in law schools. It is intended to create a continuous exchange of information and ideas concerning academic affairs, admissions, student affairs, and any other areas of responsibility for associate and assistant deans.

SUBSCRIPTION ADDRESS: listserv@cali.kentlaw.edu:
SUBSCRIPTION COMMAND: SUBSCRIBE DNSLIST <Your Name, Position, and Institution>
MAIL ADDRESS: dnslist@cali.kentlaw.edu

DOXNJ

DESCRIPTION: The New Jersey government information forum facilitates the discussion of government information (U.S., state, local, international and foreign) in New Jersey.

SUBSCRIPTION ADDRESS: listserv@rutvm1.rutgers.edu or listserv@rutvm1.bitnet
MAIL ADDRESS: doxnj@rutvm1.rutgers.edu or doxnj@rutvm1.bitnet

DUAL-USE

DESCRIPTION: This is an interactive discussion list and information source for members of congress, academics, entrepreneurs, and corporate policy makers involved with state and/or federal defense conversion programs.

SUBSCRIPTION ADDRESS: listserv@netcom.com
MAIL ADDRESS: dual-use@netcom.com

EASMNT-L

DESCRIPTION: An electronic forum discussing issues of property law and trusts.

SUBSCRIPTION ADDRESS: listserv@vw.ucs.ualberts.ca
SUBSCRIPTION COMMAND: subscribe easmnt-l <Your Name>
MAIL ADDRESS: easmnt-l@vw.ucs.ualberts.ca

ECONLAW

DESCRIPTION: This is the list for law and economics discussions.

SUBSCRIPTION ADDRESS: listproc@gmu.edu
MAIL ADDRESS: econlaw@gmu.edu

EDLAW

DESCRIPTION: This list focuses on law and education.

SUBSCRIPTION ADDRESS: listserv@ukcc.uky.edu or listserv@ukcc.bitnet
MAIL ADDRESS: edlaw@ukcc.uky.edu or edlaw@ukcc.bitnet

EFFECTOR-ONLINE

DESCRIPTION: EFFector Online is the Electronic Frontier Foundation biweekly newsletter covering privacy rights, freedom of speech in digital media, intellectual property, and other issues related to computer-based communications media. Current and back issues of EFFector Online are also available at the EFF WWW site (URL : http://www.eff.org).

SUBSCRIPTION ADDRESS: listserv@eff.org
SUBSCRIPTION COMMAND: subscribe effector-online
ARCHIVE URL: http://www.eff.org

EFJ

DESCRIPTION: This is a bilingual list for discussions including legal issues related to Japan's electronic networks. Other topics covered include, lobbying methods, roles of government agencies, cultural and social issues, etc.

SUBSCRIPTION ADDRESS: efj-request@twics.com
MAIL ADDRESS: efj@twics.com

ELAW-J

DESCRIPTION: The Murdoch University Electronic Journal of Law distribution list. As a subscriber, you will receive by email the table of contents of each issue of ELaw as it is published and instructions on how to obtain individual articles.

Although ELaw is not a discussion list it encourages readers to comment on its contents, particularly those articles that have been included in the section of the journal titled "Materials for Comment". The editors will consider comments received for publication in a subsequent edition (with permission). Comments and proposals for article submissions should be sent to the editors by email at their address: elaw-editors@csuvax1.murdoch.edu.au.

SUBSCRIPTION ADDRESS: majordomo@cleo.murdoch.edu.au
ARCHIVE: E Law is also available by gopher and ftp - for more information concerning those forms send the following commands in the body of a message to Majordomo@cleo.murdoch.edu.au: get elaw-j 2.txt

ENVIROLAW

DESCRIPTION: This is a discussion list for environmental and natural resource law students throughout the world. It is based at the University of Oregon School of Law and managed by law students.

SUBSCRIPTION ADDRESS: mailserv@oregon.uoregon.edu
MAIL ADDRESS: envirolaw@oregon.uoregon.edu

ENVLAWPROFS

DESCRIPTION: This is an international mailing list for professors in environmental law. The home base of this mailing list is at the University of Oregon School of Law.

SUBSCRIPTION ADDRESS: mailserv@oregon.uoregon.edu
MAIL ADDRESS: envlawprofs@oregon.uoregon.edu

ENV.SEASHEPHERD

DESCRIPTION: The mailing list of the Sea Shepherd Conservation Society which focuses on the enforcement of international conservation law; discusses environmental topics including marine issues. Some postings to this high traffic list are very lengthy. Flaming is not tolerated.

SUBSCRIPTION INFORMATION: Send your name, street/postal/ snail mail address, and email address to the owner, Nick

Voth (dcasmedic@aol.com or nvoth@igc.apc.org).
MAIL ADDRESS: env.seashepherd@igc.apc.org

EPA (VARIOUS LISTS)

DESCRIPTION: A mail server that will deliver the full text of documents regarding federal environmental regulations published in the Federal Register to you by email, on the day of publication.

SUBSCRIPTION ADDRESS: To subscribe send a message to listserve@unixmail.rtpnc.epa.gov and in the body of the message type: subscribe <Name of List> <Your Name>

The following subscription options are available:

- EPA-AIR—Office of Air and Radiation material
- EPAFR-CONTENTS—full Table of Contents of daily Federal Register
- EPA-GENERAL—General EPA non-program specific material; Presidential documents related to environment; other agency environment related material (except endangered species and environmental impact)
- EPA-IMPACT—Environmental impact statement related material
- EPA-MEETINGS—All EPA meeting notices
- EPA-PEST—Office of Pesticide Programs material
- EPA-PRESS—EPA press releases
- EPA-SAB—Material relating to the Science Advisory Board
- EPA-SPECIES—Endangered special related material
- EPA-TOX—Office of Pollution Prevention and Toxic Substances documents (excluding Community Right to Know)
- EPA-TRI—Community Right to Know (Toxic Release Inventory)
- EPA-WASTE—Hazardous and Solid Waste material
- EPA-WATER—Office of Water material

EURO-LEX

DESCRIPTION: All European Legal Information Exchange—discusses EC & European country legal information sources mainly.

SUBSCRIPTION ADDRESS: listserv@vm.gmd.de or listserv@dearn.bitnet
MAIL ADDRESS: euro-lex @vm.gmd.de or euro-lex@dearn.bitnet
ARCHIVE URL: gopher://gopher.law.cornell.edu:70/11s/listservs/eurolex

EXPERT-L

DESCRIPTION: An Internet mailing list for those individuals engaged in "expert witness" activities associated with itigation. It was inspired by the need for experts to communicate with each other about issues related to the "expert witness" profession, such as:

- Errors and omissions insurance
- Dealing with abusive discovery
- Dealing with abusive cross-examination
- Billing and collection practices
- Ethics and professional conduct
- Networking with other experts and attorneys

EXPERT-L is designed to be a forum for the sharing of information and expertise in a general way. It is inappropriate for specific consultations about individual concerns to be made over a computer network. EXPERT-L will send you a copy of your own messages, so that you can see that the message was distributed and did not get damaged on the way.

SUBSCRIPTION INFO: Send an email to expertl@lern.mv.com with the word "SUBSCRIBE" in the subject header.
MAIL ADDRESS: expert-l@lern.mv.com

FAMILYLAW-L

DESCRIPTION: This list is for discussion of current literature, hot topics, and upcoming events in the area of family law. The discussion list enables individuals to air ideas, problems, and issues by means of Email. Announcements of coming conferences and Continuing Legal Education, notice of legislative activity, curriculum development issues, and professional responsibility in family court are examples of possible topics of discussion here.

SUBSCRIPTION ADDRESS: listserv@lawlib.wuacc.edu
MAIL ADDRESS: familylaw-l@lawlib.wuacc.edu
The list requires that you include a subject heading to post a message.

FEDTAX-L

DESCRIPTION: The Federal Taxation list is very busy. A large number of people send messages daily asking a wide range of tax questions. Tax professionals also frequent the list, lending advice and discussing substantive issues.

SUBSCRIPTION ADDRESS: listserv@shsu.bitnet or fedtax-l-request@shsu.edu
MAIL ADDRESS: fedtax-l@shsu.bitnet

FEMJUR

DESCRIPTION: The Feminist Law list is intended to provide

a forum for discussing theories and issues regarding feminism and women and law. It is also a good place to share research questions, scholarship, calls for papers, job announcements, and provide support for people working in this area of law.

SUBSCRIPTION ADDRESS: listserv@suvm.bitnet
MAIL ADDRESS: femjur@suvm.bitnet

FIREARMS

DESCRIPTION: List for discussion of firearms.

SUBSCRIPTION ADDRESS: listserv@utarlvm1.uta.edu
MAIL ADDRESS: firearms@utarlvm1.uta.edu

FLADOCS

DESCRIPTION: Southeast Document Librarians discussion list.

SUBSCRIPTION ADDRESS: listserv@nervm.nerdc.ufl.edu
MAIL ADDRESS: fladocs@nervm.nerdc.ufl.edu

FL-LIST

DESCRIPTION: A list for discussion of newspaper reports from countries worldwide on linguistic evidence in court, courtroom discourse, ideas and controversies about expert evidence and language, language and the law generally; subscribers include linguists, lawyers, court translators and interpreters, etc.

SUBSCRIPTION ADDRESS: fl-list-request@bham.ac.uk

FOI-L

DESCRIPTION: The Freedom of Information list is sponsored by the National Freedom Information Coalition for those interested in open government, First Amendment and freedom of information issues. Advertisements and flaming are discouraged by list management.

SUBSCRIPTION ADDRESS: listserv@suvm.syr.edu
MAIL ADDRESS: foi-l@suvm.syr.edu

FOOD-LAW

DESCRIPTION: Discussion list for laws dealing with food science.

SUBSCRIPTION ADDRESS: listserv@vm1.spcs.umn.edu
MAIL ADDRESS: food-law@vm1.spcs.umn.edu

FREE-L

DESCRIPTION: Fathers' Rights and Equality Exchange discussion list.

SUBSCRIPTION ADDRESS: listserv@indycms.iupui.edu or
listserv@indycms.bitnet
MAIL ADDRESS: free-l@indycms.iupui.edu

FUTUREL

DESCRIPTION: Futures Studies for Court Systems discussion list. It is restricted.

SUBSCRIPTION ADDRESS: listserv@vm.temple.edu or
listserv@templevm.bitnet
MAIL ADDRESS: futurel@vm.temple.edu

GANGTM

DESCRIPTION: This is a list for discussion of gangs and gang-related problems. The list is open to all—gang members, ex-gang members, teachers, etc. You may discuss your situation with the group, or make a one-one connection through the list. It is also open to discussion of policies and other general issues.

SUBSCRIPTION ADDRESS: gangtmrequest@dhvx20.csudh.edu
MAIL ADDRESS: gangtm@dhvx20.csudh.edu

GAYLAW

DESCRIPTION: National Journal of Sexual Orientation Law, the first online law journal in the country and the second devoted exclusively to legal issues affecting lesbians, gay men and bisexuals. The Journal's primary purpose is to disseminate information. By virtue of being available online, subscription to the Journal is free.

SUBSCRIPTION INFO: Individuals can subscribe themselves by sending the following message to listserv@unc.edu: subscribe GAYLAW <First Name> <Last Name> Subscribers will receive bulletins with short summaries of the articles available and information on how to retrieve them when each new issue comes online.

GOVACCESS

DESCRIPTION: This list originally focused only on one specific California bill mandating free online legislation. Now, thanks to its creator, Jim Warren, it encompasses public to government records in a much broader sense. This is an information distribution list, not a discussion list.

SUBSCRIPTION ADDRESS: Email your subscription request

to: jwarren@well.sf.ca.us Include the email address you wish added to the list. If you are willing, include your traditional contact info: name, work, organization, snail mail address, voice phone, fax.
ARCHIVE: CPSR gopher service: gopher.cpsr.org
CPSR HTTP/WEB SERVER: http://cpsr.org/homepage

GOVDOC-L

DESCRIPTION: The Government Documents and Depository Libraries list is a round table discussion among librarians and other interested people that takes place across computer networks. It is moderated by a group of librarians from institutions all over the country. If you subscribe to this list you will receive an extensive message detailing the list's searchable archives, net etiquette, and describing listserv commands in detail.

SUBSCRIPTION ADDRESS: listserv@psuvm.bitnet
MAIL ADDRESS: govdoc-l@psuvm.bitnet or
govdoc-l@psuvm.psu.edu
ARCHIVE: You can get to the GOVDOC-L archive through the Library of Congress, as follows:
telnet://marvel.loc.gov
Login: marvel
then choose Search LC MARVEL Menus (then keyword search with the word GOVDOC-L)

GOVINFO

DESCRIPTION: This list is dedicated to discussion of government information in Canada.

SUBSCRIPTION ADDRESS: mailserv@sask.usask.ca
MAIL ADDRESS: govinfo@sask.usask.ca.

H-DIPLO

DESCRIPTION: Diplomatic history, foreign affairs and international relations discussion list.

SUBSCRIPTION ADDRESS: listserv@uicvm.bitnet or
listserv@uicvm.uic.edu
MAIL ADDRESS: h-diplo@uicvm.uic.edu

HEALTHLAW-L

DESCRIPTION: This list provides for discussion of current literature, hot topics (e.g., healthcare legislation, mental health law, etc.), and upcoming events in the area of health law.

SUBSCRIPTION ADDRESS: listserv@lawlib.wuacc.edu
MAIL ADDRESS: healthlaw-l@lawlib.wuacc.edu

HEALTHRE

DESCRIPTION: This list provides for discussion on health-care reform.

SUBSCRIPTION ADDRESS: listserv@ukcc.uky.edu
Type the following as the first line of the message: sub HEALTHRE <Your Name>
MAIL ADDRESS: healthre@ukcc.uky.edu

HISLAW-L

DESCRIPTION: This list focuses on the history of law.

SUBSCRIPTION ADDRESS: listserv@ulkyvm.bitnet or
listserv@ulkyvm.louisville.edu
MAIL ADDRESS: hislaw-l@ulkyvm.bitnet or
hislaw-l@ulkyvm.louisville.edu
ARCHIVE: Archived HISLAW-L messages are browsable at the Cornell Law School gopher as follows:
telnet fatty.law.cornell.edu
LOGIN: gopher
gopher gopher.law.cornell.edu
then choose:
Discussions and Listserv ARCHIVE: s

H-LAW

DESCRIPTION: This is the Legal History discussion list. H-Law exists so scholars of legal and constitutional history can communicate with one another and as a group. It is hoped that discussions will include some of the following topics: current research projects, reviews, calls for papers, reports on conferences, reports of grants, teaching methods.

SUBSCRIPTION ADDRESS: listserv@uicvm.bitnet or
listserv@uicvm.uic.edu
MAIL ADDRESS: h-law@uicvm.uic.edu or
h-law@uicvm.bitnet

HRS-L

DESCRIPTION: This list focuses on Systematic Studies of Human Rights. This is a restricted list for faculty, students and other professionals who conduct research and write on the subject of human rights. Subscription requires the listowners permission.

SUBSCRIPTION ADDRESS: listserv@bingvmb.bitnet
MAIL ADDRESS: hrs-l@bingvmb.bitnet

HUMANRIGHTS-L

DESCRIPTION: International Human Rights Law discussion list.

SUBSCRIPTION ADDRESS: listserv@lawlib.wuacc.edu
MAIL ADDRESS: humanrights-l@lawlib.wuacc.edu

ILSA-L

DESCRIPTION: International Law Students Association list.

SUBSCRIPTION ADDRESS: listserv@chicagokent.kentlaw.edu
MAIL ADDRESS: ilsa-l@chicagokent.kentlaw.edu

INFOPRO

DESCRIPTION: The Information Professionals list is a network comprised of private investigators, legal investigators for law firms, fee-based information brokers, investigative reporters, United Nations information personnel, corporate information officers, and other related professionals. Membership is determined by the list owner, James Cook. To obtain an application for membership, send a request to: jcook@netcom.com

INFOTERRA

DESCRIPTION: Infoterra is a list for communications about environmental topics and sources on a global basis, including the United Nations Environment Programme (UNEP).

SUBSCRIPTION ADDRESS: to subscribe, send the following message to listproc@pan.cedar.univie.ac.at: subscribe INFOTERRA <Your Name>
MAIL ADDRESS: infoterra @pan.cedar.univie.ac.at

INT-LAW

DESCRIPTION: The Foreign and International Law Librarians list is for those interested in exchanging information related to foreign, comparative and international legal materials and issues. Selected topics on INT-LAW include the Readex CD-ROM Index to United Nations documents, databases containing information on foreign and international law, the "European Court Reports", sources of information on careers in international law, GATT panel reports, the "National Trade Data Bank" CD-ROM, etc. INT-LAW came up on April 31, 1991.

SUBSCRIPTION ADDRESS: listserv@uminn1.bitnet or
listserv@vm1.spcs.umn.edu
MAIL ADDRESS: int-law@vm1.spsc.umn.edu or
int-law@uminn1.bitnet
ARCHIVE: Archived INT-LAW messages are browsable at the Cornell Law School gopher as follows:
telnet fatty.law.cornell.edu
LOGIN: gopher
gopher gopher.law.cornell.edu
then choose:
Discussions and Listserv ARCHIVE: s
Foreign and International Law Librarians
Foreign and International Text Search

INTVIO-L

DESCRIPTION: The Intimate Violence discussion list serves as a networking system devoted to all aspects of family violence. While various other lists may explore the topics of child abuse or violence within the family, the intimate violence list serves a wide range of areas that constitute the definition of intimate violence. The list is designed to encompass all areas of interest regarding family violence rather than limiting discussion to one interest. The list is concerned with the following topics: physical child abuse, sexual child abuse, child neglect, spousal physical violence, spousal sexual violence, psychological abuse and dating violence.

SUBSCRIPTION ADDRESS: listserv@uriacc.uri.edu
MAIL ADDRESS: intvio-l@uriacc.uri.edu

IRISHLAW

DESCRIPTION: The Irish Law list is for discussion of all topics relating to the law of Ireland and Northern Ireland. In the future, the list maybe subdivided into separate areas.

SUBSCRIPTION ADDRESS: listserv@irlearn.ucd.ie or
listserv@irlearn.bitnet
MAIL ADDRESS: irishlaw@irlearn.ucd.ie or
irishlaw@irlearn.bitnet

JEWISHLAWPROF-L

DESCRIPTION: This forum is specifically for Jewish law professors.

SUBSCRIPTION ADDRESS: listserv@lawlib.wuacc.edu
MAIL ADDRESS: jewishlawprof-l@lawlib.wuacc.edu

JLS

DESCRIPTION: The Jewish Law Student list is intended to provide a medium for Jewish law student organizations to keep in touch. Many law schools have such organizations and this list will allow them to exchange ideas for activities, programming, etc. The list is unmoderated and open to Jewish law students and Jewish law professors who have an interest in interacting with Jewish law students and/or providing ideas, comments, etc., to assist Jewish law student organizations.

Subscription Address: listserv@austin.onu.edu
Mail Address: jls@austin.onu.edu

JUDAFF

Description: Student Judicial Affairs discussion list.

Subscription Address: Send the following message to listserv@bingvmb.cc.binghamton.edu or listserv@bingvmb.bitnet:
subscribe judaff-l <Your Name>
Mail Address: JUDAFF@ @bingvmb.cc.binghamton.edu

LJO

Description: The Journal of On-line Law one-way listserv publishes scholarly essays about the law and policy of cyberspace. These are thoughtful, readable pieces that analyze current trends in the law and predict future disputes and problems.

Subscription Address: listserv@listserv.cc.wm.edu
Mail Address: jol@listserv.cc.wm.edu
Questions, problems, letters to the editor, article submissions, etc., should be addressed to: Editor@JOL.law.wm.edu

JURIST-L

Description: Dutch Lawyers list—discussion in Dutch.

Subscription Address: listserv@nic.surfnet.nl
Mail Address: jurist-l@nic.surfnet.nl

JUSTICE

Description: This is a discussion list focusing on issues of criminal punishment.

Subscription Address: justice-request@scn.org
Mail Address: justice@scn.org

JUSTINFO

Description: The goal of the Justice Information distribution list is to provide criminal justice professionals with accurate, current and useful criminal justice-related information. In order to accomplish this goal, the list publishes a biweekly newsletter that will report on a wide variety of topics, including News from the Agencies within the Office of Justice Programs, Criminal Justice in the News, etc. In addition you will receive updates about important issues, such as new services on the Internet, federal legislation, etc.This is a distribution list and requests will not be accepted if they are posted to JUSTINFO. If you have suggestions or information to be considered for distribution through this list, send it to askncjrs.aspensys.com.

Subscription Address: listproc@ncjrs.aspensys.com

JUVENILELAW-L

Description: Discussion list for juvenile law issues.

Subscription Address: listserv@lawlib.wuacc.edu
Mail Address: juvenilelaw-l@lawlib.wuacc.edu

KANSASATTORNEYS-L

Description: Kansas Attorneys list.

Subscription Address: listserv@lawlib.wuacc.edu
Mail Address: kansasattorneys-l@lawlib.wuacc.edu

LAIR

Description: A list designed to distribute the weekly newsletter Legal Automation and Internet Review (LAIR) written by the staff of the Center for Computer-Based Legal Research, Tarlton Law Library, The University of Texas at Austin School of Law. The editors of LAIR hope to use this forum to bring to light new and developing resources of professional and personal interest to law educators and librarians regarding Internet legal resources, legal automation and general library automation issues. While attempts have been made to organize entries based on topical lines, preference will go to communicating resources in a timely fashion. To this end, resources will be grouped primarily by type (i.e., World Wide Web, gopher, usenet, listserv, ftp, software, legal information services, etc.). If you have material you feel should be included or wish to submit comments, address your message to the editors at: lair-ed@tarlton.law.utexas.edu

Subscription Address: majordomo@tarlton.law.utexas.edu
Mail Address: lair-ed@tarlton.law.utexas.edu

LAWAID

Description: Law School Financial Aid discussion list.

Subscription Address: listserv@rutvm1.bitnet
Mail Address: lawaid@rutvm1.bitnet

LAWAND

Description: Law and Society list for interdisciplinary communication between scholars researching related issues.

SUBSCRIPTION INFO: Send the following message to listproc@polecat.law.indiana.edu: subscribe lawand <Your Name>
MAIL ADDRESS: lawand@polecat.law.indiana.edu

LAWARIEL-L

DESCRIPTION: Ariel Project discussion list.

SUBSCRIPTION ADDRESS: listserv@lawlib.wuacc.edu
MAIL ADDRESS: lawaid@lawlib.wuacc.edu

LAWCLINIC

DESCRIPTION: This discussion group is for clinical law teachers, including those engaged in live-client, externship, and simulation-based teaching, as well as persons interested in clinical legal education generally.

SUBSCRIPTION ADDRESS: listserv@lawlib.wuacc.edu
MAIL ADDRESS: lawclinic@lawlib.wuacc.edu

LAWCONTINUINGED-L

DESCRIPTION: Discussion list for Continuing Legal Education.

SUBSCRIPTION ADDRESS: listserv@lawlib.wuacc.edu
MAIL ADDRESS: lawcontinuinged-l@lawlib.wuacc.edu

LAWDEANS-L

DESCRIPTION: Moderated list for law school deans, sponsored by AALS. The list is restricted.

SUBSCRIPTION INFO: Send subscription requests to Mark Folmsbee, Associate Director, Washburn University School of Law Library, zzfolm@lawlib.wuacc.edu.
MAIL ADDRESS: lawdeans-l@lawlib.wuacc.edu

LAW-ECONOMICS

DESCRIPTION: This U.K.-based list is for the discussion of issues around law and economics. Upon subscription, you will also receive mail directed to the list's superlist, LAW-ALL.

SUBSCRIPTION ADDRESS: mailbase@mailbase.ac.uk
SUBSCRIPTION INFO: Include the following message in the first line of the text: join LAW- ECONOMICS <First Name> <Last Name>. To leave the list, type: leave LAW-ECONOMICS.
MAIL ADDRESS: law-economics@mailbase.ac.uk

LAW-EUROPE

DESCRIPTION: This is the European Law list. Upon subscription, you will also receive mail directed to the list's superlist, LAW-ALL. This is a high volume list.

SUBSCRIPTION ADDRESS: mailbase@mailbase.ac.uk
SUBSCRIPTION INSTRUCTIONS: Include the following message in the first line of the text: join LAW-EUROPE <First Name> <Last Name>.
MAIL ADDRESS: law-europe@mailbase.ac.uk

LAW-FAMILY

DESCRIPTION: This U.K.-based list is for the discussion of family law. Upon subscription, you will also receive mail directed to the list's superlist, LAW-ALL. This is a high volume list.

SUBSCRIPTION ADDRESS: mailbase@mailbase.ac.uk
SUBSCRIPTIONS INSTRUCTIONS: Include the following message in the first line of the text: join LAW-FAMILY <First Name> <Last Name>
MAIL ADDRESS: law-family@mailbase.ac.uk

LAWFIRMADMIN-L

DESCRIPTION: Law Firm Administration discussion list.

SUBSCRIPTION ADDRESS: listserv@lawlib.wuacc.edu
MAIL ADDRESS: lawfirmadmin-l@lawlib.wuacc.edu

LAW-IPR

DESCRIPTION: A list for the discussion of U.K. and European issues in Intellectual Property Law, with special references to the impact of information technology and the Internet.

SUBSCRIPTION ADDRESS: Send subscription requests to: mailbase@mailbase.ac.uk
To unsubscribe, send the following message to mailbase@mailbase.ac.uk: leave law-ipr
MAIL ADDRESS: law-ipr l@ mailbase.ac.uk

LAWJOBS-L

DESCRIPTION: This list allows for the posting of job openings in any law related profession, however, resumes may not be posted.

SUBSCRIPTION ADDRESS: listserv@lawlib.wuacc.edu with
MAIL ADDRESS: lawjobs-l@lawlib.wuacc.edu

LAWJOURNAL-L

DESCRIPTION: List for law journal and law review discussions.

SUBSCRIPTION ADDRESS: listserv@lawlib.wuacc.edu
MAIL ADDRESS: lawjournal-l@lawlib.wuacc.edu

LAW-LIB

DESCRIPTION: The Law Libraries list is very high traffic list. Those posting on the list are mostly law librarians. There are frequent mentions of new Internet and other sorts of legal resources, give-aways of books and periodicals no longer wanted, and the latest goings-on at WestLaw and Lexis.

SUBSCRIPTION ADDRESS: law-lib-request@ucdavis.edu or
law-req@ucdavis.edu
MAIL ADDRESS: law-lib@ucdavis.edu
ARCHIVE: Archived LAW-LIB messages are browsable at the Cornell Law School gopher. as follows:
telnet fatty.law.cornell.edu
login: gopher
gopher gopher.law.cornell.edu
then choose:
-Discussions and Listserv archives
ftp ucdavis.edu
At the login prompt, type in: anonymous
For the password, type in: guest
Once you are signed on to the anonymous account, type in:
cd/archive/law-lib-archive

LAWLIBDIR-L

DESCRIPTION: The Law Library Directors list is intended to serve the needs of directors of U.S. law school libraries (or their designated representatives). Objectives of the list include: (1) Serve as an information dissemination vehicle for those who have a legitimate need to reach directors; (2) Provide a forum for the discussion of issues of mutual concern or interest; and (3) Perform a "filtering function" for the LAWLIB list. Some directors may wish to unsubscribe or postpone mail from LAWLIB if they have the assurance that "significant" posts will be forwarded to lawlibdir-l. After you have subscribed to lawlibdir-l, the list owner will send you the first version of Law School Library Directors Internet E-mail Directory. The intention is to maintain this directory on an ongoing basis and distribute it monthly via the list.

SUBSCRIPTION ADDRESS: listserv@lawlib.wuacc.edu
MAIL ADDRESS: lawlibdir-l@lawlib.wuacc.edu

LAWLIBREF-L

DESCRIPTION: The Law Library Reference list is intended to relieve the LAWLIB listserv of reference type queries. The aim is to establish a discussion listserv for reference librarians working in law libraries. Content includes reference queries (U.S. federal and state law emphasis) and reference issues (policy, collection development, resource sharing, etc.).

SUBSCRIPTION ADDRESS: listserv@lawlib.wuacc.edu
MAIL ADDRESS: lawlibref-l@lawlib.wuacc.edu

LAWPROF

DESCRIPTION: The Law School Professors list is meant to be a forum for discussing law, legal education, and technology in legal education. It is a discussion group for persons teaching law in universities and professional schools - no one else will be permitted to join. The list management reserves the right to remove anyone who is ineligible or who abuses his or her list privileges. The list is moderated by Edward P. Richards, Associate Professor of Law, University of Missouri at Kansas City (erichard@medlaw.win.net).

SUBSCRIPTION ADDRESS: listserv@chicagokent.kentlaw.edu
SUBSCRIPTION INSTRUCTIONS: This list requires a special subscription procedure. When emailing your subscription request to the subscription address above, include the following text in the body of your message:
subscribe lawprof <Your name and position and institution here>
MAIL ADDRESS: lawprof@chicagokent.kentlaw.edu

LAWSCH-L

DESCRIPTION: The Law Students and Law Schools list discussions include how good school X really is, how difficult law school is, as well as substantive issues. This is a very high volume list.

SUBSCRIPTION ADDRESS: listserv@auvm.bitnet
MAIL ADDRESS: lawsch-l@auvm.bitnet

LAWSOC-L

DESCRIPTION: This list is a forum for sharing information and discussing issues relevant to the study of law and society in Canada.

SUBSCRIPTION ADDRESS: lawsoc-l-request@cc.umanitoba.ca
MAIL ADDRESS: lawsoc-l@cc.umnaitoba.ca

LAWSRC-L

DESCRIPTION: Internet Law Sources list.

SUBSCRIPTION ADDRESS: listserv@fattylaw.cornell.ed
MAIL ADDRESS: lawsrc-l@fatty.law.cornell.edu
ARCHIVE: Archived LAWSRC-L messages are browsable at the Cornell Law School gopher as follows:
telnet fatty.law.cornell.edu
login: gopher
gopher gopher.law.cornell.edu
then choose:
-Discussions and Listserv Archives

LEGALETHICS-L

DESCRIPTION: Legal Ethics discussion list.

SUBSCRIPTION ADDRESS: listserv@rutvm1.bitnet
MAIL ADDRESS: lawaid@rutvm1.bitnet

LEGAL-LIST

DESCRIPTION: The purpose of the Legal List is to provide a consolidated list of all law-related resources available on the Internet and beyond. Upon subscription you receivea FAQ from listowner Eric J. Heels, chock-full of information regarding the Legal List and how to use the list.

SUBSCRIPTION ADDRESS: legal-list-request@justice.eliot.me.us
SUBSCRIPTION INSTRUCTIONS: Include the following text, in the subject of the message: subscribe <Your Name>
MAIL ADDRESS: legal-list@justice.eliot.me.us

LEGAL-LISTOWNERS

DESCRIPTION: Sponsored by Cornell Law School's Legal Information Institute, this list is for listowners of law-related discussion lists and newsgroups. This is a closed-subscription list for the exchange of ideas, tips, and experiences on the management of law-related discussion lists. If you are the listowner of a law-related discussion list, a listserv administrator, or if you are interested in starting such a list, you are invited to join. The list is co-moderated by: Jim Milles
millesjg@sluvca.slu.edu
and Peter Martin
martin@law.mail.cornell.edu.

SUBSCRIPTION ADDRESS: listserv@fatty.law.cornell.edu
MAIL ADDRESS: legal-listowners@fatty.law.cornell.edu

LEGALSTUDIES

DESCRIPTION: This list promotes communication among those teaching about law at the undergraduate level. It is primarily oriented around concerns experienced by those teaching law and society or legal studies courses from an interdisciplinary or liberal arts perspective although there are, of course, many concerns shared by all who teach about law outside the law school context.

SUBSCRIPTION ADDRESS: listserv@fatty.law.cornell.edu
MAIL ADDRESS: legalstudies@fatty.law.cornell.edu
ARCHIVE: Archived LEGALSTUDIES messages are browsable at the University of Massachusetts Amherst Campus-Wide Information System as follows:
gopher gopher.ucs.umass.edu
then choose:
-Academic Department Information
-Legal Studies
-Legal Studies ARCHIVE: s

LEGALTEN

DESCRIPTION: The purpose of the LEGALTEN mailing list is to facilitate assessment of the impacts of interventions in the broad area of interface between the mental health system, criminal justice system, and the courts. This mailing list is part of the Topical Evaluation Network on Issues in Mental Health Care and Law of the Evaluation Center @ HSRI. Upon subscription to the LEGALTEN list you are automatically added to the to the Evaluation Master List TEC-TEN. Long messages to this list are discouraged.

SUBSCRIPTION ADDRESS: Send subscription requests to listserv@sjuvm.stjohns.edu
MAIL ADDRESS: legalten-l@sjuvm.stjohns.edu

LEGAL-WEBMASTERS

DESCRIPTION: LEGAL-WEBMASTERS was created to coordinate efforts between all of law people maintaining World Wide Web servers.

SUBSCRIPTION ADDRESS: Send subscription requests to listserv@listserv.law.cornell.edu
MAIL ADDRESS: legal-webmasters@listserv.law.cornell.edu
ARCHIVE: Archived LEGAL-WEBMASTERS messages are browsable at the Cornell Law School gopher as follows:
telnet fatty.law.cornell.edu
login: gopher
gopher gopher.law.cornell.edu
then choose:
-Discussions and Listserv Archives

LEGI-SLATE

DESCRIPTION: This list provides a forum for subscribers (and others) to discuss user tips and shortcuts, search strategies, applications and issues. It will also be used by LEGI-SLATE staff to announce new features and enhancements to the system.

SUBSCRIPTION ADDRESS: istserv@lists.colorado.edu
MAIL ADDRESS: legi-slate@lists.colorado.edu

LEGWRI-L

DESCRIPTION: A discussion list for legal writing instructors.

SUBSCRIPTION ADDRESS: listserv@chicagokent.kentlaw.edu
MAIL ADDRESS: legwri-l@chicagokent.kentlaw.edu

LEXISUSER-L

DESCRIPTION: This list provides users with a forum for discussing problems and sharing solutions and tips concerning Lexis.

SUBSCRIPTION ADDRESS: listserv@lawlib.wuacc.edu
MAIL ADDRESS: listserv@lawlib.wuacc.edu

LICENSE

DESCRIPTION: This list focuses on issues related to software licensing.

SUBSCRIPTION ADDRESS: listserv@bitnic.bitnet
MAIL ADDRESS: license@bitnic.bitnet

LIIBULLETIN

DESCRIPTION: This is a mailing list for the distribution of email bulletins from the Legal Information Institute of Cornell Law School. Subscribers receive email containing the syllabi of decision of the Supreme Court as they are placed on the Internet. Although set up as a listserv, it is not a discussion list. It is only intended for outgoing messages.

SUBSCRIPTION ADDRESS: listserv@fatty.law.cornell.edu.
MAIL ADDRESS: liibulletin@listserv.law.cornell.edu
ARCHIVE: WWW - http://www.law.cornell.edu
Gopher: gopher.law.cornell.edu
Ftp: ftp.cwru.edu /U.S. Supreme Court

LIS-LAW

DESCRIPTION: A list for news and discussion on legal information and law libraries, with particular reference to U.K. and EEC sources.

SUBSCRIPTION ADDRESS: mailbase@mailbase.ac.uk
SUBSCRIPTION COMMAND: join lis-law <Your Name>
MAIL ADDRESS: lis-law@mailbase.ac.uk

LIST.HEALTHPLAN

DESCRIPTION: This list functions as a conduit through which the White House distributes health-reform announcements. LIST.HEALTHPLAN does not permit interactive discussion. If you wish to participate in a discussion list on healthcare reform, subscribe to HEALTHRE (see above). Unexpected versions of most White House electronic texts can be found on the usenet newsgroup. ALT.POLITICS.CLINTON.

SUBSCRIPTION ADDRESS: sfreedkin@igc.apc.org
SUBSCRIPTION INFORMATION: To subscribe, send a message to the above address in the following exact format:
Topic: SUBSCRIBE LIST.HEALTHPLAN
Body: ADD: your-electronic-address-here
(your real name in parentheses), Your real name here, Your postal address (optional), City, State, Profession, Professional interest in health care (if any), Institutional affiliation, if relevant

To be removed from this mailing list, send email with the following Subject: REMOVE LIST.HEALTHPLAN. Include the following two lines (and nothing else) in the body of the message: REMOVE: [show your address(es) as currently appearing on the list] (Your name in parentheses)

MAALL

DESCRIPTION: Mid-America Association of Law Libraries list.

SUBSCRIPTION ADDRESS: listserv@wuvmd.wustl.edu
MAIL ADDRESS: maall@wuvmd.wustl.edu
ARCHIVE: Archived MAALL messages are browsable at the Cornell Law School gopher as follows: telnet fatty.law.cornell.edu
login: gopher
gopher gopher.law.cornell.edu
then choose:
-Discussions and Listserv ARCHIVE: s

MN-GOVT

DESCRIPTION: This is an experimental service of the Information Policy Office, Department of Administration that is part of state government in Minnesota. It is a product of the electronic government information and services initiative. This list will broadcast updates on efforts in the public electronic area and experiment with other
government information announcements.
SUBSCRIPTION ADDRESS: listserv@vm1.spcs.umn.edu
MAIL ADDRESS: none for the public

MODELUN

DESCRIPTION: Model United Nations Bulletin.

SUBSCRIPTION ADDRESS: listserv@indycms.iupui.edu or listserv@indycms.bitnet
MAIL ADDRESS: modelun@indycms.iupui.edu or modelun@indycms.bitnet

MUNEX-L

DESCRIPTION: The Municipal Information Exchange was designed to help rural communities and citizens use the emergent technological infrastructure to improve the capacity and performance of their local governments. The MUNEX list aims to grow an Internet community centered on issues of information exchange in local governments.

SUBSCRIPTION ADDRESS: listserv@cornell.edu
MAIL ADDRESS: munex-l@cornell.edu

NATODATA

DESCRIPTION: The North Atlantic Treaty Organization (NATO) uses this list to distribute public data such as: press releases, communiqués, NATO Review articles, NATO Factsheets, NATO Fellowship Programmes, Secretary General speeches, NATO Handbook, North Atlantic Assembly reports, and West European Assembly reports.

SUBSCRIPTION ADDRESS: listserv@cc1.kuleuven.ac.be
MAIL ADDRESS: natodata@cc1.kuleuven.ac.be or scheurwe@stc.nato.int, for special requests only

NCS-L

DESCRIPTION: National Crime Survey discussion list.

SUBSCRIPTION ADDRESS: listserv@umdd.bitnet
MAIL ADDRESS: ncs-l@umdd.bitnet

NET-LAWYERS

DESCRIPTION: This mailing list is intended to allow lawyers, law students, law professors and others interested in law to discuss issues relating to the use of the Internet in the study, practice, development, and marketing of law. The list is moderated.

SUBSCRIPTION ADDRESS: net-lawyers-request@webcom.com
MAIL ADDRESS: net-lawyers@webcom.com
ARCHIVE: Want to know what you missed so far at net-lawyers? Back issues of net-lawyers are available by sending the message "help" (without the quotes) to net-lawyers-digest-request@webcom.com Follow the instructions you get back to use the commands "index" and "get" to retrieve these files.

A beta version of a FAQ for net-lawyers may be obtained either by: ftp: (ftp://ftp.webcom.com/pub/lewrose/ARCHIVE: /net-lawyers-digest. ARCHIVE: /faqv8) or email: Send the command "help" (without the quotes) to net-lawyers-digest@webcom.com You will receive instructions on how to retrieve files from the archive: using the commands "index" and "get." The name of the file is faqv8.

NETWORK2D-L

DESCRIPTION: A forum for current timely and lively discussion of issues raised in Network 2d, the quarterly newsletter of the American Bar Association's Law Practice Management Computer Division.

SUBSCRIPTION ADDRESS: listserv@austin.onu.edu
subscribe network2d-l <Your Name>

In the subject line, indicate whether you are a lawyer, judge, legal academic, or what your position is that gives you an interest in this list.

To leave the list, send the following message to the listserv: signoff network2d-l
MAIL ADDRESS: network2d-l@austin.onu.edu

NEWLAWBOOKS-L

DESCRIPTION: Discussion list for new law books.

SUBSCRIPTION ADDRESS: listserv@lawlib.wuacc.edu
MAIL ADDRESS: newlawbooks-l@lawlib.wuacc.edu

NOCALL-LIST

DESCRIPTION: The Northern California Association of Law Libraries (NOCALL) list is for the dissemination of information on NOCALL business and for discussion of local interest topics. The list is open to members of NOCALL and other interested parties.

SUBSCRIPTION ADDRESS: listserv@netcom.com
SUBSCRIPTION INFORMATION: In the body of the message, type SUBSCRIBE NOCALL-LIST

Do not type your name following this subscription command, due to the Majordomo listserv software in use here.
MAIL ADDRESS: nocall-list@netcom.com

NREN-DISCUSS

DESCRIPTION: This list focuses on National Research and Education Network (NREN) legislation and development.

SUBSCRIPTION ADDRESS: nren-discuss-request@psi.com
MAIL ADDRESS: nren-discuss@psi.com

OILGASLAW-L

Description: Oil & Gas Law list.

Subscription Address: listserv@lawlib.wuacc.edu
Mail Address: oilgaslaw-l@lawlib.wuacc.edu

PARALEGAL-L

Description: A discussion list for paralegals.

Subscription Address: Send subscription requests to listserv@lawlib.wuacc.edu
Mail Address: paralegal-l@lawlib.wuacc.edu

PATENT-REQUEST

Description: This mailing list is a bit unusual. It features a weekly mailing of all patents issued by the Patent Office during the last week (or more specifically, all of the patents listed in the most recent issue of the USPTO Patent Gazette). For each patent, the patent title and number is listed. The mailings consist of three files, each on the average totaling 50K of ASCII text - one file with the mechanical patents, one file with the chemical patents and one file with the electronic patents. With each file there is provided information on how to order paper and electronic versions of patents. The service is free, and the files are not copyrighted. The list is offered by Gregory Aharonian who is not affiliated with the Patent and Trademark Office. His email address is patents@world.std.com

Subscription Address: patents-request@world.std.com
Subscription Information: To subscribe, send your name and postal and email addresses, the words MECHANICAL, CHEMICAL and/or ELECTRONIC (depending which groups you care to receive), and the words ASCII or UUZIP (depending on which format you want - UUZIP means you can receive and UNZIP a UUDECODED file, which are about half the size of the ASCII files).

If you want to receive patent news information (PTO announcements, lawsuit outcomes), send the word NEWS. If you want to receive all of the files, send the word ALL. Mr. Aharonian also requests that you include some information on what you do and how you might use this patent information.

POVERTYLAW-L

Description: A list for the general discussion of substantive pedagogical and practical issues as they relate to poverty law and the poor. Criminal issues are not covered. Law professors, public service lawyers and those interested in poverty issues are invited to participate in discussions.

Subscription Address: To subscribe, send a message to: listserv@lawlib.wuacc.edu
Mail Address: povertylaw-l@lawlib.wuacc.edu

PRELAW-STUDENTS

Description: A discussion list for Prelaw users.

Subscription Address: Send subscription requests to listserv@lawlib.wuacc.edu
Mail Address: PRELAW-STUDENTS@lawlib.wuacc.edu

PRIVACY

Description: Privacy Forum digest.

Subscription Address: privacy-request@vortex.com
Mail Address: privacy@vortex.com

PRIVATELAWLIB-L

Description: This list provides private, state, and county law librarians with a forum to exchange ideas.

Subscription Address: listserv@lawlib.wuacc.edu
Mail Address: privatelawlib-l@lawlib.wuacc.edu

PSRT-L

Description: Political Science Research and Teaching list; has the Law and Politics Book Review e-journal.

Subscription Address: listserv@mizzou1.missouri.edu or listserv@mizzou1.bitnet
Mail Address: psrt-l@mizzou1.missouri.edu or psrt-l @mizzou1.bitnet

PSYLAW-L

Description: The Psychology and Law list is for the discussion of all areas of the interface of psychology and law. PSYLAW-L is sponsored by the American Psychology-Law Society (Division 41 of APA), the Psychology and Law Division of the International Association of Applied Psychology, and the Student Section of APLS.

Subscription Address: listserv@utepa.bitnet
Mail Address: psylaw-l@utepa.bitnet

REGS-L

Description: Title 10 Rules and Regulations.

Subscription Address: listserv@albnydh2.bitnet

MAIL ADDRESS: regs-l@albnydh2.bitnet

RIGHTS-L

DESCRIPTION: Rights and Responsibilities.

SUBSCRIPTION ADDRESS: listserv@auvm.bitnet or listserv@american.edu
MAIL ADDRESS: rights-l@auvm.bitnet or rights-l@american.edu

RLGLAW

DESCRIPTION: Research Libraries Group Law Library list. It is restricted to RLG member libraries.

SUBSCRIPTION ADDRESS: rlglaw-l@vm1.spcs.umn.edu or rlglaw-l@uminn1.bitnet
MAIL ADDRESS: rlglaw-l@vm1.spcs.umn.edu

SCALL-LIST

DESCRIPTION: The Southern California Association of Law Libraries list is unmoderated and open to anyone interested in participating. Advertisements from commercial vendors/publishers are not welcome. Appropriate topics include:

- local workshops and seminars
- notice of membership changes
- committee news
- requests for volunteers for SCALL activities
- news of interest to the Southern California law library community
- reference requests that are local in nature
- hard to find ILL requests
- book give-aways or exchanges

SUBSCRIPTION ADDRESS: listserv@netcom.com
MAIL ADDRESS: scall-list@netcom.com

SPORTLAW

DESCRIPTION: Discussion list for sports law.

SUBSCRIPTION ADDRESS: listserv@cmcuvmb.cmsu.edu or listserv@cmcuvmb.bitnet
MAIL ADDRESS: sportlaw@cmcuvmb.cmsu.edu or sportlaw@cmcuvmb.bitnet

STATECOURTCOUNTYLAWLIB-L

DESCRIPTION: A discussion list for state court county law librarians.

SUBSCRIPTION ADDRESS: listserv@lawlib.wuacc.edu
MAIL ADDRESS: statecourtcountylawlib-l@lawlib.wuacc.edu

SWALL-L

DESCRIPTION: The purpose of the Southwestern Association of Law Libraries list is to disseminate information on SWALL activities and topics of local interest to law librarians. This list is open to all law librarians.

SUBSCRIPTION ADDRESS: mailserv@post-office.uh.edu
SUBSCRIPTION INFORMATION: In the body of your subscription message, type: SUBSCRIBE SWALL-L
MAIL ADDRESS: swall-l@post-office.uh.edu

TAP-INFO

DESCRIPTIONS: TAP-INFO disseminates policy notes and memoranda of the Crown Jewels Campaign (CJC—a joint effort between Essential Information and Ralph Nader's Taxpayer Assets Project (TAP). CJC aims to gain public access to several of the federal government's most important information systems. The TAP-INFO listserver issues a password when it adds your name to the list. The password provides subscriber privileges. For more information, send a 'help live' request to listserver@essential.org

SUBSCRIPTION ADDRESS: tap-info-request@essential.org
MAIL ADDRESS: tap-info@essential.org
ARCHIVE: TAP-INFO postings are ARCHIVE: d at cspr.org.
ftp: ftp.cpsr.org;
gopher: gopher.cpsr.org;
wais: wais.cspr.org

TECHNO-L

DESCRIPTION: This Issues in Technology Licensing list is intended to be a resource for people involved in the licensing of technology. By facilitating conversations among university licensing professionals, their counterparts in industry, and eventually the potential licensees themselves, list members hope to initiate more technology transfer.

Subscribers are invited to discuss issues as they come up, on a case-by-case basis. Topics may include marketing brainstorming, review of prior art for a particular invention, searches for contacts in a particular industry, discussion of creative licensing terms, nationwide policy, etc.

SUBSCRIPTION ADDRESS: listserv@mitvma.mit.edu
MAIL ADDRESS: techno-l@mitvma.mit.edu

TEKNOIDS

DESCRIPTION: This busy list focuses on computer technical support for law schools.

SUBSCRIPTION ADDRESS: listserv@law.mail.cornell.edu
MAIL ADDRESS: teknoids@fatty.law.cornell.edu

ARCHIVE: Archived TEKNOIDS messages are browsable at the Cornell Law School gopher as follows:

telnet fatty.law.cornell.edu
login: gopher
gopher gopher.law.cornell.edu

then choose:
Discussions and Listserv ARCHIVE: s

TELECOMREG

DESCRIPTION: The Telecommunications Regulation list has been established to facilitate discussion about telecommunications regulation on the local, state, and federal levels. Regulatory issues involving cable, broadcasting, telephony, and data transmission are of direct interest, as are related economic and social issues. Anyone may subscribe. Industry participants are welcome as well as regulators, academics, consumers. A feature of the list is distribution of the Cable Regulation Digest. This is a weekly publication.

SUBSCRIPTION ADDRESS: listserver@relay.adp.wisc.edu
MAIL ADDRESS: telecomreg@relay.adp.wisc.edu

TI-FORUM

DESCRIPTION: This unusually-named list is sponsored by Transparency International (TI), an organization based in Berlin dedicated to the battle against corruption. TI-forum is complemented by TI-press, which exists to distribute TI press releases and bulletins, as well as any relevant contributions to TI-forum as they appear.

SUBSCRIPTION ADDRESS: listserv@kabissa.com
In the body of the message type: SUB TI-forum <First Name> <Last Name>
MAIL ADDRESS: ti@kabissa.com

TLTP-LAW

DESCRIPTION: A discussion list for all those involved with the work of the Law Courseware Consortium, producing computer-based learning materials for legal undergraduate courses. It is intended primarily for academics who are contributing materials, but any interested parties are welcome. Upon subscription you will also receive mail directed to the list's superlist TLTP-LAW.

SUBSCRIPTION ADDRESS: mailbase@mailbase.ac.uk
SUBSCRIPTION COMMAND: join tltp-law <Your Name>
MAIL ADDRESS: tltp-law@mailbase.ac.uk

TORTSLAW

DESCRIPTION: This is list for the discussion of all areas of Tort Law.

SUBSCRIPTION ADDRESS: listserv@ulkyvm.louisville.edu
SUBSCRIPTION INFORMATION: You can only "be subscribed" to the list by the list owner. Send your subscription request (including a short biographical note with your research interests) to: rweade01@ulkyvm.louisville.edu
MAIL ADDRESS: tortslaw@ulkyvm.louisville.edu

TRADE

DESCRIPTION: The TRADE list was set up to facilitate discussion of international trade policy. Subjects include items such as NAFTA, the Uruguay Round, U.S. trade policy and related issues. Although TRADE has been organized by international trade economists participation from everyone is welcomed.

SUBSCRIPTION ADDRESS: listserv@csf.colorado.edu
MAIL ADDRESS: trade@csf.colorado.edu

TRADE-NEWS
TRADE-LIBRARY
TRADE-STRATEGY

DESCRIPTION: The Institute for Agriculture and Trade Policy in Minneapolis, Minnesota sponsors 3 lists: TRADE-NEWS (includes the weekly bulletins _NAFTA Monitor_, _Trade Week_, and _GATT Alert_); TRADE-LIBRARY (documents); TRADE-STRATEGY (issues).

SUBSCRIPTION ADDRESS: majordomo@igc.apc.org
SUBSCRIPTION INFO: To subscribe to all three lists, send the following message:

subscribe TRADE-NEWS
subscribe TRADE-LIBRARY
subscribe TRADE-STRATEGY

MAIL ADDRESS: TRADE-NEWS@igc.apc.org, TRADE-LIBRARY@igc.apc.org, TRADE-STRATEGY @igc.apc.org

TRAVEL-ADVISORIES

DESCRIPTION: U.S. Department of State Consular Information Sheets and Travel Warnings.

SUBSCRIPTION ADDRESS:
travel-advisories-request@stolaf.edu
MAIL ADDRESS: travel-advisories@stolaf.edu
ARCHIVE: ftp ftp.stolaf.edu/pub/travel-advisories/
ARCHIVE: gopher gopher.stolaf.edu
- Internet Resources
- US State Department Travel Advisories

TXDXN-L

DESCRIPTION: Texas Documents Information Network.

SUBSCRIPTION ADDRESS: listserv@uhupvm1.uh.edu
MAIL ADDRESS: txdxn-l@uhupvm1.uh.edu

UKLEGAL

DESCRIPTION: This list discusses academic and practical cases relating to English and Scottish law. The list is moderated by Graham Wilson.

SUBSCRIPTION ADDRESS:
lsg001@cck.coventry.ac.uk (US Subscribers);
lsg001@uk.ac.coventry.cck (UK Subscribers)
SUBSCRIPTION INFORMATION: To join, send mail to the list owner at the above address. In the subject heading, type UKLEGAL; in the body of the message, type your full Internet email address.
MAIL ADDRESS: lsg1@uk.ac.coventry.cck. Send postings to legal@uk.ac.coventry.cck with UKLEGAL in the subject heading.

UNCJIN-L

DESCRIPTION: This is the United Nations Justice Information Network list.

SUBSCRIPTION ADDRESS: listserv@albnyvm1.bitnet
MAIL ADDRESS: uncjin-l@albnyvm1.bitnet

UN-NEWS

DESCRIPTION: List UN-NEWS is not open for automatic subscription.

SUBSCRIPTION ADDRESS: Your request has been forwarded to the list owner(s): ART ST. GEORGE <STGEORGE@UNMB.BITNET>

VLAJUR

DESCRIPTION: This is a list for Flemish lawyers. List info sent in Flemish.

SUBSCRIPTION ADDRESS: majordomo@belnet.be
MAIL ADDRESS: vlajur@belnet.be

WESTLAWUSER-L

DESCRIPTION: This list will allow members to post questions, comments and share information relating to the WESTLAW service and its operation.

SUBSCRIPTION ADDRESS: listserv@lawlib.wuacc.edu
MAIL ADDRESS: westlawuser-l@lawlib.wuacc.edu

WH-SUMMARY

DESCRIPTION: A distribution list for White House summaries and press releases.

SUBSCRIPTION ADDRESS: Send the following message to almanac@esusda.gov:
subscribe wh-summary

Y-RIGHTS

DESCRIPTION: Y-RIGHTS is an open discussion group on the rights of kids and teenagers. The list owner Kenneth Udat (KUDUT@Hampvms.Bitnet) notes that "everyone is welcome here, no matter who or what you are. You could be a faculty member, a teenager, a parent, a manual laborer, a student working in a class about rights, or whatever. You are welcome here."

SUBSCRIPTION ADDRESS: listserv@sjuvm.bitnet
MAIL ADDRESS: y-rights@sjuvm.bitnet

Publications

LAW JOURNALS

LAW JOURNALS ON THE WEB

DESCRIPTION: This is an expanding, annotated listing of law-related journals on the Web. If you can't find the journal you want on the following pages, try this site at USC.

PROVIDER: University of Southern California Law Center
EMAIL: dfox@law.usc.edu
URL: http://www.usc.edu/dept/law-lib/legallst/journals.html

AMERICAN JOURNAL OF INTERNATIONAL LAW

DESCRIPTION: The American Journal of Law has been published by the American Society of International Law since 1907. It features articles and editorials, notes and comments by leading scholars on developments in international law and international relations. Internet access to the Journal is via the Electronic Newstand, which offers some articles and the complete table of contents from recent issues.

CONTACT: Sandra Liebel
PHONE: (202) 939-6035
PROVIDER: Electronic Newstand
CONTACT: William Love
EMAIL: love@enews.com, info@enews.com
PHONE: (617) 547-4731
URL: http://www.enews.com/magazines/ajil/

CARDOZO ELECTRONIC LAW BULLETIN

DESCRIPTION: The Cardozo Electronic Law Bulletin is the first European scholarly electronic law journal. It is the official journal of the Cardozo Institute of Comparative Law, founded in Jerusalem, 1989 at Jaffa Gate. It is presently based at the University of Trento, Faculty of Law, where the Cardozo Lectures in Law are held.

ACCESS: http://www.gelso.unitn.it/card-adm/

CORNELL LAW REVIEW

DESCRIPTION: The Review's current Net offerings include the full text of articles and notes beginning with November 1994 plus a preview of coming attractions and other information.

PROVIDER: Cornell Law School Legal Information Institute
ADDRESS: Myron Taylor Hall, Ithaca, NY 14853
PHONE: (607) 255-4619
FAX: (607) 255-7193
CONTACT: Peter W. Martin, Co-Director, Legal Information Institute
EMAIL: MARTIN@LAW.MAIL.CORNELL.EDU
URL: http://www.law.cornell.edu/clr/clr.htm

CUMULATIVE INDEX TO RISK: HEALTH, SAFETY & ENVIRONMENT

DESCRIPTION: Articles are annotated.

PROVIDER: Franklin Pierce Law Center
URL: http://www.fplc.edu/tfield/rskindx.htm

ELECTRONIC JOURNAL OF LAW (ELAW)

DESCRIPTION: ELAW includes articles on a variety of legal topics, ranging from property law to feminism to indigenous peoples. Strangely, it appears that ELAW is not available in full text at the gopher site, but rather is abstracted.

CONTACT: Michael Pendleton
PROVIDER: School of Law, Murdoch University
ADDRESS: Perth, Australia, 6150
PHONE: 61 09 360 2976
EMAIL: pendle@csuvax1.murdoch.edu.au
URL: EMAIL the message: subscribe elaw-j to: Majordomo@cleo.murdoch.edu.au
URL: gopher://infolib.murdoch.edu.au:70/11/.ftp/pub/subj/law/jnl/elaw

FEDERAL COMMUNICATIONS LAW JOURNAL (FCLJ)

DESCRIPTION: Full text of the last few issues of the FCLJ are available at this site.

PROVIDER: Indiana University School of Law and the Federal Communications Bar Association
ADDRESS: 201 South Indiana Avenue, Bloomington, IN 47405
CONTACT: Will Sadler, Systems Coordinator, IU School of Law
EMAIL: fclj@indiana.edu
URL: http://www.law.indiana.edu/fclj/fclj.html

GERMAN-AMERICAN LAW JOURNAL

URL: gopher://gal.umd.edu:72/11/

GOVERNMENT INFORMATION IN CANADA

DESCRIPTION: This journal premiered in the summer of 1994. It discusses Canadian federal, provincial/territorial, and local government. Full text is available at this site.

PROVIDER: University of Saskatchewan, Saskatoon, Saskatchewan, Canada S7N 0W0
CONTACT: Andrew Hubbertz
EMAIL: hubbertz@sklib.usask.ca
PHONE: (306) 966-5989
FAX: (306) 966-6040
URL: http://www.usask.ca/library/gic/index.html

HARVARD JOURNAL OF LAW AND TECHNOLOGY

DESCRIPTION: The Journal offers insight into the legal implications of emerging technologies

URL: http://studorg.law.harvard.edu/jolt/

INDIANA JOURNAL OF GLOBAL LEGAL STUDIES

DESCRIPTION: This site provides full text access to the Journal.

PROVIDER: Indiana University School of Law, Bloomington, IN
CONTACT: Business Editor
PHONE: (812) 855-8717
URL: http://www.law.indiana.edu/glsj/glsj.html
URL: telnet://www.law.indiana.edu
LOGIN: www

INFORMATICA E DIRITTO

DESCRIPTION: In addition to this Journal, this site also includes Italian legal databases and a Guide to Cyberspace for Lawyers.

PROVIDER: Institute for Legal Documentation of Italian National Research Council, Florence, Italy
URL: http://www.idg.fi.cnr.it/

INTELLECTUAL PROPERTY MAGAZINE (IPM)

DESCRIPTION: IPM is a quarterly online magazine that addresses issues in law and policy for high technology. The articles in IPM are written mainly by lawyers, both academics and leading practitioners. The full-text articles contain links to court decisions and other materials that are too lengthy to include in the print version of the magazine. In some cases the editors have also included email connections within the articles, so readers can communicate directly with the authors.

URL: http://www.portal.com/~recorder/recorder.html

JOURNAL OF ONLINE LAW

DESCRIPTION: The Journal of Online Law publishes scholarly essays about the law and policy of cyberspace. These are thoughtful, readable pieces that analyze current trends in the law and predict future disputes and problems.

PROVIDER: Marshall-Wythe School of Law, College of William & Mary, Williamsburg, VA 23187
CONTACT: Trotter Hardy
PHONE: (804) 221-3826
EMAIL: Editor@JOL.law.wm.edu
URL: Send email to subscribe to the Journal mailing list: listserv@listserv.cc.wm.edu
URL: http://www.law.cornell.edu/jol/jol.table.html

LAW AND POLITICS BOOK REVIEW

DESCRIPTION: This publication seeks to comprehensively review books of interest to political scientists studying law, the courts, and the judicial process. Reviews are commissioned by the editor; they are published within a week of receipt. However, the Review is organized into 12 monthly issues for each annual volume. The first issue was March 1991.

URL: To Subscribe: (NB - you must subscribe to the list, PSRT-L to receive the Review.) Send the following to LISTSERV@UMCVMB: SUBSCRIBE PSRT-L <Your Name>

NEPTUNUS LAW REVIEW

DESCRIPTION: This publication focuses on maritime law.

PROVIDER: Maritime & Oceanic Law Center at the University of Nantes, France
URL: http://palissy.humana.univnantes.fr/CDMO/WebThalassa.html

OFFSHORE

DESCRIPTION: This journal, reaches attorneys, trustees, bankers, etc. in more than 20 countries including the Caribbean

URL: Send inquiry to: offshore@dnai.com

THE RICHMOND JOURNAL OF LAW & TECHNOLOGY

DESCRIPTION: This is an online law journal - there is no printed counterpart.

PROVIDER: University of Richmond School of Law
CONTACT: Richard P. Klau, Editor in Chief
EMAIL: klaurich@uofrlaw.urich.edu // PGP 2.6.2 Key available
URL: http://www.urich.edu/~jolt/

STANFORD JOURNAL OF LAW

DESCRIPTION: This site provides information about the semi-annual Stanford Journal of Law, Business and Finance as well as abstracts.

URL: http://www-leland.stanford.edu/group/sjlbf

TELEJURIST

DESCRIPTION: Law student review of current issues in the field of communications law. It is dedicated to the emerging legal issues resulting from new communications technologies. The first edition contained articles on subjects ranging from electronic monitoring of employees in the workplace to the liability issues raised by the practice of telemedicine; the latest in cable TV must carry litigation to new multimedia techniques being used in the courtroom. It is distributed to law schools, Communications Law scholars and various communications groups and organizations.

CONTACT: Terence O'Malley
PHONE: (913) 862-9521
EMAIL: omalleyt@acc.wuacc.edu.
URL: listserv comlaw-l@acc.wuacc.edu
URL: telnet://acc.wuacc.edu
LOGIN: washlaw

TEXAS INTELLECTUAL PROPERTY LAW JOURNAL

URL: http://www.law.utexas.edu/journals/tiplj/tiplj.htm

THEMIS LAW JOURNAL

DESCRIPTION: This journal is in French.

PROVIDER: University of Montreal Centre de Recherche en Droit Public
URL: http://www.droit.umontreal.ca/Faculte/Themis/

THE WEB JOURNAL OF CURRENT LEGAL ISSUES

CONTACT: Robin Widdison, Director - Centre for Law and Computing, University of Durham, 50 North Bailey, Durham DH1 3ET United Kingdom
PHONE: 091 374 2041
EMAIL: r.c.widdison@durham.ac.uk
URL: http://www.ncl.ac.uk/~nlawwww/

LEGAL NEWSLETTERS

AUTOMATOME

DESCRIPTION: Newsletter of the American Association of Law Libraries, Automation and Scientific Development Special Interest Section.

CONTACT: Anna Belle Leiserson, Editor American Association of Law Libraries
ADDRESS: Vanderbilt Law Library, 53 West Jackson Blvd., Suite 940, Nashville, TN 37203
PHONE: (312) 939-4764
EMAIL: leiserab@ctrvax.vanderbilt.edu
URL: To Subscribe: Join the Law Librarians' Computer Conference Subscription requests to LAW-REQ@UCDAVIS.EDU

BANKRUPTCY NEWSLETTERS

DESCRIPTION: Available from the InterNet Bankruptcy Library.

URL: http://bankrupt.com/chap11.bradlees.html

CABLE REGULATION DIGEST

DESCRIPTION: This weekly Internet publication is concerned with cable television regulatory and other news.

PROVIDER: Multichannel News
CONTACT: John Higgins
EMAIL: higgins@dorsai.dorsai.org
PHONE: (212) 887-8390
ARCHIVE: ftp://ftp.vortex.com/tv-film-video/cable-reg/
ARCHIVE: gopher://gopher.vortex.com:70/1/tv-film-video/cable-reg/
URL: Distribution via the TELECOMREG mailing list
SUBSCRIPTION ADDRESS: listserver@relay.adp.wisc.edu

CIVIL LIBERTIES

DESCRIPTION: This is the ACLU's Membership Newsletter. It is available in full text at this site.

PROVIDER: American Civil Liberties Union and The Pipeline Network
ADDRESS: ACLU Public Education Department, 132 West 43rd Street, New York, NY 10036
EMAIL: infoaclu@aclu.org
URL: gopher://aclu.org

COMPUTER LAW REPORT

DESCRIPTION: The Computer Law Report covers current legal issues relating to computers and technology. The Report is specifically written for the nonlawyer. Topic suggestions and questions concerning related issues are welcome.

PROVIDER: William S. Galkin, Esq., adjunct professor of computer law at the University of School of Law, who has been practicing in the computer law area since 1986.
EMAIL: galkin@aol.com
URL: Send email to galkin@aol.com. In the body of the email, specify that you want to receive the Report and include your full, real name.

EFFECTOR-ONLINE

DESCRIPTION: EFFector Online is the Electronic Frontier Foundation biweekly newsletter covering privacy rights, freedom of speech in digital media, intellectual property, and other issues related to computer-based communications media.Current and back issues of EFFector Online are also available at the EFF WWW site -(URL : http://www.eff.org)

PROVIDER: Electronic Frontier Foundation
ARCHIVE: EFF Document and File archives can be accessed via the following:

- http://www.eff.org
- gopher://gopher.eff.org
- ftp://ftp.eff.org

ACCESS: Send email to subscribe to the following address: listserv@eff.org
In the body of the message, type: subscribe effector-online

ENVIRONMENTAL DAMAGE VALUATION AND COST BENEFIT NEWS

DESCRIPTION: The newsletter is available free via email. Send your name, and email address, and specify whether you want the plain text (ASCII) or a uuencoded (binary) WordPerfect version. If you don't specify, you'll be sent the ASCII version, which you can pull into any word processor. If you choose the binary version, note that you'll need uudecode software to access the file.

URL: Send email to: kenacks@delphi.com

FCIL NEWSLETTER

DESCRIPTION: The FCIL Newsletter is published by the Foreign, Comparative, and International Law Special Interest Section of the American Association of Law Libraries. Past issues have featured a report on the status of the new international law schedules from the Library of Congress and an article on cataloging religious law.

URL: http://law.wuacc.edu/fcil/newsl.html

FEDERAL INFORMATION NEWS SYNDICATE (FINS)

DESCRIPTION: FINS is a news column that focuses on various federal government-related cyberspace issues, including the National Information Infrastructure, etc. A subscription costs $30 a year, and includes 24 issues. Back issues are available at the UCSF gopher (below).

PROVIDER: Federal Information News Syndicate
ADDRESS: 18 9th Street N.E. #206, Washington, DC 20002-6042
CONTACT: Vigdor Schreibman
EMAIL: fins@ACCESS.digex.net
PHONE: (202) 547-6106
URL: gopher://itsa.ucsf.edu:70/1m/.i/.q/.b/.n/FINS%3A%20Federal%20Information%20News%20Syndicate

INFORMATION POLICY ONLINE (IPO)

DESCRIPTION: IPO is an online newsletter published on the Internet by the Information Industry Association and distributed free of charge. The purpose of the Newsletter is to inform readers of events and activities affecting information policy, and to present an information industry viewpoint concerning these events and activities.

CONTACT: Steven J. Metalitz, Editor of Information Policy Online
EMAIL: iia.ipo@his.com
PHONE: (202) 639-8262
FAX: (202) 638-4403
URL: Email the message "subscribe" to iiaipo-request@his.com

JUSTINFO

DESCRIPTION: This electronic newsletter is designed to provide criminal justice professionals with accurate, current and useful criminal and juvenile justice-related information. Published twice monthly, some of the topics addressed are: new products and services from NCJRS, updates on federal legislation, and other important criminal justice resources on the Internet.

PROVIDER: National Criminal Justice Reference Service
URL: Send email to: listproc@ncjrs.aspensys.com
In the body of the message, type:
subscribe justinfo <Your Name>

LADAS & PARRY NEWSLETTER

DESCRIPTION: This law firm newsletter reports intellectual property matters from around the world.

URL: http://www.ladas.com/ladasnews.html

LANGUAGE IN THE JUDICIAL PROCESS

DESCRIPTION: The intention of the editors is to maintain on a World Wide Web home page current information of interest to all scholars and legal practitioners interested in law and language. Issues list bibliographies and othertools, direct readers to relevant organizations, provide program information where appropriate, and list current bibliography in language and law. Later issues will be expanded to cite legal cases in which linguistic issues are important, and also to include abstracts of articles and summaries of relevant cases, etc. Published at the University of Tennessee, Knoxville.

URL: http://hamlet.la.utk.edu/

LEGAL AUTOMATION AND INTERNET REVIEW (LAIR)

DESCRIPTION: The editors of this weekly newsletter hope to use this forum to bring to light new and developing resources of professional and personal interest to law educators and librarians regarding Internet legal resources, legal automation and general library automation issues. While attempts have been made to organize entries based on topical lines, preference will go to communicating resources in a timely fashion. To this end, resources will be grouped primarily by type (i.e., World Wide Web, gopher, usenet, listserv, ftp, software, legal information services, etc.) If you have material you feel should be included or wish to submit comments, address your message to the editors at: lair-ed@tarlton.law.utexas.edu

PROVIDER: Center for Computer-Based Legal Research, Tarlton Law Library, The University of Texas at Austin School of Law
URL: Subscribe to the LAIR mailing list by sending email to: majordomo@tarlton.law.utexas.edu

LEGAL NET MONTHLY

DESCRIPTION: This monthly compilation focuses on the legal and ethical aspects of computer networking.

EMAIL: fergp@sytex.com

MULTINATIONAL MONITOR

DESCRIPTION: This monthly magazine tracks corporate activity, especially in the Third World, and focuses on the export of hazardous substances, worker health and safety, labor union issues and the environment.

PROVIDER: Multinational Monitor was founded by Ralph Nader and is published by Essential Information, Inc.
URL: http://www.essential.org/monitor/monitor.html

NETWATCH

DESCRIPTION: Latest netnews on legal resources.

PROVIDER: Murdoch University Library, Perth, Australia
CONTACT: Anne Greenshields
EMAIL: greenshi@portia.murdoch.edu.au
URL: Send message "get elaw-j netw2.txt" to Majordomo@cleo.murdoch.edu.au
URL: gopher://infolib.murdoch.edu.au:70/00/.ftp/pub/subj/law/jnl/elaw/netwatch/netw2.txt
URL: ftp://infolib.murdoch.edu.au/pub/subj/law/jnl/elaw/netwatch/netw2.txt

NETWATCHERS

DESCRIPTION: This cyberzine focuses on legal, ethical and policy issues of Cyberspace and the Online World.

URL: http://www.ionet.net/~mdyer/netwatch.shtml

PRISON LEGAL NEWS (PLN)

DESCRIPTION: The PLN is a monthly newsletter published and edited by Washington state prisoners Ed Mead and Paul Wright. PLN has been regularly published since May 1990. While the paper's focus is on Washington state, it PLN also has coverage of prison-related news and analysis from across the country and around the world.

ADDRESS: Prison Legal News, PO Box 1684, Lake Worth, FL 33460
ACCESS: http://weber.u.washington.edu/~lursa/PLN/pln.html

PRIVACY FORUM

DESCRIPTION: This is a moderated digest for the discussion and analysis of issues relating to the general topic of privacy (both personal and collective) in the "information age" of the 1990s and beyond. Topics include a wide range of telecommunications, information/database collection and sharing, and related issues, pertaining to the privacy concerns of individuals, groups, businesses, and government. The Privacy Forum digest is supported in part by the ACM (Association for Computing Machinery) Committee on Computers and Public Policy.

PROVIDER: Vortex Technology, Woodland Hills, CA
MODERATOR: Lauren Weinstein
EMAIL: lauren@vortex.com
EMAIL: privacy-FAX@vortex.com
PHONE: (818) 225-2800
FAX: (818) 225-7203
ARCHIVE: ftp://ftp.vortex.com/privacy
ARCHIVE: gopher://gopher.vortex.com
ARCHIVE: http://www.vortex.com/
URL: To subscribe, send a message to: privacy-request@vortex.com or listserv@vortex.com with the message: subscribe privacy your name

RESOURCES LAW NEWSLETTER

DESCRIPTION: Resources is the newsletter of the Canadian Institute of Resources Law. Published quarterly, the newsletter's purpose is to provide timely comments on current resources law issues and to give information about Institute publications and programs.

PROVIDER: Canadian Institute of Resources Law
ADDRESS: Room 3330 PFB, University of Calgary, 25090 University Drive NW, Calgary, Alberta T2N 1N4 Canada
EMAIL: cirl@acs.ucalgar
PHONE: (403) 220-3200
URL: Resources is circulated via the following listservs:

- NATRESLIB-L@cc.usu.edu: discussion list for Natural Resources Librarians. Subscription ADDRESS: annhed@library.lib.usu.edu
- OILGASLAW-L@acc.wuacc.edu: discussion list about Oil and Gas Law. Subscription ADDRESS: listserv@acc.wuacc.edu

URL: telnet://acc.wuacc.edu
LOGIN: washlaw
then choose: Campus and other Information Systems
then choose: OILGASLAWnet
then choose: Resources

THE RODENT

DESCRIPTION: A wonderful and irreverent, regular publication that thrashes the big-firm associate's personal hell (also known as the official underground newsletter for associates).

URL: http://bankrupt.com/rodent.html

TECHNOLOGY UPDATE

DESCRIPTION: This opinion-and-news column, written by G. Burgess Allison covers computer industry developments for the American Bar Association's Law Practice Management magazine.

URL: http://www.abanet.org/lpm/magazine/tu_intro.html

TELECOM POST

DESCRIPTION: The Telecom Post is published weekly "while the U.S. Congress works on the first comprehensive rewrite of legislation regarding telecommunications since the Communication Act of 1934."

PROVIDER: This publication is compiled, written, and edited by Coralee Whitcomb
EMAIL: cwhitcom@bentley.edu
URL: It is posted to various discussion lists and is also available from the CPSR listserv. To subscribe, send email to listserv@cpsr.org with the message: subscribe telecom-post <Your Name>

VTW BILLWATCH

DESCRIPTION: This weekly newsletter tracks U.S. federal legislation affecting civil liberties. BillWatch is published every Friday afternoon as long as Congress is in session.

PROVIDER: The Voters Telecommunications Watch
EMAIL: vtw@vtw.org
URL: Voice phone to request fax distribution: (718) 596-2851
URL: Send email to: vtw-announcerequest@vtw.org In the body of the message, type: subscribe vtw-announce <First Name> <Last Name>
URL: To receive the latest version of BillWatch, send email to: vtw@vtw.org In the body of the message, type: send billwatch

LAWYER DIRECTORIES

ADA ATTORNEY DIRECTORY

URL: http://www.rit.edu/~easi/easilaw/easilawlawyers.html

ATTORNEY AND LEGAL PROFESSIONAL DIRECTORIES

DESCRIPTION: A collection of lawyer directories.

PROVIDER: U.S. House of Representatives
ADDRESS: H2-613 Ford House Office Building, Washington, DC 20515-6165
CONTACT: Elliot C. Chabot, Legal Support Project Leader, House Information Systems
EMAIL: echabot@hr.house.gov
PHONE: (202) 226-6456
FAX: (202) 226-4033
URL: http://www.pls.com:8001

BANKRUPTCY PRO DIRECTORY

DESCRIPTION: The Internet Bankruptcy Library provides access to the Worldwide Directory of Bankruptcy & Insolvency Professionals (among many other unique bankruptcy resources). If you are interested in a free listing in the Directory, send email to the T&W Newswire subscription list (TWN-edit@bankrupt.com).

URL: http://bankrupt.com

CANADIAN LAWYER DIRECTORY

DESCRIPTION: If you want your firm included in the Directory, send email to: lawdir@io.org The message should contain the following:

1. Name of lawyer
2. City and province
3. Law firm name
4. Email address
5. WEB URL address, if available

URL: http://www.carswell.com/LawDir/

DIRECTORY OF LEGAL ACADEMIA

DESCRIPTION: Database of American Law School Faculty, including name, affiliation, address, mail and phone. It is not comprehensive, but interesting nonetheless.

PROVIDER: Cornell Law School Legal Information Institute
CONTACT: Thomas R. Bruce
EMAIL: tom@law.mail.cornell.edu
URL: gopher://gopher.law.cornell.edu:70/11/csodir

HIEROS GAMOS

DESCRIPTION: Hieros Gamos is a very extensive directory of bar associations, vendors, firm associations, consultants, and law schools. Unfortunately, however, for the most part, the directory includes no Internet links. The directory includes lots of North American and international listings, but the information provided is strictly contact info—addresses, phone numbers, etc. This is a useful resource, but it would be much more interesting and useful if all the relevant Internet links were included.

URL: http://www.hg.org/

WEST'S LEGAL DIRECTORY

DESCRIPTION: West Publishing provides access to its directory of lawyers for free on the Internet. This is one of the most comprehensive directories available. It is searchable by attorney name, law firm name, specialties, geographic location, and any combination of these criteria. Frequently, when Martindale Hubbell does not list an attorney or firm, they will appear in the West Directory. And of course, the price cannot be beat.

PROVIDER: West Publishing
URL: http://wld.westlaw.com (port 70) 1
URL: http://www.westpub.com/WLDInfo/WLD.htm

EXPERT WITNESS SOURCES

EXPERT WITNESSES DIRECTORIES

DESCRIPTION: This site offers a compilation of sources for expert witnesses.

PROVIDER: The Northern California Association of Law Libraries (NOCALL)
URL: http://lawlib.wuacc.edu/nocall/buddies/faq/experts.html

ECONOMIC EXPERT WITNESS

DESCRIPTION: Expert Witness in Quantitative Economics (since 1966): Conduct and evaluate studies on the economic value of business, income, pension and Social Security losses. This involves model building and quantification —extensive calculations of present and future values, indexes, interest and annuity rates, discount rates, life expectancy tables and other similar statistics. Testimony as an expert witness includes federal and state courts, arbitration and legislative hearings and depositions.

URL: http://pluto.njcc.com/~grs

LEGAL RESEARCH NETWORK (LERN)

DESCRIPTION: LERN is a fee-based bbs. However, portions of the extensive LERN expert witness database are free on the Net. Note that LERN specializes in engineering and construction and OSHA-familiar experts.

URL: http://www.witness.net

MEDSTUFF

DESCRIPTION: MEDSTUFF provides expert medical opinions on medical-legal matters to attorneys (plaintiff and defense), and to risk management professionals from hospitals, and other health institutions. Medstuff's expert division offers a preliminary evaluation of any potential medical-legal matter for a reasonable fee that is considerably less than the current fees that are charged on an hourly basis for this kind of evaluation.

The service also provides educated and honest opinions to any member of the public that may have potential grievances against physicians, clinics, hospitals or other health institutions. If you feel that the medical care you have received or the advice you have been given has not been correct or has been substandard, Medstuff will review the case and make recommendations, including appropriate legal and/or medical referrals.

URL: http://www.opennet.com/medstuff

VARIOUS EXPERT DIRECTORIES

URL: http://lawlib.wuacc.edu/nocall/buddies/faq/experts.html

LEGAL TECHNOLOGY RESOURCES

COMPUTER TECHNOLOGY LEGAL NET

DESCRIPTION: The Computer Technology Legal Net home page includes the following:

1. Computer Law Articles and Recent Case Summaries
2. Free Computer Law Email Updates
3. List of Available Computer & Technology Jobs and Resumes

PROVIDER: Law firm of Morris, Manning & Martin, Atlanta, GA
URL: To subscribe to "Computer Law Email Updates," send email to lstreet@america.net with their name, company name, mailing address, and Internet email address
URL: http://www.com/mmm/mmmhome.html

CITI LAW TECHNOLOGY CENTRE

DESCRIPTION: The CTI Law Technology Centre, based at the University of Warwick, exists to promote, coordinate and support the development of information technology in law. They offer practical support, advice and encouragement for the integration and use of new technology in all aspects of legal education throughout the U.K. Their WWW site contains a publications archive, an archive of the Law Technology Journal, a list of electronic law journals, a calendar of conferences and events of interest to those in the law and technology field, and an experimental information server for law schools. They also offer several guides, such as LTC Guide to Law on the Web and the LTC Guide to Teaching and Learning on the Web.

URL: http://ltc.law.warwick.ac.uk/

LAW OFFICE TECHNOLOGY

DESCRIPTION: This is a site where lawyers can get information on legal software and hardware. All software listed on this site has been "tested and approved."

PROVIDER: Albert Barsoochini
EMAIL: lawtech@well.com
URL: http://www.well.com/user/lawtech

TECHNOLOGY LAW COLUMN

DESCRIPTION: This site archives the monthly Technology Law column from the Chicago Daily Law Bulletin, as well as other things written by David Loundy. It also has useful links for attorneys, especially in the area of cyberspace law.

PROVIDER: David Loundy
URL: http://www.leepfrog.com/E-Law/

OTHER LEGAL RESOURCES

CITATION REPORT

DESCRIPTION: The American Assn of Law Libraries' report examines the volatile issue of legal citation formats.

URL: http://law.wuacc.edu/aallnet/aall.citation.html

COPYRIGHT FAQ

DESCRIPTION: This Frequently Asked Questions document provides answers about copyright.

PROVIDER: Terry Carroll
ACCESS: ftp://ftp.netcom.com/pub/ca/carrollt/law/copyright/faq
files: part1-part6
URL: URL: ftp://rtfm.mit.edu/pub/usenet/news.answers/law/copyright/faq/
files: part1-part6
URL: gopher://gopher.cni.org:70/11/cniftp/forums/cni-copyright/other
URL: Send email to: mail-server@rtfm.mit.edu with the following message:
send usenet/news.answers/law/Copyright-FAQ/part1
send usenet/news.answers/law/Copyright-FAQ/part2
send usenet/news.answers/law/Copyright-FAQ/part3

send usenet/news.answers/law/Copyright-FAQ/part4
send usenet/news.answers/law/Copyright-FAQ/part5
send usenet/news.answers/law/Copyright-FAQ/part6
quit

DRAFT NEGOTIATING NETWORKED INFORMATION CONTRACTS AND LICENENSES

PROVIDER: READI (Rights for Electronic Access to and Delivery of Information)
URL: http://www.cni.org/projects/READI/guide/www/READI-guide.html

INTERNET DEMO FOR LAWYERS

DESCRIPTION: The hypertext demonstration is based on a presentation to the April 1994 New York City Bar program on the Internet—Its title: Five Reasons for Lawyers and Law Firms To Be on the Internet.

PROVIDER: Legal Information Institute, Cornell Law School
CONTACT: Professor Peter W. Martin
EMAIL: martin@law.mail.cornell.edu
ADDRESS: Myron Taylor Hall, Ithaca, NY 14853
PHONE: (607) 255-4619
URL: http://www.law.cornell.edu/papers/5reasons.html

JOB CENTER

DESCRIPTION: Law Journal Extra has launched the Law Employment Center. The site is available to anyone with Web access. The site includes searchable classifieds from The National and New York Law Journals as well as articles and news about the job market.

URL: http://www.lawjobs.com

LAW LISTS

DESCRIPTION: This is a comprehensive and updated catalog of law-related email lists.

PROVIDER: Lyonette Louis-Jacques, Foreign and International Law Librarian & Lecturer in Law
ADDRESS: D'Angelo Law Library, 1121 East 60th Street, University of Chicago Law School, Chicago, IL 60637
EMAIL: llou@midway.uchicago.edu
PHONE: (312) 702-9612
URL: http://www.lib.uchicago.edu/cgi-bin/law-lists

LAW REVIEW ADDRESSES

DESCRIPTION: A rank order listing of the top general interest journals based on frequency of citation in other journals.

PROVIDER: Washington and Lee University
URL: gopher://liberty.uc.wlu.edu:70/0/library/law/lawftp/lawrevs.txt

LAW SCHOOL INDEX

DESCRIPTION: This site offers a comprehensive index of 148 U.S. law school Web and gopher servers.

URL: http://www.usc.edu/dept/law-lib/librarys/locators.html

LAWTALK

DESCRIPTION: Indiana University is producing a series of short segments for radio broadcast providing general legal information and discussion of issues. All of the files are in the standard .au format for Suns and also playable with several Windows sound players.

URL: http://www.law.indiana.edu:80/law/lawtalk.html

LEGAL DOMAIN NETWORK (LDN)

DESCRIPTION: The LDN is an attempt to consolidate and coordinate all substantive legal information and discussions on the Internet. The LDN is a private usenet newsfeed for law-related organizations only. It is currently distributed among several law schools and plans are currently in the works to increase distribution to law firms, the U.S. Congress, and areas for use with the practicing bar.

CONTACT: Laurence S. Donahue, Research Fellow, UNIX/Internet Consultant & Advisor, Chicago-Kent College of Law
EMAIL: ldonahue@chicagokent.Kentlaw.EDU
PHONE: (312) 906-5308
EMAIL: legaldom@ming.law.vill.edu
URL: http://www.kentlaw.edu/lawnet/lawnet.html

LEGALEAGLE

DESCRIPTION: Free solutions for people having difficulty communicating with their lawyers and locating lawyers for particular problems.

URL: http://pages.prodigy.com/FL/legaleagle/legaleagle.html

LEGAL INTERNET TRAINING

DESCRIPTION: The Clearinghouse for Law-Related Internet Training Materials.

PROVIDER: Jim Milles, Head of Computer Services at Saint Louis University Law Library (millesjg@sluvca.slu.edu,http://lawlib.slu.edu/milles.htm)
ACCESS: http://lawlib.slu.edu/training/train.htm

LEGAL JOB HUNTING ONLINE

DESCRIPTION: The TSW Legal-JobCenter offers free online posting of "help-wanted" and "position sought" notices.

URL: http://seamless.com/jobs

LEGAL LIST

DESCRIPTION: List of law-related resources online.

PROVIDER: Erik J. Heels
ADDRESS: 39 Main Street, Eliot, ME 03903-2234
URL: ftp://ftp.midnight.com/pub/LegalList/legallist.txt

LEGAL RESEARCH FAQ

DESCRIPTION: This document answers Frequently Asked Questions (FAQ) file concerning legal research and the structure the U.S. legal system.

PROVIDER: Mark Eckenwiler
EMAIL: eck@panix.com
URL: ftprtfm.mit.edu/pub/usenet/news.answers/law/research
URL: News groups: miscc.legal, news.answers
URL: EMAIL to mail-server@rtfm.mit.edu
send the following:
send usenet/news.answers/law/research/part1
send usenet/news.answers/law/research/part2

MARKETING HELP

DESCRIPTION: This site offers an index of free online sites where you can quickly gain exposure for your Web page by submitting your URL address to large searchable online databases, indexes and directories.

URL: http://www.vir.com/~wyatt/index.html
URL: http://ep.com/faq/webannounce.html

MARKETING ON THE WEB

DESCRIPTION: David Vandagriff's July 1995 ABA Journal column discussing law firm use of the Web is available online in hypertextual format.

URL: http://www.abanet.org/journal/julydpvcolumn.html

NET-LAWYERS FAQ

DESCRIPTION: The Net-lawyers FAQ, is a joint effort by students, librarians, lawyers and like-minded people. It is geared toward informing those engaged in law-related professions how to best make use of the Internet and other electronic communications.

URL: ftp://ftp.webcom.com/pub/lewrose/archive/net-lawyers-digest.archive/faqv1.zip

PRIVATE INVESTIGATOR HOME PAGE

DESCRIPTION: If you need a referral to a PI or simply want to do some research on your own, consider this site.

URL: http://www.indirect.com/www/montypi/privi/pihome.html

RARE LAW BOOKS

DESCRIPTION: For those interested in out-of-print and even rare books on business law and related topics, there is a bookshop on the Internet with its inventory (about 6000 books) devoted in part to this kind of book. The inventory can be searched by email. A help file may be obtained via email. Send email to: rare-lawbooks@netcom.com
In the Subject line of your message, and in the body of the message itself, type: help

URL: Send email to: rare-lawbooks@netcom.com with the word "search" as the subject and the message "search <your-word>".
For example:
To: rare-lawbooks@netcom.com
Subject: search
Message: search business
Within a short period of time, you will receive an email reply consisting of a list of those books which satisfy your search request.

VETERANS ARCHIVE

DESCRIPTION: This database purports to be for all veterans who served in the military and would like to put themselves in the database for their military buddy's to look for them easily. It includes only a handful of vets. Good idea, but where's the beef?

URL: http://www.earthlink.net/~beerborn/index.html

THE VIRTUAL LAW LIBRARY REFERENCE DESK

DESCRIPTION: The goals of this database are to provide reference access to sources of legal information, provide access to general reference sources and guides, and provide access to matter that enriches academic study.

PROVIDER: Washburn University School of Law Library, Topeka, KS 66621
CONTACT: Lissa Holzhausen
PHONE: (913) 231-1088
EMAIL: zzholz@acc.wuacc.edu
URL: telnet://law.wuacc.edu
LOGIN: reflaw
URL: http://law.wuacc.edu/washlaw/reflaw/reflaw.html

YAHOO'S NEW LEGAL RESEARCH GROUP

DESCRIPTION: Links to various legal researching organizations.

URL: http://www.yahoo.com/Business_and_Economy/Companies/Law/Research/

INTERNET RESOURCE GUIDES

A CITIZEN'S GUIDE TO INTERNET RESOURCES ON THE RIGHTS OF AMERICANS

DESCRIPTION: The guide is designed for the layperson and focuses on Internet resources that explain and discuss individual rights under the Bill of Rights, select federal statutes (e.g., the ADA, the Copyright Act), rights by status or group (e.g., women, youth, the disabled), and other rights-related resources (e.g., gateways to legal information). It has been posted on the Clearinghouse of Subject-Oriented Internet Resource Guides at the University of Michigan.

CONTACT: Michele Pfaff and David Bachman
EMAIL: um-citizen.rights@umich.edu
URL: gopher://una.hh.lib.umich.edu:70/00/inetdirsstacks/citizens:bachpfaff

CLEARINGHOUSE FOR SUBJECT ORIENTED INTERNET RESOURCE GUIDES

DESCRIPTION: This site provides access to the major guides to United States government gophers, BBSs, WWW servers, etc. on the Internet.

PROVIDER: University of Michigan
URL: http://www.lib.umich.edu/chhome.html or
URL: gopher://una.hh.lib.umich.edu/11/inetdirs

THE DESKTOP INTERNET REFERENCE

DESCRIPTION: Lists law library telnet addresses, among other things.

PROVIDER: John Buckman
ADDRESS: 3520 Connecticut Ave., Apt.33, Washington, DC 20008
PHONE: jbuckman@aas.org
URL: http://archive.uwp.edu/

DIRECTORY OF ELECTRONIC JOURNALS AND NEWSLETTERS

PROVIDER: University of Ottowa, Department of Religious Studies
CONTACT: Michael Strangelove
EMAIL: 441495@Acadvm1.Uottawa.Ca
PHONE: (613) 2372052
FAX: (613) 5646641
URL: Send the following commands as an email message to listserv@uottawa or listserv@acadvm1.uottawa.ca:
GET EJOURNL1 DIRECTRY
GET EJOURNL2 DIRECTRY
URL: Send an electronic mail message to Comserve@Rpiecs (Bitnet) or Comserve@Vm.Ecs.Rpi.Edu (Internet) with the following command appearing on the first line of the message:
Send EJournl1 Sources
Send EJournl2 Sources

No other words, punctuation, or symbols should appear in the email.

Comserve is an automated system for file retrieval; it will acknowledge receipt of your message and let you know that the files have been sent to you.

GUIDE TO INTERNET RESOURCES IN CRIMINAL LAW

DESCRIPTION: This guide is in two parts: a general description of the Internet, and a catalogue of resources.

PROVIDER: International Centre for Criminal Law Reform and Criminal Justice Policy UBC Faculty of Law
ADDRESS: 1822 East Mall, Vancouver, BC, V6T 1Z1 Canada
URL: gopher://view.ubc.ca
URL: http://view.ubc.ca

THE GUIDE TO NETWORK RESOURCE TOOLS

DESCRIPTION: The Guide to Network Resource Tools describes many of the key tools in use today among the academic networking community for accessing resources on the Net. For each tool, the guide provides a general overview and details on availability, intended audience, basic usage, and examples.

URL: Send email to: listserv@earncc.bitnet
In the body of the message, type:
GET NETTOOLS TXT

URL: ftp://naic.nasa.gov/files/general_info/earn-resource-tool-guide-v3.ps
ftp://naic.nasa.gov/files/general_info/earn-resource-tool-guide-v3.txt

THE INTERNET PUBLIC LIBRARY

DESCRIPTION: Check out reference sections on subjects ranging from gardening to the Internet to today's news. Explore an online story book with a child. Take a tutorial to help you improve your computing skills.

PROVIDER: University of Michigan, School of Information and Library
CONTACT: Joseph Janes, Director, the Internet Public Library
URL: http://ipl.sils.umich.edu/

INTERNET SOURCES OF GOVERNMENT INFORMATION

DESCRIPTION: Gumprecht's extensive guide is available at the Clearinghouse for Subject Oriented Internet Resource Guides. See the entry herein for access.

PROVIDER: Blake Gumprecht, Documents Librarian, Temple University
EMAIL: gumpbw@vm.temple.edu

ONLINE ACTIVISM RESOURCE LIST

DESCRIPTION: A list of Internet newsgroups and mailing lists of use to the online activist. Includes activism forums, and topical forums (computing futures, access to govt. info, privacy and censorship, regional politics, NII/GII/ "Data Superhighway" issues, virtual community, civil liberties & human rights, etc.).

CONTACT: Stanton McCandlish
EMAIL: mech@eff.org
URL: ftp://ftp.eff.org/EFF/activists.eff
URL: gopher://gopher.eff.org
URL: http://www.eff.org/

QUEER RESOURCES DIRECTORY (QRD)

DESCRIPTION: QRD contains information concerning lesbians, bisexuals, gay men, and transgendered persons.

PROVIDER: David Casti
EMAIL: disc@vector.casti.com
URL: gopher://gopher.casti.com:70/11/gaystuff/QRD

MISCELLANEOUS JOURNALS AND NEWSLETTERS

THE COOK REPORT ON INTERNET

DESCRIPTION: The COOK Report is a monthly newsletter focusing on the policy complexities of NREN, and National Information Infrastructure (NII) development as well as Internet commercialization. Published by the former director of a U.S. Congress Office of Technology assessment of the NREN. Subscriptions range in price from $85 for an Individual to $500 for a Corporate Site License.

PROVIDER: Gordon Cook
ADDRESS: COOK Network Consultants, 431 Greenway Ave, Ewing, NJ 08618
PHONE: (609) 882-2572
EMAIL: cook@path.net

EFF GUIDE TO THE INTERNET

DESCRIPTION: This document was formerly the Big Dummy's Guide to the Internet. This is the best free book on use of the Internet available. Look for version in your favorite word processor.
URL: ftp://ftp.eff.org/pub/EFF/netguide.eff

ELECTRONIC GREEN JOURNAL

DESCRIPTION: This is a new publication concerned with international environmental issues (the first issue covers environmental racism, China's environmental policies, recycling in America, etc.).

PROVIDER: University of Idaho, Moscow, ID
CONTACT: Marty Zimmerman
EMAIL: martyz@uidaho.edu, gopher@uidaho.edu
URL: gopher://gopher.uidaho.edu:70/11/UI_gopher/library/egj
URL: http://gopher.uidaho.edu/1/UI_gopher/library/egj/
URL: ftp://ftp.uidaho.edu/pub/docs/publications/EGJ/issue-1

ELECTRONIC JOURNAL OF INTIMATE VIOLENCE (EJINTVIO)

DESCRIPTION: The EJINTVIO is a new electronic publication that will make use of the Internet to bring you the latest information on the research and treatment of intimate violence. Topics to be included are physical child abuse, sexual child abuse, child neglect, physical spouse abuse, sexual spouse abuse, psychological abuse, elder abuse, and dating violence, as well as other related topics subscribers may wish to explore.

The EJINTVIO will permit current research briefs and clinical discussions to be published in a much shorter timespan than hard-copy journals, usually with publication occurring within eight weeks of submission for accepted manuscripts.

CONTACT: Glenn Wolfner, Assistant Director of Family Violence Research Program, University of Rhode Island
EMAIL: famviol@uri.acc.edu
URL: EJINTVIO on LISTSERV@URIACC.URI.EDU or LISTSERV@URIACC.BITNET

NASDAQ FINANCIAL EXECUTIVE JOURNAL (NFEJ)

DESCRIPTION: Hypermedia version of the NFEJ. The print version of the NFEJ is circulated to CEOs and CFOs of Nasdaq companies quarterly. The electronic version anticipates the release of the print version by approximately two weeks, and contains its full text and illustrations.

PROVIDER: The Nasdaq Stock Market (SM) and the Legal Information Institute at Cornell Law School
URL: telnet://fatty.law.cornell.edu
LOGIN: www.
then choose: NFEJ
URL: http://www.fatty.law.cornell.edu

NEW YORK TIMES

DESCRIPTION: There is a daily eight-page of edition of the New York Times available online for free. The software program Adobe Acrobat is required to read this material (so that the news it will look the way the Times intended it to look). Acrobat is available at this site for free download.

URL: http://nytimesfax.com

CENTRALIZED LEGAL SERVERS

GLOBAL LAWNET

URL: http://www.lawnet.net/

INTERNET LEGAL RESOURCE GUIDE

DESCRIPTION: This guide to Internet legal resources is a well-organized list of useful links. In addition to all the usual pointers, it also offers law student services links, such as class outlines, the latest versions of Lexis and Westlaw software, and law school exams from Ohio NU.

PROVIDER: University of Texas law student Prescott Caballero
URL: http://uts.cc.utexas.edu/~juris/

LAW LIBRARIAN'S ONLINE LIBRARY

DESCRIPTION: The American Association of Law Libraries maintains AALLNET, an expansive central site of legal info online. Included at the site are two menus. The Main Menu offers AALL materials, including news-letters, job information, and other information about the Association. The Official Menu offers a wonderful series of resources including: Directories (access info for the U.S. courts, law school faculty, AALL members, counsel connects, and West's lawyer directory, etc.), international, federal, and state law collections, the paralegal info system, central access to law library catalogs. It's truly a nicely put together collection of links. Hopefully, the entire system will become Web-accessible.

URL: telnet lawlib.wuacc.edu
LOGIN: aallnet

LAWLINKS

DESCRIPTION: This server offers information concerning the Chicago-Kent Law School, an interface into Chicago-Kent's Electronic Publishing Initiative, an interface into The Legal Domain Network, and access to LawLinks.

The Legal Domain Network was established by Chicago-Kent College of Law and Villanova University School of Law to consolidate all substantive legal discussion on the Internet. It is fully WAIS searchable and NNTP feedable to law-related organizations.

LawLinks represents Chicago-Kent College of Law's effort to consolidate all law resources on the Internet. That is, instead of pointing to servers of information, the site aims to point to the information pieces themselves without having to go through the intermediate step of connecting to a resource server.

CONTACT: Laurence S. Donahue, Research Fellow, UNIX/Internet Consultant & Advisor, Chicago-Kent College of Law
EMAIL: ldonahue@chicagokent.Kentlaw.EDU
PHONE: (312) 906-5308
URL: http://www.kentlaw.edu/

LAWLINKS LEGAL RESOURCE CENTER

DESCRIPTION: The Legal Resource Center is a one-stop legal resource gateway for both attorneys and consumers. Research pages range from judicial and administrative decisions to legislation; regulations and codes to law school libraries; governmental agencies to international authoritative sources. Includes pages for national and state bar associations, attorneys, computer consultants, sheriffs, investigators, law-related employment opportunities, expert witnesses, bail bondsmen, process servers, investigators, court reporters, review of law-related software, etc. The Action Line solves consumer problems, and answers selected legal questions of general interest.

URL: http://lawlinks.com

LAWMALL

DESCRIPTION: A central repository of legal information for the practitioner and layperson. Includes pamphlets for non-lawyers concerning how to handle some typical problems, and discussion of the provider's inventions: "legal gopher" (tm), Internet Law School (tm).

PROVIDER: Carl E. Person, "theft of idea" attorney
EMAIL: carlpers@www.lawmall.com
ADDRESS: 325 W 45 St., New York, NY 10036
PHONE: (212) 307-4444
URL: http://www.lawmall.com/

THE LAW STUDENT WEB

DESCRIPTION: A comprehensive site for law students and those interested in the study of law. The site includes an index of all law student home pages, U.S. law schools, sites of interest to law students and interesting case law, statutes, and articles.

URL: http://darkwing.uoregon.edu/~ddunn/l_schl.htm

LAW WORLD

DESCRIPTION: Excellent site of legal resources.

URL: http://www.lawworld.com

LAWYERS' DAILY INTERNET LEGAL NEEDS

DESCRIPTION: This Web site organizes Internet materials "an attorney would need most frequently." The site maintains pointers to many of the typical legal resources but also includes many unique California documents, such as state code and environmental law materials.

PROVIDER: California attorney Peter Krakaur
URL: http://users.aimnet.com/~ils/main.html

'LECTRIC LAW LIBRARY

DESCRIPTION: This site is an eclectic but well-organized resource with a sense of humor. The library is organized around the physical model and includes areas dedicated to the study of law, reference, business, law for laypeople, law for legal professionals, periodical and serials reading rooms, a forms room, and a bookstore.Some of the materials that they claim to be unique include:

- Court case filings
- Our Lawcopedia
- The 9th Circuits' Standards of Review
- Law School Course Outlines
- Legal Forms
- National Judicial College Information
- Legal Software
- Nevada Corporate Law
- The 'lectric Law Review(tm)

URL: http://www.inter-law.com/

LEGAL INFORMATION INSTITUTE

DESCRIPTION: Contains access to full text of U.S. Supreme Court rulings, plus lots of other useful stuff. This is a very well designed site.

URL: http://www.law.cornell.edu

THE LEGAL PAD

DESCRIPTION: A huge list of over 550 different legal resources.

URL: http://www.pond.com/~pinky/legal.pad/legalpad.htm

LEGAL SERVICES SECTION

DESCRIPTION: The All-Internet Shopping Directory's Legal Services Section.

URL: http://www.webcom.com/~tbrown/legal.html

P-LAW LEGAL RESOURCE LOCATOR

DESCRIPTION: Kenneth Perry has organized an impressive array of legal internet resources through his home page. Besides links to the usual sites, he also has pointers to articles on law and multimedia, a fairly detailed list of sites organized by topic (such as advertising law, ADA law, corporate law and antitrust law), and pointers to legal statistics databases.

PROVIDER: Kenneth M. Perry, a New York attorney
URL: http://www.dorsai.org/p-law/index.html

THOMAS

DESCRIPTION: As stated on the home page: "In the spirit of Thomas Jefferson, a service of the U.S. Congress through its Library." The site includes full text of legislation for the 104rd Congress; full text of the Congressional Record; an explanation of the lawmaking process from the origin of a legislative proposal through its publication as a law; and pointers to the House and C-SPAN gophers.

URL: http://thomas.loc.gov/

U.S. GOVERNMENT GOPHERS

DESCRIPTION: Provides one stop access to nearly 100 U.S. government gopher systems.

URL: gopher://gopher.tc.umn.edu:70/11/Other%20Gopher%20and%20Information%20Servers/North%20America/USA

USC LAW CENTER

DESCRIPTION: This site includes a comprehensive index of legal resources (including California and United Nations materials) on the Net, federal and state government indexes, a comprehensive, annotated listing of law-related journals, a comprehensive listing of law schools on the Net, law student/prelaw student resources, career services information, law-related computing information, and USC Law Center publications - bulletin, newsletters

PROVIDER: The University of Southern California Law Center
URL: http://www.usc.edu/dept/law-lib/index.html

WASHBURN UNIVERSITY LAW SCHOOL

DESCRIPTION: Washburn offers the WashLaw WEB. This site provides a vast collection of links to law-related materials on the Internet. The information is arranged by subject, by location (geographically), and alphabetically. In addition, Washburn provides access to the archives of several legal mailing lists.

URL: http://lawlib.wuacc.edu/washlaw/washlaw.html

Index